PRACTICAL SPANISH GRAMMAR

Marcial Prado

California State University, Fullerton

A Wiley Press Book

John Wiley & Sons, Inc.

New York • Chichester • Brisbane • Toronto • Singapore

Publisher: Judy V. Wilson
Editor: Alicia Conklin
Managing Editor: Maria Colligan
Composition and make up: Cobb-Dunlop Publisher Services, Inc.

Library of Congress Cataloging in Publication Data

Prado, Marcial, 1933-
  Practical Spanish grammar.

  (Wiley self-teaching guide)
  Includes index.
  1. Spanish language—Grammar—1950-   —Programmed
instruction.   I. Title.
PC4112.5.P7   1983   468.2'421'077   82-21785
ISBN 0-471-89894-5

Printed in the United States of America

20 19 18 17 16 15 14

Contents

Preface

Practical Spanish Grammar: A Self-Teaching Guide aims at teaching the essentials of the Spanish language at the beginning level in a practical and pleasant manner. This programmed textbook is designed for your use as a Self-Teaching Guide; as such it allows you to progress at your own pace as you practice and test yourself on the points covered in each lesson. *Practical Spanish Grammar* may also be used in a beginning college course. The content is that of the average textbook intended for a full year of college Spanish—about 70 percent of the grammatical structures of the language and some 1000 of the most frequently used Spanish words.

This book uses a practical and linguistic approach in treating grammatical structures. Concise and clear explanations are followed by completion exercises for testing and reinforcing comprehension—a unique feature not found in any other textbook. A variety of practical exercises complete each of the grammar sections. As always, new words have to be memorized. To help you in this, a variety of exercises reinforce your memorization while at the same time expanding your vocabulary.

Each of the 15 lessons contains these features:

A vocabulary list of the words used in the lesson, with some cultural notes and several practical drills for the new words.

A dialog using the key words of the previous vocabulary, with some cultural notes, followed by exercises in comprehension and vocabulary.

Three grammatical explanations, each with corresponding completion practice, followed by various exercises.

All the exercises and tests have answers for self-correction. In addition, there is a preliminary lesson on Spanish sounds. And after each five lessons there is a 100-question exam for self-testing.

Some Helpful Pointers For Using This Book

In taking the responsibility for your own progress, you'll notice your knowledge of Spanish increasing quickly. The programmed format affords both a challenge and a means of self-evaluation. The following tips should help you make the best use of this book:

1. *Do the exercises one at a time and check your answers right away.* The faster you're corrected, the faster you learn. Immediate feedback is a very important feature of this approach to learning.

2. *Use common sense in correcting your answers.* Although the answer key gives you all the correct answers as such, in some cases there are several possible synonyms; also, word order is more flexible in Spanish than it is in English, so don't let this surprise or trouble you.

3. *Master all material before going on.* If you missed more than two or three answers in one exercise, go back and review the vocabulary or the grammatical explanation. Then try your answers again. Language learning, like mathematics, is cumulative; you can't multiply without learning first how to add.

4. *Review the previous five lessons before taking the review exam.* The longer it takes you to cover the five lessons, the more you need to give them a quick review. Fifty percent of the exam is on vocabulary and the other 50 percent on grammar. You don't want this long test to be a surprise. You needn't score 90 percent or more, but you don't want to score less than 80 percent either!

To The Instructor

If you're a first-year college instructor, this programmed textbook can be used effectively in four ways:

1. *As a Self-Teaching Guide for individualized learning.* The student studies and completes every lesson; then you give him/her a test on the material covered. After completion of five lessons, you give the student the Review Exam; or you can prepare your own test. The number of credits should be proportionate to credit given for work in regular courses in your college.

2. *As an intensive review in the first year.* This course is ideal for students who have had two or three years of high school Spanish or one semester of college Spanish, or who have already learned some Spanish at home. *Practical Spanish* has been tested over several semesters in courses geared to group work, with very satisfactory results.

3. *As the textbook for a full year of beginning Spanish in college.* It's recommended that you cover the first eight or nine lessons during the first semester and the rest in the second. You might also want to supplement your course with one of the many graded readers for first-year Spanish. Obviously, your program depends on the number of hours of instruction available per week.

4. *As a supplement workbook to the main text you use, especially if you are dissatisfied with the workbook that accompanies the text.* The grammatical part with its accompanying explanations and exercises should be helpful to the student who needs further practice.

I wish to thank my colleagues who used the xeroxed manuscript in their classes. I am especially thankful to Professors Mario Díaz, Arturo Jasso, Dr. and Mrs. Walter Kline and to my wife Rita for their criticism and suggestions. I also want to express my appreciation to Judy Wilson, Alicia Conklin and Maria Colligan of John Wiley & Sons for their support and valuable suggestions.

M. Prado

Spanish Pronunciation

There are sounds in Spanish that do not exist in English, and vice versa. Still, some sounds are the same in both languages. An important fact to keep in mind is that in Spanish we run several words together to form what's called a "breath group"; in other words, we link together all the words between pauses. As a result, we omit one of two identical vowels or consonants, and we soften certain consonants (such as *b, d, g*) within the breath group. Ex.: *Ella va a ver a mi hijo* is pronounced [éyabábéramíjo].

1. *Vowels.* There are only five vowel sounds: *a, e, i, o, u*. They are clear, tense, and short sounds, stressed or not. For example, the three *a*s of *Panamá* have the same sound.
    1. Spanish [**a**] is pronounced with the mouth open as in *far*. Ex.: *mañana, banana, Canadá.*
    2. Spanish [**o**] is pronounced with the lips rounded as in *for*. Ex.: *profesor, tonto.*
    3. Spanish [**e**] is pronounced with the lips stretched and the tongue higher than for [**a**]. It sounds like the first part of the letter *a* in English without the final glide. Ex.: *este, desde, ese.*

4. Spanish [**u**] is very rounded, as in English *boot,* but shorter. Ex.: *tú, luna, su.*

5. Spanish [**i**] is pronounced with the lips very stretched and the tongue nearly touching the roof of the mouth, as in English *see,* but shorter. There are two letters for the [**i**] sound: *i* and *y.* When *y* is by itself, it means *and; y* also appears at the end of a word after another vowel. Ex.: *Juan y María, soy, sí, cita.*

6. Spanish *i, u* are pronounced shorter than [**i**], [**u**] whenever they are unstressed and are directly preceded or followed by another vowel. They are the "weak" (short) part of the two-vowel combination we call a *diphthong.* Ex.: *bien* [**ĭe**], *patio* [**ĭo**], *causa* [**aŭ**], *soy* [**oĭ**], *aire* [**aĭ**], *veinte* [**eĭ**], *hay* [**aĭ**], *puente* [**ŭe**], *muy* [**uĭ**].

2. *Consonants.* In general, Spanish consonants are pronounced with less strength and friction than English consonants, especially *b, d, g.* The following consonants are used in standard Latin American Spanish:

1. Spanish [**p**] is like English *p,* except that it's never followed by the puff of air heard in English initial *p.* Ex.: *papa, Pedro, papel.*

2. Spanish [**t**] is pronounced with the tip of the tongue against the upper teeth, never followed by the puff of air heard in English *t.* In Spanish we never write two *t*s or *th.* Ex.: *tú, tutor, total.*

3. Spanish [**k**] is like English *k,* but it's never followed by the puff of air heard in English initial *k.* The spelling is *c* in front of *a, o, u* and consonants *1* and *r,* as in *casa, cosa, cuando, crema, clase.* The spelling is *qu* (with silent *u*) in front of *i* and *e.* Ex.: *que, quien, Quito.* The spelling with *k* is used only in a few foreign words such as *kilómetro, kilogramo, kiosko, kimono.*

4. Spanish [**b**] is like English *b* at the beginning of a breath group or after a pause. In other cases, Spanish *b* is very soft, with a slight friction between the lower and upper lips. The spelling is *b* or *v.* Avoid pronouncing the [**v**] sound of English. Ex.: *labio, vamos a ver* [bámosabér], *vaca.*

5. Spanish [**d**] is pronounced with the tip of the tongue against the upper teeth at the beginning of a breath group. It becomes very soft within the breath group and in this case it sounds like English *th* in *father,* with even less friction. Ex.: *dedo.*

6. Spanish [**g**] is like English *g* of *get* when it's at the beginning of a breath group. Otherwise, it's very soft, with only a slight friction. The spelling is *g* in front of *a, o, u, r, l,* as in *lago, gato, agua, grado, iglesia.* The spelling is *gu* (with silent *u*) in front of *i* and *e,* as in *guitarra, guerra.* When the *u* of *gu* is pronounced, we write *gü,* as in *pingüino, vergüenza.*

7. Spanish [**j**] is pronounced very different from English *j* or *g.* It sounds more like English *h* in *hat,* but with more friction in the back of the mouth. The spelling is *j* in front of all five vowels or *g* in front of *i* and *e.* Ex.: *jamón, jerez, gitano, viaje, gente, Juan.* The *x* of *México* is pronounced [**j**].

8. Spanish [**s**] is exactly like English *s.* The only problem is the spelling. Four different letters are pronounced [**s**]: (a) *s* in front of any vowel and final syllable, as in *soy, casas, estos;* (b) *z* in front of *a, o, and u,* and in final position, as in *zapato, feliz, vez;* (c) *c* in front of *i* and *e,* as in *felices, felicidad, dice;* (d) *x* (the second half of the sound) as in *examen* [eksamen], *sexo* [sekso].

9. Spanish [**r**] is pronounced like English *d* and *t* in words like *ladder, matter.* Ex.: *pero, para, árbol, comer.*

10. Spanish [**rr**] has no comparable sound in English. The tip of the tongue moves five to eight times in a very fast manner against the gum ridge. It is a trilled sound. Ex.: *perro, arroz.* Besides the spelling *rr*, there is the single *r* with the [**rr**] sound. This occurs at the beginning of a word, as in *rosa* [rrosa], *rojo* [rrojo], and also after the consonants *n, l,* and *s.* Ex.: *sonrisa* [sonrrisa], *alrededor* [alrrededor], *Israel* [isrrael], *honra* [onrra].

11. Spanish [**l**] is like English *l* in words like *let,* but not like English *l* in *mill.* English *l* at the end of a syllable or word is very soft, dark, and relaxed. In Spanish the [**l**] sound is always clear, high, and tense, with the tongue almost touching the roof of the mouth. This sound will more readily betray an English accent than many others. Ex.: *los, hotel, mil, tal, alto, volver.*

12. Spanish [**f**] is like English *f,* but we never write *ph* or *ff.* Ex.: *teléfono, fuente.*

13. Spanish [**m**] is like English *m,* but we never write *mm.* Ex.: *madre, mañana, amor.*

14. Spanish [**n**] is like English *n.* Ex.: *nada, mono, hablan, antes.*

15. Spanish [**y**] is like English *y,* but there are two spellings: *y,* and *ll.* Ex.: *mayo, bello.*

16. Spanish [**ch**] is like English *ch.* Ex: *muchacho, chico, hecho.*

17. Spanish [**ñ**] is like English *ny* in words like *canyon.* Ex.: *soñar, mañana.*

18. Spanish *h* is never pronounced. Ex.: *hablar* [ablar], *prohibir* [proibir], *alcohol* [alkol].

NOTES:

1. There is no letter *w* in the Spanish alphabet except as it occurs in a few appropriated foreign words. But we have the sound [**w**] for the letter *u* preceded by *h* and followed by *e.* Ex.: *huevo* [webo], *hueso* [ueso], *huele* [wele].

2. Identical vowels between two words are pronounced as just *one* vowel. The same is true for two identical consonants within the breath group. Ex.: *va a casa* [bakasa], *le encanta* [lenkanta], *el lado* [elado].

In Summary

1. The *h* is always silent. The *u* is silent in *qu* and *gue, gui,* but not in *güe, güi.*
2. Consonants *p, t,* and *c* are never followed by the puff of air heard in English.
3. Consonants *b, d,* and *g* are very soft in Spanish within a breath group.
4. The five vowels are short, tense, and clear, with or without the stress.
5. Make a diphthong (one syllable) whenever *i* and *u* are directly preceded or followed by another vowel.
6. Keep your tongue high to pronounce the final *l* or you will betray a strong English accent.
7. Link together the words within a breath group.
8. Don't make the stressed syllable too long to avoid the *uh* sound of English in the unstressed syllables that follow the stressed vowel.
9. The Spanish speech rhythm is machine-gun-like; all the syllables are almost even.
10. Avoid the *z* sound of English in words written with the letter *z.* It is the [**s**] sound.
11. Avoid the *z* sound of English for the single *s* between vowels: *presente, visita.*
12. Strengthen the [**h**] sound of English for the Spanish *j: Juan, gente.*
13. Avoid the *a* sound of English in *Ann.* There is no such sound in Spanish, which instead employs an [**a**] sound as in *far.*
14. Avoid the lengthening of final vowels as is done in English; for example, *no* is much shorter in Spanish than it is in English.

Lesson 1

Basic Expressions

Buenos días, señor.	Good morning, sir.
Buenas tardes, señora.	Good afternoon, madam.
Buenas noches, señorita.	Good evening, miss.
¡Hola! ¿Cómo está usted?	Hi! How are you?
Muy bien, gracias. ¿Y usted?	Very well, thank you. And you?
Bastante bien, gracias.	Fairly well, thank you.
¿Cómo se llama usted?	What's your name?
Me llamo Roberto.	My name is Robert.
¿Dónde vive usted?	Where do you live?
Vivo en California.	I live in California.
¿En qué puedo servirle?	May I help you?
¿Dónde está el baño, por favor?	Where is the bathroom, please?
Allí, a la derecha.	Over there, to the right.
¿Cómo se dice *left* en español?	How do you say *left* in Spanish?
Se dice *izquierda*.	You say *izquierda*.
Hasta luego.	So long.
Hasta mañana.	See you tomorrow.
Adiós.	Goodbye.

PRACTICE THE BASIC EXPRESSIONS   *(Answers, p. 75)*

1. How do you say *Good morning* in Spanish? _____ .

2. After 12 P.M. we don't say *Buenos días* but _____ .

3. After dark we don't say *Buenas tardes* but _____ .

4. How do you say *madam* in Spanish? _____ .

5. How do you reply to *¿Cómo está usted?* _____ .

6. How do you reply to *¿Cómo se llama usted?* _____ .

7. In English we write the question and exclamation mark at the end of the
   word or sentence, whereas in Spanish we write it at the _____
   and the end.

8. How do you reply to *¿Dónde vive usted?* _____ .

9. If you are looking for the bathroom, how do you ask for directions?____
   _____ . A possible reply is
   _____ .

10. *Goodbye* is translated in Spanish as _____ . And *So long*_____
    _____ .

11. How do you say *May I help you?* _____ .

12. How do you say *please?* _____ .

PALABRAS NUEVAS (New Words)

**(You will find these words in the grammar explanations, in the
exercises, and also in later lessons. Try to memorize them.)**

acción	action	**hotel**	hotel	**papel**	paper
agua	water	**inglés**	English	**paraguas**	umbrella
águila	eagle	**lápiz**	pencil	**pared**	wall
árbol	tree	**lección**	lesson	**pluma**	pen
autobús	bus	**libro**	book	**policía**	police
avión	airplane	**lunes**	Monday	**porcentaje**	percentage
calor	heat	**luz**	light	**problema**	problem
casa	house	**mano**	hand	**sabor**	taste, flavor
clase	class	**mañana**	morning	**sol**	sun
color	color	**mar**	sea	**sur**	south
confusión	confusion	**mesa**	table	**tarde**	afternoon
día	day	**mujer**	woman	**taxista**	taxi driver
estación	station	**nariz**	nose	**tema**	theme
garaje	garage	**noche**	night	**tren**	train
gato	cat	**nombre**	name	**verdad**	truth
hambre	hunger	**nuevo**	new	**vez**	time
hombre	man	**palabra**	word		

PRACTICE THE VOCABULARY   (*Answers, p. 75*)

Match the two columns by writing the letters in the spaces provided.

1. _____ gato	16. _____ árbol	A. train	P. pencil
2. _____ lunes	17. _____ águila	B. sea	Q. taste
3. _____ tren	18. _____ noche	C. tree	R. percentage
4. _____ nariz	19. _____ nuevo	D. man	S. wall
5. _____ hambre	20. _____ vez	E. hand	T. truth
6. _____ mar	21. _____ porcentaje	F. cat	U. woman
7. _____ sol	22. _____ avión	G. new	V. station
8. _____ pared	23. _____ nombre	H. eagle	W. water
9. _____ luz	24. _____ sur	I. night	X. theme
10. _____ mano	25. _____ palabra	J. nose	Y. table
11. _____ mujer	26. _____ estación	K. time	Z. light
12. _____ lápiz	27. _____ sabor	L. sun	a. Monday
13. _____ hombre	28. _____ tema	M. name	b. heat
14. _____ verdad	29. _____ mesa	N. airplane	c. hunger
15. _____ calor	30. _____ agua	O. word	d. south

GRAMMAR I   Indefinite articles. Gender of nouns.

A.   There are two indefinite articles in English: *a* and *an,* as in "*a* book," "*an* apple." In Spanish the indefinite articles are **un** which is masculine, and **una,** which is feminine, as in *un* señor, *una* señora.

B.   Nouns referring to males are masculine, and nouns referring to females are feminine, as in *un* hombre, *una* mujer, *un* gato, *una* gata. The article distinguishes a male from a female when the noun has the same spelling for males and females.
    Ex.: *un* policía (a policeman), *una* policía (a policewoman)

C.   Nouns referring to "things" are neuter in English (=*it*). In Spanish, "things" are either masculine or feminine, and they will take either *un* or *una*. In this case the gender—that is, whether it is masculine or feminine—has nothing to do with male or female; the gender has no meaning at all.
    Ex.: *una* casa, *un* patio, *un* árbol

D.   The only way to predict the gender of a noun in Spanish is by consulting the final letter of the word:

> Nouns ending in L-O-N-E-R-S are almost always masculine (97%).
> Nouns ending in D-IÓN-Z-A are almost always feminine (98%).

Ex.: *un* pape*l*, un libro, *un* tre*n*, *un* garaj*e*, *un* colo*r*, *un* lune*s*
una pare*d*, *una* lecc*ión*, *una* lu*z*, *una* mes*a*, *una* confus*ión*

E.   There are important exceptions to these two rules, and they should be memorized.

Some nouns ending in *-ma* are masculine rather than feminine.
Ex.: *un* proble*ma*, *un* te*ma*, *un* progra*ma* (a program)

Other important exceptions are the following nouns:

una mano	*una* noche	*un* día
una clase	*una* calle (a street)	*un* lápiz
una tarde	*una* llave (a key)	*un* avión
		un mapa

PRACTICE THE ARTICLES   *(Answers, p. 75)*

1. The two indefinite articles in Spanish are _____ and _____ . The translation in English is either _____ or _____ .

2. The difference between *un* and *una* is what we call *gender: un* is _____ _____ , whereas *una* is_____ .

3. All the nouns referring to males are _____ , and all the nouns referring to females are_____ .

4. There are three genders in the English pronoun system: (1) masculine (males: *he*); (2) feminine (females: *she*); and (3) neuter: *it*, which refers to _____—that is, inanimate nouns.

5. In Spanish we don't have "neuter" nouns: they are either_____ _____ or _____ .

6. Is there any meaning attached to the gender of "things"? _____ . But the article may serve to distinguish a male from a female when it precedes a noun. For example, *un* policía means "a _____ ."

7. You can predict the gender of an inanimate noun "thing" by the last _____ of the word. Everybody knows that -*o* is usually masculine and -*a* is _____.

8. But there are more than *o*'s and *a*'s at the end of a word; nouns ending in _____ are generally *masculine*, and nouns ending in _____ are generally feminine.

9. Therefore you can predict that a word like *tacón* (heel) is_____, _____ a word like *mes* (month) is_____, and a word like *bondad* (goodness) is_____.

10. Some important exceptions to these rules are the nouns ending in -*ma*, which are_____, such as _____problema (a problem).

11. Other exceptions are *mano* and *día:* we say _____ *día* (a day); for the same reason, we don't say *buenas días*, but_____días.

12. Do we say, *una lápiz* or *un lápiz*? _____. *Una tarde* or *un tarde*? _____.

EXERCISE

(Answers, p. 75)

Write the articles *un* or *una.*

1._____árbol	11._____mañana	21._____papel
2._____casa	12._____estación	22._____acción
3._____tema	13._____hombre	23._____patio
4._____día	14._____luz	24._____corral
5._____mano	15._____avión	25._____mar
6._____lunes	16._____tren	26._____sabor
7._____libro	17._____garaje	27._____taxista (man)
8._____lápiz	18._____pared	28._____porcentaje
9._____mesa	19._____problema	29._____policía (woman)
10._____tarde	20._____color	30._____inglés

GRAMMAR II   Definite articles and contractions.

A.   In English there is only one definite article: *the*. In Spanish there are four: **el/la** (masculine/feminine singular), **los/las** (mas./fem. plural). These articles agree with the noun they precede.

B.   We use *el* and *los* with masculine nouns and *la/las* with feminine nouns. Remember that males are always masculine and females feminine. "Things" are either masculine or feminine according to the last letter of the word:

Nouns ending in L-O-N-E-R-S are generally *masculine* (97 percent).

Nouns ending in D-IÓN-Z-A are generally feminine (98 percent).

Examples: *el* tre*n*, *el* nombr*e*, *el* pape*l*, *la* lec*ción*, *la* lu*z*, *la* verda*d*.

C.   Remember that there are important exceptions to these rules. Review them.

1.   Nouns ending in *ma* are masculine rather than feminine: *el* proble*ma*.

2.   *la* mano, *el* día, *la* clase, *la* tarde, *la* noche, *el* lápi*z*.

D.   The article *la* precedes feminine nouns, but if the feminine noun begins with a stressed *a*, we use *el* instead of *la*. Actually, the noun may begin with *a* or *ha* because the *h* is always silent in Spanish.

Ex.: *el* a*gua* (it is pronounced [elágwa], with a soft *g*). Plural: *las* aguas.

el águila, *el* ham*bre* (pronounced [elámbre]). Plural: *las* águilas.

But we say *la* americana because the initial *a* of *americana* is unstressed.

E.   This same rule applies to the indefinite article *una*, which precedes all feminine nouns, except the ones beginning with a stressed *a*.

Ex.: *un águila* rather than *una águila, un hambre* instead of *una hambre*

F.   We have only two contractions in Spanish—that is, where *two* words become *one*:

1.   Preposition *de* + *el* becomes **del** (of the . . .)

2.   Preposition *a* + *el* becomes **al** (to the . . .)

Ex.: el árbol *del* patio (the tree *in the* yard), la luz *del* día (the daylight)

Voy *al* patio. (I am going *to the* yard); but Voy *a la* casa. (. . . *to the* house)

PRACTICE THE DEFINITE ARTICLES   *(Answers, p. 75)*

1. The definite article *the* has 4 possible translations: _____.

2. Inanimate nouns (things) are almost always masculine in Spanish when the last letters of the word are _____, and they are almost always feminine when the last letters are _____.

3. According to these rules, you can predict the gender of most nouns; for example, *nariz* (nose) is _____, *paraguas* (umbrella) is _____, *sol* (sun) is _____.

4. There are some exceptions to these rules; for example, nouns ending in *-ma* are _____, such as _____ *problema* (the problem).

5. A few nouns ending in *-z* are _____ rather than feminine, such as _____ *lápiz* (the pencil); but _____ *luz* (the light).

6. The preposition *de* (of) followed by the article *el* becomes one word: _____.
The preposition *a* (to) followed by the article *el* becomes one word: _____.

7. Not every feminine noun takes the feminine articles *la* and *una*; instead we use *el* and *un* if the noun begins with a _____ *a* [á], such as _____ *agua* (the water), _____ *águila* (an eagle). The plural forms require the feminine *las*. Ex.: *las* aguas, *las* águilas.

8. Which letter is always silent in Spanish? _____. This means that if a word starts with *ha* [á], it will take the definite article _____ rather than _____. For example, _____ *hambre* (the hunger).

9. Is it correct Spanish to say *la americana*? _____. Here we don't use *el* because the first *a* is not _____; [amerikána].

10. *La casa* de el *presidente* is not correct; it should be *la casa* _____ _____, because *de* + *el* contract into _____.

11. Is *la casa* de la *señora* correct? _____. Actually there is no contraction with the article _____. There are no contractions with plural articles: *a los, de los, a las, de las*.

EXERCISE

(Answers, p. 76)

Write the article *el* or *la*.

1. ____ tarde	11. ____ tren	21. ____ hospital
2. ____ agua	12. ____ programa	22. ____ patio
3. ____ mano	13. ____ mujer	23. ____ pluma
4. ____ sol	14. ____ taxista (man)	24. ____ águila
5. ____ luz	15. ____ verdad	25. ____ garaje
6. ____ pared	16. ____ hambre	26. ____ sur
7. ____ problema	17. ____ autobús	27. ____ policía (woman)
8. ____ día	18. ____ hotel	28. ____ alfalfa [alfálfa]
9. ____ lunes	19. ____ americana	29. ____ nombre
10. ____ lápiz	20. ____ confusión	30. ____ dilema

GRAMMAR III   Subject pronouns.

A.   Memorize the following chart of subject pronouns:

yo	I		
nosotros -as	we		
tú	you (familiar)	**él**	he
vosotros -as	"you-all" (familiar)	**ellos**	they(males)
usted (Ud.)	you (formal)	**ella**	she
ustedes (Uds.)	"you-all" (formal)	**ellas**	they(females)

B.   Notice the following facts concerning these pronouns:
1. *I* is always capitalized; *yo* is not. The two refer to the speaker.
2. *Nosotros* becomes *nosotras* if the speakers are all females. If the speakers are males and females, we use *nosotros*.
3. *Tú* is the familiar for *you;* it is used among friends and within the family. Its frequency as compared to *usted* may change from country to country.
4. *Vosotros* and *vosotras* is the plural form of *tú;* it is used only in Spain. Since this text employs Latin American usage, it will not be used in exercises here.
5. *Usted* and the plural *ustedes* are more formal than *tú;* they are used with persons we don't know well. In Latin America *ustedes* is the plural of *usted* and *tú*, since *vosotros* is not used at all.

6. *Ellas* refers only to females, whereas *ellos* refers to males as well as to combinations of males and females.

7. Notice the two pronouns with *acento escrito* (written stress): *tú* and *él*.

C. Notice that there is *no subject* pronoun for the neuter *it;* this is because inanimate nouns (things) can rarely be replaced by a pronoun as subjects of a sentence.

Ex.: ¿La *mujer* es americana? - Sí, *ella* es americana. (she is American) ¿La *mesa* es americana? - Sí, es americana. (it is American)

The same rule applies in the plural: *ellos* and *ellas* refer to persons or animals, never to things.

NOTE:

Usted is abbreviated into *Ud.* or *Vd.* and *ustedes* into *Uds.* or *Vds.*

PRACTICE THE SUBJECT PRONOUNS   *(Answers, p. 76)*

1. Which pronoun is always capitalized in English but not in Spanish?_____ _____ .

2. The pronoun *we* has two possible words in Spanish: _____ _____ .

3. *Vosotros* is the plural of_____ in Spain, but it is not used in Latin America. In its place, Latin Americans use _____ .

4. Which one is more familiar, *tú* or *usted?* _____ .

5. *Nosotras* is used when all the speakers are _____ , but *nosotros* can be all males or a combination of males and _____ .

6. If Mr. Pérez is talking for himself and his wife, will he say *nosotros* or *nosotras?* _____ .

7. The use of *tú* versus *usted* varies from country to country. A student would address his teacher as_____ , and the teacher would reply with _____ .

8. The mark (´) on a vowel in Spanish is called *acento,* and later you will learn the rules for its use. Which are the two pronouns with *acento?* _____ .

9. *He* is always a person (or animal) as subject of a sentence; the Spanish word is_____. The pronoun for *she* is _____. The pronoun for *it* is _____.

10. If we talk to Mary and Jane, we refer to them as *they;* the Spanish word is _____. If we talk about the boy and girl, we refer to them as *they;* the Spanish word is _____.

11. If we talk about the tables, we refer to them as *they* if the word is the subject of the sentence. Would you translate *they* (tables) in this case? _____.

12. One easy way to tell *tú* from *usted* is to compare with English. When you call a person by his or her first name (John, Mary, etc), you would use *tú*. When you use last names (Mr. Martínez), you would use _____ in Spanish.

13. *Usted* is abbreviated into _____, and *ustedes* _____.

EXERCISE   (Answers, p. 76)

Write the Spanish pronouns.

1. we (all females) _____

2. you (familiar, singular) _____

3. I _____

4. you (familiar, plural [Spain]) _____

5. they (all females) _____

6. you (formal, singular) _____

7. he _____

8. she _____

9. they (all males) _____

10. it _____

11. you (formal, plural) _____

12. they (males and females) _____

13. we (males and females) _____

14. they (things) _____

Lesson 2

En un restaurante (In a Restaurant)

Aprenda las Palabras Nuevas (Learn the New Words)

almuerzo	lunch	cuenta	bill	lechuga	lettuce
azúcar	sugar	ensalada	salad	menú (el)	menu
caja	cash register	filete	steak	papas fritas	french fries
camarera	waitress	flan	custard	postre	dessert
camarero	waiter	fruta	fruit	salsa	sauce
cerveza	beer	helado	ice cream	sopa	soup
comida	food, meal	jamón	ham	tomate	tomato
crema (la)	cream	langosta	lobster	vegetales	vegetables
aprender	to learn	estar	to be	salir	to leave
beber	to drink	estudiar	to study	ser	to be
comer	to eat	hablar	to talk	subir	to climb
completar	to complete	leer	to read	tomar	to take
creer	to believe	ordenar	to order	trabajar	to work
desear	to want	pagar	to pay	usar	to use
escribir	to write	pasar	to pass	vivir	to live
algo	something	delicioso	delicious	también	also
allí	there	dos	two	tarde	late
aquí	here	excelente	excellent	verde	green
¡cómo no!	of course!	por	by	ya	already
con	with				

PRACTICE THE NEW WORDS *(Answers, p. 76)*

A. Write the article *el* or *la* in front of these nouns.

1.____salsa	6.____azúcar	11.____helado	16.____vegetal
2.____filete	7.____postre	12.____papa	17.____cuenta
3.____jamón	8.____crema	13.____tomate	18.____lechuga
4.____caja	9.____menú	14.____comida	19.____camarero
5.____cerveza	10.____flan	15.____fruta	20.____camarera

B. Match the two columns by writing the appropriate letter.

1.____flan	10.____helado	A. beer	J. fried
2.____cuenta	11.____filete	B. to pay	K. lunch
3.____algo	12.____caja	C. here	L. to leave
4.____cerveza	13.____también	D. custard	M. steak
5.____almuerzo	14.____aquí	E. ice cream	N. to drink
6.____pagar	15.____verde	F. bill	O. green
7.____beber	16.____papa	G. to read	P. potato
8.____salir	17.____frita	H. cash register	Q. waiter
9.____leer	18.____camarero	I. something	R. also

DIÁLOGO *En un restaurante*

CAMARERO: Buenas tardes, señores. Aquí está el menú. ¿Desean ustedes beber algo?

ROBERTO: Sí, dos cervezas, por favor.

ANTONIO: También deseamos ordenar el almuerzo.

CAMARERO: Sí, ¡cómo no!

ROBERTO: Yo deseo un filete con papas fritas, ensalada de lechuga y tomate, y de postre, helado de chocolate.

CAMARERO: Y usted, señor, ¿qué desea?

ANTONIO: Sopa de vegetales, langosta en salsa verde, ensalada de tomate y lechuga, y fruta, de postre.

CAMARERO: ¿Toman ustedes café con la comida?

ROBERTO: Sí, con crema y azúcar, por favor.

• • •

> Roberto: La comida está excelente. Este restaurante es muy bueno.
> Antonio: Sí, la langosta tiene un sabor delicioso.
>
> • • •
>
> Roberto: Ya es tarde. Camarero, la cuenta, por favor.
> Camarero: Aquí está. Ustedes pagan allí en la caja. Adiós y gracias.
> Antonio: Adiós. Hasta luego.

DIALOG *In a Restaurant*

WAITER: Good afternoon, gentlemen. Here's the menu. Would you care for anything to drink?
ROBERT: Yes, two beers, please.
ANTHONY: We also want to order lunch.
WAITER: Yes, of course!
ROBERT: I want a steak with french fries, a lettuce and tomato salad, and chocolate ice cream for dessert.
WAITER: And you, sir, what do you want?
ANTHONY: Vegetable soup, lobster in green sauce, a lettuce and tomato salad, and fruit for dessert.
WAITER: Do you take coffee with your meal?
ROBERTO: Yes, with cream and sugar, please.

• • •

ROBERT: The food is excellent. This restaurant is very good.
ANTHONY: Yes, the lobster has a delicious flavor.

• • •

ROBERT: It's late. Waiter, the bill, please.
WAITER: Here it is. You pay over there at the cash register. Goodbye and thanks.
ANTHONY: Goodbye. So long.

EXERCISES   *(Answers, p. 76)*

A. Complete the sentences according to the dialog.

1. Roberto y Antonio desean beber dos _____.

2. Roberto y Antonio hablan con el _____.

3. Los dos amigos (friends) ordenan el _____ por el menú.

4. Roberto desea comer un filete con _____.

5. Antonio desea tomar una sopa de _____.

6. Los dos amigos ordenan una ensalada de _____.

7. Roberto ordena _____ de postre.

8. Antonio ordena _____ de postre.

9. La comida del restaurante está _____.

10. La langosta de Antonio tiene un sabor _____.

11. Antonio y Roberto toman el café con _____.

12. Los dos amigos pagan la cuenta en _____.

B.   Underline the word that makes sense.   *(Answers, p. 77)*

1. Ordenamos el almuerzo por (la caja, el postre, el menú).

2. Usamos el azúcar y la crema en (las papas, el café, la sopa).

3. El camarero trabaja en (el jamón, la caja, el restaurante).

4. Roberto desea beber (un helado de chocolate, una cerveza, un flan).

5. La ensalada es de (filete, crema, lechuga y tomate).

6. Roberto toma el café con (azúcar y crema, salsa verde, vegetales).

7. (El filete, el flan, la cuenta) es una clase de postre.

8. (El tomate, el azúcar, el menú) es una clase de vegetal.

9. Usamos el azúcar en (el filete, la sopa, el café).

10. El camarero pasa (la cuenta, la caja, el restaurante) a los dos amigos.

11. Los dos amigos leen (el filete, el menú, la cerveza) en el restaurante.

12. Una clase de helado es (de chocolate, de jamón, de salsa verde).

13. Antonio come la langosta con (tomates, salsa verde, fruta).

GRAMMAR I   Regular **-AR** verbs in the Present Indicative.

A. The three kinds of verbs:
    There are three kinds of verbs in Spanish, classified according to the
    ending of the infinitive. The form of the verb listed in dictionaries is
    the infinitive. Its equivalent in English is the form preceded by *to: to*
    speak, *to* study. The three kinds of verbs are called first, second, and
    third conjugations.
    1. First conjugation: Verbs ending in -**AR,** such as *hablar.* (to speak/
       to talk)
    2. Second conjugation: Verbs ending in -**ER,** such as *comer.* (to eat)

3. Third conjugation: Verbs ending in **-IR,** such as *vivir.* (to live) Every verb form is divided in two parts: *stem + ending.* The stem carries the meaning of the verb and is the same in all persons and tenses. The ending is the part of the verb that changes to signal the different tenses and persons.

Ex.: *habl + ar.* The stem is *habl,* the ending *ar* (infinitive).

B. Present Indicative of *hablar:*

SUBJECT	**habl ar**	SUBJECT	*to speak*
yo	**habl o**	I	speak/am speaking/do speak
nosotros -as	**habl amos**	we	speak/are speaking/do speak
tú	**habl as**	you	speak/are speaking/do speak
él/ella/Ud.	**habl a**	he/she/you	speaks/is speaking/does speak
ellos/ellas/Uds.	**habl an**	they/you	speak/are speaking/do speak

1. The stem *habl* is the same for all the persons, and it doesn't change for the different verb tenses. This is why we call *hablar* a regular verb.
2. The endings identify the person and the tense: *-o* means *yo* (I); *-amos* means *nosotros -as* (we);*-as* means *tú* (familiar you); *-a* means *él, ella* or *usted,* and *-an* means *ellos, ellas* or *ustedes.* These endings are not the same for all the tenses.
3. Since the subject pronoun information is given by the verb ending, we omit the subject pronouns unless we want to add emphasis to the subject. For example, *tú hablas español* means *you speak Spanish* (raising the voice on *you*).

C. Uses of the Present Indicative:
1. The Present Indicative is used to indicate an *action in progress* at the time of speaking.

Ex.: *Hablo* español ahora. (*I'm speaking* Spanish now)
2. The Present Indicative is used to show a *habit,* something we continue doing.

Ex.: *Hablo* español siempre. (*I speak* Spanish all the time)
3. The Present Indicative also translates the emphatic *I do speak* by raising the voice on the verb or by adding an adverb such as *sí* (indeed).
4. The Present Indicative can be used for an action in the future, but we need a time adverb to differentiate it from the present.

Ex.: Mañana *hablo* con el director. (*I will speak* to the director tomorrow)

PRACTICE THE PRESENT INDICATIVE   (Answers, p. 77)

1. The three kinds of verbs in Spanish are identified by the ending of the
   _____. The first conjugation ends in _____,
   the second in _____ and the third in _____.Actually we
   can say that the vowels *a, e, i* identify the three kinds of verbs and the final *r*
   identifies the infinitive of all verbs, just as *to* precedes all the infinitives in
   English.

2. The stem of a verb carries the basic _____ which is
   repeated in all the person and all the tenses. What's the stem of *hablar*?
   _____. And the stem of *vivir*? _____.

3. The ending *-amos* gives the subject pronoun information for _____
   _____. The ending *-as* repeats the subject _____,
   and the ending *-o* repeats the subject _____.

4. Any noun takes the same third-person ending as *él, ellas, ellos, ellas.* How
   do you complete the sentence *Roberto* _____*mucho*?
   (Robert talks a lot).

5. *We* is the combination of *somebody else and I;* therefore, how do you say *She
   and I speak Spanish? Ella y yo* _____
   español.

6. Notice that the stem of *estudiar* ends in an *i* after you drop the ending *-ar.*
   This means you have to keep the *i* in all the persons. How do you say *We
   study?* _____.

7. Since the verb endings repeat the information carried by the subject pronouns, we don't use subject pronouns unless we want to add _____
   _____.

8. The Present Indicative is used for an action in _____ at the
   time of speaking. For example, *she is studying now* is translated as *Ella*
   _____*ahora.*

9. The verb *usar* has a short stem: _____. How do you say *we use?*_____
   _____. And how do you say *they are using?*_____.

10. A habit is an action we repeat many times. How do you say *I use Spanish at
    home?*_____ *el español en casa.*

11. We can use the present for a future action with the help of an adverb. How do you say *I will use the book tomorrow?* _____ *el libro mañana.*

12. In Spanish we don't have an emphatic auxiliary like the *do* in *you do speak.* We use the ordinary present *hablas* and emphasize it with the voice. How do you say *They do study Spanish?* _____.

EXERCISE   *(Answers, p. 77)*

Complete the sentences with the appropriate verb form.

1. Ustedes _____ español. (estudiar)

2. Roberto y Antonio _____ el almuerzo. (ordenar)

3. Ellos _____ la cuenta en la caja. (pagar)

4. Tú _____ el café con crema y azúcar. (tomar)

5. El camarero _____ en un restaurante excelente. (trabajar)

6. En Estados Unidos nosotros _____ bastante gasolina. (usar)

7. María y yo _____ en la clase de español. (estar)

8. Yo _____ comer una ensalada de tomate. (desear)

9. Señores, ¿ _____ ustedes leer el menú? (desear)

10. La camarera _____ el menú a Roberto. (pasar)

11. El postre _____ una comida deliciosa. (completar)

12. Tú _____ beber una cerveza mexicana. (desear)

13. Ella y él _____ el autobús por la noche. (tomar)

14. José y yo _____ la lección de español. (completar)

15. Los camareros _____ en el restaurante. (trabajar)

16. ¿Dónde _____ nosotros la cuenta? (pagar)

17. El taxista _____ un taxi excelente. (usar)

18. José _____ muy tarde los lunes. (trabajar)

19. Antonio _____ el azúcar a Roberto. (pasar)

20. Yo _____ el problema en el libro. (estudiar)

GRAMMAR II   Regular verbs ending in -**ER** and -**IR**.

A.   The Present Indicative of *comer* and *vivir*:
Verbs of the second conjugation end in -*ER* in the infinitive; those of
the third conjugation end in -*IR*. Ex.: *comer* (to eat) and *vivir* (to live).
These two kinds of verbs have almost the same endings in all the
tenses. Memorize the Present Indicative.

SUBJECT	com er	viv ir	SUBJECT	to eat to live
yo	com o	viv o	I	eat/am eating/do eat
				live/am living/do live
nosotros -as	com emos	viv imos	we	eat/are eating/do eat
				live/are living/do live
tú	com es	viv es	you	eat/are eating/do eat
				live/are living/do live
él/ella/Ud.	com e	viv e	he/she/you	eats/is eating/does eat
				lives/is living/does live
ellos/ellas	com en	viv en	they/you	eat/are eating/do eat
				live/are living/do live

B.   Notice the following facts in the chart above:
1. The stem of *comer* is *com* and the stem of *vivir* is *viv*. These stems
   carry the meaning of the verb and they are the same in all the
   persons.
2. The endings are very similar to those of the first conjugation: -*o*
   means *yo;* -*emos* and -*imos* mean *nosotros -as;* -*es* means *tú;* -*e*
   means *él/ella/Ud.;* and -*en* means *ellos, ellas, ustedes.*
3. The endings of *comer* and *vivir* are the same except in the first
   person plural. Compare *comemos* with *vivimos;* the difference is
   the *e* vs. *i.*

C.   Uses of the Present Indicative:
The uses of *comer* and *vivir* in the Present Indicative are the same as
those of *hablar;* in fact, they are the same for all verbs. Let's review
them.
1. an action *in progress* at the time of speaking.
      Ex.: Ella come en este momento. (she is eating at this mo-
      ment)
2. an action as a *habit.*
      Ex.: Ella siempre come mucho. (she always eats a lot)
3. an action in the *future.*
      Ex.: ¿Dónde comes mañana? (where will you eat tomorrow?)

> 4. The Present Indicative translates the emphatic form *do + verb* by raising the voice on the verb.
>   Ex.: Usted vive aquí. (you do live here)

PRACTICE THE VERBS

(Answers, p. 77)

1. The second kind of verb is characterized by the ending _____ of the infinitive, and the third kind, by the ending _____ .

2. The stem carries the meaning of the verb. What's the stem of *comer?* _____ . The stem of *escribir?* _____ and the stem of *leer?* _____ .

3. The subject pronouns are usually omitted in Spanish because the _____ _____ of the verb carries the same information; for example, the ending *-o* means _____ .

4. You may have noticed that the difference between *habl-amos* and *com-emos* is the ending *-amos* vs. *emos,* or better yet, the two vowels *a/e.* What's the form of *vivir* in the same person? *Nosotros* _____ . The ending here is neither *-amos* nor *-emos* but _____ .

5. *Comer* and *vivir* have the same endings in all the persons of the Present Indicative except in the _____ . Note that the differences is the same vowel that indicates the difference in the infinitive, *-ER* vs. *-IR*.

6. The Present Indicative of any verb is used for an action in progress. For example, Where *are you living* now? is translated as *¿Dónde* _____ *usted ahora?*

7. A habit is an action we repeat many times. If the habit still exists, we express that action in the _____ . For example, *You drink milk all the time* is translated as *Usted* _____ *leche siempre.* (beber)

8. The present tense is often used instead of the future tense for an action still to come. Ex.: *Mañana* (yo) _____ *la lección.* (leer)

9. *Escribir* means *to write*. Can you write the four meanings of *escribimos*?

   (a) An action in actual progress: _____.

   (b) An action as a habit: _____.

   (c) An action in the future: _____.

   (d) An action with emphasis: _____.

EXERCISE

(Answers, p. 77)

Complete the following sentences with the correct forms of the verbs in parenthesis. (Remember that the pronouns can be omitted, but they are given in the exercise so that you can practice all the persons. Notice that there are a few -*AR* verbs included, and they will follow the pattern of *hablar*.)

1. Nosotros _____ español en el libro.
(aprender)

2. El policía _____ en la estación. (leer)

3. ¿Dónde _____ tú la cuenta de la comida?
(escribir)

4. Yo _____ el tren en la estación. (tomar)

5. La mujer _____ una cerveza. (beber)

6. Antonio y yo _____ la Sierra Nevada.
(subir)

7. El avión no _____ muy tarde. (salir)

8. Ellas _____ un postre delicioso. (comer)

9. Ustedes no _____ la verdad. (creer)

10. Los lunes yo _____ en un restaurante. (comer)

11. Nosotros _____ del tema del hambre.
(hablar)

12. Usted _____ el menú una vez. (leer)

13. Yo _____ la lección de español en el papel.
(escribir)

14. José _____ mañana para San Francisco. (salir)

15. El agua del mar _____ con la *marea* (tide). (subir)

16. Tú no _____ en el problema del hambre. (creer)

17. Ustedes ———————————————————— en un garaje. (trabajar)

18. ¡Cómo no! Los mexicanos ———————————————————— en México. (vivir)

19. Yo no ———————— cerveza *sino* (but) café. (beber)

20. El gato ———————— muy bien al árbol. (subir)

GRAMMAR III   Forms and usage of **ser** and **estar** *(to be)*.

A.   Memorize *ser* and *estar* in the Present Indicative:

SUBJECT	s er	est ar	to be	
yo	s oy	est oy	I	am
nosotros	s omos	est amos	we	are
tú	er es	est ás	you	are
él/ella/Ud.	es	est á	he/she/you	is
ellos/ellas/Uds.	s on	est án	they/you	are

B.   Notice the following facts in the chart:
1. These two verbs are irregular because they don't follow the conjugation of the verbs ending in *-AR, ER,* or *-IR,* or they have changes in the stem.
2. The stem of *ser* is *s* but also *er* in *tú eres* and *es* in *él es*. The stem of *estar* is *est* in the infinitive and all the persons of the Present Indicative.
3. The first-person ending is *oy* instead of *o* as in *hablo* or *como*.
4. *Estar* has three forms with the written accent: *estás, está,* and *están*. (If you pay attention to the words with written accent as you go along, you will find it easier to learn the rules about the accent when you study them later.)

C.   Uses of *ser* and *estar:*
1. *Ser* is used to identify a person or a thing.
   Ex.: Esto es un lápiz. (this is a pencil)
   Juan es maestro. (John is a teacher)

   (Notice that we don't translate *a*.)
2. *Estar* is used to show the location of a person or thing. (Compare *estar* and *stay*.)
   Ex.: El lápiz está aquí. (the pencil is here)
   Juan está en casa. (John is at home)

3. *Ser* is used with an adjective to show that a characteristic is the *norm* for the noun. For example, it is the norm for *snow* to be white, soft, etc.

  Ex.: La nieve es blanca. (snow is white) (Note that there is no translation for *la*.)
    Roberto es mexicano. (Robert is Mexican)

4. *Estar* is used with an adjective to show that the characteristic is a *change* from the norm. For example, it is not normal for *snow* to be *red, hard,* etc.

  Ex.: Esta nieve está roja. (this snow is red) (because of red paint, blood, etc.)
    Esta hierba está verde. (this grass is green) (after watering the lawn)

5. *Ser* is used with the preposition *de* to indicate:
  (a) *Origin:* Este libro es de Chile. (this book is from Chile)
  (b) *Material:* La mesa es de plástico. (the table is mad of plastic)
  (c) *Possession:* La casa es de mi amigo. (the house belongs to my friend)

PRACTICE *SER* AND *ESTAR*

              (Answers, p. 77)

1. There are two verbs in Spanish for *to be:* _____.

2. *Ser* is an *-ER* verb and *estar* is an *-AR* verb, but they don't follow the conjugations of *comer* and *hablar*. For this reason we say that they are

 _____ .

3. The first person *(yo)* of *hablar* and *comer* is marked by the vowel *o*; *ser* and *estar* don't have *o* but _____ .

4. *Estar* has three forms with *acento* (written accent): _____

 _____ .

5. Which verb is used to show the place where a person, an animal, or a thing is—*ser* or *estar*? _____ . For example, *El gato* _____ *allí*.

6. Which verb is used to identify a person or a thing, *ser* or *estar*? _____ .
For example, *Washington* ____ *la capital de Estados Unidos*.

7. An adjective shows a characteristic of a noun: red, big, good, roomy, etc. If the characteristic shown is the norm for that noun, we use the verb ____ in Spanish. If the characteristic is a change from the norm, we use ____ .

8. Usually, grass is green; in Spanish you should say *La hierba* _____ *verde.*

9. It is the norm for coffee to be brown, but not to be hot or cold; you have to heat it to make it hot. Therefore, you say *El café* _____ *caliente.*

10. To indicate the origin of a person or thing, we use the verb _____ in Spanish. For example, *El taxista* _____ *de Chicago.* After all, giving the origin of a person or thing is a way of identifying or showing the norm for a person or thing.

11. To indicate the material something is made of, we use the verb _____ . For example, *La sopa* _____ *de vegetales.* It is a way of identifying it.

12. To show possession, we use the verb _____ in Spanish. For example, *La cuenta* _____ *de Roberto y Antonio.*

EXERCISE   *(Answers, p. 78)*

Complete with the correct forms of *ser* or *estar.*

1. Yo _____ de España. ¿De dónde _____ ustedes?

2. Ella _____ americana, pero _____ en Madrid.

3. El café _____ de Colombia.

4. Los policías _____ en la estación de policía.

5. La langosta _____ del mar Caribe.

6. Ronald Reagan _____ el Presidente de Estados Unidos.

7. Tú y yo _____ americanos.

8. Las camareras _____ en el restaurante.

9. ¿Cómo _____ usted? - Yo _____ bien, gracias.

10. No tomo el café; _____ muy frío. (it's very cold)

11. La nieve de las montañas _____ blanca. (the snow in the mountains is white)

12. Ustedes _____ muy buenos con la camarera.

13. José _____ taxista; trabaja en Nueva York.

14. La ensalada _____ verde; _____ de lechuga. (it's made of lettuce)

15. El jamón _____ un producto de un animal: el puerco. (pig)

16. El helado _____ *dulce* (sweet); la cerveza no _____ dulce.

17. El filete de Roberto _____ excelente, y la langosta _____ deliciosa.

18. La cerveza _____ *fría* (cold); _____ en el *refrigerador.* (refrigerator)

19. El libro no _____ de inglés; _____ de español.

20. El agua mineral _____ buena con la comida.

Lesson 3

En un restaurante de mariscos (In a Seafood Restaurant)

aperitivo	aperitif	**idea**	idea	**pareja**	couple (people)
boca	mouth	**mante-quilla**	butter	**plato**	dish, plate
botella	bottle	**margarina**	margarine	**ración**	order, serving
camarón[1]	shrimp	**marisco**	seafood	**tarjeta**	card (credit)
cena	supper	**mundo**	world	**vaso**	(drinking) glass
cheque	check	**paella**[2]	paella	**viajero**	traveler
ciudad	city, town	**pan**	bread	**vino**	wine
aceptar	to accept	**espe-cializar**	to specialize	**pedir**	to ask for
acompañar	to accompany	**hacer**	to do, make	**preparar**	to prepare, cook
cenar	to eat supper	**ir**	to go	**saber**	to know
dar	to give	**mirar**	to look at	**servir**	to serve, help
decir	to say, tell	**necesitar**	to need	**ver**[3]	to see, look at
amarillo	yellow	**dulce**	sweet	**negro**	black
barato	cheap	**frío**	cold	**pequeño**	small
blanco	white	**grande**	large, big	**rojo**	red
caliente	hot	**malo**[4]	bad, sick	**rosado**	pink, rosé
caro	expensive	**mejor**	better, best	**seco**	dry
		mucho	much, a lot	**todo**	all, whole
además	besides	**para**	to, in order to		
a la plancha	on the grill	**por supuesto**	of course		
ahora	now	**primero**	first		
este (masculine)	this	**hacer la boca agua**	to make one's mouth water		

NOTES:

1. *Camarón* is used in Latin America. In Spain it is called *gamba*.

2. *Paella* is a popular dish in Spain and Latin America. It is made with chicken, pork, sausage, rice, saffron, and all kinds of seafood, such as shrimp, clams, lobster, crab, mussels, etc.

3. *Ver* is not only *to see,* but also *to look at* or *to watch.* In this sense *ver* overlaps with the meaning of *mirar* (watch).

4. *Malo* means *bad,* but when it is used with the verb *estar* (to be) with persons, it means *sick.*
     Ex.: María está mala. (Mary is sick)

PRACTICE THE NEW WORDS   (Answers, p. 78)

A.   Write the article *el* or *la* in front of the noun. Remember that L-O-N-E-R-S is *el* and D-IÓN-Z-A is *la*.

1. _____ paella   6. _____ cheque   11. _____ pareja

2. _____ marisco   7. _____ viajero   12. _____ vino

3. _____ pan   8. _____ ciudad   13. _____ mundo

4. _____ idea   9. _____ tarjeta   14. _____ plancha

5. _____ ración   10. _____ camarón   15. _____ viajera

B.   Complete the sentences with a word from the vocabulary.

1. La langosta y el_____son dos clases de mariscos.

2. Dos personas (o animales) es una_____.

3. Usamos un_____para beber el vino.

4. Este vino no es dulce; es_____.

5. La_____es un plato con muchos mariscos.

6. Los camarones se llaman_____en España.

7. La langosta y el camarón no son baratos; son_____.

8. El color del vino es blanco, rojo o_____.

9. El hambre es el mejor_____.

10. En este restaurante aceptamos_____de *crédito* (credit).

11. Pagamos la cuenta con un_____de viajeros.

12. Nueva York es una _____ muy grande.

13. Comemos el pan con margarina o _____.

14. ¿Cómo se dice *to ask for* en español? _____.

15. ¿Cómo se dice *a la plancha* en inglés? _____.

C. Write the antonym or contrary of.

1. El antónimo de *blanco* es _____.

2. El antónimo de *caro* es _____.

3. El antónimo de *frío* es _____.

4. El antónimo de *dulce* es _____. (talking about wines)

5. El antónimo de *grande* es _____.

6. El antónimo de *bueno* es _____.

7. El antónimo de *postre* es _____.

8. El antónimo de *hombre* es _____.

9. El antónimo de *camarero* es _____.

10. El antónimo de *viajero* es _____.

11. El antónimo de *un turista* es _____.

12. El antónimo de *un policía* es _____.

13. El antónimo de *allí* es _____.

14. El antónimo de *día* es _____.

15. El antónimo de *norte* (north) es _____.

DIÁLOGO   *En un restaurante de mariscos*

(Una pareja cena en un restaurante que se especializa en mariscos.)

CAMARERA: Buenas noches. ¿En qué puedo servirles?

JOSÉ: ¿Es verdad que este restaurante prepara los mejores mariscos de la ciudad?

CAMARERA: Sí, aquí servimos la mejor paella del mundo.

CECILIA: ¡Qué bueno! ¡La boca se me hace agua!

CAMARERA: Aquí está el menú. ¿Desean un aperitivo primero?

JOSÉ: Sí, dos vermuth dulces, por favor.

CECILIA: . . . y dos raciones de camarones a la plancha.

CAMARERA: Muy bien. ¿Desean pedir la comida ahora? La paella necesita tiempo.

CECILIA:	Sí, vamos a ordenar una paella para dos, ¡con muchos mariscos!
JOSÉ:	Además, pan con mantequilla. Y de postre, dos flanes.
CAMARERA:	¿Algo de beber con la cena?
CECILIA:	Una botella de vino blanco para acompañar la paella.
JOSÉ:	¿Aceptan ustedes tarjetas de crédito?
CAMARERA:	Por supuesto. Y cheques de viajeros también.

DIALOG   *In a Seafood Restaurant*

(A couple is going to eat supper in a restaurant that specializes in seafood.)

WAITRESS:	Good evening. May I help you?
JOE:	Is it true that this restaurant prepares the best seafood in town?
WAITRESS:	Yes, here we serve the best paella in the world.
CECILIA:	That sounds good! It makes my mouth water!
WAITRESS:	Here's the menu. Do you want an aperitif first?
JOE:	Yes, please, two sweet vermouths . . .
CECILIA:	. . . and two orders of grilled shrimp.
WAITRESS:	Very well. Do you want to order your dinner now? The paella takes time.
CECILIA:	Yes, we're going to order a paella for two, with plenty of seafood!
JOE:	And bread and butter. And two custards for dessert.
WAITRESS:	Anything to drink with your supper?
CECILIA:	A bottle of white wine to accompany the paella.
JOE:	Do you accept credit cards?
WAITRESS:	Of course. And traverler's checks too.

EXERCISES

(Answers, p. 78)

A.   Complete the sentences according to the dialog.

1. José y Cecilia cenan en un restaurante de_____.

2. La camarera habla con la_____.

3. En este restaurante sirven la mejor paella del_____.

4. La pareja desea tomar primero un_____.

5. José y Cecilia toman dos vermuth_____.

6. Cecilia ordena dos_____de camarones a la plancha.

7. La camarera da el_____a José y a Cecilia.

8. Cecilia ordena una paella_____, con muchos mariscos.

9. Además, José desea pan con_____.

10. De postre, la pareja va a comer_____.

11. Cecilia ordena una_____de vino.

12. ¿Toman vino rojo, blanco o rosado?_____.

13. En el restaurante aceptan_____de crédito.

14. También aceptan cheques de_____.

B.   Match the two columns. (One of the letters in the column to the right matches two numbers.)

1._____Deseo camarones . . .

2._____¡Cómo no!

3._____Comemos pan . . .

4._____El restaurante se especializa . . .

5._____El amarillo es . . .

6._____La boca . . .

7._____Aquí aceptamos . . .

8._____Comemos flan . . .

9._____Ahora la langosta . . .

10._____VISA es una tarjeta . . .

11._____Necesito cheques . . .

12._____Una ración de camarones . . .

13._____Deseamos dos vermuth . . .

14._____El color del vino es . . .

15._____Leemos los platos . . .

A. de crédito.

B. de postre.

C. de viajeros.

D. a la plancha.

E. de aperitivo.

F. con mantequilla.

G. por supuesto.

H. un color muy popular.

I. en mariscos.

J. se hace agua.

K. en el menú.

L. tarjetas de crédito.

M. es muy cara.

N. rojo, rosado o blanco.

GRAMMAR I   Adjective–noun agreement. Plural of nouns and adjectives.

A.   An adjective describes a noun with such characteristics as color, shape, size, quality, nationality, etc. The adjective agrees with its noun in *gender* and *number* in Spanish. In English adjectives never change; there is no agreement.

> Ex.: un libr*o* buen*o* (a good book): masculine singular
> una mes*a* buen*a* (a good table): feminine singular
> uno*s* libr*os* bueno*s* (some good books): masculine plural
> una*s* mes*as* buen*as* (some good tables): feminine plural

B. *Plural* means two or more. Nouns and adjectives follow the same rules to form the plural:

---

1. If a word ends in a vowel, we add an *s*: libro bueno/libro*s* bueno*s*.
2. If a word ends in a consonant, we add *es*: papel azul/papel*es* azul*es*. (blue)
3. If a word ends in a -*z*, we change *z* to *c* and add *es*: lápi*z*/ lápi*ces*.
4. If a word ends in an -*s*, there are two rules for the plural:
   (a) If the *s* is preceded by a *stressed* vowel, we add *es*: inglés/ingles*es*.
   (b) If the *s* is preceded by an *unstressed* vowel, there is no change.
      Ex.: *un* lunes/*dos* lunes.
           un paraguas/*dos* paraguas (umbrella)
5. There are a few words ending in *stressed* -í and *stressed* -ú; they have two plural endings (according to different regions): *s* or *es*.
      Ex.: carmesí (crimson)/*carmesís* or *carmesíes*
           rubí (ruby)/*rubís* or *rubíes*.
           Hindú (Hindu)/*hindúes* or *hindús*

C. Adjectives ending in -*o*, change to *a* in the feminine: buen*o*/buen*a*. If the adjective ends in any other letter, there is no change for the gender.

> Ex.: libr*o* verd*e*/sals*a* verd*e*   Libro mejor/paell*a* mejor

D. Adjectives ending in L-N-R-S (part of *L-O-N-E-R-S*) and *referring to countries* add an *a* to the last consonant to form the feminine. They are also used as nouns.

> Ex.: un profeso*r* españo*l*/una profeso*ra* españo*la*
> un camarero inglés/una camarera inglesa
> un libro alemá*n*/una universidad alemana

PRACTICE THE GRAMMAR   *(Answers, p. 78)*

1. An adjective describes a_____. In Spanish the adjective

   changes with the noun for gender and_____.

2. Remember that nouns ending in L-O-N-E-R-S are _____.
   This means that these six endings will match the adjectives ending in the

   letter _____.

3. Nouns ending in D-IÓN-Z-A are _____; these endings
   will

   match the adjectives ending in the letter _____.

4. Do the adjectives ending in *e* change from masculine to feminine? _____.

   For example, libro verde, tarjeta _____ (green).

5. Which is correct, *pared blanco* or *pared blanca*? _____.

6. Which is correct, *papel amarillo* or *papel amarilla*? _____.

7. Remember that nouns ending in -*ma* are *not* feminine. Would you say

   programa americano or *programa americana*? _____

   _____.

8. Which is correct, *luz rojo* or *luz roja*? _____.

9. Would an adjective ending in *e,* such as *grande, verde,* change from mas-

   culine to feminine? _____. Ex.: Un libro *grande,* una casa _____.

10. The plural of *bueno* is _____. We add an *s* because the

    last letter is a _____.

11. The plural of *camarón* is _____. We add *es* because the

    last letter is a _____.

12. The plural of *luz* is _____. We add *es* because the last

    letter is a consonant, but we change the *z* to _____.

13. The plural of *lunes* is _____. The last letter is an *s,* and

    the preceding vowel carries no _____, so there is no
    change.

14. The plural of *inglés* is _____. The last letter is an *s,* but

    it is preceded by a _____ vowel. Therefore we add *es.*

15. There are two plurals for words ending in stressed -*í* or -*ú*: For example,

    the plural of the precious stone *rubí* is _____ or

    _____. The modern tendency in most regions is simply
    to add the *s.*

EXERCISES

(Answers, p. 79)

A. Write the plural forms.

1. el aperitivo pequeño _____

2. el camarón caro _____

3. la mejor paella _____

4. el cheque amarillo _____

5. la cena grande _____

6. la idea mala _____

7. la ración deliciosa _____

8. el café caliente _____

9. el mejor papel _____

10. el vino seco _____

11. el rubí caro _____

12. la luz verde _____

13. el lunes *pasado* (last) _____

14. el vaso inglés _____

15. el agua caliente _____

B. Underline the adjective that agrees with the noun. Two answers are sometimes possible. (Remember the rules for masculine/feminine gender.)

1. Programa (bueno, buena, buenos, buenas)

2. Papeles (rojo, roja, rojos, rojas)

3. Vermuth (seco, seca, secos, secas)

4. Vinos (dulce, dulza, dulces, dulzas)

5. Mano (pequeño, pequeña, pequeños, pequeñas)

6. Hambre (grande, granda, grandes, grandas)

7. Luces (mejor, mejora, mejores, mejoras)

8. Lunes (pasado, pasada, pasados, pasadas)

9. Libros (inglés, inglesa, ingleses, inglesas)

10. Rubís (carmesí, carmesís, carmesíes) (crimson rubies)

GRAMMAR II   Present Indicative of **ir, dar, ver, saber,** and **decir.**

A.   Memorize the following chart:

SUBJECT	ir *(to go)*	d ar *(to give)*	v er *(to see)*	sab er *(to know)*	dec ir *(to say)*
yo	v oy	d oy	ve o	sé	dig o
nosotros -as	v amos	d amos	v emos	sab emos	dec imos
tú	v as	d as	v es	sab es	dic es
él/ella/Ud.	v a	d a	v e	sab e	dic e
ellos/ellas/Uds.	v an	d an	v en	sab en	dic en

B.   Notice the following facts in the chart above:
1.   *Ir* and *dar* are irregular because they add *y* to the *o,* in the first person singular the same way as *ser (soy)* and *estar (estoy).*
2.   *Ver* is irregular only in the first person singular because it adds *e* to the stem. Notice that the stem in the infinitive is *v.* The meaning of *ver* is either *to see* or *to watch,* depending on the context.
3.   *Saber* is very irregular in the first person singular. It is *sé* instead of *sabo.*
4.   *Decir* is the most irregular verb in the group. As a stem-changing verb (see p. 50), it changes *e* to *i* in *digo, dices, dice,* and *dicen;* it also changes *c* to *g* in *digo.*
5.   *Ir* is the only Spanish verb without a stem in the infinitive. In the present the stem is *v,* and has the endings of the *-AR* verbs.
6.   The person-number endings to identify the subject are the same in all these verbs: *-o* (or *-oy*) for *yo;-mos* for *nosotros;-s* for tú, and *-n* for ellos/ellas/ustedes.

NOTE:

We very frequently use *ir a + infinitive* to indicate an action in the future, parallel to the English *to be + going + infinitive. Ir* is used in the Present Indicative.
   Ex.:   Ellos van a estudiar mañana. (they are going to study tomorrow)

PRACTICE THE VERBS   *(Answers, p. 79)*

1.   The basic meaning of a verb is carried by the _____ of the verb. For example, the part of *saber* with the meaning *know* is _____ .

2.   *Dar* is an -AR verb; its stem is very short: _____ . *Ver* is an -ER verb and its stem is also very short: _____ . Remember that the stem is the only part of the verb that is repeated in all the tenses if it is regular.

3. All verbs supposedly have an *-o* for *yo* in the Present Indicative, but a few have *-oy* instead. For example, from *ir* we get *yo* _____, and from *dar, yo* _____.

4. For *saber* we don't say *yo sabo* but *yo* _____. For *decir* we don't say *yo deco,* but *yo* _____.

5. For *ver* (v-er) we don't say *yo vo,* but *yo* _____. Notice the spelling difference between *van/ven:* the first one means *they* _____.

6. The person-number endings are common to all the verbs: *-mos* means _____, *-s* means _____, and *-n* means _____.

7. We can use the simple Present form for an action in the future, for example in *Voy a clase mañana.* We can also se the verb *ir* followed by the preposition *a* and the main verb, parallel to English *I am going to see you tomorrow: Voy a ver(te) mañana.* How do you say *He is going to go . . .?* _____ _____.

8. The Present tense can be used for an action that is a habit. How do you say *I always tell the truth* in Spanish? *Yo siempre* _____.

EXERCISE
(Answers on p. 79)

Complete the sentences with the correct Present Indicative form of the verb given in parentheses. (Although the subject pronouns can be omitted in Spanish, they are given here for practice; review the verbs in the vocabulary.)

1. Jorge y yo _____ a clase todos los días. (go)

2. Ustedes _____ cheques de viajeros. (need)

3. Todas las noches tú _____ la televisión. (watch)

4. La camarera _____ el menú a la pareja. (give)

5. María _____ a su mamá. (accompany)

6. El restaurante se _____ en mariscos. (specialize)

7. Este restaurante no _____ tarjetas de crédito. (accept)

8. Ellos _____ hablar español y francés. (know [how])

9. La camarera _____ el café. (is going to serve)

10. Usted _____ unos platos deliciosos. (prepare)

11. Cecilia y yo _____ toda la verdad. (tell)

12. En casa de María ellos _____ muy tarde. (have supper)

13. Yo no _____ preparar una paella. (know [how])

14. Tú _____ a cenar a *mi* (my) casa. (are going to go)

15. Nosotras _____ dos vasos de vermuth. (ask for)

16. ¡Con *tanta* (so much) comida, la boca se me _____ agua! (make)

17. El *banco* (bank) _____ cheques de viajeros. (give)

18. Yo _____ un plato muy grande para la paella. (need)

19. José no _____ vino seco. (drink)

20. El camarero y la camarera _____ español. (know)

GRAMMAR III   Question words. Numbers in Spanish.

A.   Memorize the following question words. Notice that all of them carry a written accent *(acento):*

¿Cuándo?	When?	**¿Quién?**	Who?
¿Dónde?	Where?	**¿De quién?**	Whose?
¿Cómo?	How?	**¿Por qué?**	Why?
¿Cuánto -a?	How much?	**¿Para qué?**	What for?
¿Cuántos -as?	How many?	**¿Qué?**	What?
¿Adónde?	Where to?	**¿Cuál?**	Which?

¿Adónde? can be spelled as two words: *¿A dónde?* Notice the question *mark* (¿) at the beginning of the question.

　　Ex.: *¿Cuándo comen ustedes?*

Notice that the subject (*ustedes* in this case) *follows* the verb instead of preceding it.

B.   The written accent (´) has to be written not only in *direct* questions but also in *indirect* questions.

　　Ex.: Deseo saber *cómo* estás. (I want to know *how* you are)

C.   Memorize the numbers in Spanish:

0 cero	17 diecisiete	60 sesenta
1 un/uno/una	18 dieciocho	70 setenta
2 dos	19 diecinueve	80 ochenta
3 tres	20 veinte	90 noventa
4 cuatro	21 veintiuno -a	100 cien(to)
5 cinco	22 veintidós	101 ciento uno
6 seis	23 veintitrés	200 doscientos
7 siete	24 veinticuatro	300 trescientos
8 ocho	25 veinticinco	400 cuatrocientos
9 nueve	26 veintiséis	500 quinientos
10 diez	27 veintisiete	600 seiscientos
11 once	28 veintiocho	700 setecientos
12 doce	29 veintinueve	800 ochocientos
13 trece	30 treinta	900 novecientos
14 catorce	31 trienta y uno	1000 mil
15 quince	40 cuarenta	2000 dos mil
16 dieciséis	50 cincuenta	1.000.000 un millón

D.   Notice the following facts about numbers:

1. From 16 to 29, we write only one word and we pronounce it with only one phonetic stress. In English compound numbers carry two stresses.

    Ex.: dieciséis (sixteén), veintidós, veintitrés, veintiséis

2. Some countries use three words from 16 to 29: *diez y seis, veinte y dos*. Either way, you'll notice that in Spanish, unlike English, the conjunction *y, (and)* is placed between tens and units.

    Ex.: *dieciséis* or *diez y seis, cuarenta y cinco, setenta y ocho*, etc. But *forty-five, sixty-two*.

3. For *one* we use *un* in front of a masculine noun, *una* in front of a feminine noun, and *uno* when the masculine noun is omitted.

    Ex.: Leo *un* libro, leo *una* novela. ¿Lee Ud. *un* libro? - Sí, leo *uno*.

    This same rule applies to compounds: veinti*ún* libros, veinti*una* mesas.

4. *Ciento* (100) is used only in compound numbers: *ciento dos* (102). Notice that we don't translate *one in one hundred two*. The expression *one hundred percent* is *cien por cien* or *ciento por ciento*, according to the country and region.

5. In the hundreds, *doscientos, trescientos*, etc., change to *doscientas, trescientas*, etc., when we talk about feminine nouns.

    Ex.: *quinientas langostas*

6. *Mil* doesn't change: *dos mil, tres mil, diez mil*, etc. Notice that we don't say *un mil* for *one thousand:* simply *mil*. We use *miles* (plural form) to refer to a large but inexact amount: Toma *miles de* vasos de vino.

7. Notice the spelling of *million: millón* (not *-lion*). The plural is *millones*, and it is always followed by *de* before the noun we are counting.

Ex.: *un* millón *de* dólares, *dos* millones *de* dólares ($2.000.000)

NOTE:

In Spanish we use a period (.) to indicate *thousand* and *million*, and a comma (,) to indicate *decimals*. In English it's the other way around.

PRACTICE THE NUMBERS

(Answers, p. 79)

1. All the question words carry a written ＿＿＿＿＿＿. For example, *¿cuando?* is incorrect; it should be ¿＿＿＿＿?.

2. *¿Adónde?* can also be spelled ¿＿＿＿＿?

3. An indirect question depends on a verb of asking, knowing, telling, etc., such as *saber, decir, pedir*. Is *donde* correct in the sentence *Yo no sé donde vive Ud.?* ＿＿＿; it should be ＿＿＿＿＿.

4. In Spanish *zero* is not spelled with *z* but ＿＿. Notice that *diez* (10) has a *z*, but *dieziséis* is incorrect; it should be ＿＿＿＿＿. This same change from *z* occurs in the plural of nouns and adjectives: *lápiz/lápices*.

5. How many phonetic stresses does a compound number have in Spanish? ＿＿＿. For example, *veinticinco* has the stress in the last number: ＿＿＿＿＿.

6. There are two words for 100: ＿＿＿＿/＿＿＿＿. Before a noun such as *pesos* ($), we say ＿＿＿＿*pesos*.

7. Do we use *cien* or *ciento* in numbers over one hundred? ＿＿＿. For example, 105 would be spelled on a Spanish bank check like this: ＿＿＿＿＿.

8. The indefinite article *un/una* is exactly like the number *one* in Spanish: *un* is used before a ＿＿＿＿ noun, and *una* before a ＿＿ ＿＿ noun.

9. *Uno* is used when a ＿＿＿＿ noun is omitted—that is, when it's alone. For example, *¿Desea Ud. un lápiz? - Sí, deseo* ＿＿＿.

10. *Dos cientos* (200) is not correct; it should be _____. All multiples of 100 change from *masculine* to *feminine* just like any other adjective. How do you say *300 bottles*? _____ botellas.

11. How do you say *one thousand* in Spanish? _____. (notice that we don't translate *one!*) How do you say 2.000? _____.

12. *Millión* is not spelled correctly; it should be _____. The plural of *millón* is _____ (no written accent! you'll understand why later).

13. We use the preposition _____ between *millón* (or *millones*) and the noun being counted. For example, $2.000.000 is *dos* _____ *dólares*.

EXERCISE   *(Answers, p. 79)*

Complete the sentences with the translation of the word in the parentheses.

1. ¿_____ vas a San Francisco? (when)

2. ¿_____ es este lápiz amarillo? (whose)

3. ¿_____ ves la televisión todos los días? (why)

4. ¿_____ cheques de viajeros necesita Ud.? (how many)

5. ¿_____ clase de vino desea tomar? (what)

6. Marcos necesita saber _____ vive usted. (where)

7. María va a decir _____ es el mejor de todos. (which)

8. ¿_____ va usted con la botella? (where to)

9. ¿_____ café desea usted, señora? (how much)

10. Josefina sabe _____ *lenguas* (languages); yo sé _____.
    (2/1)

11. Jorge necesita _____ vaso, y yo también necesito _____.
    (1/1)

12. Mañana es el día _____ de *junio* (June). (16)

13. ¿Tú vas a comer _____ tacos? Es imposible. (22)

14. Necesito _____ dólares. (32)

15. Este cheque es de _____ pesos. (500)

16. Esta cuenta del gas es de _____ pesos. (110)

17. ¿Quién va a pagar los _____ dólares? (2.000)

18. Aquí cenan todos los días _____ personas. (500)

19. ¿Tú deseas leer _____ libros? (2.000.000)

20. Tú estás correcto _____. (one hundred percent)

QUESTION:

To indicate *thousand* and *million* in Spanish, do we use a comma or a period?

_____ How do we indicate decimals? _____. Write this figure in

Spanish: 2,200,300.50: _____.

Lesson 4

En el aeropuerto
(At the Airport)

aduana	customs	**empleada**	employee	**pasaporte**	passport
aerolínea[1]	airline	**empleado**	employee	**piloto**	pilot
aeropuerto	airport	**equipaje**	luggage	**puerta**	door, gate
asiento	seat	**hora**	hour	**reservación**	reservation
avión	airplane	**llegada**	arrival	**salida**	departure, exit
azafata[2]	stewardess	**maleta**	suitcase	**ventana**	window
billete	ticket	**maletín**	briefcase	**ventanilla**	window (small)
cigarrillo	cigarette	**pasaje**	ticket	**viaje**	travel, trip
cinturón[3]	belt	**pasajero**	passenger	**vuelo**	flight

abrocharse	to fasten	**inspeccionar**	to inspect	**seguir (i)**	to follow
ayudar	to help	**llegar**	to arrive	**sentarse (ie)**	to sit down
bajar (de)	to get off, go down	**mostrar (ue)**[4]	to show	**servir (i)**	to serve
comprar	to buy	**pedir (i)**	to ask for	**subir**	to get on, go up
deshacer	to undo, melt	**pensar (ie)**[5]	to think, plan	**tener**	to have
detener	to stop	**poder (ue)**	to be able	**venir**	to come
facturar	to check (luggage)	**poner**	to put	**viajar**	to travel
fumar	to smoke	**querer (ie)**	to wish, want	**volar (ue)**	to fly
hacer	to do, make	**salir**	to leave	**volver (ue)**	to come back

alto	high, tall	**fantástico**	fantastic	**rápido**	fast
bajo	low, short	**largo**	long	**simpático**	nice, cute
		medio -a	half		

antes (de)[6]	beforehand, before	en punto	sharp (exact time)
a tiempo	on time	tener que (+ infinitive)	to have to (+ verb)
después (de)	afterwards, after	salir de + place	to leave (a place)

NOTES:

1. *Aerolínea* is also called *línea aérea*.

2. *Azafata* is also called *aeromoza*.

3. *Cinturón de seguridad* (safety belt) is also used.

4. *Mostrar:* the *ue* in parentheses is explained later in this lesson.

5. *Pensar + infinitive* means to *plan to* (+ verb).
    Ex.: *Pienso ir a México.*

6. *Antes* and *después* require *de* when a noun or an infinitive follows.
    Ex.: Voy *antes de* comer. (I'll go *before* eating)
    Voy *antes de* la comida. (I'll go before dinner)

PRACTICE THE NEW WORDS   *(Answers, p. 80)*

A.   Write the article *el* or *la* before the nouns.

1._____ avión	5._____ reservación	9._____ ventanilla
2._____ azafata	6._____ equipaje	10._____ pasaporte
3._____ maletín	7._____ cinturón	11._____ billete
4._____ vuelo	8._____ pasaje	12._____ maleta

B.   Underline the word that makes sense.

1. El pasajero llega (el pasaje, la llegada, a tiempo, el cigarrillo).

2. La azafata sirve (el vuelo, la comida, la maleta, el pasaporte).

3. En el aeropuerto facturamos (la llegada, el cinturón, el billete, el equipaje).

4. En el avión nos abrochamos (la maleta, el cinturón, la puerta, el pasaje).

5. En el aeropuerto compramos (el pasaje, el pasaporte, el vuelo, la maleta).

6. Yo me siento (a la ventanilla, al equipaje, a la azafata, al cigarillo).

7. En el aeropuerto hablo con (el piloto, el empleado, la azafata, el maletín).

8. Decimos adiós antes de (subir, servir, deshacer, comprar) al avión.

9. Pensamos hacer (un asiento, una salida, un vuelo, una aduana) a Chicago.

10. ¿Quién ayuda (a los cinturones, a los pasajeros, al avión, al asiento)?

11. Salimos por la puerta de (aerolínea, equipaje, viaje, salida).

12. Vamos a comer después de (llegar, poder, poner, seguir).

13. Deseo un asiento en la sección de (bajar, volar, volver, fumar).

14. Los oficiales (officers) inspeccionan el equipaje en (el pasaje, el pasaporte, la aduana, la maleta).

15. El avión sale (a tiempo, a la ventanilla, al asiento, al empleado).

C.   Match the two columns.

1. _____ abrocharse

2. _____ llegar

3. _____ facturar

4. _____ volar

5. _____ mostrar

6. _____ sentarse

7. _____ fumar

8. _____ servir

9. _____ comprar

10. _____ hacer

11. _____ salir del

12. _____ pensar

13. _____ inspeccionar en

14. _____ ir y (opposite)

A. aeropuerto

B. en avión

C. el pasaporte

D. cigarrillos

E. el pasaje

F. volver

G. la comida

H. viajar a México

I. el cinturón

J. la aduana

K. el equipaje

L. la reservación

M. a la ventanilla

N. a tiempo

Diálogo   *En el aeropuerto*

(Un viajero llega al aeropuerto a las 2:15 de la tarde y habla con una empleada de la aerolínea.)

EMPLEADA: Buenas tardes, señor. ¿En qué puedo servirle?
PASAJERO: Quiero hacer una reservación para el vuelo 800 a Madrid.
EMPLEADA: Llega usted a tiempo. El avión sale en 45 minutos, a las 3 en punto.
PASAJERO: ¡Fantástico! ¿Puede darme un asiento con ventanilla?
EMPLEADA: ¿En la sección de fumar?
PASAJERO: No, no fumo.
EMPLEADA: En ese caso, sí puedo darle ventanilla. ¿Tiene Ud. su pasaporte?
PASAJERO: Aquí está. ¿Algo más?
EMPLEADA: No . . . Aquí está el pasaje. Su asiento es el número 20 A, con ventanilla.
PASAJERO: ¡Qué bueno! ¡Es usted muy simpática!
EMPLEADA: Gracias. ¿Dónde está su equipaje?
PASAJERO: Quiero facturar estas dos maletas.
EMPLEADA: Muy bien. Puede llevar el maletín con Ud. en el avión.
PASAJERO: ¿Cuál es la puerta de salida para el vuelo 800?
EMPLEADA: Es el número 7. ¡Buen viaje!
PASAJERO: Muchas gracias. Adiós.

DIALOG   *At the Airport*

(A traveler arrives at the airport at 2:15 P.M. and talks to an airline employee.)

EMPLOYEE: Good afternoon, sir. May I help you?
PASSENGER: I want to make a reservation for flight 800 to Madrid.
EMPLOYEE: You got here just in time. The airplane leaves in 45 minutes, at 3:00 sharp.
PASSENGER: Terrific! Can you give me a seat by the window?
EMPLOYEE: In the smoking section?
PASSENGER: No, I don't smoke.
EMPLOYEE: In that case, I can give you a window seat. Do you have your passport?
PASSENGER: Here it is. Anything else?
EMPLOYEE: No . . . Here is your ticket. Your seat is number 20 A, by the window.
PASSENGER: Great! You're very nice!
EMPLOYEE: Thanks. Where is your luggage?
PASSENGER: I want to check on these two suitcases.
EMPLOYEE: Fine. You can take the briefcase with you on the plane.
PASSENGER: Which is the departure gate for flight 800?
EMPLOYEE: It's number 7. Have a nice trip!
PASSENGER: Thank you. Goodbye.

EXERCISES

(Answers, p. 80)

A.   Complete the sentences according to the dialog.

1. El viajero _____ al aeropuerto a las 2:15 de la tarde.

2. El pasajero quiere hacer una _____ para el vuelo 800.

3. ¿Llega tarde el pasajero para el vuelo 800? No, _____

   _____ .

4. El pasajero quiere un asiento con _____ .

5. ¿Fuma o no fuma el pasajero? _____ .

6. La empleada pide el _____ al pasajero.

7. El _____ del pasajero es el número 20 A, con ventanilla.

8. La empleada es muy _____ con el pasajero.

9. El pasajero quiere facturar dos _____ .

10. ¿Cuántos maletines lleva el pasajero? _____ .

11. El pasajero puede llevar el _____ en el avión.

12. La puerta de _____ para ir al avión es el número 7.

13. El pasajero toma el _____ 800 para ir a Madrid.

14. La empleada desea buen _____ al pasajero.

15. El pasajero dice _____ antes de ir a la puerta de salida.

B.   Match the two columns.

1. ____ El avión llega a las dos . . .   A. con ventanilla.
2. ____ La azafata es una camarera . . .   B. muy simpáticas.
3. ____ El pasajero compra . . .   C. el cinturón.
4. ____ Las maletas son parte . . .   D. empleados.
5. ____ Para viajar a Europa, Ud. necesita . . . E. en el avión.
6. ____ Quiero un asiento . . .   F. en punto.
7. ____ Esta aerolínea tiene aeromozas . . .   G. a los pasajeros.
8. ____ Una maleta pequeña es . . .   H. del vuelo.
9. ____ Tengo reservación . . .   I. el billete (pasaje).
10. ____ Los pasajeros se abrochan . . .   J. un asiento.
11. ____ La aeromoza ayuda . . .   K. a tiempo.

12. ___ El piloto es responsable . . .   L. del equipaje.
13. ___ El avión sale en 30 minutos. Ud. llega . . . M. para el vuelo 800.
14. ___ Quiero *reservar* (reserve) . . .   N. tener pasaporte.
15. ___ Todas las personas del avión son . . .   O. un maletín.

GRAMMAR I   Present Indicative of **tener, venir, poner, salir,** and **hacer.**

A. Memorize the following chart:

SUBJECT	**ten er** *(to have)*	**ven ir** *(to come)*	**pon er** *(to put)*	**sal ir** *(to leave)*	**hac er** *(to do, make)*
yo	**teng o**	**veng o**	**pong o**	**salg o**	**hag o**
nosotros -as	**ten emos**	**ven imos**	**pon emos**	**sal imos**	**hac emos**
tú	**tien es**	**vien es**	**pon es**	**sal es**	**hac es**
él/ella/Ud.	**tien e**	**vien e**	**pon e**	**sal e**	**hac e**
ellos/ellas/Uds.	**tien en**	**vien en**	**pon en**	**sal en**	**hac en**

B. Notice the following features of the chart:
   1. These five verbs add a *g* to the stem in the first person singular. Actually *hacer* doesn't add the *g* but rather changes *c* to *g*: *hac* to *hag*.
   2. *Poner, salir,* and *hacer* are regular in all the forms except for the subject *yo*.
   3. *Tener* and *venir* change *e* to *ie* in the second and third persons: *tienes, tiene, tienen*. They belong to a large group of stem-changing verbs where the *e* switches to *ie*. These verbs are studied in Grammar II (see p. 50).
   4. There are many compounds of these five verbs. They have the same changes as the original verb. There are two of them in the vocabulary of this lesson: *detener* (*de* + *tener*) meaning *to stop*, and *deshacer* (*des* + *hacer*) meaning *to undo, to melt*.
      Ex.: Ella se detiene en la luz. (she stops at the light)
           Yo deshago la maleta. (I am unpacking the suitcase)

C. Uses of *tener, salir,* and *venir:*
   1. *Tener* means *to have, to possess*.
      Ex.: Tengo un carro azul. (I have a blue car)

      Tener + que + infinitive indicates obligation; it translates *to have to + verb*.
      Ex.: ¿Cuándo tienes que volar a Chicago? (when do you have to fly to Chicago?)

2. *Salir* means *to go away, to leave,* and it requires *de* if the point of departure is mentioned in the sentence.
> Ex.: El avión sale de Los Angeles. (the airplane leaves [from] Los Angeles)

3. *Venir* means *to come* and it's the opposite of *ir (to go)*. *Venir* is to move from anywhere to the place of the speaker, and *ir* is to move from the speaker to somewhere else. Note that both *ir* and *venir* can mean *to come*.
> Ex.: ¿Cuándo *vienes* a verme? - *Voy* mañana. (when are you *coming* to see me? - I *am coming* tomorrow)

PRACTICE THE VERBS   *(Answers, p. 80)*

1. *Tener* has three different stems in the Present Indicative: _____, _____ and all three carry the same basic meaning: _____ .

2. *Vengo, tengo, pongo,* and *salgo* are irregular because they add the letter _____ to the stem. *Hacer* changes the c to _____ in *yo hago*.

3. *Vienes* y *tienes* change the original *e* to _____ . Are *venimos* and *tenemos* iregular? _____ .

4. In order to translate *to have to* (+ verb), we add _____ to *tener*. How would you say *I have to leave*? _____ .

5. *Salir* is *to leave*. If we mention the place we leave, we need the preposition _____ in front of the place. For example, *I'm leaving home* is translated as _____ .

6. *Venir* means _____ ; but in English *to come* can mean *to move in any direction*, whereas in Spanish it is *to move from somewhere to where the* _____ *is*.

7. A child who replies *I'm coming, mom* is moving from his place to hers. How would you translate *I'm coming, mom* into Spanish? *Ahora* _____, *mamá*.

8. Compound verbs follow the same changes as the original verb. If *deshacer* is *to undo, unpack*, how would you say *I am unpacking*? _____ .

9. If *detener* is *to stop,* how do you say *They are stopping at the light? Ellos se*

_____ en la luz.

EXERCISE   *(Answers, p. 80)*

Complete with the correct forms of the Present Indicative. (first review the new verbs in the vocabulary of this lesson)

1. Este avión _____ de Madrid. (come)

2. Mañana yo _____ comprar un libro. (have to)

3. La azafata _____ a los pasajeros. (help)

4. ¿Cuándo _____ *tú para* (for) México? (to leave)

5. Carmen _____ la comida todos los lunes. (make)

6. Los pasajeros se _____ los cinturones. (fasten)

7. ¿_____ usted reservación en este vuelo? (have)

8. Yo _____ el maletín en el avión. (put)

9. ¿Cuándo _____ el vuelo 304? (arrive)

10. El policía _____ al criminal. (detain, stop)

11. Paco _____ todo el equipaje. (check in)

12. Yo no _____ en la clase. (smoke)

13. Carmen y yo _____ a tiempo. (come)

14. Los pasajeros _____ ahora del avión. (get off)

15. Yo _____ la maleta antes del viaje. (do, pack)

16. Después del viaje José _____ las maletas. (unpack)

17. Los policías _____ las maletas en la aduana. (inspect)

18. ¿_____ usted un asiento reservado? (have)

19. El niño dice a su mamá: *I'm coming now, mom: Ahora* _____, *mamá.*

20. Nosotros _____ el pasaje en el aeropuerto. (buy)

GRAMMAR II ¿Qué hora es? (What time is it?).

A. Memorize the following chart to tell the time:

1. *Exact time:* (hora exacta)	**Es** la una. **Son** las dos. **Son** las diez.	(it's one o'clock) (it's two o'clock) (it's ten o'clock)
2. *After the hour:* (+) = **y**	Es la una *y* diez. Son las dos *y* **cuarto.** Son las dos *y* **quince.** Son las dos *y* **media.** Son las dos *y* **treinta.**	(it's 1:10) (it's 2:15) (it's 2:30)
3. *Before the hour:* (–) = **menos**	Es la una *menos* diez. Son las dos *menos* cuarto. Son las dos *menos* quince. Son las dos *menos* viente.	(it's 12:50) (it's 1:45) (it's 1:40)

B. *De la mañana/de la tarde/de la noche:* A.M. and P.M.

    1 A.M. is **de la mañana.**   (from midnight to noon)
    2 P.M. is **de la tarde.**   (from noon to dark, officially, 6:00 P.M.)
         de la noche.   (from dark to midnight, officially, 6:00–midnight)

C. Notice that we say *es la una* (hora); the word *hora* (feminine) is understood. The verb *es* changes to the plural *son* from 2 to 12—they are more than *one.*

D. To translate *sharp,* we say **en punto** or **exactamente.** To say *about,* we can translate by **más o menos** (more or less) and **como.** To translate *at,* we use the preposition **a** followed by the article **la** or **las.**
        Ex.: Son las dos *más o menos.*
             Son *como* las dos.
             Llegamos *a la* una.

E. *De la tarde/de la noche* will change with the season of the year, just like the greetings *Buenas tardes/Buenas noches.* The official change in schedules is at 6:00 P.M.

PRACTICE THE NUMBERS AND TELLING TIME

(Answers, p. 81)

1. *Son* and *es* belong to *ser,* the verb for identification. We use the singular *es* with _____, and the plural *son* with _____.

2. In telling time, *15* minutes has two possible words: _____ and _____.

3. In telling time, *30* minutes also has two possible words in Spanish: _____ and _____.

4. To tell the minutes *after* the hour, we add the minutes with the conjunction _____.To subtract minutes *before* the next hour, we use the word _____.

5. How do you translate *sharp* when talking about time?_____ _____. How do you translate *about*?_____ _____.

6. There is only one translation for A.M.:_____.

7. There are two translations for P.M.:_____ and _____.

8. Is it correct to say *Salgo a una* (I'm leaving at 1:00)?_____; the article _____ is missing before *una.*

9. We say *a las dos, a la una,* with the feminine article *la/las/una* because the feminine word_____ is understood.

10. How do you translate What time is it?_____.

EXERCISE

(Answers, p. 81)

Translate the following time expressions.

1. It's 3:10 P.M. _____.

2. It's 2:15 A.M. _____.

3. It's 1:30 P.M. _____.

4. It's 5:50 A.M. _____.

5. It's 11:00 P.M. _____.

6. It's 11:20 A.M. _____.

7. It's 12:45. _____.

8. It's 1:05 A.M. _____.

9. El avión sale _____. (at 2:00 sharp)

10. En mi casa cenamos todos los días _____.
    (at 8:30)

11. Todos los días salgo de casa _____. (at
    7:00 A.M.)

12. Josefina mira la televisión _____. (at
    11:00 P.M.)

13. El vuelo 800 llega a Madrid _____. (at
    about 2:00)

14. ¿ _____ vienes a mi casa? (At what time?)

GRAMMAR III   Present Indicative of stem-changing verbs.

A. Memorize the following chart:

SUBJECT	pens ar *(to think)*	volv er *(to return)*	ped ir *(to ask for)*	segu ir *(to follow)*
yo	piens o	vuelv o	pid o	sig o
nosotros -as	pens amos	volv emos	ped imos	segu imos
tú	piens as	vuelv es	pid es	sigu es
él/ella/Ud.	piens a	vuelv e	pid e	sigu e
ellos/ellas/Uds.	piens an	vuelv en	pid en	sigu en

B. Notice the following features of this chart:
    1. All these verbs are called *stem-changing verbs* because they
       change a vowel in the stem; there are many verbs in Spanish with
       this same feature.
    2. Notice that the stem of *pensar* is *pens,* but the *e* changes to *ie* in all
       the persons except *pensamos* which is regular.
    3. *Volver* changes *o* to *ue* in all the persons except *volvemos.*
    4. *Pedir* and *seguir* have the same stem change: *e* to *i* in all the
       persons except the first person plural: *pedimos* and *seguimos.*
    5. Notice that *seguir* has the stem *segu* with a silent *u* when it is
       followed by *i* or *e: seguir, sigues, siguen.* But the *u* is lost in front of
       o: sigo.

C. A partial list of stem-changing verbs:

    Notice that in the vocabulary and most dictionaries you see (ie), (ue),
    or (i) after certain verbs. This is to remind you that it's a stem-
    changing verb. You will find many more in the coming lessons since
    there are about 600 stem-changing verbs in Spanish. Here is a list of
    the stem-changing verbs that you've encountered so far:

e to *ie*	*o* to *ue*	*e* to *i*
pensar (to think, to plan)	**mostrar** (to show)	**pedir** (to ask for)
querer (to wish, to love)	**poder** (to be able, can)	**seguir** (to follow)
sentarse (to sit down)	**volar** (to fly)	**servir** (to serve)
tener (to have)	**volver** (to return)	**decir** (to say, to tell)
venir (to come)		

D. Uses of *pedir, querer,* and *volver:*
   1. *Pedir* means *to ask for.* Notice that *for* is not translated in Spanish.
      Ex.: Voy a pedir café. (I'm going to ask *for* coffee)
   2. *Querer* means *to wish, want* with things and actions, but it is *to love* with people.
      Ex.: Quiero una casa grande. (I want a big house)
      ¿Quieres a tu mamá? (do you love your mother?)
   3. *Volver* means *to return, to come back.* But *volver a + infinitive* means *to do it again.*
      Ex.: ¿Cuándo vuelves a clase? (when are you returning to class?)
      Ella vuelve a viajar. (she is traveling again)

PRACTICE THE STEM-CHANGING VERBS

(Answers, p. 81)

1. The stem of *querer* is _____, and the stem of *quieres* is

   _____. This means that the vowel *e* from the infinitive

   has changed to _____ in the Present Indicative.

2. The stem of *decir* is _____,and the stem of *dices* is _____.

   This means that the vowel *e* from the infinitive has changed to_____
   in the Present Indicative.

3. The stem of *poder* is _____, and the stem of *puedo* is_____

   _____. In this case the vowel *o* has changed to_____.

4. Is the stem of *pedimos* the same as the stem of *pedir*?_____.
   Then *pedimos* is regular because the stem doesn't change.

5. *Querer* means to *wish, want* when it is used with things, but it means *to love*

   when it is used with _____. For example, *Tú*_____
   a papá.

6. In the expression *ask for*, the word_____ has no translation in Spanish. How do you say *we ask for?*_____.And *they ask for?* _____ .

7. *Servir* (i) is a stem-changing verb like *pedir*. How do you say *I'm serving?* _____ . And *they are serving?*_____ .

8. *Volar* (ue) is a stem-changing verb like *volver*. How do you complete this sentence? *El avión*_____ *a San Francisco*.

9. *Mostrar* (ue) is also a stem-changing verb. Remember that we can use the Present Indicative with future meaning. How do you say *I'll show you? Yo te* _____ .

10. There is no special auxiliary in Spanish for the emphatic *do* in expressions like *We do come*. One way to give emphasis is to raise the voice on the verb. How do you say *I do love you?* Yo te_____ .

11. The stem of *seguir* is _____ , and the stem of *sigues* is _____ . But the_____ is silent and it's lost before an *o*. How do you say *I follow?* _____ .

12. *Volver* is *to return*, but *volver a + infinitive* means *to do (verb) it* _____ _____ . For example, *volvemos a volar* means _____ _____ .

13. The spelling change from *e* to *ie* also occurs in adjectives and nouns. For example, you remember the numbers *setenta* and *siete*. Notice the change from *o* to *ue: noventa* and *nueve*.

EXERCISE   *(Answers, p. 81)*

Complete the sentences with the correct form of the Present.

1. Usted no_____fumar en esta sección del avión. (can)

2. Sí, ellos_____de Miami a Nueva York. (fly)

3. ¿Cuándo_____usted a México? (return)

4. Nosotros_____hacer un viaje a Perú. (plan)

5. ¿Por qué_____(tú) comer en este restaurante? (wish)

6. José _____ a la derecha, y yo _____ a la izquierda. (follow)

7. ¿Para qué _____ (tú) doscientos dólares? (ask for)

8. Yo me _____ a la ventanilla derecha. (sit)

9. El turista _____ el pasaporte en la aduana. (show)

10. Las azafatas _____ la comida en el avión. (serve)

11. ¿A dónde _____ viajar usted? (wish)

12. ¿Qué día _____ usted a clase? (return)

13. Sí, yo _____ estudiar más español. (plan)

14. El águila _____ muy rápido y muy alto. (fly)

15. No, yo no _____ ir el lunes. (be able)

16. Paquito _____ mucho a su mamá. (love)

17. Por favor, ¿_____ darme un cigarrillo? (can)

18. ¿Cómo se _____ *ask for* en español? (say)

19. ¿Quién _____? (follow, be next)

20. ¿Quiénes (plural *who*) _____ el billete? (have)

21. Mañana nosotros no _____ venir aquí. (can)

22. Ustedes _____ los pasajes a la azafata. (show)

23. Nosotros _____ a las cuatro más o menos. (arrive)

24. Este avión _____ muy alto. (fly)

25. El lunes que viene yo _____ a verte. ([see you] again)

Lesson 5

La familia y la casa
(The Family and the House)

abuela	grandmother	garaje	garage	padre	father
abuelo[1]	grandfather	hermana	sister	padres	parents
baño	bathroom	hermano	brother	papá	father
cama	bed	hija	daughter	pariente	relative
carro, coche	car	hijo	son	piso	floor
chimenea	fireplace	invitación	invitation	primo -a	cousin (m/f)
cocina	kitchen	jardín	garden	reloj (el)[2]	clock, watch
cocinero -a	cook (m/f)	lavaplatos	dishwasher	silla	chair
comedor	dining room	nieta	grand-daughter	sillón	armchair
cuarto	room	nieto	grandson	sobrina	niece
dormitorio	bedroom	niño -a	boy/girl	sobrino	nephew
ducha	shower	novio -a	fiancé/fiancée	suegra	mother-in-law
esposo -a	spouse	madre	mother	suegro	father-in-law
familia	family	mamá	mom	tejado	roof
flor (la)[2]	flower	mueble[3]	furniture	tío -a	aunt/uncle

aparecer	to appear	destruir	to destroy	presentar	to present
apreciar	to appreciate	dormir (ue)	to sleep	producir	to produce
caer	to fall	huir	to flee	reconocer	to recognize
concluir	to conclude	importar	to matter	recordar (ue)	to remember
conducir	to drive, conduct	invitar	to invite	traducir	to translate
conocer	to know	lavar	to wash	traer	to bring
construir	to build	ofrecer	to offer	morir (ue)	to die
creer	to believe	oír[4]	to hear, listen	nacer	to be born
deber	must, should	parecer	to seem	bañarse	to bathe

alegre	happy, glad	**feo**	ugly	**poco**	a little
amable	kind	**futuro**	future	**rico**	rich
bonito	pretty	**guapo**	handsome	**soltero**	single
casado	married	**joven**	young	**terrible**	terrible
corto	short	**lindo**	pretty	**triste**	sad
fantástico	fantastic	**mucho**	a lot	**viejo**	old
feliz	happy	**pobre**	poor		

ayer	yesterday	**mi/mis**[5]	my	**temprano**	early
desde	from	**pero**	but	**tener...años**	to be ... years old
entonces	then	**que**	that	**todavía**	still, yet
hasta	until, to	**sobre**	about	**tu/tus**[5]	your
hoy	today	**solamente**	only		

NOTES:

1. The plural masculine form *abuelos* means *grandparents* (masculine and feminine). The same thing happens with all the pairs in family words.
    Ex.: *hermanos* (brothers and sisters), *hijos* (daughters and scns), *tíos* (aunts and uncles), *sobrinos* (nieces and nephews), etc.

2. Notice that *flor* is an exception to the gender rules; it is feminine: *la flor. Reloj* is masculine: *el reloj.*

3. *Mueble* is a *count* noun in Spanish—that is, unlike *furniture* (never *furnitures*), *mueble* is used in both singular and plural forms.
    Ex.: La silla y la mesa son *dos muebles.* (the chair and the table are *two pieces of furniture*)

4. *Oír* has two meanings: *to hear* or *to listen,* just like *ver* is *to see* or *to watch.* The verb *to listen* is *escuchar,* but it is used less frequently than *oír.*

5. We will study the possessive adjectives in Lesson 7. In the meantime notice that *mi* (my) changes to the plural *mis* if the thing possessed is plural. The same goes for *tu* (your) and *tus* (no written accent!).

EXERCISE   *(Answers, p. 81)*

A.   Write *el* or *la* in front of the noun.

1. _____ mueble
2. _____ pariente
3. _____ madre
4. _____ flor
5. _____ garaje
6. _____ reloj
7. _____ silla
8. _____ sillón
9. _____ papá
10. _____ comedor
11. _____ coche
12. _____ lavaplatos
13. _____ chimenea
14. _____ invitación
15. _____ tejado

B. Complete the following sentences.

1. El padre de mi padre es mi _____ .

2. El hermano de mi padre es mi _____ .

3. El hijo de mi hermano es mi _____ .

4. El hijo de mi hijo es mi _____ .

5. La hija de mis tíos es mi _____ .

6. Las hermanas de mi papá son mis _____ .

7. Mis abuelos son los padres de mis _____ .

8. Los hijos de mis tíos son mis _____ .

9. La madre de mi esposa es mi _____ .

10. Los hijos de mis padres son mis _____ .

11. El papá de mi esposo es mi _____ .

12. Mi abuela es la mamá de mi _____ .

C. Write the opposite word.

1. alegre_____   8. mucho_____

2. bonito_____   9. nacer_____

3. joven_____   10. construir_____

4. soltero_____   11. llevar_____

5. largo_____   12. terrible_____

6. pobre_____   13. tarde_____

7. lindo_____   14. desde_____

D. Match the two columns.

1._____Conducimos . . .   A. del inglés al español.

2._____Oímos . . .   B. en un hospital.

3._____Construimos . . .   C. en una silla o sillón.

4._____Traducimos . . .   D. a los amigos y parientes.

5._____Dormimos . . .   E.   en la ducha, en el mar, etc.

6._____Morimos y nacemos . . .   F.   el radio, la televisión.

7._____Ofrecemos . . .   G.   el coche, el carro, el avión.

8._____Nos bañamos . . .   H.   una cerveza, un aperitivo.

9._____Conocemos . . .   I.   en la cama por la noche.

10._____Nos sentamos . . .   J.   una casa, un avión, un hospital.

E.   Underline the word that makes sense.

1. El cocinero trabaja en (el piso, el jardín, el reloj, la cocina).

2. Ponemos los coches en (el garaje, el tejado, la ducha, el cuarto).

3. Hacemos el *fuego* (fire) en (el jardín, lavaplatos, la chimenea, la flor).

4. Mi jardín es bonito; tiene much*os[-as]* (cuartos, flores, camas, muebles).

5. Mi casa es grande; tiene cinco (muebles, relojes, dormitorios, lavaplatos).

6. Un mueble de la cocina es (el lavaplatos, la cama, el sillón, el comedor).

7. Un mueble del comedor es (la ducha, la mesa, la chimenea, el baño).

8. Un mueble del dormitorio es (el piso, el tejado, la cama, el baño).

9. Nos bañamos en (el jardín, la ducha, las flores, el lavaplatos).

10. *Coche* también se dice (sobrino, reloj, carro, sillón).

11. Sabemos la hora por (el lavaplatos, tejado, el mueble, el reloj).

12. *Hijos* también se dice en español (nietos, sobrinos, niños, tíos).

13. La parte alta de la casa es (el tejado, el cuarto, el comedor, la cama).

14. La rosa y el geranio son dos (muebles, flores, sillones, baños).

15. La cama y el sillón son dos (muebles, baños, relojes, tejados).

16. Toda la familia cena en (el cuarto, el comedor, el sillón, el garaje).

17. Ella y él no son esposos todavía. Son (padres, sobrinos, novios, nietos).

18. José no tiene hijos; es (abuelo, rico, soltero, pariente).

19. No tengo muchos dólares; soy (casado, viejo, triste, pobre).

20. Los abuelos no son muy (jóvenes, casados, solteros, cortos).

DIÁLOGO   *La familia de Carlos*

(Carlos es mexicano y Debbie es americana; los dos son muy amigos.)

CARLOS: ¿Por qué no vienes a comer a mi casa hoy?
DEBBIE: Pero no conozco bien a tus padres todavía.
CARLOS: No importa. Ellos quieren conocerte mejor también.
DEBBIE: Está bien. Acepto tu invitación. ¿Cuántos hermanos tienes?
CARLOS: Somos dos hermanos y una hermana.
DEBBIE: ¿Viven los abuelos con ustedes?
CARLOS: Solamente mi abuela materna, y también una hermana de mi padre.
DEBBIE: Entonces deben tener una casa grande.
CARLOS: Sí, tiene cinco dormitorios, un garaje grande, un patio con jardín con árboles y flores. ¡También tenemos tres baños!
DEBBIE: Quiero conocer a tu abuelita. ¿Es muy vieja?
CARLOS: Tiene 76 años, pero está joven todavía. Trabaja en la casa desde temprano hasta la noche.
DEBBIE: Ustedes los latinos saben apreciar a la familia mejor que nosotros los americanos.
CARLOS: Bueno . . . ¡pero las suegras son terribles!
DEBBIE: No lo creo. Conozco un poco a mi futura suegra y sé que es ¡fantástica!

DIALOG   *Carlos's Family*

(Carlos is Mexican and Debbie is American; they are very good friends.)

CARLOS: Why don't you come eat at my house today?
DEBBIE: But I don't know your parents very well yet.
CARLOS: It doesn't matter. They want to get to know you better too.
DEBBIE: OK. I accept your invitation. How many brothers and sisters do you have?
CARLOS: One brother and one sister.
DEBBIE: Do your grandparents live with you?
CARLOS: Just my maternal grandmother and one of my father's sisters.
DEBBIE: Then you must have a big house.
CARLOS: Yes, it has five bedrooms, a large garage, [and] a yard with a garden with trees and flowers. We also have three bathrooms.
DEBBIE: I want to meet your grandma. Is she very old?
CARLOS: She's 76, but she still looks young. She works in the house from morning 'til night.
DEBBIE: You *Latinos* know how to appreciate your families better than we Americans.

CARLOS: Yeah . . . but mothers-in-law are terrible!

DEBBIE: I don't believe so. I know my future mother-in-law a little bit, and I know that she's *fantastic!*

EXERCISES

(Answers, p. 82)

A. Complete the sentences according to the dialog.

1. Carlos y Debbie no son novios todavía, pero son muy_____.

2. Los dos hablan sobre _____ de Carlos.

3. Carlos invita a Debbie a_____en su casa.

4. Debbie dice que no_____bien a los padres de Carlos.

5. Los padres de Carlos también_____conocer mejor a Debbie.

6. Debbie acepta la _____ de Carlos.

7. En la familia de Carlos son dos _____ y una

   _____.

8. La_____materna de Carlos vive en la casa.

9. Una hermana del_____también vive en la casa.

10. La casa de Carlos tiene cinco _____.

11. ¿Cuántos baños tiene la casa de Carlos?_____.

12. El patio de la casa tiene un _____muy bonito.

13. Los árboles y las flores están en el_____.

14. ¿Cuántos años tiene la abuelita de Carlos? Tiene_____

    _____.

15. La abuelita es vieja, pero está _____.

16. Ella trabaja todo el día; desde temprano_____ la noche.

17. Debbie dice que los latinos saben_____mucho a la familia.

18. Pero Carlos dice que las_____son terribles.

19. ¿Cree Debbie a Carlos, o no lo cree?_____.

20. Debbie cree que su futura suegra es_____.

B. Match the two columns.

1._____En el jardín tenemos . . .		A.	joven.
2._____Preparamos la comida . . .		B.	sillón.
3._____La parte alta de la casa es . . .		C.	en el garaje.
4._____Para saber la hora leemos . . .		D.	árboles y flores.
5._____Una silla grande es un . . .		E.	vieja.
6._____Toda la familia cena . . .		F.	en el comedor.
7._____Ponemos los carros . . .		G.	en la cocina.
8._____Una persona de 80 años es . . .		H.	casados.
9._____Los novios todavía no son . . .		I.	el tejado.
10._____Si Ud. tiene pocos años es . . .		J.	el reloj.

GRAMMAR I   Present Indicative of **oír, traer, conocer,** and **huir.** Contrast between **saber** and **conocer.**

A. Memorize the following chart:

SUBJECT	o ír *(to hear)*	tra er *(to bring)*	conoc er *(to know)*	hu ir *(to flee)*
yo	oig o	traig o	conozc o	huy o
nosotros	o ímos	tra emos	c-onoc emos	hu imos
tú	oy es	tra es	conoc es	huy es
él/ella/Ud.	oy e	tra e	conoc e	huy e
ellos/ellas/Uds.	oy en	tra en	conoc en	huy en

B. Notice the following features in the chart:
1. *Oír* has a short stem, *o*. It expands to *oig* for the first person, and *oy* for all the other persons except *oímos* which is regular.
2. The stem of *traer* is *tra,* and it is expanded to *traig* in *traigo.*
3. *Conocer* has the stem *conoc.* The final *c* of *conocer* changes to *z,* and the stem in *conozco* adds the letter *c* with the [k] sound. Remember that *c* (followed by *e* or *i*) and *z* are pronounced *s* in Latin America.
4. *Huir* has the stem *hu* and it is expanded to *huy* in all the forms except in *huimos* which is regular.

C. Verbs conjugated like *conocer* and *huir:*

Most of the verbs ending in *-cer* and *-cir* add the *c* like *conocer*. All the verbs ending in *-uir* add *y* like *huir*. Look again at the stem-changing verbs from the vocabulary list for this lesson:

	-cir/-cer	*-uir*
aparecer (to appear)	**producir** (to produce)	**concluir** (to conclude)
conducir (to drive)	**reconocer** (to recognize)	**construir** (to build)
ofrecer (to offer)	**traducir** (to translate)	**destruir** (to destroy)
parecer (to seem)	**nacer** (to be born)	**huir** (to flee, escape)

D. Differences between *saber* and *conocer:*

  1. *Conocer* is *to be acquainted with, to meet people* (in the past tense).
    Conocer is *to know places, countries,* and *people.*
      Ex.: ¿Conoces a mi tío? (are you acquainted with my uncle?)
      ¿Conoces [a] Cuba? (do you know Cuba?)

NOTE:

Some regions use the preposition *a* before cities and countries following *conocer.* Other regions omit *a.*

      Ex.: Conozco Chile./Conozco a Chile.

  2. *Saber* is *to know facts.*
      Ex.: *Sé que México es grande.* (I know that Mexico is large)

    Saber is *to know by heart,* like numbers.
      Ex.: *¿Sabes mi teléfono?*

    Saber is *to know how,* but we don't translate the word *how.*
      Ex.: Pablo sabe hacer paella. (Paul knows how to make paella)

PRACTICE THE VERBS   *(Answers, p. 82)*

1. *Oír* has three different stems in the Present: _____.

  The only regular form is *nosotros* _____. (with written acento!)

2. *Traer* and *caer* are irregular in the first person only: _____
_____. Both add two letters to the stem: _____.

3. *Conocer* changes to *yo* _____. The *c* has changed to *z* because of a spelling rule, but it has added the sound [**k**], which is the letter

_____.

4. Most of the verbs ending in -cer, -cir are irregular like conocer. For example, from ofrecer, yo_____; from conducir, yo_____ _____.

5. The stem of huir is hu, but it adds the letter _____ in huyo, huyes, huye(n). The only form that is regular is _____.

6. All the verbs ending in -uir add the y like huir. Ex.: from construir, yo _____ and Ellos _____.

7. Nacer is a passive verb in English, to be born. We use this verb in the past more often than in the present: I was born; but it is possible to say I am born: _____.

8. Saber and conocer mean to know. Which one do you use for to know people? _____. And to know facts? _____.

9. To know how implies knowledge and practice. Do you use saber or conocer? _____. And how do you translate the word how in to know how? _____.

10. If you know a city, a state, etc., do you use saber or conocer?_____ _____. For example, Nosotros_____ a Nueva York.

11. If you know my telephone number and my address, it means that you have memorized numbers and names. Would you use saber or conocer? _____.

12. How do you say I know how to write?_____.

EXERCISE

(Answers, p. 82)

Complete the sentences with the Present Indicative of the verbs in parentheses.

1. Venezuela y México_____mucho petróleo. (produce)

2. Yo no _____ este coche: es muy viejo. (drive)

3. Mis padres _____ el radio todos los días. (listen)

4. Los criminales _____ de los policías. (flee)

5. ¿Por qué tú no _____ en tu casa? (sleep)

6. Los empleados _____ un hospital grande. (build)

7. Muchos niños _____ de hambre todos los días. (die)

8. Yo no_____el carro a la universidad. (bring)

9. Tu novio_____que es muy simpático. (seem)

10. Mi suegra no_____sus errores. (recognize)

11. Mi abuela no _____ que hoy es lunes. (remember)

12. Yo _____ muchas palabras del inglés al español. (translate)

13. Esta clase _____ a las doce menos diez. (conclude)

14. Por la mañana yo _____ el radio del coche. (listen)

15. José _____ muy bien la ciudad de Nueva York. (know)

16. Cuando bebo mucho vino, yo me _____ al piso. (fall)

17. Yo no _____ preparar paella. (know how)

18. Las *guerras* (wars) _____ a muchas personas inocentes. (destroy)

19. La azafata _____ el menú a los pasajeros. (offer)

20. Ella _____ muy bien mi teléfono. (remember)

GRAMMAR II (Written Accent Rules).

A. Spanish words carry *one* and *only one* phonetic stress. This stress is marked with the *acento* (´) according to the following fixed rules. In order for these rules to be effective you should be able to "hear" the stress. For example, *mesa* has the stress on *me*, not on *sa*.

B. The following three rules show you when to mark the *acento:*

> 1. Words with phonetic stress on the *last* syllable need *acento* if the last letter is any of the five vowels or the consonants *n* or *s*. Also, the word must have two or more syllables: *Estás, están, está, aquí, papá, menú, dieciséis*
> 2. In words with stress on the *next-to-last* syllable, we write the *acento* if the last letter is any consonant except *n* or *s*.
>   Ex.: *árbol, lápiz;* but *hotel*
> 3. All words with the stress appearing *two syllables before the last* need *acento: números, fantástico, águila, gramática.* Here the last letter has nothing to do with the accent.

C. The only exceptions to these three rules are for reasons other than the stress. These are the two additional rules:

> 1. We write *acento* on the vowels í or ú to break a diphthong—i.e., when the *í* or the *ú* carries the stress and is before or after the other three vowels: *a-e-o.*
>   Ex.: *oír, día, maíz* (corn), *tío, rubíes, hindúes, reúno* (I get together)
> 2. We have *pairs* of words with the same spelling but different *meanings:* the only way to tell them apart is the *acento* on one of them.
>   Ex.: *él* (he) /*el* (the); *tú* (you) / *tu* (your); *sé* (know) / *se* (himself)

D. Remember that *question* words carry an *acento* without following the previous rules, even in an *indirect* question.
    Ex.: Ella sabe *cuándo* vamos a llegar.

No spelling rule, including the *acento,* is as good as a "visual memory." Try to pay attention to the full spelling of the words when you learn their meanings.

PRACTICE THE ACCENT   *(Answers, p. 83)*

1. How many stresses does a Spanish word carry? _____. For example, *diecinueve* has no stress on *diec-* but on _____.

2. *Café* has an *acento* because the stress is on the _____ syllable, and the last letter is a _____, as in *menú, está.*

3. *Avión, menús* need *acentos* because the stress is on the _____ syllable, and the last letter is_____ and_____.

4. *Pared, verdad, hotel* don't carry *acento* because the stress is on the _____ _____syllable, but the *last* letter is neither a _____ _____nor the consonants _____.

5. *Lápiz, árbol* carry the *acento* because the stress is *one syllable* before the _____, and the last letter is a_____, but not *n, s.*

6. *Lápices, número, águila* carry the *acento* because the stress is _____ syllables before last. The last letter doesn't matter at all.

7. Both *María* and *oír* carry *acento* for the same reason: to mark the break of

the _____ between the *i* and the vowels *a* and *o;* they are pronounced in two syllables.

8. In English *read* can be two different things (Past or Present), but the spelling is the same. In Spanish we indicate such differences, with the *acento*. For example, *él* means _____, whereas *el* means_____.

9. The word *tú* means _____, whereas *tu* means _____.

10. Words with just one syllable don't need an *acento: dos, va, ve, tres, son,* etc.; but if these words appear in compound words, they will need *acento*. How do you write 22 in Spanish? _____. And 23? _____.

EXERCISE

(Answers, p. 83)

Be a good word-watcher! And a good listener! (All the following words are in previous lessons: write the *acento* when needed.)

1. amarillo	8. carmesi	15. feliz	22. papeles	29. veintiun
2. luz	9. mama	16. avion	23. dieciseis	30. el (the)
3. aguila	10. tu (you)	17. camarera	24. dia	31. se (I know)
4. rubi	11. traemos	18. lapices	25. novio	32. arbol
5. creer	12. huimos	19. el (he)	26. estudio	33. rubis
6. oir	13. oimos	20. arboles	27. seis	34. estas (you are)
7. numero	14. estan	21. flores	28. tres	35. piloto

GRAMMAR III   Negative constructions.

A.   Memorize the following negative-affirmative words:

nunca/siempre (never/always)	**nadie/alguien** (nobody/somebody)
jamás/siempre (never/always)	**nada/algo** (nothing/something)
tampoco/también (neither, either/also)	**sin/con** (without/with)
ninguno/alguno (no one, none/some)	**no/sí** (no/yes)

B.   Notice the following rules about the words in the chart:
   1. *Jamás* and *nunca* mean *never*, but *jamás* is more emphatic.

Actually the two words can be used in the same sentence to make the negation even stronger.

Ex.: Carlos nunca jamás estudia. (Charles never never studies)

2. *Nadie* and *alguien* refer to people only. They are pronouns. *Nada* and *also* refer only to things, and they are also pronouns.

Ex.: ¿Alguien sabe esta palabra? (does anybody know this word?)

Nadie dice eso. (nobody is saying that)

3. *Alguno* and *ninguno* refer to people or things. They change to *alguna* and *ninguna* for the feminine. *Algunos/as* is the plural of *alguno a*, but *ninguno* rarely appears in the plural. Alguno becomes *algún* and *ninguno* becomes *ningún* when they precede masculine noun.

Ex.: *algún hombre, ningún libro.*

4. *Alguno* is used only before a noun, or as a pronoun when the noun has already been mentioned, whereas *alguien* is always used without a noun. The same rule exists for *ninguno* vs. *nadie*. In other words, *nadie* and *alguien* are always pronouns.

Ex.: No viene nadie. (nobody is coming)

¿Cuántos niños vienen? - No viene ninguno. (none are coming)

¿Conoces esos países? - Sí, conozco algunos. (yes, I know some)

C. Double negative in Spanish:

1. If we start a sentence with a negative word, we cannot use an affirmative word after the verb. It must be another negative word. For example, it's incorrect to say *No viene alguien;* it must be *No viene nadie.* We can summarize the double negative in this chart:

$\dfrac{\text{Negative word}}{\text{No}}$	+	$\dfrac{\text{verb}}{\text{dice}}$	+	$\dfrac{\text{Negative word}}{\text{nada}}$	+	$\dfrac{\text{Negative word}}{\text{nunca}}$

Ex.: Ella no dice nada. (she doesn't say anything)

Ella no dice nada tampoco. (she doesn't say anything either)

As you can see from the examples and the chart, it is possible to use three negative words in one sentence: one before the verb and two after the verb.

D. Simple negative and double negative:
We can often use a simple negative or double negative to carry the same message. The double negative is more emphatic.

> Ex.: Nadie habla español aquí./No habla nadie español aquí. (nobody speaks Spanish here)
> Ella tampoco habla español./Ella no habla español tampoco. (she doesn't speak Spanish either)

PRACTICE THE NEGATIVE WORDS   *(Answers, p. 83)*

1. Lo contrario de *alguno* es _____, y lo contrario de *algo* es _____.

2. Lo contrario de *también* es _____, y lo contrario de *con* es _____.

3. Which is more emphatic, *nadie habla* or *no habla nadie*? _____ _____.

4. ¿Cuál es correcto, *él es no bueno* or *él no es bueno*? _____ _____.

5. ¿Cuál es correcto, *él está no aquí* or *él no está aquí*? _____ _____.

6. *Alguno, ninguno* become *algún, ningún* in front of a _____ noun.

7. When we say in Spanish *nadie*, we mean *ninguna* _____, and when we say *nada*, we mean *ninguna* _____.

8. *Tú no sabes inglés también* is incorrect; it should be: *Tú no* _____ _____.

EXERCISE   *(Answers, p. 83)*

Complete the sentences.

1. Lo contrario de (the opposite of) *nadie* es _____.

2. Lo contrario de *tampoco* es _____.

3. Lo contrario de *alguno* es _____.

4. Lo contrario de *siempre* es _____.

5. Lo contrario de *algo* es _____.

6. Lo contrario de *sin* es _____.

7. Lo contrario de *ninguno* es _____.

8. ¿Cómo traduce usted *I know nothing?* _____.

9. ¿Cómo traduce usted *I don't know anything?* _____.

10. ¿Cómo traduce usted *I don't know nothing?* _____.

11. *No digo algo* es incorrecto. Debe ser _____.

12. *No habla alguien* es incorrecto. Debe ser _____.

13. *Nunca digo algo* es incorrecto. Debe ser _____.

14. *No trabaja también* es incorrecto. Debe ser _____.

15. *No tengo alguno* es incorrecto. Debe ser _____.

16. *Ella es no americana* es incorrecto. Debe ser _____.

17. *Ella está no bien* es incorrecto. Debe ser _____.

18. There are two words for *anything* in Spanish: _____.

19. There are two words for *also* in Spanish: _____.

20. There are two words for *never* in Spanish: _____.

REVIEW EXAM FOR LESSONS 1–5

Part I   VOCABULARY

(Answers, p. 83)

A.   Match the two columns.

1. ____ Camarón   A. es un mueble para dormir.

2. ____ Almuerzo   B. es la maleta, el matetín, para viajar.

3. ____ Postre   C. es el hijo de mi hermana.

4. ____ Sillón   D. es el padre de mi esposa.

5. ____ Cinturón   E. es lo contrario de *triste*.

6. ____ Cama   F. es la camarera del avión.

7. ____ Reloj   G. es comida o bebida antes de comer.

8. ____ Equipaje   H. es la comida a las 12:00, 1:00, 2:00 P.M.

9. ____ Cocina   I. es llegar a la hora exacta.

10. ____ Vaso   J. es el flan, el helado, la fruta, etc.

11. ____ Primo   K. es un grupo de dos personas o animales.

12. ____ Aperitivo   L. es para comer con pan, con vegetales, etc.

13. ____ Suegro   M. es un marisco muy caro, pero delicioso.

14. ____ En punto   N. es para abrocharse en el avión, el carro, etc.

15. ____ Sobrino   O. es lo contrario de *salida*.

16. ____ Alegre   P. es el hijo de mis tíos.

17. ____ Azafata   Q. es un mueble para sentarse.

18. ____ Mantequilla R. es para servir la cerveza, el vino, etc.

19. ____ Pareja   S. es para saber la hora.

20. ____ Llegada   T. es donde preparamos la comida.

B.   Complete the sentences with an appropriate word.

21. Una futura esposa es una _____.

22. Pago la cuenta con una _____ de crédito.

23. Quiero un _____ con ventanilla para el vuelo 800.

24. La parte alta de la casa es el _____.

25. Para decir *30 minutos* también decimos _____.

26. Para decir *15 minutos* también decimos _____.

27. Quiero la langosta en _____ verde.

28. Lo contrario de *caro* es _____.

29. La comida española de la noche (9:00 P.M.) es la _____.

30. Los hijos de mis hijos son mis _____.

31. Mi jardín tiene árboles y _____.

32. Lo contrario de *casado* es _____.

33. Nueva York y Los Angeles son _____ muy grandes.

34. Tenemos dos manos: la _____ y la izquierda.

35. Usted puede pagar la cuenta con cheques de _____.

C.   Underline the answer that best completes the sentence.

36. La cocinera prepara (la ducha, la nariz, el filete, el águila).

37. La maleta es parte (del carro, del equipaje, de la pared, de la lechuga).

38. Necesito comprar (un pasaje, un calor, una aduana, un lavaplatos) para viajar.

39. Deseo una ensalada de tomate y (botella, lechuga, luz, mantequilla).

40. Tenemos vino blanco, rosado y (verde, amarillo, excelente, rojo).

41. El criminal (trae, huye, cree, nace) de la policía.

42. José conduce muy bien (el sabor, la luz, el postre, el coche).

43. Yo siempre me detengo en (el tejado, la aduana, el maletín, la luz).

44. Queremos dos (parejas, raciones, clases, manos) de camarones a la plancha.

45. El vuelo 800 tiene (salida, puerta, piloto, hora) de Miami a las 2 P.M.

D.   Write the letter for the best reply.

46. _____Jorge tiene que lavar el coche esta tarde; no puede ir con nosotros.
   A. ¡Por supuesto! ¡Hoy es lunes, las veinticuatro horas del día!
   B. No importa. Mi cocina tiene lavaplatos.
   C. ¡Por supuesto! Tiene que facturar la maleta.
   D. No importa. Nosotros podemos ayudar*le* (him).

47._____En esta sección del autobús nadie puede fumar.
    A. Está bien. Los pasajeros también fuman.
    B. Está bien. Yo tampoco voy a fumar.
    C. Está bien. Los cigarrillos son baratos.
    D. Está bien. Vamos a fumar un cigarrillo.

48._____El jamón, el filete, la ensalada, todo está delicioso.
    A. Es verdad. Este restaurante se especializa en mariscos.
    B. Es verdad. Mi sopa de vegetales está excelente también.
    C. Es verdad. Todas las camareras son muy simpáticas.
    D. Es verdad. La cocinera inspecciona bien el equipaje.

49._____De aperitivo deseamos dos vermuth y una ración de camarones a la plancha.
    A. ¡Cómo no! Aquí servimos la mejor paella del mundo.
    B. Muy bien. Los mariscos siempre son caros.
    C. Por supuesto. Los camarones viven en el mar.
    D. Muy bien. Voy a traer la orden *ahora mismo*. (right now)

50._____¿Quién va a pagar la cuenta después del almuerzo? Aquí no aceptan tarjetas.
    A. No sé. Yo no puedo pagar. Solamente traigo un dólar.
    B. Está bien. Los mariscos de aquí son fantásticos.
    C. No importa. La caja está a la derecha de la puerta.
    D. Muy bien. Pasamos la cuenta a una de las camareras.

Part II   GRAMMAR   *(Answers, p. 84)*

A. Complete the sentences with the correct form of the Present Indicative.

1. ¿Quién _____ tu futura suegra? (be)

2. Iberia _____ de Madrid a Nueva York todos los días. (fly)

3. ¿Cuándo _____ (tú) venir a verme? (can)

4. Mis hijos _____ nueve horas todos los días. (sleep)

5. ¿Por qué _____ (tú) ese programa de televisión? (watch)

6. Usted _____ por la derecha hasta la luz. (continue)

7. Yo siempre _____ vino rosado con la cena. (ask for)

8. Mis padres no _____ que digo la verdad. (believe)

9. Este cigarrillo _____ de Panamá. (be)

10. Mi abuela tiene 70 años, pero _____ joven todavía. (be)

11. ¿Cuándo _____ ustedes a España? (return)

12. ¿Dónde _____ usted pasar la noche? (plan)

13. Las camareras _____ la comida en el restaurante. (serve)

14. ¿A dónde _____ (tú) a viajar en el futuro? (go)

15. ¿Cuántas cervezas _____ Uds.? (wish)

16. Yo no _____ nada en casa los lunes. (do)

17. Nosotras _____ bien el nombre de él. (remember)

18. El vuelo de Miami a Tampa _____ muy corto. (be)

19. Carlos dice que él _____ un libro todos los días. (read)

20. Yo siempre _____ a mis amigos. (recognize)

21. Después del viaje ella _____ las maletas. (unpack)

22. Después de 3 cervezas, tú no _____ nada. (remember)

23. Yo siempre _____ dos dólares a los pobres. (give)

24. Nosotros _____ casa muy temprano. (leave)

25. Carlos _____ pagar la cuenta hoy. (have to . . .)

B.   Only one of the choices correctly completes the sentence here. Try figuring out the answer on your own first; then look at the four choices, and write the letter in the space.

26. _____ Veinte menos cuatro son . . .
    A. diez y seis.   C. dieciséis.
    B. dieziséis.   D. deciséis.

27. _____ En el Caribe . . . camarones son grandes.
    A. el   C. las
    B. la   D. los

28. _____ El plural de *feliz lunes* es . . .
    A. felices lunes.   C. felices lúneses
    B. felizes lunes.   D. felizes lúneses

29. _____ El plural de *papel inglés* es . . .
    A. papels ingleses.   C. papeles ingléses
    B. papeles ingleses.   D. papeles inglés

30. _____ ¿Cómo se dice en español *It's 1:30 P.M.*?
   A. Es la una y media de la mañana.
   B. Son la una y media de la tarde.
   C. Es la una y treinta de la tarde.
   D. Son la una y treinta de la mañana.

31. _____ ¿Cómo se dice en español *It's 2:45 A.M.*?
   A. Son las dos y cuarto de la mañana.
   B. Son quince para las tres de la tarde.
   C. Son las tres menos quince de la tarde.
   D. Son las tres menos cuarto de la mañana.

32. _____ Treinta menos siete son . . .
   A. veinte y tres.   C. ventitrés.
   B. veintitrés.   D. veintitres.

33. _____ ¿Cómo se escribe y se dice *Two million dollars*?
   A. Dos millón de dólares.
   B. Dos millones dólares.
   C. Dos millones de dólares.
   D. Dos million de dólares.

34. _____ ¿Cómo se escribe en un cheque 110?
   A. Un ciento y diez.   C. Cien y diez.
   B. Ciento diez.   D. Ciento y diez.

35. _____ Ustedes . . . la clase a las dos menos diez. (conclude)
   A. concluyen   C. concluen
   B. conclúen   D. concluyan

36. _____ Yo siempre me . . . antes de llegar a la luz roja. (stop)
   A. detieno   C. detengo
   B. deteno   D. detiengo

37. _____ *José nunca viene* means approximately that *José no viene* . . .
   A. alguna vez.   C. siempre.
   B. jamás.   D. tampoco.

38. _____ Yo no . . . radio por la tarde *sino* (except) por la mañana. (listen to)
   A. oyo al   C. oyo el
   B. oigo al   D. oigo el

39. _____ Yo voy por la derecha, y tú . . . por la izquierda. (follow)
   A. siges   C. sigues
   B. seges   D. segues

40. _____ El *nido* (nest) . . . está en la montaña alta. (eagle's)
   A. del águila   C. de el águila
   B. de la águila   D. dela águila

41. _____ Yo no . . . hablar italiano. (know how)
   A. sabo cómo   C. sé cómo
   B. sabo   D. sé

42. _____ El nombre . . . americana no es María; es Mary.
     A. del   C. de la
     B. dela   D. de el

43. _____ El oxígeno es un elemento . . . agua.
     A. dela   C. del
     B. de la   D. de el

44. _____ José nunca estudia . . .
     A. algo.   C. alguno.
     B. también.   D. nada.

45. _____ Yo siempre . . . la mano a mis amigos. (offer)
     A. ofrezo   C. ofreso
     B. ofrezco   D. ofreco

46. _____ Para ir allí no necesitas tomar . . . (any bus)
     A. ninguna autobús.   C. algún autobús.
     B. alguna autobús.   D. ningún autobús.

47. _____ Ustedes nunca tienen . . . (any problem)
     A. ningún problema.   C. algún problema.
     B. ninguna problema.   D. alguna problema.

48. _____ Después del viaje yo . . . las maletas. (unpack)
     A. deshaco   C. deshago
     B. deshazo   D. deshaso

49. _____ Este avión lleva . . . maletas más o menos. (300)
     A. tres cientos   C. trescientos
     B. tres cientas   D. trescientas

50. _____ Todos mis abuelos . . . de Colombia. (be)
     A. están   C. son
     B. estan   D. són

ANSWERS FOR LESSONS 1–5

Lesson 1

Basic Expressions

1. Buenos días
2. Buenas tardes
3. Buenas noches
4. Señora
5. Estoy bien, gracias
6. Me llamo . . .
7. beginning
8. Vivo en
9. ¿Dónde está el baño? — Allí, a la derecha
10. Adiós/Hasta luego
11. ¿En qué puedo servirle?
12. Por favor

Vocabulary

1. F	6. B	11. U	16. C	21. R	26. V
2. a	7. L	12. P	17. H	22. N	27. Q
3. A	8. S	13. D	18. I	23. M	28. X
4. J	9. Z	14. T	19. G	24. d	29. Y
5. c	10. E	15. b	20. K	25. O	30. W

Grammar I

Practice
1. un/una/a-an
2. masculine/feminine
3. masculine/feminine
4. things(inanimate)
5. masculine/feminine
6. No/policeman
7. letter/feminine
8. L-O-N-E-R-S/D-IÓN-Z-A
9. masculine/masculine/feminine
10. masculine/un
11. un/buenos
12. un/una

Exercise

1. un	6. un	11. una	16. un	21. un	26. un
2. una	7. un	12. una	17. un	22. una	27. un
3. un	8. un	13. un	18. una	23. un	28. un
4. un	9. una	14. una	19. un	24. un	29. una
5. una	10. una	15. un	20. un	25. un	30. un

Grammar II

Practice
1. el/la/los/las
2. L-O-N-E-R-S/D-IÓN-Z-A
3. feminine/masculine/masculine
4. masculine/el
5. masculine/el/la
6. del/al
7. stressed/el/un
8. h/el/la/el
9. yes/stressed
10. del presidente/del
11. yes/la

Exercise   1. la   6. la   11. el   16. el   21. el   26. el
              2. el   7. el   12. el   17. el   22. el   27. la
              3. la   8. el   13. la   18. el   23. la   28. la
              4. el   9. el   14. el   19. la   24. el   29. el
              5. la   10. el   15. la   20. la   25. el   30. el

Grammar III

Practice   1. I/yo   8. tú/él
              2. nosotros/nosotras   9. él/ella/∅
              3. tú/ustedes   10. ellas/ellos
              4. tú   11. No
              5. females/females   12. usted
              6. nosotros   13. Ud./Uds. (capital U!)
              7. usted/tú

Exercise   1. nosotras   6. usted (Ud.)   11. ustedes
              2. tú   7. él   12. ellos
              3. yo   8. ella   13. nosotros
              4. vosotros -as   9. ellos   14. ∅
              5. ellas   10. ∅

Lesson 2

Vocabulary

A.   1. la   5. la   9. el   13. el   17. la
      2. el   6. el   10. el   14. la   18. la
      3. el   7. el   11. el   15. la   19. el
      4. la   8. la   12. la   16. el   20. la

B.   1. D   4. A   7. N   10. E   13. R   16 P
      2. F   5. K   8. L   11. M   14. C   17. J
      3. I   6. B   9. G   12. H   15. O   18. Q

Dialog Exercises

A.   1. cervezas   5. vegetales   9. excelente
      2. camarero   6. tomate y lechuga   10. delicioso
      3. almuerzo   7. helado de chocolate   11. crema y azúcar
      4. papas fritas   8. fruta   12. la caja

B.   1. el menú   6. azúcar y crema   10. la cuenta
     2. el café   7. el flan   11. el menú
     3. el restaurante   8. el tomate   12. de chocolate
     4. una cerveza   9. el café   13. salsa verde
     5. lechuga y tomate

Grammar I

Practice   1. infinitive /-ar/-er/-ir   2. meaning (idea) /habl/viv
             3. nosotros (we) /tú (you) / yo (I)   4. habla
             5. hablamos   6. estudiamos
             7. emphasis   8. progress / estudia
             9. us / usamos / usan   10. uso
             11. uso   12. (ellos) estudian español

Exercise   1. estudian   6. usamos   11. completa   16. pagamos
             2. ordenan   7. estamos   12. deseas   17. usa
             3. pagan   8. deseo   13. toman   18. trabaja
             4. tomas   9. desean   14. completamos   19. pasa
             5. trabaja   10. pasa   15. trabajan   20. estudio

Grammar II

Practice   1. *er / ir*   2. *com / escrib / le*   3. ending / *yo* (I)
             4. *vivimos/imos*   5. first person plural   6. *vive*
             7. present indicative / *bebe* 8. *leo*
             9. (a) we are writing, (b) we write, (c) we will write (we are going to write),
                and (d) we do write

Exercise   1. aprendemos   6. subimos   11. hablamos   16. crees
             2. lee   7. sale   12. lee   17. trabajan
             3. escribes   8. comen   13. escribo   18. viven
             4. tomo   9. creen   14. sale   19. bebo
             5. bebe   10. como   15. sube   20. sube

Grammar III

Practice   1. ser/estar   5. estar/está   9. está
             2. irregular   6. ser   10. ser/es
             3. oy   7. ser/estar   11. ser/es
             4. estás/está/están   8. es   12. ser/es

Exercise   1. soy/son   5. es   9. está/estoy   13. es   17. está/está
             2. es/está   6. es   10. está   14. es/es   18. está/está
             3. es   7. somos   11. es   15. es   19. es/es
             4. están   8. están   12. son   16. es/es   20. es

Lesson 3

Vocabulary

A.   1. la   4. la   7. el   10. el   13. el
     2. el   5. la   8. la   11. la   14. la
     3. el   6. el   9. la   12. el   15. la

B.   1. camarón   5. paella   9. aperitivo   13. mantequilla
     2. pareja   6. gambas   10. tarjetas   14. pedir (forget *for*)
     3. vaso   7. caros   11. cheque   15. on the grill
     4. seco   8. rosado   12. ciudad

C.   1. negro   5. pequeño   9. camarera   13. aquí (acá)
     2. barato   6. malo   10. viajera   14. noche
     3. caliente 7. aperitivo 11. una turista 15. sur
     4. seco   8. mujer   12. una policía

Dialog Exercises

A.   1. mariscos   5. dulces   9. mantequilla   13. tarjetas
     2. pareja   6. raciones   10. dos flanes   14. viajeros
     3. mundo   7. menú   11. botella
     4. aperitivo   8. para dos   12. blanco

B.   1. D   4. I   7. L   10. A   13. E
     2. G   5. H   8. B   11. C   14. N
     3. F   6. J   9. M   12. D   15. K

Grammar I

Practice   1. noun/number   6. papel amarillo   11. camarones/consonant
             2. masculine/-o   7. programa americano   12. luces/c
             3. feminine/-a   8. luz roja   13. lunes/stress
             4. no/verde   9. No/grande   14. ingleses/stressed
             5. pared blanca   10. buenos/vowel   15. rubís/rubíes

A.
1. los aperitivos pequeños
2. los camarones caros
3. las mejores paellas
4. los cheques amarillos
5. las cenas grandes
6. las ideas malas
7. las raciones deliciosas
8. los cafés calientes
9. los mejores papeles
10. los vinos secos
11. los rubís (rubíes) caros
12. las luces verdes
13. los lunes pasados
14. los vasos ingleses
15. las aguas calientes

B.
1. bueno
2. rojos
3. seco
4. dulces
5. pequeña
6. grande
7. mejores
8. pasado/pasados
9. ingleses
10. carmesís/carmesíes

Grammar II

Practice
1. stem/sab
2. d/v
3. voy/doy
4. sé/digo
5. veo/go(are going)
6. we(nosotros)/you(tú)
   /they(ellos -as, Uds.)
7. (él) va a ir . . .
8. digo la verdad

Exercise
1. vamos
2. necesitan
3. ves(miras)
4. da
5. acompaña
6. especializa
7. acepta
8. saben
9. va a servir
10. prepara
11. decimos
12. cenan
13. sé
14. vas a ir
15. pedimos
16. hace
17. da
18. necesito
19. bebe(toma)
20. saben

Grammar III

Practice
1. accent/cuándo
2. a dónde
3. No/dónde
4. c/dieciséis
5. one/cinco
6. cien/ciento/cien
7. ciento/ciento cinco
8. masculine/feminine
9. masculine/uno
10. doscientos/trescientas
11. mil/dos mil
12. millón/millones
13. de/millones de

Exercise
1. Cuándo
2. De quién
3. Por qué
4. Cuántos
5. Qué (cuál)
6. dónde
7. cuál
8. Adónde
   (a dónde)
9. Cuánto
10. dos/una
11. un/uno
12. dieciséis
13. veintidós
14. treinta y dos
15. quinientos
16. ciento diez
17. dos mil
18. quinientas
19. dos millones
    de
20. cien por cien
    /ciento por
    ciento

Question: period/comma 2.200.300,50

Lesson 4

Vocabulary

A.
1. el	4. el	7. el	10. el
2. la	5. la	8. el	11. el
3. el	6. el	9. la	12. la

B.
1. a tiempo	5. el pasaje	9. un vuelo	13. fumar
2. la comida	6. a la ventanilla	10. a los pasajeros	14. la aduana
3. el equipaje	7. el empleado	11. salida	15. a tiempo
4. el cinturón	8. subir	12. llegar	

C.
1. I	4. B	7. D	10. L	13. J
2. N	5. C	8. G	11. A	14. F
3. K	6. M	9. E	12. H	

Dialog Exercises

A.
1. llega	6. pasaporte	11. maletín
2. reservación	7. asiento	12. salida
3. llega a tiempo	8. simpática	13. vuelo
4. ventanilla	9. maletas	14. viaje
5. No fuma	10. Lleva uno	15. gracias/adiós

B.
1. F	4. L	7. B	10. C	13. K
2. E	5. N	8. O	11. G	14. J
3. I	6. A	9. M	12. H	15. D

Grammar I

Practice
1. ten/tien/teng/have	4. que/Tengo que salir	7. voy
2. g/g	5. de/salgo de casa	8. Deshago
3. ie/yes	6. to come/speaker	9. detienen

Exercise
1. viene	6. abrochan	11. factura	16. deshace
2. tengo que	7. Tiene	12. fumo	17. inspeccionan
3. ayuda	8. pongo	13. venimos	18. Tiene
4. sales	9. llega	14. bajan	19. voy
5. hace	10. detiene	15. hago	20. compramos

Grammar II

Practice
1. una(sing)/
   2–12(plur.)
2. quince/cuarto
3. treinta/media
4. y/menos

5. en punto/como
   (más o menos)
6. de la mañana
7. de la tarde/
   de la noche

8. No/la
9. hora
10. ¿Qué hora es?
    ¿Qué horas son?
    (México)

Exercise
1. Son las tres y diez de la tarde.
2. Son las dos y cuarto (quince) de la mañana.
3. Es la una y media (treinta) de la tarde.
4. Son las seis menos diez de la mañana.
5. Son las once de la noche.
6. Son las once y veinte de la mañana.

7. Es la una menos cuarto (quince).
8. Es la una y cinco de la mañana.
9. a las dos en punto
10. a las ocho y media (treinta.)
11. a las siete de la mañana
12. a las once de la noche
13. a las dos más o menos (como)
14. A qué hora

Grammar III

Practice
1. quer/quier/ie
2. dec/dic/i
3. pod/pued/ue
4. Yes

5. persons (people)/quieres
6. for/pedimos/piden
7. sirvo/sirven

8. vuela
9. muestro
10. quiero
11. segu/sigu/u/sigo
12. again/we are flying again

Exercise
1. puede
2. vuelan
3. vuelve
4. pensamos
5. quieres
6. sigue/sigo
7. pides
8. siento
9. muestra
10. sirven
11. quiere
12. vuelve
13. pienso
14. vuela
15. puedo
16. quiere
17. puede
18. dice
19. sigue
20. tienen
21. podemos
22. muestran
23. llegamos
24. vuela
25. vuelvo

Lesson 5

Vocabulary

A.
1. el
2. el
3. la
4. la
5. el
6. el
7. la
8. el
9. el
10. el
11. el
12. el
13. la
14. la
15. el

B. 1. abuelo   4. nieto   7. padres   10. hermanos
    2. tío   5. prima   8. primos   11. suegro
    3. sobrino   6. tías   9. suegra   12. madre/padre

C. 1. triste   5. corto   9. morir   13. temprano
    2. feo   6. rico   10. destruir   14. hasta
    3. viejo   7. feo   11. traer
    4. casado   8. poco   12. fantástico

D. 1. G   3. J   5. I   7. H   9. D
    2. F   4. A   6. B   8. E   10. C

E. 1. la cocina   6. lavaplatos   11. el reloj   16. el comedor
    2. el garaje   7. la mesa   12. niños   17. novios
    3. la chimenea   8. la cama   13. el tejado   18. soltero
    4. muchas flores   9. la ducha   14. flores   19. pobre
    5. dormitorios   10. carro   15. muebles   20. jóvenes

Dialog Exercises

A. 1. amigos   7. hermanos/   12. jardín   18. suegras
    2. la familia   hermana   13. jardín   19. No lo cree
    3. comer   8. abuela   14. setenta y seis 20. fantástica
    4. conoce   9. padre/papá   15. joven
    5. quieren   10. dormitorios   16. hasta
    6. invitación   11. Tiene tres   17. apreciar

B. 1. D   3. I   5. B   7. C   9. H
    2. G   4. J   6. F   8. E   10. A

Grammar I

Practice 1. oig/o/oy/oímos   6. construyo/   9. saber/Ø
            2. traigo/caigo/ig   construyen   10. conocer/conocemos
            3. conozco/c   7. nazco   11. saber
            4. ofrezco/conduzco   8. conocer/saber   12. (yo) sé escribir
            5. y/huimos

Exercise 1. producen   6. construyen   11. recuerda   16. caigo
            2. conduzco   7. mueren   12. traduzco   17. sé
            3. oyen   8. traigo   13. concluye   18. destruyen
            4. huyen   9. parece   14. oigo   19. ofrece
            5. duermes   10. reconoce   15. conoce   20. recuerda

Grammar II

Practice   1. One/   5. last/consonant   9. you/your
             2. last/vowel   6. two   10. veintidós/veintitrés
             3. last/n/s   7. diphthong
             4. last/vowel/n/s   8. he/the

Exercise   3. águila   9. mamá   18. lápices   29. veintiún
             4. rubí   10. tú   19. él   31. sé
             6. oír   13. oímos   20. árboles   32. árbol
             7. número   14. están   23. dieciséis   33. rubís
             8. carmesí   16. avión   24. día   34. estás

Grammar III

Practice   1. ninguno/nada   4. él no es bueno   7. persona/cosa (thing)
             2. tampoco/sin   5. él no está aquí   8. sabes inglés tampoco
             3. no habla nadie   6. masculine

Exercise   1. alguien   9. no sé nada   17. ella no está bien
             2. también   10. no sé nada   18. algo/nada
             3. ninguno   11. no digo nada   19. también/tampoco
             4. nunca(jamás)   12. no habla nadie   20. siempre/
             5. nada   13. nunca digo nada   nunca(jamás)
             6. con   14. no trabaja tampoco
             7. alguno   15. no tengo ninguno
             8. no sé nada   16. ella no es americana

Review Exam

Vocabulary

 1. M   11. P   21. novia   31. flores(frutas)   41. huye
 2. H   12. G   22. tarjeta   32. soltero   42. el coche
 3. J   13. D   23. asiento   33. ciudades   43. la luz
 4. Q   14. I   24. tejado   34. derecha   44. raciones
 5. N   15. C   25. media(hora)   35. viajeros   45. salida
 6. A   16. E   26. cuarto(de hora) 36. el filete   46. D
 7. S   17. F   27. salsa   37. del equipaje   47. B
 8. B   18. L   28. barato   38. un pasaje   48. B
 9. T   19. K   29. cena   39. lechuga   49. D
10. R   20. O   30. nietos   40. rojo   50. A

Grammar

1. es	11. vuelven	21. deshace	31. D	41. D
2. vuela	12. piensa	22. recuerdas	32. B	42. C
3. puedes	13. sirven	23. doy	33. C	43. C
4. duermen	14. vas	24. salimos de	34. B	44. D
5. ves(miras)	15. quieren/desean	25. tiene que	35. A	45. B
6. sigue	16. hago	26. C	36. C	46. D
7. pido	17. recordamos	27. D	37. B	47. A
8. creen	18. es	28. A	38. D	48. C
9. es	19. lee	29. B	39. C	49. D
10. está	20. reconozco	30. C	40. A	50. C

Lesson 6

En el hotel
(At the Hotel)

ascensor	elevator	**fecha**	date	**peso**[2]	peso
banco	bank	**habitación**	room	**piso**	floor, story
botón	button	**hotel**	hotel	**plaza**	square
botones[1]	bellboy	**jabón**	soap	**precio**	price
dinero	money	**llave (la)**	key	**recepción**	front desk
desayuno	breakfast	**lluvia**	rain	**recepcionista**	receptionist
divisa	foreign money	**mozo**	bellboy	**servicio a los cuartos**	room service
época	season, epoch	**nieve (la)**	snow	**toalla**	towel
escalera	staircase	**nube (la)**	cloud	**vista**	sight, view
estaciona-miento	parking	**pensión**	boarding-house		

abrir	to open	**firmar**	to sign	**preferir (ie)**	to prefer
cambiar	to change	**interesar**	to interest	**registrarse**[4]	to register
cerrar (ie)	to close	**incluir (y)**	to include	**reservar**	to reserve
cobrar[3]	to charge	**llover (ue)**	to rain		
decidir	to decide	**nevar (ie)**	to snow	**subir**	to take up/go up
divertirse(ie)	to have fun	**perdonar**	to pardon	**tratar de (+ infinitivo)**	to try to (+ verb)
entrar a	to come in	**permitir**	to allow	**visitar**	to visit
estacionar	to park				

ancho	wide	**disponible**	available	**nuevo**	new
animado	lively	**doble**	double	**razonable**	reasonable
antiguo	ancient	**estrecho**	narrow	**sencillo**	single/simple
bastante	enough	**nublado**	cloudy	**tercero**[5]	third

¿A cómo está . . .?	What's the price of . . .?	estar nublado	to be cloudy
aquí tiene la llave	here is the key	lejos	far away
cerca	near	por día	per day
dar a + (place)	to face + (place)	porque	because
en seguida/enseguida	right away	por eso	because of that

	buen tiempo	good weather		años		years old
	calor	hot		calor		hot
	frío	cold		éxito		successful
Hacer +	mal tiempo = *to be*	bad weather	*Tener* +	frío	= *to be*	cold
	sol	sunny		ganas de		feel like
	viento	windy		hambre		hungry
	fresco	cool		sed		thirsty
				suerte		lucky

NOTES:

1. Notice that the plural of *botón* (button) is *botones* (buttons), but this plural form becomes the name of the person "with many buttons": a *bellboy*. In this case we say *un botones* (one bellboy).

2. *Peso* is the currency in México, Argentina, Chile, Cuba, Colombia, and Uruguay. One dollar is approximately 150 Mexican pesos.

3. *Cobrar* is to charge and also *to get paid*—for example, for a job. In this sense, is the opposite of *pagar:* Yo *pago* la cuenta del cuarto./ El recepcionista *cobra* la cuenta de mi cuarto.   También él *cobra* todas las *semanas* (weeks).

4. *Registrarse* is used in the hotel, city hall, motor vehicles, where they have a *registro*. But we use *matricular* or *inscribir* (register) when we talk about a student in a school.

5. *Tercero* becomes *tercer* in front of a masculine noun, just as *bueno* becomes *buen* and *malo* becomes *mal:* El *tercer* piso, but la *tercera* puerta.
    Un *buen* café / un café *bueno* (The first sentence emphasizes *good* [buen].)

PRACTICE THE VOCABULARY   *(Answers, p. 185)*

A.   Write *el* or *la* in front of the following nouns.

1. ____ascensor   4. ____precio   7. ____divisa   10. ____lluvia

2. ____hotel   5. ____recepción   8. ____jabón   11. ____pensión

3. ____llave   6. ____botón   9. ____nube   12. ____botones (person)

B. Write the opposite word.

1. ancho_____
2. antiguo_____
3. calor_____
4. hambre_____
5. doble_____
6. cerca_____

7. abrir_____
8. cobrar_____
9. buen tiempo_____
10. salir de_____
11. bajar_____
12. joven_____

C. Word Families:

The dictionary of a language has many words that are related to each other; however, the meaningful *roots* are far fewer in number than the dictionary entries. Try to relate the words you know to the new words, as if they were grouped by families. For example, if you know *comer,* you can relate it to *comedor, comida, comestible* (foodstuff). If you remember *beber,* you can relate it to *bebida* (drink), *bebedor* (drinker). The following list includes words you studied before and that are associated with others you know. Write as many related words as you can think of.

1. servicio_____
2. baño_____
3. desayuno_____
4. fumador_____
5. perdón_____
6. registro_____
7. lluvia_____
8. nieve_____
9. reservación_____
10. turista_____
11. caliente_____
12. oído (ear)_____
13. vista_____
14. viajar_____
15. pasajero_____

16. rosa (rose)_____
17. lavar_____
18. invitar_____
19. dormir_____
20. asiento_____
21. casado_____
22. estado (state)_____
23. nube_____
24. cocinero_____
25. señora_____
26. cena_____
27. llegar_____
28. mar_____
29. salir_____
30. volar_____

D. Write an appropriate word to complete these sentences.

1. La comida por la mañana temprano es el _____.

2. El dinero de México no se llama dólar; se llama _____.

3. Subimos al tercer piso en el _____ o la

   _____.

4. El agua que cae cuando llueve es la _____.

5. Una pareja duerme mejor en una cama _____.

6. Para cambiar divisas vamos a un _____.

7. Todas las ciudades antiguas del mundo español tienen una _____ central en medio de la ciudad.

8. Mi casa no está cerca; al contrario, está _____ de aquí.

9. Para bañarnos usamos agua y _____.

10. La persona del hotel que lleva las maletas es el _____.

11. Un precio que no es caro ni (nor) barato, decimos que es _____

    _____.

12. Los cuartos (rooms) del hotel también se llaman _____.

13. Cuando hace _____, me pongo las botas (boots).

14. Cuando tengo _____, voy a tomar agua fría.

15. Cuando está _____, llevo el paraguas.

E. Match the two columns.

1. _____ Nos bañamos . . .   A. dólares en pesos.

2. _____ Firmamos . . .   B. aprender español muy rápido.

3. _____ Abrimos . . .   C. un error en un amigo.

4. _____ Subimos . . .   D. la comida en el precio.

5. _____ Cobramos . . .   E. el nombre en el registro del hotel.

6. _____ Estacionamos . . .   F. en una fiesta, en un viaje, etc.

7. _____ Cambiamos . . .   G. con agua y jabón en la ducha.

8. _____ Tratamos de . . .   H. el coche en el garaje.

9. _____ Nos divertimos . . .   I. el equipaje a la habitación.

10. _____ Perdonamos . . .   J. la puerta con la llave.

11. _____ Incluimos . . .   K. cuatrocientos pesos por día.

F. **Practice the new verbs by filling in the correct form of the Present. (The verb is the core of the Spanish language: once you master the verb system, you master the language. Since there is no explicit practice for verbs in this lesson, practice the present indicative of the verbs in the vocabulary of this lesson. Review them on page 85, and notice the irregular ones indicated (ie), (ue), (i).)**

1. En Arizona y California _____ muy poco. (rain)

2. En Nueva York y en Colorado _____ mucho. (snow)

3. Cuando voy a una fiesta, siempre me _____ mucho. (have fun)

4. Todos los años mi esposa y yo _____ Las Vegas. (visit)

5. Esta habitación _____ un patio antiguo. (face)

6. José _____ doscientos dólares en el trabajo. (get paid)

7. ¿_____ ustedes un cuarto doble? (prefer)

8. Los Señores Roy se _____ en el hotel. (register)

9. El inspector de la aduana _____ las maletas. (open)

10. El mozo del aeropuerto _____ las maletas al autobús. (take up)

11. Todos los pasajeros _____ al avión. (enter)

12. Las puertas del hotel se _____ a las 12:00 P.M. (close)

13. ¿A cómo _____ el *cambio* (exchange) del dólar hoy? (be)

14. El precio de la pensión _____ también la comida. (include)

15. ¿Por qué no _____ Ud. _____ hablar siempre español? (try . . . to)

16. Los libros de Cervantes me _____ mucho. (interest)

17. Ella _____ estudiar español para visitar a México. (decide)

18. Mi padre no nos _____ fumar en casa. (permit)

19. Cuando vamos a México, _____ dólares en pesos. (exchange)

20. ¿Dónde _____ ustedes el hotel? (reserve)

21. Mi esposa y yo nos_____en el viaje. (have fun)

22. Hoy hace calor; (yo)_____ir a la *playa* (beach). (prefer)

23. Esta escalera_____antigua; por eso_____muy estrecha. (be/be)

DIÁLOGO   *En un hotel en México*

(Los señores González llegan a México para visitar la ciudad. Deciden pasar tres días en un hotel. Hablan con el recepcionista del hotel.)

RECEPCIONISTA: Buenas noches. ¿En qué puedo servirles?
SR. GONZÁLES: Queremos una habitación con cama doble para tres días.
RECEPCIONISTA: ¿Tienen ustedes reservación?
SRA. GONZÁLES: Pues no. Pero no es época de turismo ahora.
RECEPCIONISTA: Tiene usted razón, señora. Tenemos un cuarto disponible en el tercer piso. Tiene dos ventanas que dan a la plaza central.
SR. GONZÁLEZ: ¿Cuánto cobran ustedes por día?
RECEPCIONISTA: Mil quinientos pesos, sin incluir la comida. También tiene televisor.
SR. GONZÁLEZ: Bueno . . . No es el precio de una pensión, pero me parece razonable.
SRA. GONZÁLEZ: ¿Tiene agua caliente el baño?
RECEPCIONISTA: Por supuesto. Y fría también. Y toallas . . . y jabón.
SR. GONZÁLEZ: ¿A qué hora abren el comedor por la mañana?
RECEPCIONISTA: El desayuno se sirve desde las 8:00 hasta las 11:00. Por la noche cerramos el comedor a las diez y media.
SR. GONZÁLEZ: Está bien. Tomamos el cuarto por tres días.
RECEPCIONISTA: ¿Quiere firmar el registro, por favor? Aquí tienen la llave. El botones sube el equipaje.
SRA. GONZÁLEZ: Muchas gracias. Muy amable.

DIALOG   *In a Hotel in Mexico*

(Mr. and Mrs. González arrive in Mexico to visit the city. They decide to spend three days at a hotel. They talk to the hotel receptionist.)

RECEPTIONIST: Good evening. May I help you?
MR. GONZÁLEZ: We want a room with a double bed for three days.
RECEPTIONIST: Do you have a reservation?
MRS. GONZÁLEZ: Well, no. But this isn't the tourist season.
RECEPTIONIST: You're right, madam. We have a room available on the third floor. It has two windows facing the central square.

MR. GONZÁLEZ:	How much do you charge a day?
RECEPTIONIST:	One thousand five hundred pesos, without meals. There's a TV set too.
MR. GONZÁLEZ:	Well . . . It's not the price of a boarding-house, but it seems reasonable.
MRS. GONZÁLEZ:	Does the bathroom have hot water?
RECEPTIONIST:	Of course. And cold too. And towels . . . and soap.
MR. GONZÁLEZ:	At what time does the dining room open in the morning?
RECEPTIONIST:	Breakfast is served from eight to eleven. We close the dining room at 10:30 in the evening.
MR. GONZÁLEZ:	OK. We'll take the room for three days.
RECEPTIONIST:	Sign the register, please. Here's the key. The bellboy will take your luggage up.
MRS. GONZÁLEZ:	Thank you. You're very kind.

EXERCISES

(Answers, p. 185)

A. Answer the questions according to the dialog. (Try short answers.)

1. ¿A dónde llegan los señores González?_____.

2. ¿Cuánto tiempo van a pasar en el hotel?_____.

3. ¿Con quién hablan los señores González?_____
_____.

4. ¿Qué clase de habitación quieren los González?_____
_____.

5. ¿Tienen reservación los González?_____.

6. Cuando los González llegan a México no es época de_____.

7. ¿En qué piso tienen un cuarto disponible?_____.

8. Las ventanas de la habitación dan a la_____.

9. ¿Cuántos pesos cobran por día por un cuarto doble?_____
_____.

10. ¿Incluye la comida el precio, o no?_____
_____.

11. ¿Qué le parece el precio al Sr. González?_____
_____.

12. ¿Cuál es más caro, un hotel o una pensión?_____.

13. El baño tiene agua fría y _____.

14. El baño también tiene toallas y _____ para bañarse.

15. ¿A qué hora abren el comedor por la mañana? _____.

16. ¿A qué hora cierran el comedor por la noche? _____

_____.

17. ¿Toman el cuarto los señores González, o no? _____.

18. El Sr. González tiene que firmar el _____.

19. El recepcionista da _____ del cuarto a los González.

20. ¿Quién sube el equipaje al cuarto? _____.

B.   Underline the correct answer.

1. Subimos en el ascensor o por (la toalla, el dinero, la escalera, la llave).

2. Cuando está muy nublado nieva o (firma, incluye, cambia, llueve).

3. Para comer en el cuarto pido (servicio, toalla, fecha, jabón) a los cuartos.

4. Esta ventana (cobra, baja, sube, da) a la plaza central.

5. El precio de la habitación es (doble, razonable, disponible, estrecho).

6. Para cambiar (desayunos, divisas, cuartos, visitas) vamos a un banco.

7. Cuando hablamos de (sencillo, bastante, doble, nuevo) pensamos en una pareja.

8. Subimos a un piso alto en (el dinero, la plaza, el servicio, el ascensor).

9. Cuando hace buen tiempo, no tenemos (nubes, escaleras, épocas, toallas).

10. Tomo una cerveza cuando tengo (hambre, suerte, frío, sed).

11. Cuando firmamos, escribimos *nuestro -a* (our) (vista, nombre, precio, dinero).

12. Comemos cuando tenemos (éxito, sed, suerte, hambre).

13. Voy a la fiesta para (perdonar, reservar, divertirme, permitir).

14. En el trabajo cobramos (un servicio, un cheque, una divisa, una toalla).

15. José prefiere (el hotel, la vista, la plaza, la fecha) a la pensión.

GRAMMAR I   Idiomatic Expressions with **tener** and **hacer**.

A.   **¿Qué tiempo hace?** (how's the weather?) When we talk about the weather, we use *hacer* in the third person—*hace,* followed by nouns like *calor, frío, sol.*

Memorize these expressions:

Hace calor (it's hot)	**Hace viento** (it's windy)
Hace frío (it's cold)	**Hace buen tiempo** (it's good weather)
Hace fresco (it's cool)	**Hace mal tiempo** (it's bad weather)
Hace sol (it's sunny)	**Hace *mucho* frío** (it's very cold)

B. Note that *calor, sol, viento,* etc., are nouns; in English *hot, sunny,* etc., are adjectives. This means that to translate *very* in *very hot,* we use *mucho* rather than *muy.* Both *mucho* and *poco* are adjectives and must agree with the noun.
   Ex.: Hoy hace *mucho viento* y *poco sol.*

C. To express sensations of cold, hunger, thirst, etc., in English we usually use *to be.* In Spanish the expression is *tener + noun,* such as *calor, hambre,* etc.

   Memorize these expressions:

Tener frío (cold)	**Tener hambre** (hungry)	**Tener ganas de** (feel like)
Tener calor (hot)	**Tener sed** (thirsty)	**Tener cuidado** (careful)
Tener suerte (lucky)	**Tener sueño** (sleepy)	**Tener éxito** (successful)
Tener razón (right)	**Tener años** (years old)	**Tener ansias de** (feel like)

D. *Tengo muy frío* is incorrect because *frío* is a noun, so it doesn't take *muy* but *mucho.* The correct expression is *tengo mucho frío.* The opposite of *mucho -a* is *poco -a* (a little). Both *mucho* and *poco* are adjectives and must agree with the noun.
   Ex.: Tengo poca hambre hoy.   Ella tiene muchos años.

E. If *tener razón* is *to be right, no tener razón* is *to be wrong.*
   Ex.: Mi suegra nunca tiene razón. (my mother-in-law is always wrong)

   Notice that *tener ganas* and *tener ansias* require the preposition *de.*
   Ex.: ¿Tienes ganas *de* una cerveza? / de desayunar?
   do you feel like a beer? / having breakfast?)

F. Remember that *estar* is used to indicate states that exist as the result of a change.
   Ex.: El agua *está* fría; no *está* caliente.

   The verb *ser* indicates a characteristic that is the norm for a noun.
   Ex.: La nieve *es* blanca, no *es* dulce, no *es* verde.

PRACTICE THE EXPRESSIONS   *(Answers, p. 186)*

1. In the expression *hace frío,* is *frío* an adjective or a noun?_____
   _____. This is why we don't say *Hace muy frío* but *Hace*
   _____.

2. *Hace muy sol* is not correct. It should be_____.

3. In Spanish people and animals "have" cold, hunger, etc. For example,
   *Ellos*_____. (are hungry)

4. *Tenemos muy hambre* is not correct because *hambre* is a noun (hunger).
   Tenemos mucho hambre is also wrong, because *hambre* is feminine:
   *Tenemos*_____.

5. *To be wrong* is the opposite of *to be right.* The opposite of *tener razón*
   is_____.

6. What is the literal translation of *Tengo sed*?_____.

7. *Tener ganas* (or *ansias*) always needs *de* before a noun or an infinitive of a
   verb. How do you say *I feel like having a beer*?_____
   _____.

8. Remember that *ser* identifies a noun with another noun or with a characteristic that is the norm for that noun. *The staircase is narrow:* _____
   _____.

9. *Estar* indicates the result of a change; it does not express the norm for a
   noun. For example, *This room is very cold: Este cuarto*_____
   _____.

EXERCISE   *(Answers, p. 186)*

Complete the sentences with the correct form of *ser/estar/hacer/ tener.*

1. En Alaska_____más frío que en California.

2. En California y en La Florida_____mucho sol.

3. Creo que el Presidente_____70 años.

4. Mi profesora_____furiosa hoy, no sé por qué.

5. Mi cuenta del banco _____ muy baja ahora.

6. Vamos a comer algo porque (yo) _____ mucha hambre.

7. El piso de esta clase _____ muy *sucio* (dirty).

8. ¿Qué hora _____? — Creo que _____ las cinco más o menos.

9. Quiero saber cómo _____ mis padres; voy a llamar por teléfono.

10. ¿Por qué en Chicago siempre _____ mucho viento?

11. No puedo tomar este café porque _____ muy frío.

12. Voy a dormir porque _____. (I'm sleepy)

13. Yucatán está en México. Usted _____. (You're right)

14. Creo que va a llover porque _____. (it's bad weather)

15. *Ésta* (This) es la antigua casa de George Washington: _____ muy vieja, pero _____ *bien conservada* (well preserved).

16. Siempre que vas a Las Vegas, _____. (you're very lucky)

17. Prefiero *mayo* (May) porque _____.(it's cool)

18. El niño *llora* (is crying) porque _____. (he's hungry)

19. Cuando conduzco el coche siempre _____. (I'm careful)

20. Josefina _____ viajar a Madrid. (feels like)

GRAMMAR II   Demonstrative Adjectives and Pronouns.

A.   Memorize the following chart:

DISTANCE	MASCULINE	FEMININE	NEUTER	ENGLISH
Near speaker	**este/estos**	**esta/estas**	**esto**	this / these
Near listener	**ese / esos**	**esa / esas**	**eso**	that / those
Far from listener	**aquel /aquellos**	**aquella /aquellas**	**aquello**	

B. Notice the following:
1. These demonstrative adjectives show the *distance* a noun is from the speaker, the listener or from both of them. When the speaker talks about a noun *near* her, she will use *este/estos, esta/estas*.
2. When the speaker is talking about a noun *near the listener,* he will use *ese/esos, esa/esas*.
Ex.: ¿Cómo se llama *ese* libro que *tú* lees?

3. When the speaker refers to a noun *far from the listener* (and speaker), she will use *aquel/aquellos, aquella/aquellas*.
Ex.: ¿Quién es *aquel* niño *allí lejos?*

C. The neuter *esto/eso/aquello* are used to refer to a noun when we don't specify which noun we're talking about (remember: there are no neuter nouns in Spanish). We would use *esto/eso* to refer to a whole statement, a speech, a discourse, etc.
Ex.: ¿Qué es *eso* que tienes en la mano? - *Esto* es un conejo.
(What's *that* you have in your hand? - *This* is [It's] a rabbit.)
Eso que dices es un error muy grande. (what you're saying is a very big mistake)

D. The demonstratives can be used in two ways: (1) as adjectives in front of a noun as in the examples above in (*B*); (2) as *pronouns,* when a noun is omitted because it is understood. In this case the demonstratives carry a written **acento.**
Ex.: ¿Quieres *este* libro? - No, quiero *ése*. (do you want this book? - No, I want *that one*)
¿Vas a comprar *ese* carro? - No, voy a comprar *aquél*.
(are you going to buy that car? - no, I'm going to buy *that one*.)

Notice that in English you add *one* when you omit the noun; however, *one* is not translated into Spanish.

PRACTICE THE DEMONSTRATIVES   *(Answers, p. 186)*

1. If I'm talking about things (or persons) *near me,* I use any of these four demonstratives: _____.

2. If I'm talking about things or people *near you* (the listener), I use any of these four demonstratives: _____.

3. Demonstrative adjectives must agree with the noun in gender (masc./fem.) and _____, just like any other adjective.

4. Notice that in English *that/those* are used for something near the listener or far from the listener; you would have to add *over there* or the like to specify what you mean. In Spanish we have two different demonstratives for

   that/those **ese** vs. _____ , **esos** vs. _____ , etc.

5. Which word don't we translate in *this one?* _____ .

6. *Éste, ése, ésta, ésa,* etc, carry *acento* when they are _____ , because the noun has been omitted. The idea of nearness-distance doesn't change.

7. *No quiero este libro; quiero ese* is not spelled correctly. The *acento* is

   missing on _____ .

8. The neuter demonstratives *esto/eso/aquello* are never used in front of a

   _____ . In other words, they are pronouns. Do they carry

   acento? _____ .

9. Have you noticed that the masculine form of the demonstratives doesn't end in *o* like many other descriptive adjectives? Actually it ends in the vowel

   _____ or nothing, as in *aquel+Ø.*

10. The difference in distance between *ese* and *aquel* (what's *near* or *far* from the listener) is relative. The tendency today is to use *ese* more than *aquel;* the

    same is true for their neuter counterparts: _____ .

EXERCISE

(Answers, p. 186)

Complete the sentences with the correct demonstrative. (Pay close attention to number and gender.)

1. ¿Conoces a _____ hombre que está allí con Roberto? (that)

2. _____ café está frío (this); _____ está caliente. (that one)

3. ¿Qué es _____ que llevas en la maleta? (that)

4. _____ lápices son de mi amigo José. (these)

5. _____ libro que yo leo (this) es más interesante que

   _____ que tú lees. (that one)

6. ¿Qué es _____ que vemos allí lejos? (that)

7. Puedes lavarte las manos con＿＿＿＿＿＿＿＿＿＿jabón. (this)

8. No quiero＿＿＿＿＿＿＿＿＿llave (this); prefiero＿＿＿＿＿＿＿＿.
   (that one)

9. No puedo aceptar＿＿＿＿＿＿＿＿＿que usted dice. (that + what =
   what)

10. ＿＿＿＿＿＿＿＿＿es un día muy importante para los novios. (this)

11. Voy a comprar＿＿＿＿＿＿＿＿reloj que está allí en la pared. (that)

12. El taxista siempre se detiene en＿＿＿＿＿＿＿＿＿luz cuando está
    roja. (this)

13. No sé qué es＿＿＿＿＿＿＿que llevas en la mano. (that)

14. ＿＿＿＿＿＿(this) pensión es más barata que＿＿＿＿＿＿＿＿＿＿
    hotel (that).

15. José cree que siempre tiene razón;＿＿＿＿＿＿＿no me parece bien. (that)

GRAMMAR III   Possessive Adjectives and Pronouns.

A.   Memorize the following chart:

PERSONS	SHORT FORMS	LONG FORMS		ENGLISH	
		Masculine	Feminine	Adjective	Pronouns
First	mi/mis	mío/míos	mía/mías	my	mine
Second	tu/tus	tuyo/tuyos	tuya/tuyas	your	yours
Third	su/sus	suyo/suyos	suya/suyas	his/her/its	his/hers
				their	theirs
First pl.	nuestro/ -a -s	nuestro/-s	nuestra/-s	our	ours

B.   Notice these facts about the chart above:
   1. The short forms are used only *before* the noun. They change from
      singular to plural according to the things "possessed," not accord-
      ing to the owner.
      Ex.: *Mi* libro está aquí./*Mis* libros están aquí.

   2. *Nuestro -a -s* never shortens; it always agrees in gender and
      number with the thing possessed, rather than with the possessor
      (owner).
      Ex.: Nuestro hijo se llama Carlos./Nuestros hijos viven en
         nuestra casa.

3. The short forms (including *nuestro* in front of the noun) *are unstressed.* They are pronounced as if they belonged to the next word. In English *my/your,* etc, are *stressed,* and therefore you can emphasize them phonetically. In Spanish you should not emphasize *mi/tu/su.* A new speech pattern has developed in Spanish whereby some native speakers do stress *mi/tu/su* for emphasis.

C. The long forms are used *after* the noun or alone (as pronouns). They carry the stress and we can emphasize them in our intonation.

> Ex.: El libro *mío* está aquí; *el tuyo* está en casa. (*my* book is here; *yours* is at home)

D. Notice that *mine/yours/hers,* etc., never take an article; in Spanish *mío/tuyo,* etc., always need the article *el, la, los, las,* except after the verb *ser.*

> Ex.: Este libro es *mío.* ¿Dónde está *el tuyo?* (this book is *mine.* where's *yours?*)

We use *el mío/el tuyo* with *ser* if the noun is being differentiated from other nouns.

> Ex.: ¿Los libros? No sé cuál es el tuyo, pero éste es el mío. (the books? I don't know which one is yours, but this one is mine)

E. Notice that in English the third person has more forms than others, because there are three different subjects to refer to: *he/his, she/her* (hers), *it/its,* and the plural *they/their* (theirs). In Spanish we have *only one* form for all of them: *su* (long form: *suyo*). This means that *su/sus* can be very ambiguous, and it is impossible to distinguish between them without a clear context. Sometimes we prefer to use the preposition *de* + *él, ella, Ud., ellos, ellas, Uds.* But never use *su* AND *de él/ella.*

> Ex.: Conozco a tus abuelos; *su* casa es grande. (I know your grandparents; *their* house is large)
> Aquí están *Carlos* y María; el carro *de él* es éste.
> (here are *Carlos* and María; *his* car is this one)

PRACTICE THE POSSESSIVES   *(Answers, p. 186)*

1. There are three short forms of the possessives in the singular:_____

_____ , and three in the plural:_____

_____ .

2. Do you put a stress on *mi/tu/su*?_____. Can you stress *my/your/his/ her*?_____.

3. *Su* can be translated many ways in English, including the possessive for *Ud.* and *Uds*. The other possible translations are _____ _____.

4. *Tu hijos* is incorrect because *hijos* is plural; so *tu* should be_____.

5. Are the long forms *mío/tuyo/suyo* used *before* and *after* the noun?_____.

6. *Mine/yours*, etc, stand alone (without a noun). Which form stands alone in Spanish, *mi* or *mío*?; *tu* or *tuyo*?_____.

7. The plural of *mi* is_____, and the plural of *tu* is_____.

8. Remember that the spelling *tu* can mean two different things: *tú* with *acento* means_____, and *tu* without *acento* means_____ _____.

9. *Yo uso mi libro y tú usas tuyo* is incorrect. Something is missing in front of *tuyo:*_____.

10. Is *la casa de ella* correct?_____. Is *su casa* correct?_____. Is *su casa de ella* correct?_____. (It has to be one or the other!)

11. All the Spanish possessives (adjectives or pronouns) agree not with the owner but with the things_____. For example, in *Yo tengo mis libros en casa: mis* agrees with *libros,* not with *yo* (the owner).

12. Which forms are *unstressed,* the short or the long ones?_____ _____.

13. Should you emphasize phonetically *mi/tu/su*?_____. Instead, it's better to use the long forms and emphasize them.

14. Which is correct, *nuestra jabón* or *nuestro jabón*?_____ _____.

EXERCISE

(Answers, p. 186)

Translate the possessives in parentheses.

1. Te doy_____(my) reloj por un día solamente, pero debes recordar que no es_____. (yours)

2. _____ habitación está en el tercer piso. (our)

3. Este lápiz es _____ (mine); _____ está en la mesa. (yours)

4. Jorge y Elena tienen una casa en la montaña. _____ casa no es grande, pero es muy agradable. (their)

5. Tengo la toalla _____ (mine) en la maleta. Jorge me va a dar _____ . (his)

6. Este hotel es del Sr. Pérez. _____ (its) precios son muy razonables.

7. Ud. debe bajar por la escalera del hotel. _____ (its) ascensor está *roto* (broken).

8. _____ (our) pensión tiene solamente ocho habitaciones.

9. _____ (my) padres viven en España. _____ (their) casa es antigua pero grande.

10. Las luces de _____ comedor son amarillas. (our)

11. José y María tienen _____ (their) propios carros: el _____ (his) es un Toyota, y el _____ (hers) es un Chevy.

12. Tú siempre me invitas a _____ fiestas (your), y yo siempre te invito a _____ . (mine)

NOTE:

If we talk about the parts of our own bodies and the clothes we are wearing, the possession seems obvious: they belong to the *subject*. Therefore, it is customary to omit the possessive adjectives in these cases. Instead of the possessive adjective, we use the definite article.

    Ex.: John washes *his* hands: Juan se lava *las* manos.
         John puts on *his* hat: Juan se pone *el* sombrero.

(We will consider this further in a later section.)

Lesson 7

Una fiesta de cumpleaños (A Birthday Party)

arroz (el)	rice	**jueves**	Thursday	**refresco**	refreshment
bebida	drink	**limonada**	lemonade	**residencia**	residence
botana	snack (Mex.)	**lunes**	Monday	**ritmo**	rhythm
champán	champagne	**mariachi**[1]	mariachi	**sábado**	Saturday
chocolate	chocolate	**martes**	Tuesday	**sangría**[3]	wine cooler
compañero	schoolmate	**mes**	month	**semana**	week
copa	glass	**miércoles**	Wednesday	**sueño**	dream, sleep
cumpleaños	birthday	**música**	music	**teléfono**	telephone
domingo	Sunday	**país**	country	**tocadiscos**	record player
entremés	appetizer	**piano**	piano	**torta**	cake
felicidad	happiness	**pollo**	chicken	**vela**	candle
fiesta	party	**rato**[2]	a while	**viernes**	Friday
guitarra	guitar	**recado**	message	**resfriado**	cold

apagar	to turn off	**cumplir**[4]	to fulfil	**felicitar**	to congratulate
avisar	to warn	**dejar**	to leave	**merecer (c)**	to deserve
bailar	to dance	**dejar de**[5]	to stop	**molestar**[6]	to bother
celebrar	to celebrate	**encantar**	to charm	**prometer**	to promise
cocinar	to cook	**encargarse de**	to take charge of	**sonar (ue)**	to ring, to sound
comenzar (ie)	to start	**encender (ie)**	to light	**soñar (ue)**	to dream
comprender	to understand	**entender (ie)**	to understand	**tocar**	to play, to touch

aburrido[7]	boring/bored	**feliz**	happy	**puntual**	punctual
alegre	cheerful	**gracioso**	funny	**sabroso**	tasty, delicious
antipático	unpleasant	**moderno**	modern	**simpático**	nice

| atrasado | late (adj.) | oscuro | dark | **típico** | typical |
| **claro** | clear | **próximo** | next, coming | **varios** | various |

a veces	sometimes	**esta noche**	tonight
Aló!.. dígame[8]	Hello!	**felicidades**	congratulations
así que	so	**hágame el favor**	please, (do me a favor)
casi	almost	**junto a**	close to, near
con mucho gusto	it's a pleasure	**por casualidad**	by chance

NOTES:

1. *Mariachi* is the typical Mexican street band as well as each individual in the band. *Mariachis* are very popular in California, Texas, Arizona, and other states with heavy Mexican American populations.

2. *Rato* means *a while,* but in Spanish *rato* is always *a short period of time.* In English *while* can be days and even weeks; in Spanish it is no more than a few hours.

3. *Sangría* is a wine cooler, made with red or rosé wine mixed with fruits and light soda or lemonade (1/3 or less). It's served cold.

4. *Cumplir* is *to fulfil* when talking about a duty. *Cumplir años* is *to reach one's birthday* (literally, *to fulfil years);* from this we get the noun *el cumpleaños.*

5. *Dejar* is *to leave something, someplace, or somebody.* When *dejar de* is followed by an infinitive, it means *to stop.*
   Ex.: Carlos *deja* los libros en casa. Carlos *deja de fumar.* (Charles stops smoking)

6. *Molestar* is not to *molest,* as the spelling suggests; it is *to bother.*

7. *Aburrido* means *boring* with *ser* and *bored* with *estar.*
   Ex.: Este libro *es* aburrido. (this book is boring) vs. José *está* aburrido. (Joe is bored)

8. Different countries use different expressions to answer the phone. *Oigo* (I'm listening) is another one. *Aló* seems to copy the English *Hello!*

EXERCISES

(Answers, p. 187)

A. Write *el* or *la* in front of the following nouns.

1._____champán	5._____país	9._____copa
2._____mes	6._____semana	10._____arroz
3._____felicidad	7._____tocadiscos	11._____chocolate
4._____martes	8._____entremés	12._____sangría

B. Write the plural forms.

1. mes_____   6. alegre_____

2. feliz_____   7. mariachi_____

3. viernes_____   8. tocadiscos_____

4. país_____   9. entremés_____

5. puntual_____

C. Match the two columns (some answers require the plural form).

1. ____champán   A. Colombia es un . . . diferente de Venezuela.

2. ____vela   B. Si ponemos frutas y refresco con vino rojo tenemos una . . . .

3. ____torta   C. No tengo mucho tiempo; solamente voy a pasar un . . . a su casa.

4. ____teléfono   D. Vamos a comer algunos . . . antes de la cena.

5. ____país   E. La música de los . . . es muy popular en México y California.

6. ____compañero   F. Margarita va a cocinar una . . . de chocolate para tu cumpleaños.

7. ____recado   G. Muchas personas celebran el Año Nuevo con una copa de . . . .

8. ____semana   H. Generalmente trabajamos los lunes, pero no los . . . .

9. ____mariachi   I. Cuando cumplimos 12 años, encendemos 12 . . . en la torta.

10. ____sangría   J. La camarera me sirve una . . . de champán frío.

11. ____entremés   K. Tengo que hacer muchos . . . para la fiesta de mi amiga.

12. ____tocadiscos   L. Un plato típico de Cuba es arroz con . . . .

13. ____domingo   M. ¿Quieres preparar el tocadiscos? - Sí, ...

14. ____sueño   N. Tengo que llamar por . . . a mis amigos de Miami.

15. ____pollo   O. En un cumpleaños deseamos . . . a la persona que cumple años.

16. ___ refresco

P. Carlos y Elena son . . . de universidad, pero no de cuarto.

17. ___ rato

Q. Necesitamos un . . . para poner música moderna o clásica.

18. ___ felicidad

R. Las botanas están muy . . ., y nos las vamos a comer todas.

19. ___ copa

S. El maestro Segovia toca muy bien la . . . .

20. ___ con mucho gusto

T. ¿Por qué no vamos al teatro . . .?

21. ___ guitarra

U. Cuando hablamos de *siete días* queremos decir una . . . .

22. ___ resfriado

V. Muchos . . . no son nunca una realidad.

23. ___ piano

X. Mi amigo Julio no viene a la fiesta porque tiene . . . .

24. ___ esta noche

Y. No voy a tomar sangría; solamente quiero un . . . .

25. ___ sabroso -a -s

Z. Liberace es un gran maestro de . . . .

DIÁLOGO   *El cumpleaños de Carlos*

(Jorge llama por teléfono a Lola. Son compañeros de universidad.)

LOLA: Aló . . . Dígame.

JORGE: ¡Hola! ¿Cómo estás, Lola?

LOLA: ¡Ah! ¿Eres tú, Jorge? Yo, bastante bien, pero tu amiga Elena tiene un resfriado terrible.

JORGE: Lo siento. Te llamo para invitarte a la fiesta de cumpleaños de Carlos el viernes próximo.

LOLA: ¿Así que el viernes es su cumpleaños? ¿Quién va a preparar la fiesta?

JORGE: Bueno, todos un poco. Josefina trae los entremeses, Luisa va a cocinar un arroz con pollo muy sabroso, Marcos hace una buena ensalada. . . .

LOLA: ¿Y tú, qué? ¿Vas a ser el inspector de operaciones?

JORGE: Yo me encargo de las bebidas, del tocadiscos y de la música. Tú puedes encargarte de la torta, ¿no?

LOLA: Sí, claro. Por eso la invitación, ¿no es verdad?

JORGE: Ya sabes que la fiesta es para todos, y tú te diviertes más que nadie.

. . .

(En la fiesta. Llega Lola con la torta.)

JORGE: ¿Quieres tomar algo, Lola? ¿Cerveza, sangría, champán?
LOLA: Una sangría o un refresco bien frío, por favor.
JORGE: ¿Un cigarrillo?
LOLA: Gracias, tú sabes que no fumo.
JORGE: Entonces yo tampoco. ¿Bailamos?
LOLA: Con mucho gusto. Los ritmos modernos me encantan.

DIALOG   *Charles's Birthday Party*

(George is calling Lola on the phone. They are friends at the university.)

LOLA: Hello!
GEORGE: Hi! How are you, Lola?
LOLA: Oh! Is that you, George? I'm pretty well, but your friend Ellen has a terrible cold.
GEORGE: I'm sorry. I'm calling to invite you to Charles's birthday party next Friday.
LOLA: So his birthday is Friday? Who's giving the party?
GEORGE: Well, everyone's going to pitch in. Josephine is bringing the snacks, Louise is going to cook a delicious chicken and rice, Mark is making a good salad . . .
LOLA: What about you? Are you going to be the supervisor?
GEORGE: I'm in charge of the beverages, the record player, and the music. You can take care of the cake, can't you?
LOLA: Yes, sure. That's the reason for the invitation, isn't it?
GEORGE: You know the party is for everybody, and you have more fun than anybody else.
          (At the party. Lola arrives with the cake.)
GEORGE: Do you want anything to drink? Beer, sangria, champagne?
LOLA: Sangria or soda, very cold, please.
GEORGE: Cigarette?
LOLA: No thanks. You know I don't smoke.
GEORGE: Then I won't either. Shall we dance?
LOLA: It's a pleasure. I love the modern rhythms.

D.   Write the opposite of the words given.   *(Answers, p. 187)*

1. claro_____   6. aburrido_____

2. apagar_____   7. moderno_____

3. antipático_____   8. nadie_____

4. atrasado_____   9. triste (sad)_____

5. comida_____   10. comenzar a_____

E.   You have a list of new verbs in the vocabulary section of this
     lesson. Review them and pay attention to the irregular ones:
     they are marked with *ie, ue, c.* Try to remember the correct
     endings for the Present Indicative, and complete the sen-
     tences with the verb forms.

1. ¿A qué hora _____ usted a trabajar? (start)

2. En Estados Unidos (nosotros) _____ el
    Año Nuevo. (celebrate)

3. José Greco _____ muy bien el flamenco. (dance)

4. ¿Usted _____ bien el italiano? (understand)

5. Ellos _____ a viajar el miércoles. (start)

6. Creo que mi teléfono _____ en este momento. (ring)

7. Cuando salgo de la clase, yo siempre _____ la luz. (turn
    off)

8. Si bebes mucha agua antes de dormir, _____ mucho.
    (dream)

9. Mis hijos siempre me _____ con sus pro-
    blemas. (bother)

10. ¿Por qué (tú) no _____ el piano en la fiesta? (play)

11. María Elena se _____ de las bebidas.
    (take charge)

12. Yo sé un poco de francés, pero no lo _____
    bien. (understand)

13. Creo que yo no _____ este honor. (deserve)

14. La secretaria _____ a su *jefe* (boss). (warn, let
    know)

15. ¿Dónde _____ (tú) el carro todos los días?
    (leave, park)

16. Los niños siempre _____ ser buenos. (promise)

17. Mi esposa y yo siempre _____ con el deber.
    (fulfil)

18. ¿Quién _____ las velas de la torta? (light)

19. Creo que Enrique _____ 22 años el próximo sába-
    do. (reach)

20. Mi reloj es puntual; siempre _____ a las 7 en pun-
    to. (ring)

EXERCISES

(Answers, p. 187)

A. Fill in the blanks with the correct word to form a narrative summary of the dialog.

Jorge llama a Lola para (1)_____*la* a la
fiesta de (2)_____de Carlos el viernes que
viene. Ellos son (3)_____de universidad. Lola
dice que ella (4)_____bastante bien, pero Elena tiene
un (5)_____terrible. Todos van a (6)_____
_____la fiesta. Josefina va a traer los (7)_____
_____, Luisa cocina un (8)_____
_____muy sabroso, Marcos hace la (9)_____, Jorge se encarga
de las (10)_____y la música y Lola va a hacer la (11)
_____de cumpleaños.

El viernes próximo Lola (12)_____a la fiesta con
la torta. Jorge la invita a (13)_____cerveza, sangría o
(14)_____. Ella acepta una sangría o un (15)_____
_____bien frío. Lola no acepta el cigarrillo de Jorge porque
ella nunca (16)_____. Entonces Jorge la invita a (17)
_____y ella acepta (18)_____
porque le encantan los (19)_____modernos.

B. Circle the answer that best completes the following sentences.

1. En una fiesta de cumpleaños encendemos (botanas, velas, recados, cigarrillos) en la torta.

2. Si hoy es martes, mañana es (lunes, jueves, sábado, miércoles).

3. Bebemos el champán en (una copa, una vela, un vaso, una torta).

4. De aperitivo comemos entremeses o (platos, sangría, botanas, mariachis).

5. Muchas personas no trabajan (los domingos, los martes, los jueves, los viernes).

6. Carlos no toca el piano *sino* (but) (el ritmo, la guitarra, el recado, el teléfono).

7. ¿Por qué (enciendes, prometes, entiendes, comienzas) el cigarrillo en la clase?

8. Elena no puede ir a la fiesta porque tiene (sueño, cumpleaños, resfriado, refresco).

9. Siete días es (un mes, un rato, un año, una semana).

10. Cuando dormimos (sonamos, avisamos, soñamos, molestamos).

11. Jorge (merece, comienza, prepara, avisa) a Lola del cumpleaños de Carlos.

12. Luisa no entiende inglés porque no es de (esta residencia, este país, este ritmo).

13. Carlos (promete, sueña, enciende, cumple) veintitrés años el viernes.

14. Antes de entrar al ascensor, debes (encender, comenzar, encargar, apagar) el cigarrillo.

15. Para oír la música necesitamos (el recado, el champán, el tocadiscos, la guitarra).

C.   Circle the adjective that best completes these sentences.

1. Juanito llega (moderno, típico, atrasado, oscuro, claro).

2. Por la noche no vemos porque está (simpático, próximo, oscuro, alegre, feliz).

3. El pollo frito está (aburrido, sabroso, claro, gracioso, puntual).

4. María vive junto a mi casa; ella está muy (aburrida, típica, graciosa, próxima, feliz).

5. Ese libro no es interesante; es muy (feliz, gracioso, aburrido, claro, moderno).

6. Hoy hace muy mal tiempo; el día está (claro, atrasado, oscuro, sabroso, típico).

D.   Form sentences with the following words. Use the verbs in the Present Indicative. Watch out for the agreement between nouns and adjectives as well as articles. You will have to add the correct prepositions and articles. The words are given in the right order.

1. José / tener ganas / leer / libro Hawaii /.

_____

2. ¿Por qué / tú /no dejar / fumar / hoy /?

_____

3. fiesta / mi cumpleaños / ser / sábado / próximo /.

_____

4. torta / cumpleaños / Carlos / tener / 23 / velas /.

_____

5. María / querer / bailar / ritmos / moderno /.

_____

6. Ustedes / llegar / atrasado / fiesta /.

_____

7. Este / entremeses / estar / muy / sabroso /.

_____

8. Tu / sobrinos / ser / bastante / gracioso /.

_____

GRAMMAR I　Direct object nouns and pronouns. Personal A.

A.　The direct object is the noun or pronoun which completes the meaning of a transitive verb. For example, _to buy_ makes no sense without "something" you buy.
    Ex.: Bebemos _el champán_. (_champán_ is the direct object)

B.　In English you see/hear/understand _things_ or _people_. In Spanish we differentiate _things_ from _people_ by adding the preposition _a_ in front of _people_.
    Ex.: Yo veo _la casa_. / Yo veo _a la niña_. (I see _the house/the girl_)

Verb + **a** + person (definite)	Verb + **things**

Notice that if the person is indefinite, _a_ is omitted, and the person becomes "depersonalized."
    Ex.: Necesito _médico_. (I need _medical help_)

NOTE:
Remember that **a** + **el** = **al**.
    Ex.: Veo _al_ muchacho.

C. Memorize the chart with the direct object pronouns:

SUBJECT	DIRECT OBJECT	ENGLISH
yo	**me**	me
tú	**te**	you (familiar)
nosotros -as	**nos**	us
tél	**lo***	him, it
tella	**la**	her, it
tellos	**los***	them
tellas	**las**	
usted	**lo/la**	you (formal)
ustedes	**los/las**	you (formal pl.)

D. Notice the following facts about the chart above:
1. *Lo/los* are used in Latin America for masculine people or things. In Spain *le/les* is used if the direct object is a *person* and *lo/los* if it is a thing.
    Ex.: *Spain:* ¿Ve usted *a Juan?* - Sí, *le* veo.
    America: ¿Ve usted *a Juan?* - Sí, *lo* veo.

    Following our policy in this book, we will use the Latin American pronouns.
2. The direct object pronouns in Spanish are *unstressed,* and they cannot be emphasized phonetically. In English they are usually *stressed.* In Spanish you pronounce them as if they were part of the verb.
3. These pronouns *precede* the verb in Indicative in Spanish. In English they always *follow* the verb.
    Ex.: Usted *me* entiende muy bien. (you understand *me* very well)

    If the infinitive is involved in the sentence, the pronoun may follow the infinitive by forming only *one word,* or it may *precede* the Indicative.
    Ex.: Quiero ver*te.*/ *Te* quiero ver. (*one* meaning: I want to see *you*)

PRACTICE THE PRONOUNS   *(Answers, p. 188)*

1. A transitive verb completes its meaning in the _____

    _____ of the sentence. For this reason some books call it a *complement.*

2. *Yo conozco esa chica* is incorrect because *chica* is a person. It should be *Yo conozco* _____ .

3. Remember that *nadie* is the negative form of *alguien* and that both refer to persons. Is it correct to say *Conozco alguien aquí?* _____; *a* is missing in front of _____ .

4. The direct object pronouns in Spanish never carry a phonetic _____ _____ ; this is why they are always pronounced as if they were part of the _____ that follows.

5. The *third person* direct object pronouns are almost identical to the definite articles, and there are also four of them: _____ .

6. In Spain people would say *¿Juan? no le veo,* whereas Latin Americans would say *¿Juan? no* _____ . The same is true in the plural: *les* becomes _____ .

7. Do the direct object pronouns precede or follow a verb in the Indicative? _____ . Do the direct object pronouns precede or follow the Infinitive? _____ .

8. An infinitive usually follows another verb form in the Indicative. In this case the pronoun may follow the _____ or precede the _____ .

9. Which sentence is better: *Quiero ayudarte* or *Te quiero ayudar?* _____ _____ .

10. If the *person* who is the direct object is indefinite, we treat him/her as a "thing" by omitting the preposition _____. For example, how do you say *We need waitresses in the restaurant? Necesitamos* _____ *en el restaurante.*

EXERCISES   (Answers, p. 188)

A.   Answer the questions by replacing the noun direct object with the pronoun. Pay special attention to the verb forms.

1. *¿Trae usted las plumas?* - Sí, _____ .

2. ¿Oye usted *el radio*? - Sí, _____.

3. ¿Hace usted *su trabajo*? - Sí, _____.

4. ¿Conoce Ud. a *mi tía*? - Sí, _____.

5. ¿Quiere Ud. *más café*? - No, no, _____.

6. ¿Habla usted *japonés*? - No, no _____.

7. ¿Fuma usted *cigarrillos*? - No, no _____.

8. ¿Ve usted *a su amiga*? - No, no _____.

9. ¿Quiere Ud. leer *este libro*? - Sí, _____.

10. (answer 9. differently) Sí, _____.

11. ¿Tiene que oír *el radio*? _____.

12. (answer 10. differently) - No, no _____.

B. Fill in the blank with the personal *a* if required. Remember that *a* + *el* = *al*.

1. ¿Por qué no invitas_____mi novia?

2. No pienso invitar_____nadie.

3. Josefina no entiende bien_____esta lección.

4. En este restaurante necesitan_____camareros.

5. Voy a llamar_____camarero porque quiero pagar la cuenta.

6. ¿_____quién piensas invitar? ¿_____José?

C. Answer the questions with direct object pronouns *me/te/nos/*, etc.

1. ¿Quién *me* llama? ¿José? - Sí, José_____.
   (familiar)

2. ¿Quién *nos* (fem.) felicita? ¿Marcos? - Sí, Marcos_____

   _____.

3. ¿Puede Ud. llamar*me* (fem.) a las 7:00? - Sí,_____

   _____. (formal)

4. ¿*Nos* (masc.) ayudan ustedes? - Sí,_____.

5. ¿Vas a ver*me* mañana? - Sí,_____. (familiar)

6. ¿*Te* dejamos en la casa? - Sí, ustedes_____.

GRAMMAR II   Reflexive constructions and reflexive pro-
              nouns.

A.   *Reflexive* means that a pronoun repeats (reflects) the subject of the
     sentence—in other words, the subject acts upon itself.
               Ex.: José ve *a María;* José *la* ve. (nonreflexive: *doer* and *object*
               are different persons)
               José ve *a José;* José *se* ve. (reflexive: *doer* and *object* are
               one person)

B.   Memorize the following chart with reflexive constructions:

SUBJECT	divertir*se*	lavar*se*	ENGLISH		(reflexives)
yo	me div*ie*rto	me lavo	I	wash	myself
nosotros -as	nos diver- timos	nos lavamos	we	wash	ourselves
tú	te div*ie*rtes	te lavas	you	wash	yourself
él/ella/Ud.	se div*ie*rte	se lava	he/she/	washes/	him/herself/
			you	wash	yourself
ellos/ellas	se div*ie*rten	se lavan	they	wash	themselves

C.   Notice these facts about the chart above:
     1. The reflexive pronouns precede the verb in the Indicative, but
        they follow the Infinitive, just like the direct object pronouns.
            Ex.: Yo m*e* lavo, but Yo voy a lavar*me,* or Yo *me* voy a lavar.
     2. *Se* is the reflexive pronoun for all third-person subjects: *él/ella/
        ellos -as,* and also for *usted -es.*
            Ex.: Él/Ella/Ud. *se* divierten.
            Ellos/Ellas/Uds. *se* divierten.
     3. The reflexive in English always follows the verb. It is formed with
        -self/selves after the object pronoun. The reflexives carry a stress
        in English and can be emphasized, whereas in Spanish they are
        unstressed; they cannot be emphasized.

D.   Emphatic reflexive:
     Reflexive pronouns are used with intransitive verbs such as *ir, salir,
     llegar,* etc., to show that the action has been planned *for full comple-
     tion.*
               Ex.: *Me* voy a casa a las tres. (I'm GOING HOME at three)
               Voy a casa a las tres. (I'm going home at three)
     This is also done with some transitive verbs to show the same kind of
     emphasis on *completion of action.*
               Ex.: Ella *se* come la torta. (she is EATING UP the cake)
               Ella come la torta. (she is eating the cake)

E. Obligatory *se* with inanimate subjects:
    Look at this sentence: La ventana *se* cae a pedazos. (the window is
        falling apart)
    Notice that there is no translation in English for this *se*, which is
    obligatory because the subject is inanimate (*ventana,* in this case).
        Ex.: El carro *se* detiene en la luz. (the car stops at the light)

F. Impersonal *se:*
    The reflexive *se* mentioned in (E) is also called the "impersonal *se*"
    because the verb has no personal subject. Typical examples of this
    use are *Se habla español* (Spanish is spoken) and *Se vende la casa*
    (literally, the house is selling).
    More examples: *Se* compra un carro. / *Se* compran carros.
    Notice the change from singular *carro* to plural *carros;* the verb has
    to change to the plural form *compran.* This shows that *carro* has
    become the subject of the verb.

G. Frequent personal actions require the reflexive pronouns in Span-
    ish, such as *sentarse* (to sit), *vestirse* (to get dressed). In English the
    pronoun (oneself, etc.) is usually omitted. Spanish dictionaries show
    the reflexive verbs with the pronoun *se* attached to the infinitive:
    sentarse, bañarse, etc.
        Here is a partial list of reflexive verbs. You may remember
    having seen some of them before.

abrocharse	to fasten	**divertirse** (ie)	to have fun	**ponerse**	to put on (clothes)
acostarse (ue)	to go to bed	**lavarse**	to wash	**quitarse**	to take off (clothes)
afeitarse	to shave	**levantarse**	to get up	**sentarse (ie)**	to sit down
bañarse	to take a bath	**llamarse**	to be named	**sentirse (ie)**	to feel
despertarse (ie)	to wake up	**peinarse**	to comb (one's hair)	**vestirse (i)**	to get dressed

PRACTICE THE REFLEXIVE   *(Answers, p. 188)*

1. A reflexive pronoun repeats the _____ of the sentence.

    The reflexive pronoun for *yo* is _____ , and for *tú* it is _____

    _____ .

2. There is only one reflexive pronoun for all third-person subjects: _____ .
    This is the same pronoun used to translate *one* in "impersonal" senten-

    ces, such as *One speaks Spanish* (or *Spanish is spoken*): _____

    _____ .

3. Which action is more emphatic, (a) *Ya vas a casa* or (b) *Ya te vas a casa?*
_____.

4. *Se* is obligatory when the subject of a sentence is an _____ noun, such as *El plato_____ lava con jabón y agua.*

5. *La copa cae de la mesa* is not correct. The reflexive _____ is missing in front of the verb_____.

6. *Se compra carros viejos* is not correct because *carros* is plural; the verb should be plural too:_____.

7. Such personal actions as *bañarse, peinarse, lavarse,* etc., require the _____pronoun when the action is performed on oneself.

8. Notice the difference between *sentarse* and *sentirse;* the first one is *-AR* and the second *-IR.* How would you say *She is feeling? Ella*_____
_____. And how would you say *She is sitting?* Ella
_____.

EXERCISES

(Answers, p. 188)

A. Fill in the blanks with the forms of the Present Indicative. Pay attention to the irregular verbs as shown in the list in *(G)*

1. Los pasajeros_____los cinturones en el avión. (fasten)

2. Yo todos los días_____temprano. (go to bed)

3. ¿A qué hora_____Ud. normalmente? (wake up)

4. Lola siempre_____en las fiestas. (have fun)

5. ¿Cómo_____Ud.? - Yo_____Paco. (be named)

6. Después de bañar*me,*_____. (shave)

7. Ella_____un *suéter* (sweater) porque hace frío. (put on)

8. Esta señora siempre_____muy bien. (dress)

9. Los camareros no _____ nunca en el restaurante. (sit down)

10. Antes de acostar*me*, _____ la *ropa* (clothes). (take off)

11. Mi abuelo _____ muy bien hoy. (feel)

12. Jorge no _____ muy temprano. (get up)

13. Lola y yo _____ en la casa. (comb the hair)

14. Si hace buen tiempo (nosotros) _____ en el mar. (bathe)

B. **Translate the following sentences using reflexive pronouns, although in some cases other forms may be possible.**

1. One lives well here. _____.

2. In Argentina Spanish is spoken. _____ _____.

3. I'm GOING HOME now. _____.

4. He is eating all the cake up. _____.

5. The car is stopping now. _____ _____.

6. The cars are stopping now. _____ _____.

7. Cars are being bought. _____.

GRAMMAR III Preterite (past tense) of regular verbs. Spelling changes.

A. Memorize the following chart:

SUBJECT	habl-ar	com-er	viv-ir	ENGLISH	
yo	habl *é*	*com í*	*viv í*	I	talk*ed*
nosotros -as	habl amos	com imos	viv imos	we	
tú	habl aste	com iste	viv iste	you	*ate*
él/ella	habl *ó*	com *ió*	viv *ió*	he/she	live*d*
ellos/ellas	habl aron	com ieron	viv ieron	they	

B. Notice these facts about the chart:
1. The stems *habl, com, viv* are the same as in the Present. They carry the dictionary meaning of the verbs: *talk, eat, live*.
2. The person-number endings are *-mos* for *we*, *-ste* for you (familiar), and *-n* for *they* and formal *ustedes*.
3. *Comer* and *vivir* (verbs ending in *-ER* and *-IR*) follow exactly the same pattern.
4. *Hablamos* and *vivimos* are the same in the Present and Preterite; we need a context or an adverb to tell us how to interpret the forms.

> Ex.: *Ahora hablamos* con el niño. (now we are talking to the boy)
>
> *Antes hablamos* con el niño. (before we talked to the boy)

5. The most important difference from the Present forms is the *stress* on the last syllable in *hablé/habló, comí/comió, viví/vivió*.

C. *Preterite* means "past." There is another tense for a past action that we will study in Lesson 9. For the time being, try to associate the Spanish Preterite with the simple past in English: *lived, spoke, did, heard, came, ate*, etc.

D. Spelling changes:
Some verbs show changes in spelling without changes in sound. We don't call these verbs irregular. Here are four kinds of spelling changes:

---

1. *Pagar, llegar, encargar,* and any verb with a *g* before the *-AR* add a *u* after the *g* before the ending *é*. This *u* is not pronounced.
    > Ex.: *pagar* → *pagué*, but *pagó*. *Llegar* → *llegué*, but *llegó*.

2. *Comenzar, especializar,* and any verb with a *z* before the *-AR* change the *z* to *c* before *é*, just as *feliz* changes to *felices* and *felicidad*.
    > Ex.: *comenzar* → *comencé*, but *comenzó*.

3. *Tocar, practicar,* and any verb with a *c* before *-AR* change *c* to *qu* before the vowel *e*.
    > Ex.: *practicar* → *practiqué*, but *practicó*.

4. *Leer, caer, oír,* and any verb with two consecutive vowels change the vowel *i* to *y* whenever it is caught between two other vowels.
    > Ex.: *leer* → *leyó* → *leyeron*, but *leí, leíste* (acento to break up the diphthong) *oír* → *oyó* → *oyeron*, but *oí, oíste, oímos*.

NOTE:

From *ver* we get *yo vi* (I saw), *él vio* (he saw). The *acento* is not needed because these forms are only one syllable; however, a compound verb such as *prever* will need *acento: yo preví* (I foresaw).

PRACTICE THE PRETERITE *(Answers, p. 189)*

1. The stem of a verb carries the basic_____ of the verb. The stem of *comer* is_____, and the stem of *ver* is_____.

2. The person ending *-mos* is for_____, and the ending *-ste* for_____.

3. *Hablar* has two forms with *acento* in the Preterite:_____ and_____.

4. *Vivir* also has two forms with *acento:*_____and_____.

5. *Hablamos* and *vivimos* (and all the verbs ending in *-AR*, *-IR*) are the same in two tenses of the Indicative:_____.

6. From *apagar* we don't write *apagé* in the Preterite. It should be _____, because we write_____in front of the vowels *e* and *i*.

7. From *creer* we don't write *creió*, but_____. The reason is that the *i* is between two other vowels (in this case, *e* and *ó*).

8. From *tocar* we don't write *tocé*, but_____. The reason is that the *c* changes to_____in front of the vowels *e* and *i*.

9. From *comenzar* we don't write *comenzé*, but_____. The reason is that we change *z* to_____in front of the vowels *e* and *i*.

10. The word Preterite means_____. In Spanish we usually call it *Pretérito* rather than *Pasado*, which is the word for *past*. How would you usually translate Yo *practiqué*?_____

_____.

EXERCISES

(Answers, p. 189)

A.   Fill in the blanks with the correct form of the Preterite. If the verb is reflexive, write the reflexive pronoun also.

1. Mi amiga _____ a las 8 de la mañana, pero yo _____
   _____ a las 7:00 en punto. (llegar)

2. Todos los estudiantes _____ la novela. (leer)

3. Esta mañana yo no _____ . (bañar*se*)

4. ¿Dónde _____ usted esa información?
   (ver)

5. ¿A qué hora _____ usted *anoche* (last night)? (acostar*se*)

6. Yo no _____ tenis el domingo pasado.
   (practicar)

7. Ella _____ a las ocho, pero yo _____
   a las 7:00 en punto. (comenzar)

8. Tú _____ el cigarrillo, y yo lo _____
   también. (apagar)

9. Mis hijos _____ de la fiesta con nosotros.
   (volver)

10. La noche pasada yo solamente _____ seis horas. (dormir)

11. Mi vaso de vino _____ y se *rompió* (broke). (caer*se!*)

12. Diana _____ el piano y yo _____
    la guitarra. (tocar)

13. Tú _____ el vino y yo _____
    la comida. (pagar)

14. ¿Cuántos años _____ (tú) en esa ciudad? (vivir)

15. Jorge _____ el sombrero en la casa. (quitar*se*)

16. ¿Cuándo _____ ustedes eso? (oír)

17. El pasado mes _____ mucho en Colorado. (nevar)

18. Carlitos _____ toda la torta. (comer*se*)

19. El avión _____ de Chicago a las dos y media. (salir)

20. El año pasado no _____ mucho en California. (llover)

B. Change the Present to the Preterite of the verb forms in the following story.

Esta mañana (1) *me despierto* a las siete y cuarto, (2) *me levanto* de la cama, y (3) *me baño* con agua y jabón. Después (4) *me seco (secarse = to dry)* y (5) *me visto.* (6) *Me desayuno* café con pan y (7) *salgo* de casa para la universidad. (8) *Llego* a la clase a las 8 menos cinco, y (9) *oigo* las explicaciones del profesor . . . . A las doce y media (10) *como* una ensalada en la cafetería y (11) *vuelvo* a clase con mis amigos. La clase de la tarde (12) *comienza* a la una en punto. El profesor (13) *explica (explicar = to explain)* por qué el *imperio romano* (Roman Empire) (14) *se cae* y (15) *se destruye* en poco tiempo.

1._____   9._____

2._____   10._____

3._____   11._____

4._____   12._____

5._____   13._____

6._____   14._____

7._____   15._____

8._____

Lesson 8

En un supermercado[1]
(In a Supermarket)

aguacate	avocado	**hamburguesa**	hamburger	**pescado**	fish
ajo	garlic	**jugo**	juice	**plátano**[6]	banana, plantain
atún	tuna	**lata**	can	**puerco**	pig, pork
banana	banana	**leche (la)**	milk	**queso**	cheese
bocadillo	sandwich	**maíz (el)**	corn	**res (la)**	beef, livestock
burrito[2]	burrito	**manzana**	apple	**sánguich (el)**	sandwich
carne (la)	meat	**mercado**	market	**solomillo**	sirloin
cebolla	onion	**merienda**[4]	snack	**supermercado**	supermarket
cerdo	pig, pork	**naranja**	orange	**taco**[7]	taco
chuleta	chop	**paquete**	package	**té**[8]	tea
cordero	lamb	**pastel**	cake, pastry	**ternera**	veal, young cow
enchilada[3]	enchilada	**pavo**[5]	turkey	**tortilla**[9]	omelette, tortilla
frijol	bean	**pepino**	cucumber	**vaca**	cow, beef
grasa	grease, fat	**pera**	pear	**verdura**	vegetable, green
guisante	green pea	**pierna**	leg	**zanahoria**	carrot
				caloría	calorie

andar	to walk	**condimentar**	to season	**parar**	to stop
asar	to roast	**haber**	to have (auxiliary)	**pescar**	to fish
atender (ie)	to wait on	**jugar (ue)**	to play	**recomendar (ie)**	to recommend
buscar	to look for	**merendar (ie)**	to snack	**vender**	to sell

asado	roasted	**fresco**	fresh, cool	**peruano**	Peruvian
chileno	Chilean	**lleno**	full	**picante**	hot (spicy)
colombiano	Colombian	**mexicano**	Mexican	**texano**	Texan
enfermo	sick	**nervioso**	nervous	**tierno**	tender, soft

estupendo	fantastic	**pálido**	pale	**tinto**	red (for wine)
		saludable	healthy		

a menudo	frequently	**ir de compras**	to go shopping
acabar de (+ infinitive)	to have just done	**no poder ver**	can't stand
ayer	yesterday	**ponerse a (+ infinitive)**	to begin (+ verb)
decir que sí/no	to say yes/no	**ponerse (+ adjective)**	to turn (+ adjective)
hay que (+ infinitive)	it's necessary to	**saber a**	to taste like
estar a dieta	to be on a diet	**tener buena pinta**	to look good

NOTES:

1. *Supermercado* (supermarket). In the Hispanic countries, small shops are still very popular: bakery, meat shop, fruit store, fish store, etc. After many years of competition, supermarkets are finally catching on, especially in Venezuela, Spain, and Argentina.

2. *Burrito* is made of a flat flour tortilla stuffed with meat, cheese, and beans. It is not of Mexican origin despite its name. It's from Texas.

3. *Enchilada* is made with rolled corn tortillas and stuffed with all kinds of things. Then it is baked in the oven with red or green sauce, hot or mild.

4. *Merienda* is a small meal between lunch and supper. Since supper is around 9 P.M., the *merienda* is a snack in midafternoon. The verb is *merendar*.

5. *Pavo* is called *guajolote* in Mexico and *chompipe* in Central America.

6. In Spain *plátano* is used for banana, but in some countries, such as Cuba, *plátano* is used for the cooking banana or plantain, and *banana* is used for the fresh fruit.

7. *Taco* is made with a crisp corn shell and stuffed with meat, lettuce, cheese, etc.

8. *Té* is written with *acento* to differentiate it from the pronoun *te* (you).

9. *Tortilla* is an omelette in Spain, usually pretty thick because they add ham, potatoes, shrimp, etc. In Mexico the *tortilla* is thin and flat, made with wheat or corn flour. It's the base for the enchilada, burrito, taco, etc.

10. *Buscar* means *to look for. For* is not translated, as in *to ask for* (*pedir*).

EXERCISES

(Answers, p. 189)

A. Write the articles *el, la, los, las* as needed.

1. ____ carne
2. ____ atún
3. ____ aguacate
4. ____ cebollas
5. ____ maíz

6. ____ hamburguesa
7. ____ frijoles
8. ____ sángüiches
9. ____ té
10. ____ reses

11. ____ paquetes
12. ____ pastel
13. ____ guisantes
14. ____ leche
15. ____ terneras

B. Fill in the blanks with one of the words in the box. You can use some words twice.

leche	solomillo	zanahoria	jugo	hamburguesa
pepino	merendar	picante	a menudo	queso
cebolla	buena pinta	pavo	pierna	bocadillo

1. En el desayuno siempre tomo_____de naranja.

2. La carne de_____es carne de res.

3. El jamón se hace con la_____del puerco.

4. En la fiesta de *Thanksgiving* comemos_____.

5. Los tacos tienen carne, lechuga, tomate y_____.

6. Rita va al supermercado_____.

7. La_____es muy buena para los niños.

8. Los latinos comen muchas cosas con_____y ajo.

9. Voy a comer un_____de jamón con queso.

10. Para_____prefiero fruta o café.

11. Comemos una ensalada de tomate, lechuga y_____.

12. La_____es una verdura color naranja.

13. El queso se hace con_____de vaca.

14. Estas chuletas de cerdo tienen_____.

15. La carne más cara es el_____.

16. La comida mexicana es_____generalmente.

C. Write the adjectives related to the countries.

(No capital letters!)

1. Las personas de Colombia son_____.

2. Las personas de México son_____.

3. Las personas de Chile son_____.

4. Las personas de España son_____.

5. Las personas de Texas son_____.

6. Las personas de Perú son_____.

D. **Word families: Write a word that is related by origin to the ones given here, such as nouns, adjectives, verbs, etc.**

1. verde_____
2. pescar_____
3. merendar_____
4. torta_____
5. burro_____
6. asar_____
7. boca_____
8. refresco_____

9. comprar_____
10. cafetería_____
11. enfermedad_____
12. recomendación_____
13. llenar_____
14. vendedor_____
15. atención_____
16. caloría_____

E. **Fill in the blanks with a form of the verbs given in the box below. Use the Present Indicative in your answers.**

recomendar	buscar	asar	condimentar	andar
vender	parar	merendar	atender	jugar

1. Mi madre_____las papas y los pollos a menudo.
2. ¿Cuántos kilómetros_____ (tú) todos los días.
3. Si estás enferma, María, te_____ un doctor.
4. Alicia siempre_____en la luz roja.
5. Nosotros_____el carro viejo, pero no hay compradores.
6. En los mercados_____mejor que en los supermercados.
7. Esta tarde (yo)_____un bocadillo.
8. ¿A qué hora_____(tú) al tenis?
9. Los latinos_____mucho la comida.
10. No tengo casa, por eso_____una.

F. **Fill in the blanks with a form of the verbs given above in exercise (E), but this time use the Preterite tense.**

(Answers, p. 189)

1. ¿Quién_____este cordero tan sabroso?
2. Ayer por la tarde Julita_____unos bocadillos con mi esposa.

3. El gran Pelé_____*soccer* muchos años en Brasil y Nueva York.

4. Los carros_____en el STOP.

5. Después de la clase yo_____a mi novia.

6. La semana pasada_____el carro viejo y compré uno nuevo.

DIÁLOGO   *De compras en el supermercado*

(Rita y Mimi están en el supermercado para hacer las compras de la semana.)

MIMI: No vengo mucho al supermercado. Atienden mejor en los mercados pequeños.

RITA: Pues yo vengo aquí a menudo. Creo que los precios son bastante bajos.

MIMI: Tienes razón. ¡Mira estas chuletas de puerco a 3,00 pesos el kilo!

RITA: La verdad. No tienen ninguna grasa. Voy a llevarme este paquete de cuatro kilos y medio.

MIMI: Esta carne de res tiene muy buena pinta. Me llevo 6 kilos de carne de hamburguesa y dos kilos de solomillo.

RITA: Nosotros comemos bastante cordero asado. Voy a cocinar esta pierna el domingo.

MIMI: Tengo que ir a la sección de verduras. Necesito zanahorias, frijoles verdes, lechuga, aguacate, . . .

RITA: Vas a ver que aquí hay vegatales bien frescos: pepinos, guisantes, ajo, de todo.

MIMI: Yo no puedo ver los vegetales en lata. No saben a nada.

RITA: A mí las latas también me ponen enferma, con la excepción del atún.

MIMI: Yo compro mucha fruta siempre. Mis niños la prefieren al pastel.

RITA: Sí, es más saludable y tiene menos calorías.

MIMI: Mi esposo está a dieta ahora. No toca nada dulce.

RITA: La mejor dieta es el ejercicio. Hay que trabajar mucho.

DIALOG   *Shopping at the Supermarket*

(Rita and Mimi are in the supermarket to do the shopping for the week.)

MIMI: I don't come to the supermarket often. They wait on you better in the small stores.

RITA: Well, I come here often. I think the prices are quite low.

MIMI: You're right. Look at these pork chops at 3 pesos a kilo!

RITA: It's true. They don't have any fat. I'm going to take this four-and-a-half kilo package.

MIMI: This beef looks really nice. I'll take six kilos of hamburger and two kilos of sirloin steak.

RITA: We eat a lot of roasted lamb. I'm going to cook this leg for Sunday.

MIMI: I have to go to the produce section. I need carrots, green beans, lettuce, avocado, . . .

RITA: You'll see that the vegetables are very fresh here: cucumbers, green peas, garlic, everything.

MIMI: I can't stand canned vegetables. They have no taste at all.

RITA: Canned food makes me sick too, with the exception of tuna.

MIMI: I always buy lots of fruit. My children like it better than cake.

RITA: Of course, it's healthier and has fewer calories.

MIMI: My husband is on a diet now. He doesn't touch anything sweet.

RITA: The best diet is exercise. You have to work hard.

EXERCISES

(Answers, p. 190)

A. Fill in the blanks with an appropriate word to form a narrative summary of the dialog.

Rita y Mimi (1)_____en el supermercado para hacer las

(2)_____de la semana. Mimi prefiere los (3)_____

_____pequeños al supermercado porque la atienden (4)

_____allí. Rita viene al supermercado (5)_____

porque los precios son más (6)_____. Las chuletas de (7)

_____están a 3 pesos el kilo, y además no

tienen ninguna (8)_____. Rita compra un (9)_____

de cuatro kilos y medio. La carne de res tiene buena (10)_____,

por eso Mimi compra dos kilos de (11)_____. En

casa de Rita comen bastante (12)_____asado, y

se lleva una (13)_____para cocinarla el domingo. Mimi

necesita muchas (14)_____: lechuga, zanahorias,

etc. Rita piensa que en este supermercado hay vegetales bien (15)_____

_____: pepino, cebollas, ajo, de todo. Mimi no (16)_____

ver los vegetales en lata porque no saben (17)_____. A

Rita las (18)_____ le ponen enferma con la excepción

del atún. Los niños de Mimi prefieren la (19)_____

al pastel. Ella tiene razón porque la fruta es más saludable y tiene pocas (20)

_____. El esposo de Mimi está (21)_____

y no come nada (22)_____, pero la mejor dieta es el

(23)_____.

B.   Circle the word that best completes the statement.

1. La carne de res, como el solomillo, va bien con (el pescado, el vino tinto, el jugo de tomate, los burritos).

2. De merienda prefiero (maíz picante, chuletas de cerdo, un bocadillo de pavo, zanahorias fritas).

3. Este cordero asado está (lleno, pálido, estupendo, tinto).

4. En los países tropicales hay un plato de (plátanos fritos, burritos asados, pepino fresco).

5. Los ingleses tienen la costumbre de beber mucho (café, té, leche, jugo).

6. En México se comen muchas tortillas de (zanahoria, pavo, cordero, maíz).

7. Prefiero poner (ajo, frijoles, queso, pastel) en mi hamburguesa.

8. En Estados Unidos hay sángüiches de pavo, jamón, (ternera, atún, cerdo, verdura).

9. El burrito no es un plato de origen mexicano *sino* (but) (español, chileno, colombiano, texano).

10. Una vaca joven es una (res, chuleta, cordera, ternera).

11. Las verduras de (leche, cebolla, lata, paquete.) no están frescas y no saben a nada.

12. Si estás a dieta de vegetales no debes comer (verduras, grasas, maíz, guisantes).

13. El azúcar tiene muchas (proteínas, calorías, grasas, peras).

14. Un vegetal tropical muy popular es (el plátano, la manzana, el guisante, el aguacate).

15. El atún es un tipo de (carne, vegetal, pescado, fruta).

C. Match the two columns

1. ____Una . . . española tiene papas, jamón, huevo, etc.   A. ternera

2. ____La hamburguesa se hace con . . . de res.   B. queso

3. ____En México y Guatemala se comen muchos. . . .   C. picante

4. ____El . . . es más grande que el pollo.   D. pepino

5. ____La carne de . . . es más tierna que la de vaca.   E. tortilla

6. ____El pavo de México es el . . . que es palabra india.   F. maíz

7. ____Prefiero el cordero . . . o a la plancha.   G. guajolote

8. ____El . . . es un producto importante de la leche.   H. pavo

9. ____Se comió una buena ensalada de lechuga y . . . .   I. calorías

10. ____Los tacos se hacen con tortillas de . . . .   J. frijoles

11. ____La comida mexicana es más . . . que la americana.   K. carne

12. ____Las verduras tienen menos . . . que las carnes.   L. asado

D. Form sentences using the words provided in the order given. Write all the verbs in the Preterite. Add other words when necessary. Watch out for noun-adjective agreement.

1. Rita / buscar / el / verduras / más / fresco /.

_____

2. Ellas / salir de compras / supermercado / en / carro /.

_____

3. domingo pasado / yo / pescar / en / mar /.

_____

4. ¿Cuándo / vender / tú / tu / libros / viejo /?

_____

5. Nuestro / tías / merendar / este / restaurante /.

_____

GRAMMAR I   Preterite of stem-changing verbs.

A.   Memorize the Preterite forms of *dormir, pedir,* and *sentir:*

SUBJECT	dorm ir	ped ir	sent ir
yo	dorm í	ped í	sent í
nosotros -as	dorm imos	ped imos	sent imos
tú	dorm iste	ped iste	sent iste
él/ella/Ud.	d**u**rm ió	p**i**d ió	s**i**nt ió
ellos/ellas/Uds.	d**u**rm ieron	p**i**d ieron	s**i**nt ieron

B.   Notice these features from the chart above:
   1. The Preterite of *dormir* changes *o* to *u* only in the third person, singular and plural. *Morir* shows the same changes in the stem: *murió* and *murieron.*
   2. *Pedir* changes *e* to *i* only in the third person singular and plural. This change in the stem also occurs in the Present, as you will recall, in *pido, pides, pide, piden,* but not in *pedimos.*
   3. Notice that both *dormir* and *pedir* are third-conjugation verbs— in other words, they are regular verbs ending in *-IR* in the infinitive. Only stem-changing verbs of the third conjugation change *e* to *i* or *o* to *u* in the Preterite and other tenses that you will study later.

C.   Look at some more stem-changing verbs ending in *-IR:*
   Here are a few verbs that you studied in previous lessons. Note that they follow the same stem changes as *pedir.*

divertir (ie, i) (to have fun)	**pedir (i)**	(to ask for)
preferir (ie, i) (to prefer)	**seguir (i)**	(to follow)
sentir (ie, i) (to feel, sense)	**servir (i)**	(to serve)
repetir (i) (to repeat)	**vestir (i)**	(to dress)

   1. Notice the vowels in parentheses. The change from *e* to *ie* occurs in the Present, and *e* to *i* occurs in the Preterite. Ex.: *sentir / yo siento* (I feel), but *él sintió* (he felt). The verbs indicated with (i) have the change from *e* to *i* in the Present and Preterite: *pedir / yo pido* and *él pidió.*
   2. The stem-changing verbs ending in *-AR* and *-ER* change the stem in the Present but not in the Preterite.
   Ex.: *volver / él vuelve* but *él volvió.*

PRACTICE THE PRETERITE   *(Answers, p. 190)*

1. The stem of *dormir* is _____, and the stem of *durmió* is
   _____. There has been a change in the stem from *o* to_____.
   How do you say *they slept?* _____.

2. *Pedir* has the stem_____, and the stem of *pidieron* is_____
   The *e* has changed to____. How do you say *he asked for?* (remember that
   you don't translate *for!*) _____.

3. The verb *morir* is a stem-changing verb like_____.
   How do you say *he died?*_____. How do you say *they died?*
   _____.

4. *Sentir* (ie, i) is also a stem-changing verb, with different changes in the
   Present and the Preterite. In the Present it changes *e* to_____;
   for example, *yo*_____ and *él*_____. In the
   Preterite it changes *e* to_____in the third person singular and
   plural: for example, *él*_____(he felt).

5. Stem-changing verbs with changes in the Present and Preterite belong to
   the_____conjugation, in other words, ending in *-IR*.
   Verbs ending in *-AR* or *-ER* change the stem in the Present but not
   in the_____.

6. *Volver* changes *o* to *ue* in the Present; for example, *yo*_____
   and *él*_____. But there is no change in the Preterite: *él*
   _____and *ellos*_____.

7. *Dormir* (ue, u) has a double change in the stem. In the Present it changes
   o to_____; for example, *él*_____. In the Preterite it
   changes *o* to_____; for example, *él*_____and *ellos*
   _____.

EXERCISES   *(Answers, p. 190)*

**A. Complete the sentences with the correct form of the verbs in
the Preterite tense. (Remember the reflexive pronouns!)**

1. Mi hermana_____mal después del viaje, pero yo
   _____muy bien. (sentirse)

2. ¿Cuándo _____ tu abuelo? (morir)

3. Mi esposa _____ en una hora, pero yo _____
   en diez minutos. (vestirse)

4. Los Arana _____ una comida peruana el
   sábado pasado. (servir)

5. Nosotros _____ café y ella _____ un refresco.
   (pedir)

6. Cecilia *sólo* (only) _____ cinco horas, pero nosotros

   _____ ocho horas. (dormir)

7. Muchos americanos _____ en la guerra de Vietnam.
   (morir)

8. Carlitos _____ una hamburguesa y yo _____
   dos tacos. (preferir)

9. ¿Cuántas veces _____ usted el ejercicio? Yo lo _____

   _____ cinco veces *por lo menos* (at least). (repetir)

10. Todos los muchachos _____ en la fiesta.
    (divertirse)

B. Change the verbs from the Present to the Preterite.

1. Diana *vuelve* a casa de sus padres
   y *prefiere* vivir con ellos por un tiempo. _____

2. Cuando *me siento* enfermo,
   voy a ver al médico enseguida. _____

3. Ellas *se divierten* mucho en
   la fiesta, y *piden* más champán. _____

4. Arturo *se despierta* temprano
   esta mañana y *se viste* en seguida. _____

5. Cuando *llego* al supermercado,
   sigo hasta la sección de carne. _____

6. Este señor *es* muy rico,
   pero *muere* muy pobre. _____

7. Por la noche *me quito* la
   ropa (clothes) y *me acuesto* a dormir. _____

GRAMMAR II   Preterite of irregular verbs.

A.   Memorize the Preterite of these verbs:

SUBJECT	ser / ir	d ar	ven ir	dec ir	est ar
yo	fu i	d i	vin *e*	dij *e*	estuv *e*
nosotros -as	fu imos	d imos	vin imos	dij imos	estuv imos
tú	fu iste	d iste	vin iste	dij iste	estuv iste
él/ella/Uds.	fu e	d io	vin *o*	dij *o*	estuvo
ellos/ellas/Uds.	fu eron	d ieron	vin ieron	dij eron	estuv ieron

B.   Notice these facts about the chart above:

1. *Ser* and *ir* have the same forms in the Preterite. We need a context to distinguish between them.
   Ex.: El año pasado *fui* a México. (I *went* to Mexico last year)
   Fui camarero en Washington. (I *was* a waiter in Washington)

2. *Dar* is irregular because it doesn't take the endings of the *-AR* verbs, but rather of the *-ER* verbs. This is the only cross-conjugation in the Spanish verb system.

3. Notice that *fui, fue, di, dio* don't take *acento* because they have only one syllable. The same rule applies to *va, ve, vi, vio* (he saw).

4. *Venir, decir,* and *estar* are irregular for two reasons: (a) they have changes in the stem: *ven / vin;   dec / dij;   est / estuv;* (b) they have special endings in the first and third person singular: *e* instead of í and *o* instead of *ió.*

5. *Decir* is irregular for the same two reasons mentioned above, but also because it takes the ending *-eron* rather than *-ieron.* This same change occurs with the verbs for which the stem of the preterite ends in *j,* such as *traer / traje / trajeron.*

C.   The following verbs are irregular in the Preterite, with the same kinds of change in the ending as *venir, decir,* and *estar.* Pay close attention to the changes in the stem. These are very important verbs because they are used very frequently.

andar / anduve / anduvo	poner / puse / puso
conducir / conduje / condujo	producir / produje / produjo
decir / dije / dijo	querer / quise / quiso
deshacer / deshice / deshizo	saber / supe / supo
detener / detuve / detuvo	tener / tuve / tuvo
haber / hube / hubo	traer / traje / trajo
hacer / hice / hizo	estar / estuve / estuvo
poder / pude / pudo	

NOTES:

1. *Hacer* has the stem *hic* in the Preterite, and the *c* changes to *z* to *hizo*. This is a spelling change similar to that of *feliz* / *felices* and *comenzar* / *comencé*.

2. Most of the verbs above have compound forms such as *hacer* / *deshacer* and *tener* / *detener*. The compound verbs share the same features of the simple verbs.
    Ex.: *poner* / *puse*,　　*componer* / *compuse* (I fixed).

3. All verbs ending in *-ducir*—like *conducir*, *producir*—change the *c* to *j* in the Preterite. Like *decir* and *traer*, these verbs take the ending *-eron* rather than *-ieron*.
    Ex.: *conducir* / *conduje* / *condujeron*.

PRACTICE THE PRETERITE　　　　　　　　*(Answers, p. 191)*

1. *Dijo* is a Preterite form and it means *he/she said; digo* is a _____ form and it means _____.

2. From *saber* we say *yo sé* (I know) in the Present. How do you say *I knew*?

    _____.

3. *Hacer* has a triple stem: *Hac* in the infinitive, _____ and

    _____ in the Preterite.

4. *Dijeron* has an irregular ending because the *j* "swallows up" the vowel

    _____. So instead of *ieron*, the ending is _____.

5. All the verbs in *-ducir* change the *c* to _____ in the Preterite. How

    do you translate *they drove*? *Ellos* _____.

6. *Ponió* (from *poner*) is incorrect. It should be _____.

7. *Trajieron* is also incorrect. It should be _____, because of the *j*.

8. *Vino* (he came) and *vino* (wine) show the same spelling. How can you tell one

    from the other in a conversation (or writing)? _____

    _____.

9. *Yo andé* sounds like good Spanish, but it isn't. It should be *Yo* _____

    _____.

10. *Detener* is a compound of _____. How would you
    say *He stopped the criminal?* _____ *al criminal.*

11. *Fue* means two different things: _____ or _____.
    This is because *ser* and _____ have the same forms in the
    Preterite.

12. *Dar* is irregular in the Preterite because it follows the conjugation of *-ER*
    ending verbs rather than _____ verbs. For example, we
    don't say *ellos daron* but *ellos* _____.

13. *Dió* and *fué* are misspelled because of the _____.
    They must be spelled _____ and _____ because they have
    only one syllable.

EXERCISES

(*Answers, p. 191*)

A. Fill in the blanks with the correct forms of the Preterite.

1. Mi tía no _____ vender el carro viejo. (can)

2. ¿Quién _____ los frijoles y tacos en la mesa? (put)

3. Lolita _____ ir, pero no _____.
   (want/can)

4. México y Venezuela _____ mucho petróleo. (produce)

5. ¿Dónde _____ (tú) ayer todo el día? (be)

6. Ellos _____ que no, pero yo _____ que sí. (say)

7. Yo no _____ mi dinero al supermercado. (bring)

8. Cuando José vio a su esposa, no _____ qué decir. (know)

9. José y yo _____ en mi carro hoy. (come)

10. ¿Quién _____ el carro, tú o tu esposa?
    (drive)

11. Diana _____ los bocadillos, y yo _____
    el pastel de postre. (make)

12. La señora Pérez _____ en la sección de ver-
    duras. (stop)

B. Change the verbs from Present to Preterite.

Margarita no (1) *anda* al trabajo esta mañana *sino que* (but) (2) *conduce* su carro nuevo. Hoy no (3) *está* en su oficina a las 8 en punto como de costumbre, porque (4) *tiene* que hacer el desayuno a su hijo. Después que (5) *llega*, (6) *pone* las cosas en la mesa y (7) *se pone* a trabajar. Sus amigas (8) *hacen* café y le (9) *traen* una taza. Ella les (10) *dice* "mil gracias" y (11) *toma* su café sin crema y sin azúcar. En ese momento (12) *suena* el teléfono . . .

1._____   7._____

2._____   8._____

3._____   9._____

4._____   10._____

5._____   11._____

6._____   12._____

GRAMMAR III   Idiomatic expressions with verbs: **hay, hay que, acabar de, ponerse a.**

A. To indicate the idea of *there is/are,* we use *hay* from the verb *haber*. In the Past we use *hubo* for *there was/were.*
> Ex.: *Hay* muchas chuletas en este supermercado. (*there are* many . . .)
> El viernes pasado *hubo* una fiesta. (*there was* a party . . .)

B. *Estar* is used with a *definite* noun. *Hay* and *hubo* are used with an *indefinite* noun.
> Ex.: *Hay* un taco en la mesa. (*there is a* taco on the table)
> *Está* el taco en la mesa. (*the* taco *is* on the table)

C. *Hay* and *hubo* are used with a noun to describe the *weather,* with the same meaning of *hace* and *hizo*.
> Ex.: Esta mañana *hace/hay* mucho sol. (it's very sunny . . .)

D. *Hay que (+ infinitive)* indicates obligation to do something, just like *tener que,* but without a subject.
> Ex.: *Hay que* estudiar mucho. (it's necessary to study hard)
> *Tengo que* estudiar mucho. (I have to study hard)

E. *Acabar de (+ infinitive)* indicates that the action just took place; "to have just done something."
> Ex.: José *acaba de salir* para casa. (José has just left for home)

F. *Ponerse a (+ infinitive)* indicates the beginning of an action with more determination or speed than *comenzar*. *Ponerse* can be used in different tenses.
> Ex.: Cuando llegó a casa *se puso a escribir* una carta.

G. *Ponerse (+ adjective)* carries the idea of *to turn red, pale,* etc. It suggests a sudden change. The adjective has to agree with the subject of the sentence in gender and number.

> Ex.: Cuando María vio al policía *se puso roja.* (when Mary saw the policeman, she turned red)

PRACTICE THE IDIOMS   *(Answers, p. 191)*

1. To translate *there is/are*, we use the Present of *haber:* _____.

   For the past, we use the Preterite *there was/were:* _____.

2. *Estar* is used to indicate the location of people and things, but the noun has

   to be _____. A noun is made definite with the definite article, the short possessives, and the demonstratives *(este, ese,* etc).

3. *Hay* and *hubo* are third person singular forms, and they indicate the

   location of an _____ noun.

4. *Está un libro aquí* is wrong. It should be *Está* _____

   _____ .

5. *Hay que (+ infinitive)* carries the idea of _____ to do something, but in an impersonal way, since there is no subject involved.

6. To describe the weather, we can use *hace* as well as _____

   in the Present, and *hizo* and _____ in the Preterite.

7. *Hay muy viento* is wrong, because *viento* is a noun; you have to change *muy*

   to the adjective _____ .

8. *Acabar* is *to finish,* and *acabar de (+ infinitive)* shows that the action

   has _____ .

9. *Ponerse a (+ infinitive)* means to _____ an *action* with certain determination or speed.

10. How do you say *He began to eat (suddenly)?* _____ .

    _____ .

EXERCISES

(Answers, p. 191)

A. Combine the words from the first column with the words in
    the second and third columns. The 0 in the second column
    means that you don't need a word from that group. Example:
    Hay que practicar. (it's necessary to practice)

1. Hay
2. Está   practicar
3. Hubo   0   una fiesta aquí
4. Acabamos   de   viento
5. Hace   que   alegre
6. José se puso   a   el libro aquí
7. Me pongo   pálida
8. Tenemos

Complete your answers below:

1. Hay _____.

   Hay _____.

   Hay _____.

2. Está _____.

   Está _____.

   Está _____.

3. Hubo _____.

   Hubo _____.

   Hubo _____.

4. Acabamos _____.

   Acabamos _____.

   Acabamos _____.

5. Hace _____.

6. José se puso _____.

   José se puso _____.

7. Me pongo _____.

   Me pongo _____.

   Me pongo _____.

8. Tenemos_____.

   Tenemos_____.

   Tenemos_____.

B.   Complete the sentences with *a, de, que,* or nothing.

1. Hay_____comer hamburguesas esta tarde.

2. Ella quiere_____invitarte_____su fiesta de cumpleaños.

3. Rita se puso_____trabajar después que llegó.

4. Jorge dejó_____fumar la semana pasada.

5. ¿Usted acaba_____llegar de Europa?

6. No puedo_____ir con ella porque tengo_____trabajar.

7. Cuando vi_____Carlos, me puse_____pálido.

8. Ayer traté_____llamarte por la tarde a tu casa.

9. Nosotros quisimos_____parar, pero no pudimos.

10. Pepe acabó_____salir cuando llegó su amiga.

11. Cuando estoy_____dieta, debo_____comer poco.

12. Mi suegra se fue_____compras temprano.

13. No invité_____Rosaura porque siempre me dice_____no.

14. Esta pizza sabe mucho_____ajo y cebolla.

15. Venimos_____menudo_____este supermercado.

Lesson 9

En el banco
(At the Bank)

banco	bank	**dinero**	money	**moneda**	currency, coin
billete	bill, ticket	**divisa**	foreign money	**necesidad**	necessity need
cajero -a	cashier	**factura**[2]	bill	**peseta**[3]	peseta (Spain)
cartera[1]	wallet	**ganancia**	earnings	**préstamo**	loan
centavo (Amer.)	cent (Amer.)	**ganga**	bargain	**presupuesto**	budget
céntimo (Spain)	cent (Spain)	**gasto**	expense	**salario**	salary
cheque	check	**hipoteca**	mortgage	**sueldo**	salary
chequera	checkbook	**impuesto**	tax	**tienda**	store
cuenta	account	**interés**	interest	**valor**	value

agradar	to please	**encontrar(ue)**	to find	**nadar**	to swim
ahorrar	to save	**faltar**	to miss	**parecer**[5]	to seem
alegrarse de	to be happy	**ganar**	to win, earn	**prestar**	to lend
aumentar	to increase	**gastar**	to spend	**quejarse**	to complain
cargar	to load, charge	**gustar**	to like	**reducir**	to reduce
descubrir	to discover	**importar**[4]	to matter	**sacar**	to take out
convenir(ie)	to suit	**interesar**	to interest	**sobrar**	to be left
encantar	to like, please	**meter**	to put into	**valer**	to be worth

actual	present	**fuerte**	strong	**encantado**	pleased
agradecido	thankful	**lujoso**	luxurious	**serio**	serious
débil	weak	**necesario**	necessary	**valioso**	valuable

a fines de	by the end of	**¡ni modo!**	no way!
a plazos (en plazos)	in installments	**por fin**	finally
a propósito	by the way	**por ciento**	percent

al contado	cash (to pay . . .)	**sobre todo**	above all
aunque	although	**tarjeta de crédito**	credit card
cuenta corriente	checking account	**un par de**	a couple of
cuenta de ahorros	savings account	**giro postal**	money order
de lujo (lujoso)	delux (luxurious)	**giro internacional**	international money order
en fin	in short, finally	**valer la pena**	to be worthwhile

NOTES:

1. *Cartera* is *wallet,* also *purse* (and sometimes *briefcase*).

2. *Factura* means *bill,* used for the bills you get in the mail (gas, electricity, telephone). It's also used for the things you buy, such as a car, books, appliances. *Cuenta* is for smaller bills, such as those you get in a restaurant, drugstore, etc. Do not confuse it with *billete,* which is used for currency bills as well as for a travel ticket.

3. *Peseta* is the currency of Spain. The dollar is about 140 *pesetas,* and *céntimos* are used only in exchange transactions. There is no coin for the *céntimo.* In Latin America *peseta* is a *quarter* of the *peso.*

4. *Importar* can be two different things: to *import* from another country, and *to matter.* With the first meaning, we use the verb like *hablar,* with different subjects: *yo, tú, él,* etc. With the meaning of *to matter,* it is used in the third person only, like *gustar* (to like), which is explained in this lesson.

5. *Parecer* means *to seem,* and it's used only in the third person, like *gustar,* followed by an indirect object (explained later in this lesson). *Parecerse,* a reflexive verb, means *to take after* or *resemble;* it is conjugated in all the persons:
   Ex.: Le *parece* bien a Juan. (it seems OK to John)
   Juan *se parece* a su padre. (John takes after his father)

EXERCISES

(Answers, p. 192)

A. Write *el, la los,* or *las* before these nouns.

1. ___ billete
2. ___ cheques
3. ___ necesidad
4. ___ interés

5. ___ fin
6. ___ valor
7. ___ impuestos
8. ___ tiendas

9. ___ ahorros
10. ___ divisas
11. ___ ganancia
12. ___ fines

B. Word Families: Write one or more words related to each of the following.

1. ahorros_____

2. alegre_____

3. encantado_____

4. interés_____

5. valioso_____

6. lujo_____

7. conveniente_____

8. préstamo_____

9. centavo_____

10. cheque_____

11. necesitar_____

12. cuenta (ue → o)_____

13. encargarse_____

14. ganar_____

15. gasto_____

16. pareja_____

17. peseta_____

18. gastar_____

19. importancia_____

20. reducción_____

C. **Fill in the blanks with one of the words given in the box. You may need the plural forms of nouns and adjectives. The verbs are given in the infinitive, but you may need the Present Indicative, or the Preterite.**

por ciento	ganar	nadar
un par de	descubrir	a plazos
tienda	ahorrar	préstamo
moneda	ganga	giro postal
cartera	de lujo	divisa

1. Necesito un_____del banco para comprar el coche.

2. Todo el mundo cree que el Cadillac es un carro_____.

3. En California se paga 6_____de impuestos.

4. La_____de España se llama peseta.

5. Con la *inflación* (inflation) es *defícil* (difficult)_____dinero.

6. El turismo trae muchas_____a España y a México.

7. Tengo cinco billetes de un dólar en mi _____.

8. ¿Cuánto _____ usted por semana?

9. Si hace sol mañana vamos a _____ al mar.

10. ¿Puedes prestarme _____ dólares para almorzar?

11. En esta venta todo está barato. Hay muchas _____.

12. Me gusta pagar las facturas _____ y no al contado.

13. Cristóbal Colón _____ América en el año 1492.

14. Mi tía me *mandó* (sent) un _____ de 30 dólares.

15. En esta _____ solamente se venden mariscos.

D. Complete the sentences with one of the verbs below. Use only the Preterite tense.

reducir	gastar	valer	alegrarse	aumentar
encontrar	sacar	meter	quejarse	prestar

1. Mi novia me _____ su carro ayer.

2. Nosotros _____ del sueldo bajo que nos pagan.

3. ¿A qué hora _____ (tú) el carro en el garaje?

4. Ellos _____ de tu buena suerte en Las Vegas.

5. Algunos conquistadores _____ *oro* (gold) en América.

6. Los bancos _____ el interés en los préstamos. (increased)

7. Yo _____ un billete de la cartera y pagué la cuenta.

8. José vendió su casa y ésta _____ más de 100,000 dólares.

9. ¿Por qué _____ Ud. todo el dinero que cobró?

10. Los carros _____ la *velocidad* (speed) antes del STOP.

E. Write True or False (T/F).

1. ___ Abrimos una cuenta de ahorros en una tienda de mariscos.

2. ___ Una cuenta corriente da más interés que una cuenta de ahorros.

3. ___Lo contrario de *reducir* el interés es *aumentarlo*.

4. ___En España se usan céntimos; en América Latina se usan centavos.

5. ___Un Mercedes Benz es más lujoso que un Volkswagen.

6. ___En California no se pagan impuestos federales.

7. ___Una hipoteca es un préstamo muy grande.

8. ___Si Ud. usa dólares en México, Ud. deja divisas a los mexicanos.

9. ___Lo contrario de *fuerte* es *valioso*.

10. ___Vale la pena tener una dieta para reducir de *peso* (weight).

11. ___El señor George Washington está en los billetes de 10 dólares.

12. ___Estados Unidos importa muchas bananas de América Central.

13. ___Si Ud. paga a plazos, Ud. paga facturas todos los meses.

14. ___Cuando Ud. está muy feliz, Ud. está encantado.

DIÁLOGO *En un banco de Madrid*

(Susana es de Estados Unidos y acaba de llegar a Madrid para estudiar un año allí y conocer el país. Entra a un banco para cambiar dinero y abrir una cuenta corriente.)

CAJERO: Buenos días, señorita. ¿En qué puedo servirle?

SUSANA: Necesito cambiar 200 dólares a pesetas. ¿A cómo está el cambio?

CAJERO: Hoy está a 140 pesetas el dólar si está en cheques de viajeros y a 138[1] si está en moneda.

SUSANA: ¡Qué suerte! Todo mi dinero está en cheques de viajeros.

CAJERO: Por favor, necesito el número de su pasaporte para poder cambiar el dinero.[2]

SUSANA: Aquí lo tiene. También quiero abrir una cuenta corriente.

CAJERO: Muy bien. ¿Cuánto dinero va a depositar?

SUSANA: Este giro postal de 500 dólares. A propósito, ¿me pueden hacer un préstamo si algún día me hace falta?

CAJERO: Sí, si tiene una tarjeta de crédito, y el préstamo no es muy grande, como una hipoteca.

SUSANA: No, no pensaba comprarme ningún piso. Pero me gusta pagar a plazos mejor que al contado.

CAJERO: Sí, claro. ¡Ustedes los americanos viven del futuro!

SUSANA: ¡Ni modo! yo vine a España a descubrir los valores del pasado.

NOTES:

1. Traveler's checks have a higher exchange than the currency because of the mailing operations involved. The foreign money exchange goes up and down every day like the stock market.

2. The reason for asking for the passport number is to find out if you are a foreigner or a tourist living in another country. There are strict international regulations as to the amount of money you can "import" or "export."

DIALOG   *In a Bank in Madrid*

(Susan is from the United States and has just arrived in Madrid to study for one year there and to get to know the country. She goes into a bank to exchange money and to open a checking account.)

TELLER: Good morning, miss. May I help you?
SUSAN: I need to exchange $200 to pesetas. What's the rate of exchange?
TELLER: Today the rate is 140 pesetas to the dollar if it's in traveler's checks, and 138 if it's currency.
SUSAN: How lucky! All my money is in traveler's checks!
TELLER: I need the number of your passport to exchange the money, please.
SUSAN: Here it is. I also want to open a checking account.
TELLER: Fine. How much money are you going to deposit?
SUSAN: This money order for $500. By the way, can you make me a loan in case I need it some day?
TELLER: Sure, if you have a credit card, and the loan is not a big one, like for a mortgage.
SUSAN: No, I'm not thinking of buying an apartment. But I like to pay in installments rather than in cash.
TELLER: Of course. You Americans live in the future!
SUSAN: No way! I came to Spain to discover the values of the past!

EXERCISES   (Answers, p. 192)

A. **Fill in the blanks with an appropriate word to form a narrative summary of the dialog. Suppose that the story happened in the past and use the Preterite tense.**

Susana llegó a Madrid para (1)＿＿＿＿＿＿＿＿＿allí y conocer el

(2)＿＿＿＿＿＿＿＿. Ella entró a un banco para (3)＿＿＿＿＿＿＿

200 dólares a pesetas. Un (4)＿＿＿＿＿＿＿＿atendió a Susana en

las operactiones bancarias. Ese día el cambio (5)_____

a 140 pesetas por dólar en cheques de (6)_____y 138 en

(7)_____. Susana (8)_____suerte,
porque solamenta *tenía* (had) cheques de viajeros. El cajero le pidió el (9)

_____a Susana para escribir el número en la transacción.

Susana (10)_____una cuenta corriente con un

giro (11)_____de $500. El cajero le dijo que el banco le

puede dar un (12)_____si lo necesita. Susana no *pensaba* (wasn't planning) comprar ningún (13)_____

en Madrid. A ella le gusta más pagar (14)_____

que pagar (15)_____.

Para el cajero, los americanos viven del (16)_____,

pero Susana vino a España a (17)_____los valores del

(18)_____.

B.   Complete the sentences with an appropriate word.

1. Para comprar una casa necesitamos una_____,
   excepto si Ud. paga ¡al contado!

2. Visa, Master Charge, American Express son tres_____
   _____.

3. Sí, claro, no puedes escribir un cheque porque no trajiste la_____
   _____.

4. Lo contrario de *fuerte* es_____, y lo contrario de *actual*

   es_____.

5. En esta tienda me pagan un_____semanal
   de 250 dólares.

6. En California el_____de venta es el 6 por ciento.

7. Lo contrario de *gastar* es_____, y lo contrario de *meter*

   es_____.

8. Algunos bancos pagan_____en las cuentas corrientes.

9. Hay dos expresiones para *finally: en fin* y_____.

10. Vale la_____estudiar la lengua de otro país.

11. El dinero_____su valor adquisitivo todos los años.

12. ¿Es tu novio una persona_____? (serious)

C. Circle the word that best completes the sentence.

1. Pagué la factura con (una moneda, una cuenta, un cheque, una ganga).

2. Para viajar en tren hay que comprar (una cartera, un billete, un valor, un interés).

3. Cuando hay mucho sol voy a (ahorrar, encantar, ganar, nadar).

4. Si te sientes débil, debes (gastar, comer, ganar, ahorrar) algo.

5. Un carro de lujo es (barato, una ganga, encantado, valioso).

6. Me alegro mucho cuando me (reducen, aumentan, cargan, sacan) el salario.

7. Los países árabes necesitan (facturas, tiendas, divisas, gangas) de Estados Unidos.

8. En España se usan pesetas y (céntimos, pesos, dólares, centavos).

9. Mis sobrinos (gustan, se alegran, se parecen, se agradan) a su madre.

10. Fui a la *agencia de viajes* (travel agency) a sacar (el billete, la factura, las divisas).

GRAMMAR I   Indirect Object pronouns.

A. When you give a book *to your friend, friend* functions as the Indirect Object (I.O.), and *book* as the Direct Object (D.O.). In Spanish when a noun functions as the I.O., it always takes the preposition *a:* Usted dio el libro *a* su *amiga.*

B. In this chart we see the D.O., I.O., Reflexive, and Object of Preposition pronouns:

SUBJECT	Dir. Obj.	Indir. Obj.	Reflexive	Object of Prep.	ENGLISH	(objects)
yo	me	**me**	me	a **mí**	me	to me
tú	te	**te**	te	a **ti**	you	to you
nosotros -as	nos	**nos**	nos	a **nosotros**	us	to us
él (Ud.)	lo	**le**		a **él** (a Ud.)	him	to him
ella	la	**(se)**	se	a **ella**	her	to her
ellos (Uds.)	los	**les**		a **ellos** (a Uds.)	them	to them
ellas	las			a **ellas**		

Notice in the chart that first and second persons have the same pronouns for the D.O., I.O., and reflexive: *me/te/nos/*. The third person has different pronouns: *lo/la/los/las* are D.O., *le/les (se)* are I.O., and *se* is reflexive.

C. Meaning of the Indirect Object. In English only certain verbs are followed by a noun or pronoun that function as I.O. In Spanish any verb can take an I.O. with a wide range of meanings:
1. *Benefit: Le* di el libro *a Juan.* (I gave the book to John)
2. *Loss: Le* quité el libro *a Juan.* (I took the book away from John)
3. *Possession: Le* vi el libro *a Juan.* (I saw John's book)
4. *General interest or involvement: Le* gusta el libro *a Juan.* (John likes the book) Se *le* cayó el libro *a Juan.* (John dropped . . .)

D. D.O. and I.O. pronouns in the same sentence:

If both the D.O. and I.O. nouns become pronouns, they precede the verb in the Indicative, and they follow the infinitive:
Ex.: Jorge *me* dio el libro *a mí*→ Jorge *me lo* dio. (George gave *it to me*)

1. The I.O. Pronoun precedes the D.O. pronoun: Jorge *me lo* dio. An example with the infinitive: Jorge va a dár*melo* or Jorge *me lo* va a dar.
2. If both the D.O. and I.O. are *third* person, the I.O. pronouns *le/les* become *se* as shown in parentheses in the chart.
Ex.: Jorge dio el libro a su amiga → Jorge *le lo* dio. → Jorge *se lo* dio.

E. The pronouns used as Object of Preposition can be added to the D.O. and I.O. in order to add *emphasis.*
Ex.: *Usted me vio a mí* is more emphatic than *Usted me vio.*

Usted vio a mí is incorrect. It needs *me* before the verb. This means that we cannot use the Object of Preposition pronouns for D.O. and I.O. without the matching unstressed pronoun: *me/te/lo/la/le,* etc.

F. When the I.O. is a noun, it is frequent but not obligatory to add *le/les* to anticipate the noun.
Ex.: *Le di el libro a Juan* is more frequent than *di el libro a Juan.* Both sentences are used by natives speakers.

PRACTICE THE PRONOUNS   *(Answers, p. 193)*

1. The pronouns *me/te/nos* are the same for the reflexive, direct object, and

_____ .

2. The pronouns *lo/la/los/las* are D.O. pronouns, _____ are I.O. pronouns, and *se* is their matching _____ pronoun.

3. The I.O. has a wide range of uses and meanings in Spanish: benefit, loss, possession, and general _____ .

4. Do the D.O. pronouns precede or follow the I.O. pronouns? _____ .
The two pronouns stay together *before* the verb in the _____
_____ tenses.

5. If the infinitive follows the Indicative in the same sentence, the D.O., I.O., and reflexive pronouns may precede the _____
or follow the _____ .

6. The pronouns *le/les* become _____ when they are in front of lo/la/los/las.
Therefore *Le lo vendo* is wrong. It should be _____ .

7. The sentence *Te vi ayer con María* is less _____
than *Te vi a ti ayer con María*. It seems obvious because *te* and *a ti* are a repetition of the same information.

8. If the I.O. is a noun (third person), we frequently anticipate this noun with the unstressed pronouns _____ , but it's not obligatory.

9. *Yo invité a ella* is not correct. We have to add _____ in front of *invité*.

EXERCISES

(Answers, p. 193)

A. Complete the sentences with a D.O. or I.O. pronoun.

1. Elena _____ prestó el carro a su hija.

2. ¿Por qué tú _____ dijiste que no a mí?

3. Señora, se _____ cayó la cartera a usted.

4. Creo que mi hijo no _____ dijo toda la verdad a nosotros.

5. El carro se _____ paró a mí en *medio de la avenida*. (in the middle of the avenue.)

6. A tu novio, ¿ _____ gusta la comida italiana?

7. ¿La chequera? _____ dejé en casa.

8. ¿El libro? _____ di a Carmen.

9. ¿Las monedas? _____ dejé a mi hijo para su colección.

10. ¿ _____ gusta nadar a ustedes?

**B. Answer the questions and change the Direct and Indirect
     Objects to pronouns. Pay attention to the verbs. Example:
     ¿Quién oye el radio? → Yo *lo* oigo.**

1. ¿Cuándo vas a pagarme la cuenta? - Mañana voy_____

    _____. (use the familiar)

2. ¿Cuándo va Ud. a pagarme la cuenta? - Mañana voy_____

    _____. (use the formal)

3. ¿Quién dio el cheque a Susana? - El cajero_____.

4. ¿Quién prestó 5 dólares a mi primo? - Cecilia_____.

5. ¿Quién trajo este flan a mi mamá? - Tu esposa_____.

6. ¿Desea Ud. abrir la ventana? - Sí, deseo_____.

7. ¿Por qué van a lavar el coche a su papá? - Vamos_____

    _____porque él está enfermo.

8. ¿Aumentó Ud. el sueldo a las camareras? - Sí, yo_____

    _____.

9. ¿Dónde quieres poner estas maletas? - Aquí_____

    _____.

10. ¿Quién pidió un préstamo al banco? -Susana_____.

**C. Form sentences using the words in the order given. Make any
     changes and add words when necessary, especially the In-
     direct Object pronouns. Use the Preterite tense.**

1. tú / comprar / bocadillos / sabroso / nosotros /.

    _____

2. camareros / servir / la comida / pasajeros /.

    _____

3. tu / tíos / vender / Volkswagen / mí /.

    _____

4. botones / subir / maletas / turistas /.

_____

5. Enrique / prestar / carro / nadie /.

_____

GRAMMAR II   The Indirect Object with **gustar,** and Unplanned Occurrences.

A.   The sentence *El libro me gusta* translates literally as *The book is
pleasing to me* (I like the book). *Libro* is the Subject and always needs
a definite article, possessive, or demonstrative. If we change *libro* to
libros, we have to change the verb to the plural *(gustan):* Los libros
me gusta*n.*
What is the function of *me*? It is the Indirect Object, and it is
obligatory with *gustar* and other verbs listed in (B) below.

More examples:

(a mí)   me   I
(a ti)   te   gusta(n)   la(s)   casa(s). you like(s) the house(s)
(a él)   le   he

B.   Verbs functioning like *gustar* are important. Here are some of them:

agradar (to like)	**sobrar** (to be left)	**molestar**	(to bother)
encantar (to like)	**parecer** (to seem)	**importar**	(to matter)
faltar (to miss)	**doler (ue)** (to hurt)	**interesar**	(to interest)
pasar (to happen)	**convenir** (to be suitable)*	**valer la pena**	(to be worth-while)

Convenir is a compound of *venir;* it has the same irregular changes.
For example, *me conviene* in the Present, *me convino* in the Preterite.
Convenir means to agree when it is used with an ordinary subject:
yo/tú/él, etc.
        Ex.: Tú y yo convinimos en eso. (you and I agreed on that)

All the verbs in the list above are used with an I.O. pronoun. More
examples:
        A Lucía le duelen las manos. (Lucy's hands hurt)
        A Ud. le interesa más el dinero. (money interests you more)

C. Unplanned occurrences:
When we talk about an action that is/was not planned, especially
something unwanted or unpleasant, we use an impersonal construc-
tion with *se*. We don't plan actions like *to forget, to fall, to drop, to
break;* these actions seem to "just happen."
Ex.: El vaso se me cayó. (I dropped the glass) (literally, *the
glass dropped itself on me*. It was an accident, not my
fault).

In this example *vaso* (an inanimate noun) is the subject of *cayó*, and
me is the Indirect Object. If we change *vasos* to the plural, *cayó* has to
change to *cayeron: Se me cayeron los vasos*. (I dropped the glasses)
(literally, *the glasses dropped themselves on me*).
More examples: ¿Se te olvidó el libro? (did you forget the book?)
¿Se te olvidaron los libros? (did you forget the
books?)
A María se le paró el carro. (Mary's car
stopped)

PRACTICE THE GRAMMAR   *(Answers, p. 193)*

1. In a sentence like *me gusta el libro,* the subject is_____. If
    we change *libro* to *libros,* we say_____ *los
    libros.*

2. *Usted -es* is the second person in meaning (you), but grammatically it is
    the_____person. This is why the I.O. of *usted -es* are
    the pronouns_____.

3. Which is more emphatic, (a) *me gusta eso* or (b) *a mí me gusta eso?*____.

4. If *Me duele la mano* means *My hand hurts,* it seems obvious that the I.O. *me*
    means_____in this case.

5. When we say *Se me cayó el plato,* se is the same reflexive-impersonal
    pronoun as in *Se habla español. Se* is required because *plato* is an_____
    _____noun.

6. In *Se me cayó el plato, me* functions as_____,
    and it means that I *(me)* was involved with the dish—that is, because I own
    it, or I was holding it at the time of the fall. The I.O. can be very ambiguous.

7. *Plato* is the subject of the verb in *Se le cayó el plato*. How would you write the sentence with *platos* as subject?_____*los platos.*

8. Like *gustar, parecer* (to seem) needs an I.O. How would you say *The idea seems good to me? La idea*_____.

EXERCISES

(Answers, p. 193)

A.   Complete the sentences with one of the verbs suggested. Use Present forms. Don't forget the I.O. pronouns.

1. A mis padres_____los camarones a la plancha. (like)

2. ¿Qué_____a usted? - A mí no_____nada. (happen)

3. ¿Qué_____, mi hijo? - _____las manos. (hurt)

4. Esa cajera_____muy simpática a mí. (seem)

5. A ustedes_____una casa grande. (be suitable)

6. ¿A ti no_____ahorrar dinero? (interest)

7. Pepito, ¿qué_____en esa mano? (happen)

8. Este carro viejo_____siempre a mí. (stop)

9. Al camarero_____siempre los vasos. (fall/drop)

10. Después de pagar la cuenta_____un dólar a ella. (be left over)

B.   Form complete sentences, using the words in the order given. Add any necessary words. Use the Present Indicative.

1. nadie / gustar / cosas / malo /.

_____

2. tu / abuelos / encantar / comida / español /.

_____

3. alumnos / interesar / clases / serio /.

_____

4. mí / faltar / dos / dólar / de / cartera /.

_____

5. usted / no / gustar / nadar / en / mar /.

_____

6. A ella / parar / carro / en / Avenida 5 /.

_____

7. ti / caer / dos / billetes / de / 10 / dólar /.

_____

C.   Translate the following sentences.

1. My children like to listen to the radio.

_____.

2. That girl looks very pretty to me.

_____.

3. My hands hurt a lot today.

_____.

4. What's happening to you, my son?

_____.

5. My watch fell on the floor.

_____.

6. Your problems interest us.

_____.

7. This class is suitable for her.

_____.

GRAMMAR III   The Imperfect Indicative.

A.   Memorize the following chart:

SUBJECT	habl ar	com er	viv ir	ir	s er	v er
yo	habl aba	com ía	viv ía	iba	era	ve ía
nosotros -as	habl ábamos	com íamos	viv íamos	íbamos	éramos	ve íamos
tú	habl abas	com ías	viv ías	ibas	eras	ve ías
él/ella/Ud.	habl aba	com ía	viv ía	iba	era	ve ía
ellos/ellas/Uds.	habl aban	com ían	viv ían	iban	eran	ve ían

B.   Notice these features of the chart above:
1.   The stems of *hablar, comer,* and *vivir* are the same as for the Present and Preterite: *habl, com, viv.* But the endings are different: *-aba* for the *-AR* verbs, and *-ía* for the *-ER* and *-IR* verbs.
2.   All verbs are regular in the Imperfect except *ir, ser,* and *ver. Ir* has *iba* as the Imperfect tense, and *ser* has *era* which resembles the Present *eres. Ver* adds an *e* to the stem, so that it's *veía* rather than *vía.*
3.   Notice the accent on *-ía* in all the persons, and also the *acento* in the first person plural of all the verbs: *hablábamos, éramos, íbamos, vivíamos, veíamos.*
4.   The stem-changing verbs do not change the stem in the Imperfect. Compare the Present of *volver* with the Imperfect: *yo vuelvo/ volvía.* Stem-changing verbs like *pedir* change the stem in the Present and the Preterite but not in the Imperfect. Compare *yo pido* and *él pidió* with *yo pedía.*

C.   Basic use of the Imperfect:
The Imperfect is a *past* tense like the Preterite, but it is used in a different way. The Preterite indicates an entire action completed in the past, whereas the Imperfect shows the action *going on* in the past, with no reference to a beginning or an end. For this reason the Imperfect tense is usually translated by *was + (verb-ing)* in English. This will be explained further in the next lesson.

   Ex.:   Ella hablaba por teléfono cuando yo llegué. (she was talking on the phone when I arrived) Los aztecas comían maíz. (the Aztecs used to eat corn)

PRACTICE THE IMPERFECT

(Answers, p. 194)

1. The verbs ending in -*AR* take the ending_____for the Imperfect tense. For example, from *gustar* we say *Me*_____*ese presidente*.

2. The verbs ending in -*ER* and -*IR* have the same ending for the Imperfect: _____. For example, from *beber* and *vivir*, we have *Él*_____ and *Ella*_____.

3. *Ir* (to go) is irregular in the Imperfect; instead of *yo ía*, the correct form is *yo*_____.

4. *Ser* (to be) is also irregular. Remember *tú eres* in the Present. The Imperfect shows this same stem: yo_____,nosotros _____.

5. *Ver* (to see, watch) should be *yo vía* in the Imperfect. Instead we say *yo* _____.

6. All the persons with the ending *ía* need the *acento* to break up the diphthong as in *día*. Hablar *carries acento* only in_____, and *ir* carries the *acento* only in_____.

7. We have two tenses to refer to the past: the Preterite and the Imperfect. The Imperfect is used when we are referring to *an action*_____ *in the past*.

8. We use *hay* for *there is/are*. How do you say *there was/were* in the Imperfect?_____.

EXERCISES

(Answers, p. 194)

A. Fill the blanks with the Imperfect forms of the verbs.

1. Mis abuelos_____mucho dinero. (ahorrar)

2. Ella siempre_____los libros nuevos. (leer)

3. ¿Dónde_____(tú) cuando te llamé? (estar)

4. ¿Por qué Juanita no_____con sus amigas? (ir)

5. Mi esposa y yo_____españoles, pero ahora somos americanos. (ser)

6. Todos los bancos_____el por ciento de interés. (reducir)

7. ¿Cuánto_____el dólar en 1960? (valer)

8. Esa señora me_____magnífica para el Congreso. (parecer)

9. Los platos se me_____de las manos. (caer)

10. Juan y yo_____cuando tú llegaste. (nadar)

11. Mis hijos_____ese programa antes. (ver)

12. En la fiesta_____25 invitados. (haber)

B. Change the verbs from Present to Imperfect. Remember that irregular verbs in the Present are not necessarily irregular in the Imperfect. (Write only the verb.)

1. A ti te *conviene* este préstamo. _____

2. José *carga* todo en la tarjeta de crédito. _____

3. No *vale* la pena comenzar otro Vietnam. _____

4. Ustedes *encuentran* muchos errores. _____

5. Los niños *duermen* 8 horas todos los días. _____

6. ¿Cuánto te *falta* para pagar la cuenta? _____

7. Después de pagar la cuenta me *sobran* dos dó-lares. _____

8. ¿Dónde *metes* tu dinero, en el banco? _____

9. ¿Dónde *ve* usted esos programas terribles? _____

10. Camila y yo *vamos* a nadar en el mar. _____

11. Mi suegra se *queja* de todo. _____

12. Yo siempre *comienzo* a las 8:00 en punto. _____

13. ¿Qué *piensas* hacer con esos cheques de viajeros? _____

14. Esta mano me *duele* después de trabajar. _____

15. Yo siempre *tengo* que hacer la comida. _____

16. Ella siempre se *viste* muy elegante. _____

17. Muchos niños se *mueren* de hambre en África. _____

18. Yo no *conozco* a tu novia. _____

19. Esta mañana *hace* un sol estupendo. _____

20. *Hay* muchas personas en el banco esta mañana. _____

C. Crossword Puzzle (Crucigrama)

Across

2 Ponemos el dinero en la _____ .
9 Lola _____ Paco comieron langosta.
10 The opposite of *algo*
13 ¿A _____ te gusta nadar en el mar?
14 Imperfect of *ir*
15 Preterite of decir (él _____)
17 *They come in.*
19 Imperfect of *ser* (Uds. _____)
20 El camarero nos trajo el _____ .
21 ¿Quieres carne de res _____ carne de puerco?
22 Demonstrative adjective (fem.)
24 Present of *caer* (tú _____)
26 Siempre _____ detengo en la luz roja.
27 Possessive adjective

Down

1 Indefinite article
2 Woman who works in a bank
3 A nosotros nos gusta pagar _____ plazos.
5 Fuimos a la _____ para comprar verduras.
7 En la fiesta bailamos a los _____ modernos.
8 The opposite of *cierra*
11 Cuando Ud. se va, dice _____ .
12 Preterite of *dar* (yo _____)
16 A valuable metal
18 Creo que va a llover; hay muchas _____ .
22 Present of *ser*
23 Los ingleses toman mucho _____
25 ¿Cuándo vienen?? -Vamos _____ seguida.
26 Possessive adjective (Quiero presentarte a _____ familia.)

Lesson 10

En la estación del tren (At the Railroad Station)

andén	platform	**ida**	one-way ticket	**salida**	exit, departure
bar	bar	**litera**	berth	**salud**	health
boleto	ticket	**llegada**	arrival	**taquilla**	ticket window
calle (la)	street	**locomotora**	engine (train)	**taquillero**	ticket agent
coche	car, coach	**maletero**	porter	**tranvía (el)**[3]	trolley, train
cochecama (el)	sleeping car	**mapa (el)**	map	**tren**	train
cochecomedor	dining car	**milla**[2]	mile	**vacación**[4]	vacation
electrotrén	electric train	**parada**	stop	**vagón**	car, wagon
exprés[1]	express	**partida**	departure	**velocidad**	speed
ferrocarril	railroad	**propina**	tip ($)	**vía**	railroad
horario	schedule	**rapidez**	fastness	**vuelta**[5]	return, change ($)

confirmar	to confirm	**entregar**	to deliver	**olvidar**[6]	to forget
correr	to run	**funcionar**	to work, function	**perder (ie)**	to lose, miss
cruzar	to cross	**informar**	to inform	**reservar**	to reserve
demorar	to delay	**mandar**	to send, order	**romper**	to break

descontento	discontent	**fácil**	easy	**ocupado**	busy
desocupado	free, vacant	**gratis**[7]	free ($)	**rápido**	fast
difícil	difficult	**limpio**	clean	**roto**	broken
eléctrico	electric	**lento**	slow	**sucio**	dirty
entero	all, entire	**medio**[8]	half, average	**vacío**	empty

a mediodía	at noon	**hacer la maleta**	to pack the suitcase
deshacer la maleta	to unpack the suitcase	**ida y vuelta**	roundtrip

159

despacio	slowly	**millas por hora**	miles per hour
en medio de	in the middle of	**sin falta**	without fail
estar de vacaciones	to be on vacation	**tomar una copa**	to have a drink
hacer caso	to pay attention	**tomar el _pelo_[9]**	to pull one's leg

NOTES:

1. _Exprés_ is used less frequently today than _rápido,_ the fastest train in Spain. Usually the train is called by the city of its destination: _el rápido de León, el rápido de Bilbao,_ etc.

2. _Milla_ is approximately 1.6 kilometers. _Metro_ is a little bigger than a _yard._

3. _Tranvía_ is the old streetcar, which has disappeared and been replaced by _autobuses_ (buses). But _tranvía_ is still used to refer to a kind of train that travels rather short distances and stops at every station, for example from Madrid to Valladolid. Notice that we say _el tranvía_ and _el cochecama_ with the _masculine_ article _el._ In general, all compound nouns are masculine. Remember _el paraguas_ (umbrella).

4. _Vacación_ is rarely used in the singular; usually it's in the plural _(vacaciones)._

5. _Vuelta_ is _return_—and also _change_ when we talk about money (the money they _return_ to you after you pay). _Dar una vuelta_ is _to go for a ride or walk._

6. _Olvidar_ is _to forget,_ as is _olvidarse de._ Notice that when it is used as a reflexive verb, it requires _de._
   Ex.: _Me olvidé de la llave._ (I forgot the key)

7. _Gratis_ as well as _gratuito -a_ means _free_ when we're talking about money, but not when we refer to _freedom_ (libertad) or when we mean _vacant,_ which is _desocupado._

8. _Medio -a_ is _half,_—for example in _compré medio kilo_ (I bought a half kilo). When it is used with another number, it doesn't follow the number directly, but rather the thing you buy; For example, _Compré dos kilos y medio._ (I bought _two and a half_ kilos).

9. _Pelo_ means _hair. Tomar el pelo_ is an idiomatic expression: _to pull one's leg._

EXERCISES

(Answers, p. 194)

A.   Write _el, la, los,_ or _las_ before the following nouns.

1. ____ bar
2. ____ andén
3. ____ calles
4. ____ exprés
5. ____ velocidad

6. ____ vías
7. ____ vagón
8. ____ rapidez
9. ____ trenes
10. ____ mapa

11. ____ vacaciones
12. ____ ferrocarril
13. ____ cochecamas
14. ____ electrotrén
15. ____ andenes

16. ____ estación
17. ____ tranvía
18. ____ salud
19. ____ expreses
20. ____ cochecomedor

B.   Complete the sentences with a word or expression from the box below.

horario	a mediodía	exprés
salud	andén	taquilla
ida y vuelta	sin falta	bar
parada	hacer caso	milla
despacio	en medio de	litera

1. Este tren tiene _____ en todas las estaciones.

2. Si quieres dormir en el tren, tienes que comprar un billete con _____

   _____.

3. Vamos a la _____ a comprar los boletos.

4. Hay que tomar el electrotrén en el _____ número 8.

5. Para muchas personas, el dinero es más importante que la _____

   _____.

6. Una _____ tiene un poco más de un km. y medio.

7. Aquí está el _____ con todos los trenes que salen
   de Madrid.

8. Todavía no llega el tren en media hora. Vamos a tomar una copa al____

   _____.

9. Antes de entrar a la estación, el tren va muy _____.

10. Si quiere Ud. llegar pronto, debe tomar el _____.

11. Si tengo que ir y volver necesito billete de _____.

12. Si no quiere perder el tren, debe estar en el andén a las 8:00 de la mañana

   _____.

13. El carro se me rompió _____ la calle.

14. El taquillero almuerza _____ todos los días.

15. Ahí dice "No fumar", pero nadie le _____.

C.   Write a synonym for each of the following. Be sure to include articles *el/la* with the nouns.

1. el boleto_____   3. el vagón_____

2. la partida_____   4. todo_____

5. la vía_____   7. gratuito_____
6. el rápido_____   8. olvidarse de_____

D.   Write the opposite of these words.

1. la salida_____   8. ocupado_____
2. la ida_____   9. lento_____
3. la enfermedad_____   10. ganar_____
4. a medianoche_____   11. contento_____
5. sucio_____   12. medio_____
6. lleno_____   13. hacer_____
7. fácil_____   14. encontrar_____

E.   Fill the blanks with one of the following verbs in the Preterite.

| correr | mandar | perder | mandar | informar | hacer caso |
| cruzar | olvidar | romper | demorar | funcionar | tomar el pelo |

1. Mi abuela me_____un giro postal de treinta dólares.

2. Por supuesto. Yo_____la calle cuando no había tráfico.

3. El tranvía_____tres horas entre Madrid y Ávila.

4. El vaso se me cayó, y_____me_____.

5. Mis amigos_____mucho dinero en Las Vegas.

6. Sí, ahí estaba el anuncio; pero nadie le_____.

7. Ellos me_____la factura por *correo* (mail).

8. No tengo el mapa porque_____me_____en casa.

9. Eso no es verdad. ¡Ud. me_____!

10. Este electrotrén_____95 kilómetros por hora.

11. José nos_____que su novia está enferma.

12. El elevador no_____y tuvimos que bajar por la escalera.

F. Go back to the sentences in Exercise *E* and change the verbs from the Preterite to the Imperfect.

1._____ 5._____ 9._____

2._____ 6._____ 10._____

3._____ 7._____ 11._____

4._____ 8._____ 12._____

Dɪᴀ́ʟᴏɢᴏ   *Un americano en la estación de ferrocarril*

(Un turista americano habla con el taquillero de la estación de trenes de Chamartín en Madrid.)

Tᴀǫᴜɪʟʟᴇʀᴏ:	Buenas tardes. ¿Desea algo?
Aᴍᴇʀɪᴄᴀɴᴏ:	Tengo que ir a Santander y necesito información sobre los trenes.
Tᴀǫᴜɪʟʟᴇʀᴏ:	Ud. Puede tomar diferentes trenes. Tenemos el exprés, el electrotrén y el tranvía. ¿Cuál prefiere Ud.?
Aᴍᴇʀɪᴄᴀɴᴏ:	¿Cuál es el más rápido?
Tᴀǫᴜɪʟʟᴇʀᴏ:	El electrotrén. Solamente tiene parada en las ciudades grandes.
Aᴍᴇʀɪᴄᴀɴᴏ:	¿Cuánto tiempo se demora en llegar?
Tᴀǫᴜɪʟʟᴇʀᴏ:	Cinco horas y media. La velocidad media es 90 kilómetros por hora.
Aᴍᴇʀɪᴄᴀɴᴏ:	¿Tiene cochecomedor y literas?
Tᴀǫᴜɪʟʟᴇʀᴏ:	No, solamente un bar pequeño.
Aᴍᴇʀɪᴄᴀɴᴏ:	Bueno. Quiero un boleto de ida a Santander en la sección de no fumar.
Tᴀǫᴜɪʟʟᴇʀᴏ:	Aquí todo el mundo puede fumar en todas partes. Esto no es América.
Aᴍᴇʀɪᴄᴀɴᴏ:	Ud. me toma el pelo. ¿Por qué ese anuncio que veo en todas partes en esta estación "Tabaco o salud: Decide"?
Tᴀǫᴜɪʟʟᴇʀᴏ:	Bueno. Ésas son cosas del Ministerio de Salud. Nadie hace caso.
Aᴍᴇʀɪᴄᴀɴᴏ:	No entiendo. . . . ¿Cuánto es el billete?
Tᴀǫᴜɪʟʟᴇʀᴏ:	Aquí tiene. Son 2,800 pesetas.
Aᴍᴇʀɪᴄᴀɴᴏ:	Muy agradecido. Adiós.

DIALOG   *An American at the Railroad Station*

(An American tourist is talking to the ticket agent at the Chamartín train station in Madrid.)

AGENT: Good afternoon. May I help you?
AMERICAN: I have to go to Santander and I need information about the trains.
AGENT: You can take several trains. We have the express, the electric train, and the "tranvía." Which one do you prefer?
AMERICAN: Which is the fastest?
AGENT: The electric train. It stops only in the large cities.
AMERICAN: How long does it take to get there?
AGENT: Five and a half hours. The average speed is 90 kilometers an hour.
AMERICAN: Does it have a dining car and berths?
AGENT: No, it has only a small bar.
AMERICAN: O.K. I want a one-way ticket to Santander in the non-smoking section.
AGENT: Here everybody can smoke everywhere. This isn't America.
AMERICAN: You're pulling my leg. Why that ad that I see all over this station: "Tobacco or health: You decide"?
AGENT: Well, those are things from the Department of Health. Nobody pays any attention.
AMERICAN: I don't understand. . . . How much is the ticket?
AGENT: Here it is. The ticket is 2.800 pesetas.
AMERICAN: Thanks a lot. Goodbye.

EXERCISES

(Answers, p. 195)

A. Fill in the blanks with an appropriate word to make a summary of the dialog.

El turista americano habla con el (1)_____de la estación

de la ciudad de (2)_____ . El turista quiere (3)_____

_____a Santander, y le pide (4)_____sobre

los trenes. El taquillero le informa que el tren más (5)_____

es el electrotrén, porque solamente tiene (6)_____en las

ciudades grandes. Este tren (7)_____cinco

horas y media para llegar a Santander, a una velocidad (8)_____

de 90 Kms. por hora. El electrotrén no tiene comedor ni (9)_____

_____, pero tiene un pequeño (10)_____ . El americano

compra un billete de (11)_____, y lo quiere en la sección de (12)_____

_____. Pero en los trenes españoles no hay (13)

_____de fumar y no-fumar. El americano

piensa que el taquillero le toma (14)_____porque en

la estación hay muchos (15)_____que dicen: "TABACO o

(16)_____: DECIDE." El anuncio está en español y es

para los españoles, pero éstos no le (17)_____ .

El americano paga el billete que vale (18)_____pesetas.

B. Write True (T) or False (F).

1.___ Una milla es más pequeña que un kilómetro.

2.___ El tren tranvía es más lento que el tren exprés.

3.___ El ministerio de salud puso anuncios contra el tabaco.

4.___ Si Ud. quiere dormir en el tren, pide un boleto de ida y vuelta.

5.___ Para saber la hora de partida y llegada de trenes leemos el horario.

6.___ El electrotrén corre más rápido que el tranvía.

7.___ Damos una propina al maletero porque nos lleva el equipaje.

8.___ Ud. debe cruzar la calle en contra de la luz roja.

9.___ Ella se sentó donde encontró un asiento ocupado.

10.___ La locomotora eléctrica lleva todo el tren por el ferrocarril.

11.___ El taquillero vende diferentes clases de trenes.

12.___ Si el tren está roto, no puede funcionar.

13.___ El taquillero sube y baja las maletas de los trenes al andén.

14.___ Cuando Ud. no tiene que pagar nada, es gratuito.

C. Complete the sentences with an appropriate word or expression.

1. Aprender bien una lengua no es_____; al contrario, es

bastante_____ .

2. Eso no es verdad. Tú me_____ .

3. Si no hay nadie en esta casa, la casa está_____ .

4. Alguien rompió la ventana; está_____ .

5. Esos americanos son turistas; están de_____.

6. No puedo hablar con ella ahora porque estoy muy_____.

7. Fuimos al mercado y compramos dos kilos y_____de carne de res.

8. Ya le dije que fumar es malo, pero él nunca me_____.

9. Antes de llegar al STOP con mi carro, siempre voy muy_____.

10. Si el camarero nos da buen servicio, le dejamos una_____.

11. Por favor, tienes que llegar a las 2:00 sin_____.

12. Ud. no tiene que pagar nada para entrar a verlo; es_____

_____.

D. Write complete sentences, using the Imperfect tense only. Add any necessary words, and don't forget the Indirect Object if needed.

1. mi / esposa / deshacer / maletas / después / viaje /.

_____

2. su / tíos / siempre / mandar / dinero / a él /.

_____

3. niños / hacer caso / nadie / en / fiesta /.

_____

4. carro / viejo / siempre / romper / a mí /.

_____

5. todo / días / parar / carro / a ella /.

_____

6. Carlos / gustar / libros / americano / de ficción /.

_____

GRAMMAR I   Preterite and Imperfect in contrast.

A. Use of the Preterite:
There are two tenses in the Indicative to refer to an action in the past: the Preterite and the Imperfect. In order to understand the

difference, we must think of an action as having three consecutive stages or aspects: *beginning, middle* and *end.* We use the Preterite to mark the beginning or end of an action, or to show the whole action as a completed event. Look at the examples:

1. Ayer *comimos* a las 8. (yesterday we *ate* at 8) (emphasis on the *beginning:* we started to eat)
2. Julia *llegó* a las 8. (Julia *arrived* at 8) (emphasis on the *end:* no action after 8)
3. José *vivió* en Chile. (Joe *lived* in Chile) (the whole action is completed in the past)

B. Uses of the Imperfect:
The Imperfect shows the middle of the action, the event in progress, without saying anything about the beginning or end. The English progressive form *was + verb-ing* translates the Imperfect. Consider the Imperfect as a sense that shows an action in its middle stage, and look at some specific examples of its use.

  Ex.: Cuando llegué, él *no estaba* allí. (when I arrived, he *wasn't* there)
  (my arrival [end] occurred in the *midst* of his not being there)

  Trabajaba en la escuela en ese tiempo. (I *was working* at the school . . .)
  (I was in the *midst* of working there at some past time)

1. *Habit.* We use the Imperfect to indicate a habit in the past, since a habit is an action that occurs repeatedly as if there were no beginning or end.
  Ex.: Mi tío fumaba mucho. (my uncle used to smoke a lot)

2. *Description.* To describe persons, things, places, etc., in the past, we use the Imperfect, even when the situation no longer exists.
  Ex.: El pueblo estaba cerca de la playa. (the village was near the beach)
  Los indios vivían en la montaña, tenían su religión y eran felices.
  (the Indians lived in the mountains, had their religion, and were happy)

3. *Time and age.* To tell time and age with *ser* and *tener* respectively, the Imperfect must be used. The Preterite cannot be used in these instances, perhaps because time is always in the *middle* of its course, and cannot be stopped.
  Ex.: Cuando entré eran las 12. (it was 12 o'clock when I came in)
  Cuando murió tenía 70 años. (he was seventy when he died)

PRACTICE THE PRETERITE AND THE IMPERFECT

(Answers, p. 196)

1. An action has three stages or aspects: beginning,_____, and_____.

2. The word *imperfect* suggests that something was going on, but is as yet incomplete, unfinished. Actually, the Imperfect shows the_____ of an action, without reference to its beginning or end.

3. The Preterite shows the action as *whole* upon completion, but this tense often emphasizes either the_____or the_____ _____of the action. For example, *Cenamos a las siete* shows clearly that seven o'clock is only the *beginning* of supper, whereas *Llegamos a las siete* shows the *end,* since there is no more action after seven.

4. To describe places, people, things in the past, we use the_____ _____because a description doesn't seem to have limits.

   Ex.: *Roma*_____(was) *una ciudad grande y*_____ (had) *monumentos muy bellos.*

5. A habit is something unfinished and suggests repetition, as if it were always in a middle stage. For this reason we use the_____ for a habit in the past. Ex.: *Mi abuelo*_____ pero no_____. (fumar/beber)

6. To tell time in the past, do we use the Imperfect or the Preterite?_____ _____. This is perhaps because time has no limits, it cannot be stopped. Ex.: *Cuando llegué a casa ya*_____*las tres de la mañana.*

7. To tell someone's age with *tener,* do we use the Imperfect or the Preterite? _____. Ex.: *Ella*_____ *24 años cuando se casó.*

8. The progressive form, as in *I was working,* shows the ongoing nature of the action. Is it translated better by the Imperfect or by the Preterite?_____ _____.

9. The ending *-ed* as in *I walked* usually suggests the completion of an action. Is it translated better by the Imperfect or by the Preterite?_____ _____.

10. Very often the Imperfect indicates the *background* for the Preterite—that is, to show an action that continued in the background (Imperfect) when something else happened (Preterite). For example, *Carmen* _____ por la calle cuando_____el accidente. (ir/tener) (Carmen was going down the street when she had the accident.)

EXERCISES

(Answers, p. 196)

A. Use the cues in parentheses to answer these questions in the Preterite or Imperfect.

1. ¿Dónde *vivía* su familia cuando Ud. *nació*? (Kansas)

   _____

2. ¿Cuántos años *tenía* su abuelo cuando *murió*? (80)

   _____

3. ¿Qué hora *era* cuando *llegaron* los tíos? (3:00)

   _____

4. ¿Quién *llamó* cuando yo *estaba* en el jardín? (Estela)

   _____

5. ¿Qué le *pasó* a tu hermano cuando se *cayó*? (nada)

   _____

6. ¿A quién *vio* Ud. cuando *abrió* la ventana? (nadie)

   _____

B. Complete the sentences, using the Imperfect or the Preterite. (Remember: the Imperfect is like the background of a picture and the Preterite, the foreground.)

1. A la medianoche me_____a dormir porque_____

   _____sueño. (ir/tener)

2. Mi esposa_____en la cocina cuando el teléfono_____

   _____. (estar/sonar)

3. Cuando nosotros_____en Canadá,_____

   _____buenos amigos. (vivir/hacer)

4. Cuando el turista _____ a la taquilla, _____
   un boleto de ida y vuelta. (llegar/pedir)

5. El doctor me _____ que mi padre _____
   buena salud. (decir/tener)

6. El tren _____ por la estación pero no se _____
   _____ . (pasar/parar)

7. El taquillero siempre _____ a mediodía, y
   después se _____ un cigarrillo. (almorzar/fumar)

8. Ayer Uds. no _____ su coche porque _____
   _____ roto. (traer/estar)

C. **Complete the story with the Preterite or Imperfect of the verbs given. Read through the entire paragraph first to get an understanding of the story; that will help you determine the correct tense.**

Cuando Josefina y yo (1. llegar) ayer al hotel, ya (2. ser) las 11:30 de la noche. Nosotras (3. estar) muy *cansadas* (tired) del viaje, y nos (4. acostar) enseguida. Esta mañana nos (5. despertar) temprano, y (6. tener) un desayuno delicioso. El día (7. estar) nublado, pero (8. hacer) mucho calor. Nosotras (9. tomar) un autobús para ir de compras al *centro* (downtown). Después de varias horas de compras y de andar, (10. estar) muy cansadas y con mucha hambre, y (11. almorzar) en el restaurante *Los Caracoles* (The Snails). *Mientras* (While) (12. almorzar) en el restaurante, (13. comenzar) a llover y (14. tener) que volver al hotel en taxi. El taxista nos (15. llevar) por unas calles muy antiguas donde (16. haber) tiendas pequeñas, templos antiguos y muchas personas con paraguas. Después de llegar al hotel nos (17. poner) a dormir la siesta hasta las seis de la tarde.

1. _____   7. _____   13. _____

2. _____   8. _____   14. _____

3. _____   9. _____   15. _____

4. _____   10. _____   16. _____

5. _____   11. _____   17. _____

6. _____   12. _____

GRAMMAR II   **Hacer** + *time* (time ago). **Llevar** + *time* (to be).

A.   (1) *Hace 3 años que* vivo aquí.
     (2) Vivo aquí *hace 3 años.*   I have been living here *for 3 years.*
     (3) Vivo aquí *desde hace 3 años.*

We use **hace** + **time** + **que** + **main verb** in the Present, as in (1), to indicate the *duration* of an action up to the present time. Notice that *que* disappears, as in (2), when the main verb precedes *hace*. *Desde,* as in (3), can be added or omitted.

B.   (1) *Hace un mes que* fui a Chile.   I went to Chile *a month ago.*
     (2) Fui a Chile *hace un mes.*

We use **hace** + **time** + **que** + **main verb** in the Preterite to indicate the time *elapsed* between an action carried out in the past and the present time. *Que* is omitted, as in (2), when the expression *hace* + *time* follows the main verb.

C.   (1) *Hacía una hora que* llovía.
     (2) Llovía *hacía una hora.*   It had been raining *for one hour.*
     (3) Llovía *desde hacía una hora.*

The Imperfect **hacía** + **time** combines only with another Imperfect in the main verb. Notice that if we put *hacía* + *time* after the verb, the word *que* is omitted, as in (2), and in this case we can add *desde* as in (3), but it's not obligatory.

D.   **Llevar** + **time** is used without any other verb to indicate how long a person or a thing has been in a place. The preposition *de* is added if a job or a condition is added: *de secretario, de casado,* etc.
     Ex.: Mis padres *llevan* 20 años *de* casados.
           Llevo una hora en la oficina = *Hace una hora que* estoy en la oficina.

(Later on we will see that this verb can be combined with a participle or an infinitive.)

PRACTICE THE IDIOMS   *(Answers, p. 196)*

1. *Hace* + *time* can be placed before or after the main verb. For example, another way to say *Hace un mes que llegué* is_____

   _____.

2. In the sentence *No te veo desde hace un año,* the word_____
   can be omitted without change of meaning.

3. *Hace una hora se fue* is incorrect; the word _____ is necessary before the main verb, *se fue*.

4. The expression *hacía + time* requires the main verb to be in the _____ _____ tense. For example, *Hacía media hora que* _____ _____.(comer)

5. *Hacía dos días no trabajaba* is incorrect; the word_____ is missing before the main verb *no trabajaba*.

6. Another way to say *No trabajaba hacía 2 meses.* is_____ _____.

7. *Llevar + time* is another way to convey the idea of being in a place. Therefore we can say *Hace diez minutos que estoy aquí,* or_____ _____.

EXERCISES

(Answers, p. 196)

A. The following questions are directed to you. To answer them, use the cues given.

1. ¿Cuánto tiempo hace que usted vive aquí? (cinco años)

_____

2. ¿Cuánto tiempo hace que Ud. viajó a Panamá? (ocho años)

_____

3. ¿Cuánto tiempo hace que Ud. toca el piano? (media hora)

_____

4. ¿Cuántos años hace que Ud. salió de España? (veinte años)

_____

5. ¿Cuántos días hace que Ud. no viaja en tren? (una semana)

_____

6. ¿Cuánto tiempo hacía que no llovía aquí? (dos meses)

_____

7. ¿Cuánto tiempo hacía que Ud. hablaba por teléfono? (diez minutos)

_____

8. ¿Cuánto tiempo hacía que Ud. vivía en Cuba? (cuatro años)

_____

B.   Rewrite the sentences, changing the position of *hace* or *hacía* in the sentence. Remember that *desde* is optional.

1. Hace mil años que murió el Cid.

_____

2. Hacía un año que no llovía.

_____

3. Mi amiga se fue hace doce años.

_____

4. Tú fumas desde hace veinte años.

_____

5. Hace cinco minutos que pasó el tren.

_____

6. Tu amigo trabajó en esta taquilla hace unos tres años.

_____

7. Saqué los billetes hace una hora.

_____

8. Hacía veinte minutos que hablaba por teléfono.

_____

9. Llevo aquí ya diez años.

_____

10. Kennedy llevaba tres años de Presidente cuando murió.

_____

GRAMMAR III   Ordinal Numbers, Days of the Week, Seasons, and Months of the Year.

A.   These are the ten ordinal numbers in Spanish. They agree in gender and number with the noun. After 10 we use ordinary, or cardinal, numbers: *once, doce, trece, veinte,* etc.

| 1st **primero** | 3rd **tercero** | 5th **quinto** | 7th **séptimo** | 9th **noveno** |
| 2nd **segundo** | 4th **cuarto** | 6th **sexto** | 8th **octavo** | 10th **decimo** |

1. *Primero* and *tercero* drop the *-o* when they precede a masculine noun.

   Ex.: Estamos en el *primer* piso, no en el *tercero*.

2. The ordinal numbers can precede or follow the noun without change of meaning.

   Ex.: Vivo en la *calle décima.*/Vivo en la *décima calle.*

3. To show the order of kings, queens, popes, etc., we use ordinal numbers after the noun, omitting the definite article.

   Ex.: La reina Isabel Segunda (Queen Elizabeth The Second)
   Felipe Segundo fue rey de España. (Philip The Second was king of Spain)

B. The seven days of the week are not capitalized in Spanish. Note that the five weekdays end in the letter *-s* and the two weekend days end in *-o*.

lunes	(Monday)	**martes**	(Tuesday)
miércoles	(Wednesday)	**jueves**	(Thursday)
viernes	(Friday)	**sábado**	(Saturday)
domingo	(Sunday)		

We don't translate *on* in expressions such as *on Monday, on Sundays,* etc., but we use the definite articles *el/los.*

   Ex.: José llegó *el lunes.*   No trabajo *los lunes.*

C. The four seasons of the year are:

| **primavera** | (spring) | **verano** | (summer) |
| **otoño** | (fall) | **invierno** | (winter) |

D. Memorize the months of the year:

enero	**abril**	**julio**	**octubre**
febrero	**mayo**	**agosto**	**noviembre**
marzo	**junio**	**septiembre**	**diciembre**

1. The months are capitalized at the beginning of a letter, a memo, a bill, etc., but they are not capitalized in a narrative.
   Ex.: Se fue el dos de enero.

2. When giving the date, we use cardinal numbers for the days of the month with the article *el* if *día* is omitted. Notice that in English the ordinals are used.
   Ex.: Hoy es el (día) 12 de marzo. (today is march [the] twelfth)

3. The only ordinal ever used for the days of the month is *primero*, and even in this case, *uno* is used as much as *primero: Hoy es el primero/el uno de enero.*

PRACTICE YOUR GRAMMAR (Answers, p. 197)

1. The ordinal numbers are adjectives with four endings; they change in gender and _____ according to the noun.
   Ex.: libro *primero,* mesa _____ .

2. The two numerals that drop the ending *-o* are *primero* and _____ .
   When is the ending dropped, before or after the masculine noun? _____
   _____ .

3. The ordinal numbers can be placed before or _____
   the noun they modify. Ex.: *los primeros días* is the same as _____
   _____ .

4. *Carlos el Primero* is not correct for *Charles The First.* It should be _____
   _____ , because we don't use the article in Spanish.

5. Do we capitalize the days of the week in Spanish in a narrative? _____ .
   Do we capitalize the months of the year in the headline of a letter or bill? _____ .

6. *La primavera* starts *el* ____ *de marzo* and ends _____ .

7. *El invierno* starts *el* ____ *de diciembre* and ends _____ .

8. *El otoño* starts *el* ____ *de septiembre* and ends _____ .

9. *El* _____ is the coldest season of the year, and *el*
   _____ is the hottest season.

10. The first month of the year is _____ , and the shortest
    month is _____ .

11. We celebrate the Independence of the U.S. in the month of_____,
    and Christmas falls in the month of_____.

12. There are two ways to say the *first* of the month:_____
    _____.

13. Do you translate *on* in expressions such as *on Monday*?_____. Instead
    we use the definite article_____. How do you say *On Saturdays*?
    _____.

EXERCISES   *(Answers, p. 197)*

A.   Complete the sentences with an appropriate word.

1. Después de septiembre viene el mes de_____,
   y después del mes de abril viene el mes de_____.

2. Los tres meses de primavera son_____.

3. Si hoy es el primero de enero, mañana es_____
   _____.

4. Si hoy es el 28 de febrero, mañana es el_____.

5. En Estados Unidos celebramos la Independencia el_____
   _____.

6. Celebramos la fiesta de *Navidad* (Christmas) el_____
   _____.

7. Celebramos el Año Nuevo el día_____.

8. La fiesta de Thanksgiving, ¿qué día de la semana es?_____.

9. ¿Cuál es la estación más fría del año en Norteamérica?_____
   _____.

10. ¿Cuál es la estación de más calor en Estados Unidos?_____
    _____.

11. ¿Cómo dice Ud. *Elizabeth The Second* en español?_____
    _____.

12. ¿Cuál es el primer mes del año?_____.

13. ¿Vive Ud. en el primer piso o en el segundo?_____

_____ .

14. Después del piso *quinto* viene el piso_____, y después

del piso *séptimo* viene el piso_____ .

15. La calle próxima a la calle *novena* es la calle_____ .

La calle que está antes de la calle *veinte* es la calle_____ .

B. Write sentences using the words in the order given. Make the necessary changes and add words when needed. Use the Present.

1. mí / gustar / primavera / y / verano /.

_____

2. Emilio / vivir / en / 8 / calle /.

_____

3. Uds. / viajar / México / 12 / junio /.

_____

4. Nosotros / tener / vacación / 1 / abril /.

_____

5. hoy / ser / lunes, / 8 / septiembre /.

_____

C. Translate the following sentences.

1. I bought the tickets on Tuesday.

_____

2. We like the Fourth of July.

_____

3. Spring goes from March 21st to June 21st.

_____

4. Henry (Enrique) the Eighth had eight wives.

_____

5. Today is November the second.

_____

REVIEW EXAM FOR LESSONS 6–10

PART I VOCABULARY

(Answers, p. 198)

A. Match the two columns. Cross out the article where it is not needed.

1. ____ el sobrino   A. María cocinó . . . para tu cumpleaños.

2. ____ el sillón   B. El dinero de . . . en otro, se llama divisas.

3. ____ el tejado   C. Un tiempo corto; unos minutos; unas horas.

4. ____ la cama   D. No pude ir a la fiesta por . . . .

5. ____ el jabón   E. Voy a comer una ensalada de lechuga y . . . .

6. ____ la llave   F. Una vaca joven es . . . .

7. ____ el botones   G. Ayer comimos . . . de puerco.

8. ____ la escalera   H. También se llama botana, bocadillo, antojito, tapa.

9. ____ el arroz   I. Es uno de los productos de la leche.

10. ____ el resfriado   J. Mueble para sentarse.

11. ____ el entremés   K. Si está roto el ascensor, subimos por . . . .

12. ____ el rato   L. El hijo de mi hermana es mi . . . .

13. ____ el país   M. Nos bañamos con agua y . . . .

14. ____ la torta   N. Me gusta mucho . . . con pollo.

15. ____ la ternera   O. Abrimos y cerramos la puerta con . . . .

16. ____ el queso   P. Mueble para dormir.

17. ____ el pepino   Q. La parte más alta de la casa es . . . .

18. ____ la chuleta   R. El mozo que lleva las maletas a los cuartos.

B. One of the four choices given is the best; underline it.

19. Si Ud. no quiere perder el tren, debe ir enseguida (al maletero, al andén, a la propina, al horario).

20. Si Ud. desea dormir bien en el viaje, es mejor tomar (una vuelta, una vacación, un exprés, una litera).

21. Para escribir cheques Ud. necesita (una cuenta corriente, un préstamo a plazos, un giro postal, un presupuesto grande).

22. Si usted no tiene dinero ahora, puede pagarnos (al contado, sin falta, a plazos, al por ciento).

23. Si Ud. trabaja para una tienda, Ud. cobra (una hipoteca, un sueldo, un préstamo, un interés).

24. La carne más tierna y sabrosa es (el pescado, el cerdo, el solomillo, la res).

25. Hay muchas clases de vino (tinto, picante, lleno, asado).

26. En el pastel de cumpleaños de Josefina pusimos veintiuna (zanahorias, copas, velas, divisas).

27. Me gusta mi habitación porque (da a, trata de, deja de, entra a) la calle.

28. No me gustan las zanahorias porque son (amarillas, color café, muy rojas, color naranja).

C. Write the word that is the opposite of the one given.

29. lleno_____, fuerte_____

30. sucio_____, difícil_____

31. rápido_____, ancho_____

32. disponible_____, doble_____

33. abrir_____, gracioso_____

34. gastar_____, entrar_____

35. apagar_____, ganar_____

D. Complete the sentences with the correct word.

36. Si el camarero nos da buen servicio, le dejamos_____

    _____ .

37. Cuando hace calor en el verano vamos al mar para bañarnos y_____

    _____ .

38. Una casa vale mucho dinero. Para comprarla necesitamos_____

    _____ .

39. Por la mañana me gusta tomar un vaso de_____ de tomate.

40. Los hijos de mis hijos son mis_____ .

41. La semana pasada hizo frío, y las montañas tienen mucha_____ para *esquiar* (ski).

42. Después de bañarme, me *seco* (dry) con_____.

43. El atún, la sardina, el salmón no son carnes *sino* (but)_____.

E.   One of the four answers is the best; circle the letter.

44. A mí me encantan las verduras frescas sin excepción.
    - A. Sí, ya veo que no puede ver el maíz.
    - B. Sí, muchas verduras saben a chocolate.
    - C. Sí, algunos creen que son más saludables que la carne.
    - D. Sí, ya veo que estás a dieta hace un mes.

45. El taquillero dice que el tranvía se demora mucho tiempo.
    - A. Claro; tiene parada en todas las estaciones.
    - B. Tiene razón; ese tren corre 90 millas por hora.
    - C. Por supuesto; ese hombre no hace caso a nadie.
    - D. ¡Cómo no! Este tren siempre nos toma el pelo.

46. ¿Quieres comprar ese carro el lunes que viene sin falta?
    - A. Sí, es un carro valioso y de lujo.
    - B. A propósito; cobran un 20 por ciento de interés.
    - C. No, no me conviene abrir una cuenta de ahorros.
    - D. ¡Ni modo! Me faltan dos cosas: dinero y crédito.

47. Estas chuletas de cordero tienen muy buena pinta.
    - A. Sí, aquí la carne de res siempre es buena.
    - B. Por supuesto; el pescado en este mercado es excelente.
    - C. Tienes razón; me parecen muy frescas y con poca grasa.
    - D. Es verdad. Esta carne siempre tiene muchas calorías.

48. ¿Por qué se puso usted a merendar cuando se levantó de la siesta?
    - A. Porque era ya mediodía.
    - B. Porque me encanta jugar a menudo.
    - C. Porque acababa de desayunar.
    - D. Porque tenía un hambre terrible.

49. Te mereces un buen pastel porque cumples veinte años.
    - A. Sí, no puedo creer que comencé la universidad hace dos años.
    - B. No, el cumpleaños de mi hermana no es hasta mañana.
    - C. No, los mariachis ya tocaron en la fiesta.
    - D. Sí, pero mi cumpleaños fue hace dos años.

50. Usted tuvo mucho éxito en la venta de su casa.
    - A. Con mucho gusto. Voy a salir enseguida.
    - B. Sí, tuve suerte en venderla enseguida.
    - C. Aquí tiene la llave. La salida está allí.
    - D. Sí, el pagar impuestos no vale la pena.

PART II GRAMMAR   *(Answers, p. 198)*

A. **Complete the sentences with the correct forms of the Preterite.**

1. Cuando _____ me fui a dormir. (be sleepy)

2. El domingo pasado _____ y fuimos a las montañas. (be sunny)

3. Cuando ella _____ se bebió una cerveza. (be thirsty)

4. Ayer me puse mucha ropa porque _____. (be very cold)

5. Ellos no _____ dormir en toda la noche. (can)

6. Los niños _____ mucho en la fiesta. (have fun)

7. No puedes quejarte; yo _____ a las 3 en punto. (arrive)

8. Mi padre _____ ir también, pero no _____. (want/can)

9. Nuestra prima _____ otra botella de champán. (ask for)

10. Pepe _____ enfermo y _____ a casa. (feel/go)

11. Esta mañana no _____ porque no tuve tiempo. (shave)

12. Yo no sé cómo ella _____ en diez minutos. (get dressed)

13. Mi hijo _____ el violín y yo _____ el piano. (play)

14. ¿Por qué _____ Uds. estos entremeses tan sabrosos? (bring)

15. La semana pasada _____ una fiesta en casa de los Arana. (there was)

B. **In the following story, change the verbs from present to past. You will have to decide between the Preterite and the Imperfect. (Write the answers below.)**

Carlitos (16) *se levanta* temprano esta mañana porque (17) *quiere* desayunar bien antes de ir al colegio. Su madre ya (18) *está* en la cocina cuando él (19) *va* a buscar café. Primero él (20) *se baña* con agua y jabón, pero no (21) *se seca* bien el pelo hasta después del desayuno. Como (22) *tiene* mucha hambre, (23) *se come* dos huevos, jamón, tostadas y mermelada. Le (24) *dice* a su mamá que no (25) *duerme* muy bien esa noche porque (26) *sueña* en cosas muy difíciles en los exámenes del colegio. . . . Esta mañana (27) *anda* al colegio porque (28) *tiene* la *bicicleta* (bicycle) rota. (29) *Hace* un día estupendo para caminar y no (30) *hay* una sola nube en el *cielo* (sky) . . . .

16._____ 24._____

17._____ 25._____

18._____ 26._____

19._____ 27._____

20._____ 28._____

21._____ 29._____

22._____ 30._____

23._____

C.   Select the best answer and circle the letter.

31. El supermercado de la ciudad no . . . lejos del hotel.
    A. había   C. tenía
    B. estaba   D. hacía

32. Me gusta mucho más este tren que . . . porque es más rápido.
    A. ese uno,   C. aquél,
    B. aquel uno,   D. ése uno,

33. Si José no tiene lápiz, yo le puedo prestar . . . .
    A. el mío.   C. mío.
    B. la mía.   D. mía.

34. Cuando mi hija era niña, ella . . . hablar español.
    A. supo   C. sabía
    B. conoció   D. conocía

35. Cuando Felipe II . . . *rey* (king) de España, preparó la Armada Invencible.
    A. fue   C. estuvo
    B. estaba   D. era

36. Hoy estoy *cansado* (tired) porque ayer . . . tenis por dos horas.
    A. jugaba   C. jugué
    B. juegué   D. juegaba

37. . . . a las diez las puertas de este supermercado.
       A. Las cierran   C. Se cierra
       B. Se cierran   D. Lo cierra

38. ¿Qué pasó con el billete? - . . . a mi madre.
       A. se lo dí   D. se la di
       B. le la di   E. se lo di
       C. se la dí   F. le lo di

39. . . . dio dinero a Cristóbal Colón para el viaje a América.
       A. Isabel la Primera   C. Isabel Primera
       B. La Primera Isabel   D. Primera Isabel

40. Mi abuelo siempre . . . mucho, pero mi abuela, poco.
       A. fumaba   C. fumó
       B. fumía   D. fumió

41. A Margarita . . . ocho dólares en el mercado.
       A. le cayeron   D. se les caieron
       B. le caieron   E. se le caieron
       C. se le cayeron   F. se les cayeron

42. La pobre niñita . . . mucho frío cuando la encontramos.
       A. hacía   C. estaba
       B. había   D. tenía

43. Cuando volvimos de la fiesta, la ventana ya . . . rota.
       A. fue   C. estuvo
       B. era   D. estaba

44. Ayer ustedes . . . el carro por dos horas.
       A. condujieron   D. conducían
       B. condujeron   E. condujieron
       C. conduzían   F. conduzieron

45. Tu abuela . . . 85 años cuando murió.
       A. era   C. tenía
       B. fue   D. tuvo

46. Después que llegué a mi cuarto, el teléfono . . . *dos veces* (twice).
       A. suenó   D. suenaba
       B. sueñó   E. sonó
       C. sonaba   F. soño

47. No tienes que pagar la cuenta. Ya . . . yo hace cinco minutos.
       A. le pagué   D. la pagué
       B. le pagé   E. la pagaba
       C. la pagé   F. le pagué

48. Cuando conocimos esta ciudad, . . . buenas tiendas.
       A. habían   C. había
       B. hubo   D. hubieron

49. Los platos . . . a la camarera cuando iba a servir la comida.
        A. se rompieron   C. se le rompió
        B. se les rompió   D. se le rompieron

50. ¿Dónde . . . ayer cuando te llamé a las 4:00?
        A. estabas   C. estuviste
        B. eras   D. fuiste

ANSWERS FOR LESSONS 6–10

Lesson 6

A.
1. el	4. el	7. la	10. la
2. el	5. la	8. el	11. la
3. la	6. el	9. la	12. el

B.
1. estrecho	4. sed	7. cerrar	10. entrar a
2. nuevo (moderno)	5. sencillo (simple)	8. pagar	11. subir
3. frío	6. lejos	9. mal tiempo	12. viejo (nuevo)

C.
1. servir	9. reservar	17. lavaplatos	25. señor/señorita
2. bañarse	10. turismo	18. invitación	26. cenar
3. desayunar	11. calor	19. dormitorio	27. llegada
4. fumar	12. oír	20. sentarse	28. mariscos/marina
5. perdonar	13. ver (visión)	21. casar (la casa)	29. salida
6. registrar	14. viaje (viajero)	22. estar	30. vuelo
7. llover	15. pasar (pasaje)	23. nublado	
8. nevar (nevada)	16. rosado	24. cocina (cocinar)	

D.
1. desayuno	5. doble	9. jabón	13. frío (mal tiempo)
2. peso	6. banco	10. botones (mozo)	14. sed
3. ascensor/escalera	7. plaza	11. razonable	15. nublado
4. lluvia	8. lejos	12. habitaciones	

E.
1. G	4. I	7. A	10. C
2. E	5. K	8. B	11. D
3. J	6. H	9. F	

F.
1. llueve	7. prefieren	13. está	19. cambiamos
2. nieva	8. registran	14. incluye	20. reservan
3. divierto	9. abre	15. trata . . . de	21. divertimos
4. visitamos	10. sube	16. interesan	22. prefiero
5. da a	11. entran (suben)	17. decide	23. es/es
6. cobra	12. cierran	18. permite	

Dialog Exercises

A.
1. A México (hotel)	8. plaza central	15. A las ocho
2. Tres días	9. Mil quinientos pesos	16. A las diez y media (treinta)
3. El recepcionista	10. No incluye la comida	17. Sí, lo toman
4. Habitación doble	11. Le parece razonable	18. registro
5. No tienen	12. Un hotel	19. la llave
6. turismo	13. caliente (toallas)	20. El botones (el mozo)
7. En el tercer piso	14. jabón	

B.   1. la escalera   5. razonable   9. nubes   13. divertirme
      2. llueve   6. divisas   10. sed   14. un cheque
      3. servicio   7. doble   11. nuestro/nombre 15. el hotel
      4. da   8. el ascensor   12. hambre

Grammar I

Practice   1. A noun/mucho frío   4. mucha hambre   7. tengo ganas de una cerveza
             2. Hace mucho sol   5. no tener razón 8. la escalera es estrecha
             3. tienen hambre   6. I have thirst   9. está frío

Exercise   1. hace   6. tengo   11. está   16. tienes mucha suerte
             2. hace   7. está   12. tengo sueño   17. hace fresco
             3. tiene   8. es/son   13. tiene razón   18. tiene hambre
             4. está   9. están   14. hace mal tiempo 19. tengo cuidado
             5. está   10. hace   15. es/está   20. tiene ganas de

Grammar II

Practice   1. este/esta/estos -as   6. pronouns
             2. ese/esa/esos/esas   7. ése
             3. number   8. noun/No
             4. aquel/aquellos   9. *e*
             5. one   10. eso/aquello

Exercise   1. aquel   6. aquello   11. aquel
             2. este/ése (aquél)   7. este   12. esta
             3. eso   8. esta/ésa (aquélla)   13. eso
             4. Estos   9. eso   14. Esta/ese (aquel)
             5. Este/ése   10. Éste   15. eso

Grammar III

Practice   1. mi, tu, su, nuestro -a/   5. After   10. Yes/Yes/No
                mis, tus, sus, nuestros -as   6. mío/tuyo   11. possessed
             2. No/Yes   7. mis/tus   12. The short ones
             3. his/her/its/their   8. you/your   13. No
             4. tus   9. el (tuyo)   14. nuestro jabón

Exercise   1. mi/tuyo   5. mía/la suya   9. Mis/Su
             2. nuestra   6. Sus   10. nuestro
             3. mío/el tuyo (el suyo)   7. Su   11. sus/de él/de ella
             4. Su   8. Nuestra   12. tus/las mías

Lesson 7

Vocabulary

A. 1. el   3. la   5. el   7. el   9. la   11. el
    2. el   4. el   6. la   8. el   10. el   12. la

B. 1. mes/meses   4. país/países   7. mariachi/mariachis
    2. feliz/felices   5. puntual/puntuales   8. tocadiscos/tocadiscos
    3. viernes/viernes   6. alegre/alegres   9. entremés/entremeses

C. 1. G   6. P   11. D   16. Y   21. S
    2. I   7. K   12. Q   17. C   22. X
    3. F   8. U   13. H   18. O   23. Z
    4. N   9. E   14. V   19. J   24. T
    5. A   10. B   15. L   20. M   25. R

D. 1. claro/oscuro   6. aburrido/gracioso (alegre) (interesante)
    2. apagar/encender   7. moderno/antiguo
    3. antipático/simpático   8. nadie/alguien
    4. atrasado/puntual   9. triste/alegre (gracioso) (contento)
    5. comida/bebida   10. comenzar a/dejar de (terminar de)

E. 1. comienza   6. suena   11. encarga   16. prometen
    2. celebramos   7. apago   12. entiendo   17. cumplimos
    3. baila   8. sueñas   13. merezco   18. enciende
    4. entiende   9. molestan   14. avisa   19. cumple
    5. comienzan   10. tocas   15. dejas   20. suena

Dialog Exercises

A. 1. invitar   6. preparar   11. torta   16. fuma
    2. cumpleaños   7. entremeses   12. llega   17. bailar
    3. compañeros   8. arroz con pollo   13. tomar (beber)   18. con mucho
    4. está   9. ensalada   14. champán   gusto
    5. resfriado   10. bebidas   15. refresco   19. ritmos

B. 1. velas   5. los domingos   9. una semana   13. cumple
    2. miércoles   6. la guitarra   10. soñamos   14. apagar
    3. una copa   7. enciendes   11. avisa   15. el tocadiscos
    4. botanas   8. resfriado   12. este país

C. 1. atrasado   3. sabroso   5. aburrido
    2. oscuro   4. próxima   6. oscuro

D.   1. José tiene ganas de leer el libro *Hawaii.*
      2. ¿Por qué tú no dejas de fumar hoy?
      3. La fiesta de mi cumpleaños es el sábado próximo.
      4. La torta del cumpleaños de Carlos tiene veintitrés velas.
      5. María quiere bailar (los) ritmos modernos.
      6. Ustedes llegan atrasados a la fiesta.
      7. Estos entremeses están muy sabrosos.
      8. Tus sobrinos son bastante graciosos.

Grammar I

Practice   1. direct object   5. lo/la/los/las   9. They're the same
             2. a esa chica   6. lo veo/los   10. a/camareras
             3. no/alguien   7. precede/follow
             4. stress/word (verb)   8. infinitive/indicative

A.   1. las traigo   5. lo quiero   9. quiero leerlo
      2. lo oigo   6. lo hablo   10. lo quiero leer
      3. lo hago   7. los fumo   11. tengo que oírlo
      4. la conozco   8. la veo   12. lo tengo que oír

B.   1. a   2. a   3. Ø (nothing)   4. Ø   5. al   6. A/A

C.   1. te llama   3. puedo llamar*la* (la puedo llamar)   5. voy a verte/te voy a ver
      2. las felicita   4. los ayudamos   6. me dejan en casa

Grammar II

Practice   1. subject/me/te   4. inanimate/se   7. reflexive
             2. se/Se habla español   5. se/cae   8. se siente/se sienta
             3. (b)   6. compran

A.   1. se abrochan   5. se llama/me llamo   9. se sientan   13. nos peinamos
      2. me acuesto   6. me afeito   10. me quito   14. nos bañamos
      3. se despierta   7. se pone   11. se siente
      4. se divierte   8. se viste   12. se levanta

B.   1. Se vive bien aquí.   5. El coche se detiene (para) ahora.
      2. En Argentina se habla   6. Los coches se detienen (paran)
         español.   ahora.
      3. Me voy a casa ahora.   7. Se compran carros.
      4. Se come la torta.

Grammar III

Practice
1. meaning/com/v
2. nosotros -as/ (we)/tú(you)
3. hablé/habló
4. viví/vivió
5. Present/Preterite
6. apagué/gu
7. creyó
8. toqué/qu
9. comencé/c
10. "past"/I practiced

A.
1. llegó/llegué
2. leyeron
3. me bañé
4. vio
5. se acostó
6. practiqué
7. comenzó/comencé
8. apagaste/apagué
9. volvieron
10. dormí
11. se cayó
12. tocó/toqué
13. pagaste/pagué
14. viviste
15. se quitó
16. oyeron
17. nevó
18. se comió
19. salió
20. llovió

B.
1. me desperté
2. me levanté
3. me bañé
4. me sequé
5. me vestí
6. me desayuné
7. salí
8. llegué
9. oí
10. comí
11. volví
12. comenzó
13. explicó
14. se cayó
15. se destruyó

Lesson 8

Vocabulary

A.
1. la
2. el
3. el
4. las
5. el
6. la
7. los
8. los
9. el
10. las
11. los
12. el
13. los
14. la
15. las

B.
1. jugo
2. hamburguesa
3. pierna
4. pavo
5. queso
6. a menudo
7. leche
8. cebolla
9. bocadillo
10. merendar
11. pepino
12. zanahoria
13. leche
14. buena pinta
15. solomillo
16. picante

C.
1. colombianas
2. mexicanas
3. chilenas
4. españolas
5. texanas
6. peruanas

D.
1. verdura
2. pescado
3. merienda
4. tortilla
5. burrito
6. asado
7. bocadillo
8. fresco
9. comprador/compra
10. café
11. enfermo
12. recomendar
13. lleno
14. vender
15. atender
16. calor/caliente

E.
1. asa
2. andas
3. recomiendo
4. para
5. vendemos
6. atienden
7. meriendo
8. juegas
9. condimentan
10. busco

F.
1. asó
2. merendó
3. jugó
4. pararon
5. busqué
6. vendí

Dialog Exercises

A. 1. están   6. bajos   11. solomillo   16. puede   21. a dieta
    2. compras   7. puerco   12. cordero   17. a nada   22. dulce
    3. mercados   8. grasa   13. pierna   18. latas   23. ejercicio
    4. mejor   9. paquete   14. verduras   19. fruta
    5. a menudo   10. pinta   15. frescos   20. calorías

B. 1. el vino tinto   6. maíz   11. lata
    2. un bocadillo de pavo   7. queso   12. grasas
    3. estupendo   8. atún   13. calorías
    4. plátanos fritos   9. texano   14. el aguacate
    5. té   10. ternera   15. pescado

C. 1. E   3. J   5. A   7. L   9. D   11. C
    2. K   4. H   6. G   8. B   10. F   12. I

D. 1. Rita buscó las verduras más frescas.
    2. Ellas salieron de compras al supermercado en el carro.
    3. El domingo pasado yo pesqué en el mar.
    4. ¿Cuándo vendiste tú tus libros viejos?
    5. Nuestras tías merendaron en este restaurante.

Grammar I

Practice   1. dorm / durm / *u* / Ellos durmieron
             2. ped / pid / i / Él pidió
             3. dormir / Él murió / Ellos murieron
             4. ie / siento / siente / i / sintió
             5. third / Preterite
             6. Vuelvo / vuelve / volvió / volvieron
             7. ue / duerme / u / durmió / durmieron

A. 1. se sintió / me sentí   6. durmió / dormimos
    2. murió   7. murieron
    3. se vistió / me vestí   8. prefirió / preferí
    4. sirvieron   9. repitió / repetí
    5. pedimos / pidió   10. se divirtieron

B. 1. volvió/prefirió   5. llegué/seguí
    2. me sentí/fui   6. fue/murió
    3. se divirtieron/pidieron   7. me quité/me acosté
    4. se despertó/se vistió

Grammar II

Practice
1. Present/I say
2. Yo supe
3. hic/hiz
4. i/eron
5. j/condujeron
6. puso
7. trajeron
8. From the context
9. anduve
10. tener/Él detuvo
11. He went or was / ir
12. -*AR* (first conjugation) / dieron
13. accent / dio / fue

A.
1. pudo	4. produjeron	7. traje	10. condujo (manejó)
2. puso	5. estuviste	8. supo	11. hizo / hice
3. quiso/pudo	6. dijeron/dije	9. vinimos	12. se detuvo

B.
1. anduvo	4. tuvo	7. se puso	10. dijo
2. condujo	5. llegó	8. hicieron	11. tomó
3. estuvo	6. puso	9. trajeron	12. sonó

Grammar III

Practice
1. hay/hubo
2. definite
3. indefinite
4. el libro aquí
5. obligation
6. hay/hubo
7. mucho
8. just taken place
9. begin (start)
10. Él se puso a comer

A.
1. Hay una fiesta aquí.
   Hay viento.
   Hay que practicar.
2. Está el libro aquí.
   Está alegre.
   Está pálida.
3. Hubo una fiesta aquí.
   Hubo que practicar.
   Hubo viento
4. Acabamos de practicar.
   Acabamos una fiesta aquí.
   Acabamos el libro aquí.
5. Hace viento.
6. José se puso a practicar
   José se puso alegre.
7. Me pongo a practicar.
   Me pongo alegre.
   Me pongo pálida.
8. Tenemos que practicar.
   Tenemos una fiesta aquí.
   Tenemos el libro aquí.

B.
1. que	4. de	7. a / Ø	10. de	13. a / que
2. Ø / a	5. de	8. de	11. a / de (or Ø)	14. a
3. a	6. Ø / que	9. Ø	12. de	15. a / a

Lesson 9

Vocabulary

A. 1. el   3. la   5. el   7. los   9. los   11. la
    2. los   4. el   6. el   8. las   10. las   12. los

B. 1. ahorrar
2. alegrarse/alegría
3. encantar/encanto
4. interesar/interesante
5. valer/valor/valiente
6. lujoso
7. convenir
8. prestar
9. céntimo/cien(to)
10. chequera
11. necesario/necesidad
12. contado/contar
13. cargar/cargo
14. ganancia
15. gastar/gastador
16. par
17. peso/pesar
18. gasto/gastador
19. importar/importador/importante
20. reducir

C. 1. préstamo
2. de lujo
3. por ciento
4. moneda
5. ahorrar
6. divisas
7. cartera
8. gana
9. nadar
10. un par de
11. gangas
12. a plazos
13. descubrió
14. giro postal
15. tienda

D. 1. prestó
2. nos quejamos
3. metiste
4. se alegraron
5. encontraron
6. aumentaron
7. saqué
8. valió
9. gastó
10. redujeron

E. 1. F   3. T   5. T   7. T   9. F   11. F   13. T
    2. F   4. T   6. F   8. T   10. T   12. T   14. T

Dialog Exercises

A. 1. estudiar
2. país
3. cambiar
4. cajero
5. estuvo
6. viajero(s)
7. moneda
8. tuvo
9. pasaporte
10. abrió
11. postal
12. préstamo
13. piso (apartamento)
14. a plazos
15. al contado
16. futuro
17. descubrir
18. pasado

B. 1. hipoteca
2. tarjetas de crédito
3. chequera
4. débil/antiguo (viejo)
5. sueldo (salario)
6. impuesto
7. ahorrar/sacar
8. interés
9. al fin (por fin)
10. pena
11. reduce (baja)
12. seria

C. 1. un cheque
2. un billete
3. nadar
4. comer
5. valioso
6. aumentan
7. divisas
8. céntimos
9. se parecen
10. el billete

Grammar I

Practice
1. Indirect Object
2. le/les/reflexive
3. interest (involvement)
4. follow/Indicative
5. Indicative/infinitive
6. se/Se lo vendo
7. emphatic
8. le/les
9. la (Direct Object)

A.
1. le
2. me
3. le
4. nos
5. me
6. le
7. La
8. Se lo
9. Se las
10. Les

B.
1. a pagártela
2. a pagársela
3. se lo dio
4. se los prestó
5. se lo trajo
6. abrirla
7. a lavárselo
8. se lo aumenté
9. las quiero poner (quiero ponerlas)
10. se lo pidió

C.
1. Tú nos compraste (los) bocadillos sabrosos a nosotros.
2. Los camareros (les) sirvieron la comida a los pasajeros.
3. Tus tíos me vendieron el Volkswagen a mí.
4. El botones (les) subió las maletas a los turistas.
5. Enrique no le prestó el carro a nadie.

Grammar II

Practice
1. libro/me gustan.
2. third/le/les
3. (b) a mí me gusta eso
4. possession (my)
5. inanimate
6. Indirect Object
7. Se le cayeron
8. me parece buena

A.
1. les gustan
2. le pasa/me pasa
3. te duele/me duelen
4. me parece
5. les conviene
6. te interesa
7. te pasa
8. se me para
9. se le caen
10. le sobra

B.
1. A nadie le gustan las cosas malas.
2. A tus abuelos les encanta la comida española.
3. A los alumnos les interesan las clases serias.
4. A mí me faltan dos dólares de la cartera.
5. A usted no le gusta nadar en el mar.
6. A ella se le para el carro en la Avenida 5.
7. A ti se te caen dos billetes de diez dólares.

C.
1. A mis hijos les gusta oír el radio.
2. (A mí) me parece bonita esa muchacha (chica).
3. (A mí) me duelen mucho las manos hoy.

4. ¿Qué te pasa (a ti), mi hijo (hijo mío)?
5. Se me cayó el reloj en el piso (a mí).
6. (A nosotros) nos interesan tus (sus) problemas.
7. (A ella) le conviene esta clase.

Grammar III

Practice	1. -aba/gustaba	4. era/éramos	7. going on (in progress)
	2. -ía/bebía/vivía	5. veía	8. había
	3. iba	6. hablábamos/íbamos	

A.
1. ahorraban	5. éramos	9. caían
2. leía	6. reducían	10. nadábamos
3. estabas	7. valía	11. veían
4. iba	8. parecía	12. había

B.
1. convenía	6. faltaba	11. quejaba	16. vestía
2. cargaba	7. sobraban	12. comenzaba	17. morían
3. valía	8. metías	13. pensabas	18. conocía
4. encontraban	9. veía	14. dolía	19. hacía
5. dormían	10. íbamos	15. tenía	20. Había

C.

Lesson 10

Vocabulary

A.
1. el	4. el	7. el	10. el	13. el/los	16. la	19. los
2. el	5. la	8. la	11. las	14. el	17. el	20. el
3. las	6. las	9. los	12. el	15. los	18. la	

B. 1. parada   5. salud   9. despacio   13. en medio de
    2. litera   6. milla   10. exprés   14. a mediodía
    3. taquilla   7. horario   11. ida y vuelta 15. hace caso
    4. andén   8. bar   12. sin falta

C. 1. el billete   3. el coche   5. el ferrocarril   7. gratis
    2. la salida   4. entero   6. el exprés   8. olvidar

D. 1. la llegada (entrada)   8. desocupado (disponible)
    2. la vuelta   9. rápido
    3. la salud   10. perder
    4. a mediodía   11. descontento (triste)
    5. limpio   12. entero (completo)
    6. vacío   13. deshacer
    7. difícil   14. perder

E. 1. mandó   4. se . . . rompió   7. mandaron   10. corrió
    2. crucé   5. perdieron   8. se . . . olvidó 11. informó
    3. se demoró   6. hizo caso   9. tomó el pelo   12. funcionó

F. 1. mandaba   4. se . . . rompía   7. mandaban   10. corría
    2. cruzaba   5. perdían   8. se . . . olvidaban 11. informaba
    4. se demoraba 6. hacía caso   9. tomaba el pelo 12. funcionaba

Dialog Exercises

A. 1. taquillero   6. parada   11. ida   16. salud
    2. Madrid   7. se demora   12. no-fumar   17. hacen caso
    3. ir (viajar)   8. media   13. sección   18. 2,800
    4. información   9. literas   14. el pelo
    5. rápido   10. bar   15. anuncios

B. 1. F   3. T   5. T   7. T   9. F   11. F   13. F
    2. T   4. F   6. T   8. F   10. T   12. T   14. T

C. 1. fácil/difícil   5. vacaciones   9. despacio
    2. tomas el pelo   6. ocupado (a)   10. propina
    3. vacía (desocupada)   7. medio   11. falta
    4. rota   8. hace caso   12. gratis (gratuito)

D. 1. Mi esposa deshacía las maletas después del viaje.
    2. Sus tíos siempre le mandaban dinero a él.
    3. Los niños no (le) hacían caso a nadie en la fiesta.

4. El carro viejo siempre se me rompía a mí.

5. Todos los días se le paraba el carro a ella.

6. A Carlos le gustaban los libros americanos de ficción.

Grammar I

Practice   1. middle/end   6. Imperfect/eran
2. middle   7. Imperfect/tenía
3. beginning/end   8. Imperfect
4. Imperfect/era/tenía   9. Preterite
5. Imperfect/fumaba/bebía   10. iba/tuvo

A.   1. Mi familia vivía en Kansas cuando yo nací.
2. Mi abuelo tenía 80 años cuando murió.
3. Eran las tres cuando llegaron los tíos.
4. Estela llamó cuando estabas (estaba) en el jardín.
5. No le pasó nada a mi hermano cuando se cayó.
6. No vi a nadie cuando abrí la ventana.

B.   1. fui/tenía   4. llegó/pidió   7. almorzaba/fumaba
2. estaba/sonó   5. dijo/tenía   8. trajeron/estaba
3. vivíamos/hicimos   6. pasó/paró

C.   1. llegamos   7. estaba   13. comenzó
2. eran   8. hacía   14. tuvimos
3. estábamos   9. tomamos   15. llevó
4. acostamos   10. estábamos   16. había
5. despertamos   11. almorzamos   17. pusimos
6. tuvimos   12. almorzábamos

Grammar II

Practice   1. Llegué hace un mes   5. que
2. desde   6. Hacía dos meses
3. que   que no trabajaba
4. Imperfect/comía   7. Llevo aquí diez minutos.

A.   1. Hace cinco años que vivo aquí. / Vivo aquí hace cinco años.
2. Hace ocho años que viajé a Panamá. / Viajé a Panamá hace ocho años.
3. Hace media hora que toco el piano. / Toco el piano (desde) hace media hora.
4. Hace veinte años que salí de España. / Salí de España hace veinte años.
5. Hace una semana que no viajo en tren. / No viajo en tren (desde) hace
una semana.
6. Hacía dos meses que no llovía aquí. / No llovía aquí (desde) hacía dos
meses.

7. Hacía diez minutos que hablaba por teléfono. / Hablaba por teléfono hacía diez minutos.

8. Hacía cuatro años que vivía en Cuba. / Vivía en Cuba (desde) hacía cuatro años.

B. 1. El Cid murió hace mil años.
    2. No llovía (desde) hacía un año.
    3. Hace doce años que se fue mi amiga.
    4. Hace veinte años que fumas.
    5. El tren pasó hace cinco minutos.
    6. Hace unos tres años que tu amigo trabajó en esta taquilla.
    7. Hace una hora que saqué los billetes.
    8. Hablaba por teléfono (desde) hacía veinte minutos.
    9. Hace diez años que estoy (vivo) aquí. / Estoy aquí (desde) hace diez años.
    10. Hacía tres años que Kennedy era Presidente cuando murió.

Grammar III

Practice
1. number/primera
2. tercero/before
3. after/los días primeros
4. Carlos Primero
5. No/Yes
6. 21/el 21 de junio
7. 21/el 21 de marzo
8. 21/el 21 de diciembre
9. invierno/verano
10. enero/febrero
11. julio/diciembre
12. primero/uno
13. No/el/los sábados

A. 1. octubre/mayo
    2. marzo/abril/mayo
    3. el dos de enero
    4. el primero (uno) de marzo
    5. 4 de julio
    6. 25 de diciembre
    7. uno (primero) de enero
    8. jueves
    9. el invierno
    10. el verano
    11. Isabel Segunda
    12. enero
    13. en el primero (segundo)
    14. sexto/octavo
    15. décima/diecinueve

B. 1. A mí me gustan la primavera y el verano.
    2. Emilio vive en la Octava calle (calle octava) (calle Ocho).
    3. Ustedes viajan a México el doce de junio.
    4. Nosotros tenemos vacaciones el uno (primero) de abril.
    5. Hoy es lunes, el ocho de septiembre.

C. 1. (Yo) compré los boletos (billetes) el martes.
    2. (A nosotros) nos gusta el Cuatro de Julio.
    3. La primavera va del 21 de marzo al 21 de junio.
    4. Enrique Octavo tuvo ocho mujeres (esposas).
    5. Hoy es el dos de noviembre.

REVIEW EXAM

Vocabulary

1. L
2. J
3. Q
4. P
5. M
6. O
7. R
8. K
9. N
10. D
11. H
12. C
13. B
14. A
15. F
16. I
17. E
18. G

19. al andén
20. una litera
21. una cuenta corriente
22. a plazos
23. un sueldo
24. el solomillo
25. tinto
26. velas
27. da a
28. color naranja
29. vacío/débil
30. limpio/fácil
31. lento/estrecho
32. ocupado/sencillo
33. cerrar/aburrido
34. ahorrar/salir
35. encender/perder

36. (una) propina
37. nadar
38. una hipoteca
39. jugo
40. nietos
41. nieve
42. (una) (la) toalla
43. pescados
44. C
45. A
46. D
47. C
48. D
49. A
50. B

Grammar

1. tuve sueño
2. hizo (hubo) sol
3. tuvo sed
4. hizo mucho frío
5. pudieron
6. se divirtieron
7. llegué
8. quiso/pudo
9. pidió
10. se sintió/(se)fue
11. me afeité
12. se vistió
13. tocó/toqué
14. trajeron
15. hubo
16. se levantó
17. quería

18. estaba
19. fue
20. se bañó
21. se secó
22. tenía
23. se comió
24. dijo
25. durmió
26. soñó
27. anduvo
28. tenía
29. Hacía
30. había
31. B
32. C
33. A
34. C

35. D
36. C
37. B
38. E
39. C
40. A
41. C
42. D
43. D
44. B
45. C
46. E
47. D
48. C
49. D
50. A

Lesson 11

Las partes del cuerpo (The Parts of the Body)

barbilla	chin	**diente**	tooth	**ojo**	eye		
boca	mouth	**escalera**	stairs	**oreja**[5]	ear (outer)		
brazo	arm	**espalda**	back	**par**[6]	couple (things)		
cabello[1]	hair	**frente (la)**[3]	forehead	**párpado**	eyelid		
cabeza	head	**garganta**	throat	**patilla**	sideburn		
cadera	hip	**hombro**	shoulder	**pecho**	breast		
cara	face	**hueso**	bone	**pelo**	hair		
cejas	eyebrow	**labios**	lips	**pestaña**	eyelash		
cintura	waist	**mejilla**	cheek	**pie**[7]	foot		
codo	elbow	**muleta**	crutch	**pierna**	leg		
cuello	neck	**muñeca**	wrist	**rodilla**	knee		
dedo[2]	finger, toe	**muslo**	thigh	**tobillo**	ankle		
deportes	sports	**nariz**[4]	nose	**yeso**	cast (plaster)		

cojear	to limp	**ocurrir**	to occur, happen
doler (ue)	to hurt, ache	**oler (hue)**	to smell
encontrarse (ue)	to meet (find)	**pasar**	to happen
enyesar	to put in a cast	**torcer (ue)**	to twist, sprain

cojo	lame, crippled	**increíble**	incredible
estúpido	silly, stupid	**ligero**	light, quick
imprevisto	unexpected	**serio**	serious

tener mala pata	to be unlucky (lit. "to have bad foot")
tener mala estrella	to be unlucky (lit. "to have bad star")
hacer ver las estrellas	to make one feel a terrible pain (lit. "to see the stars")
echar de menos	to miss
en serio	seriously
a mal tiempo, buena cara	to smile in the face of adversity (lit. "to bad weather, nice face")

NOTES:

1. *Cabello* is the hair on a person's head. *Pelo* is also the hair on the head or any other part of the body of a person or an animal.

2. *Dedo* is *finger* as well as *toe*. To tell the difference, we sometimes add *de la mano* or *del pie*.

3. *La frente* is the *forehead*. *El frente* is the *front* of a house or any other place. *El frente* is also the *battlefront*. The change of gender makes a difference in the meaning.

4. *Nariz* is *nose*. We use the plural *narices* to refer to the *nostrils* and also in idiomatic expressions such as *dar con la puerta en las narices* (to say absolutely no).

5. *Orejas* is the standard word for *ears*, actually the "outer ear." The word for "inner ear" is *oído*. Since Spanish tends to have a different word for the same organ in animals and in persons, some dialects use *oreja* for animals and *oído* for persons.

6. *Par* means a *couple* of something. *Pareja* is a *couple of people*. The expression *un par de* is used also to mean *a few*.

7. *Pie* is the *foot* of a person. *Ir a pie* is *to go on foot*. We use the word *pata* for the foot or leg of an animal, but in idiomatic expressions we also use *pata* for people. *Meter la pata* is *to stick one's foot in it*. *Tener mala pata* is *to be unlucky*.

EXERCISES   *(Answers, p. 310)*

A. Write *el, la, los, las* in front of the nouns.

1. ____diente	6. ____pestañas	11. ____cuello
2. ____nariz	7. ____cabello	12. ____frente (forehead)
3. ____deportes	8. ____rodilla	13. ____frente (front)
4. ____pie	9. ____par	14. ____patillas
5. ____cejas	10. ____ojos	15. ____estrella

B. Complete the sentences with one of these idioms.

tener mala pata	meter la pata	a mal tiempo, buena cara
echar de menos	en serio	hacer ver las estrellas

1. El año pasado perdí a mi padre, y ahora todavía lo_____

   _____ .

2. ¿Lo dices en broma o_____?

3. El verano pasado perdí 75 dólares en Las Vegas; siempre que juego dinero

   yo_____ .

4. Si no sabes nada de eso, no debes_____ .

5. Este dolor es tan grande que me *hace*_____ .

6. No debes estar triste por eso; *a mal*_____ .

C.   Complete the sentences with a word from the list below.

hueso	rodilla	imprevisto -a	ligero -a	cojear
nariz	dedo	cabello	espalda	párpado
frente	escalera	codo	muleta	

1. Tenemos veinte_____: 10 en las manos y 10 en los pies.

2. Ayer tuve una visita_____de mis tíos.

3. Parece que José tiene un problema en el pie porque_____
   un poco.

4. Si no hay ascensor bajamos y subimos por la_____ .

5. Algunas mujeres se pintan las cejas y los_____ .

6. El tobillo y la_____son parte de la pierna.

7. Vemos con los ojos y olemos con la_____ .

8. Delante tenemos el pecho, y detrás tenemos la_____ .

9. No tengo mucha hambre; voy a comer algo_____ .

10. La cabeza está cubierta de pelo o_____ .

11. El_____más grande del cuerpo está en el muslo.

12. Si Ud. no puede caminar puede usar dos_____ .

13. La parte del brazo que se *dobla* (bends) es el_____ .

14. La parte de la cabeza entre el pelo y los ojos es la_____

D. **Word Families: Write a word related to each of the following.**
    Examples: cojo/cojear   yeso/enyesar   diente/dentista

(Answers, p. 310)

1. abrazar_____
2. collar_____
3. creer_____
4. dolor_____
5. olor_____
6. serio_____

7. pata_____
8. escalar_____
9. labial_____
10. caricatura_____
11. rodar_____
12. capilar_____

E. **Complete the sentences with the correct form of the verbs in the Preterite.**

1. Ayer me caí y me_____el tobillo. (torcer)

2. ¿Qué le_____a Juan después del baile? (pasar)

3. Lolita y yo_____en la cafetería. (encontrarse)

4. La semana pasada tuve un problema en el pie y_____ bastante. (cojear)

5. Los médicos me_____la pierna derecha. (enyesar)

6. Ahora no me duele el pie, pero ayer me_____mucho. (doler)

7. ¿Qué te_____después del accidente? (ocurrir)

8. Los perros de la policía_____la cocaína. (oler)

F. **Complete the sentence with a word for the appropriate part of the body.**

1. Abrimos y cerramos los ojos por medio de los_____.

2. Vemos con los ojos; *besamos* (kiss) con los_____.

3. Mi_____no es rojo ni *rubio* (blond) sino negro.

4. Doblamos el brazo en el codo, y doblamos la pierna en la_____.

5. A los lados del cuello tenemos los dos_____.

6. Detrás tenemos la espalda; delante tenemos el_____.

7. La parte entre el brazo y la mano es la_____.

8. El fémur es el _____ más grande del cuerpo humano.

9. El fémur está en la parte de la pierna que llamamos _____ .

10. No es lo mismo *el frente* de batalla que *la* _____ de la cabeza.

11. Las dos _____ están a los lados de la cara.

DIÁLOGO   *Un accidente imprevisto*

(Graciela y Esteban son amigos y se encuentran antes de la clase. Esteban tiene el pie derecho enyesado, y camina con muletas.)

GRACIELA:	¡Hola, chico! ¿Qué te pasó en la pierna?
ESTEBAN:	Nada. Me caí por la escalera de casa y me torcí el tobillo.
GRACIELA:	¡Increíble! Yo pensé que esos accidentes sólo ocurrían en los deportes o con el carro.
ESTEBAN:	Ya ves; parece que yo siempre tengo mala pata. Todo me ocurre de la manera más estúpida.
GRACIELA:	¿Estás seguro que no fue un accidente con el carro cuando volvías de la fiesta de Carmen?
ESTEBAN:	No, hablo en serio. Si no me crees pregúntale a mi hermana.
GRACIELA:	Bueno, ¿y te duele mucho?
ESTEBAN:	No, apenas si siento un ligero dolor.
GRACIELA:	¿Te dolió mucho cuando te pusieron el yeso?
ESTEBAN:	Bastante. Sobre todo cuando el doctor me ponía los huesos en su lugar. Me hizo ver las estrellas.
GRACIELA:	¿Y cuánto tiempo llevarás el yeso y las muletas?
ESTEBAN:	Un par de semanas, si todo va bien. Voy a echar de menos el baile del cumpleaños de Margarita.
GRACIELA:	Bueno, chico, ¿qué le vas a hacer? ¡A mal tiempo, buena cara!

Dialog   *An Unexpected Accident*

(Grace and Steve are friends and they meet before class. Steve has a cast on his right foot and walks with crutches.)

GRACE:	Hi! Steve. What happened to your leg?
STEVE:	Nothing much. I fell down the stairs at home and twisted my ankle.
GRACE:	Incredible! I thought such things happened only in sports or with the car.
STEVE:	As you can see, it seems I always have bad luck. Everything happens to me in the silliest way.

GRACE: Are you sure it wasn't an accident with the car when you were
          coming back from Carmen's party?
STEVE: Of course not, I'm serious. If you don't believe me, ask my sister.
GRACE: Well, does it hurt a lot?
STEVE: No, I hardly feel any pain.
GRACE: Did it hurt a lot when they put on the cast?
STEVE: Plenty. Especially when the doctor was setting the bones. He made
          me see stars!
GRACE: And how long will you have the cast and the crutches?
STEVE: A couple of weeks if everything goes well, I'm going to miss the
          dance on Margaret's birthday.
GRACE: Well, what can you do? Smile in the face of adversity!

EXERCISES   *(Answers, p. 310)*

A. Complete the sentences to form a narrative summary of the dialog.

Graciela y Esteban se (1)_____antes de las clases.
Esteban tiene un pie (2)_____, y por esta razón tiene
que caminar con dos (3)_____. Él se cayó por la
(4)_____de su casa y se (5)_____el
tobillo derecho. Con frecuencia ocurren accidentes en los (6)_____
_____y también con el automóvil. Esteban cree que él siempre tiene
(7)_____porque le ocurren cosas estúpidas. Graciela
piensa que Esteban no habla (8)_____, pero él le dice
que puede preguntar a su (9)_____si no le cree. En
ese momento Esteban sólo tiene un dolor (10)_____
en el tobillo pero éste le dolió mucho cuando le pusieron el (11)_____
_____. El doctor le puso primero los (12)_____en su lugar, y eso
le hizo ver las (13)_____. Esteban tiene que llevar el
yeso y las (14)_____por un par de (15)_____
_____. Él va a echar de (16)_____el baile del cumpleaños de
su amiga Margarita, pero, ¡qué le va a hacer! ¡A mal tiempo, (17)_____
_____!

B.   Answer True (T) or False (F).

1. ____Graciela y Esteban se encuentran y hablan después de la clase.

2. ____Esteban tiene enyesado el pie izquierdo.

3. ____Él se cayó por la escalera de su casa y se torció un tobillo.

4. ____Graciela siempre tiene mala pata; por eso le ocurren accidentes estúpidos.

5. ____El accidente de Esteban ocurrió en la calle con un automóvil.

6. ____Esteban dice que él habla en serio, que no es una broma.

7. ____En este momento él sólo siente un poco de dolor en el tobillo.

8. ____Cuando el doctor le puso el yeso, Esteban no sintió mucho dolor.

9. ____El doctor tuvo que poner los huesos de la pierna en su lugar.

10. ____Esteban tiene que llevar el yeso y las muletas por una semana nada más.

11. ____Él va a echar de menos un baile de cumpleaños de una amiga.

12. ____Graciela cree que es mejor estar alegre en una dificultad que ponerse triste.

C.   Underline the best answer.

1. Si Ud. tiene un problema para caminar puede usar (cinturas, muletas, rodillas, patillas).

2. Sentimos los olores con (los ojos, los oídos, la nariz, la boca).

3. Graciela y Esteban forman un (a) buen (a) (pareja, muñeca, par, deporte).

4. El fútbol y el béisbol son dos clases de (huesos, deportes, muslos, caderas).

5. El fémur es una clase de (tobillo, muslo, hueso, hombro).

6. La (garganta, espalda, cara, pestaña) es muy importante para hablar.

7. Para doblar el brazo usamos (la rodilla, el cuello, el hombro, el codo).

8. Un accidente que usted no espera es un accidente (ligero, increíble, imprevisto, serio).

9. Unas personas se besan en los labios; otras se besan en (las mejillas, las patillas, las rodillas, las cejas).

10. Nos ponemos el reloj en (el brazo, el pecho, la muñeca, las pestañas).

D. **Form sentences in the Preterite with these words. Make all necessary changes.**

1. Esteban / caerse / por / escalera / su casa /.

_____

2. Él / torcerse / tobillo / derecho / en / accidente /.

_____

3. Graciela / no / creer / Esteban / primero /.

_____

4. Esteban / sentir / bastante / dolor / en / operación /.

_____

5. doctor / poner / huesos / en / su / lugar /.

_____

6. doctor / hacer ver / estrellas / Esteban / del dolor /.

_____

7. Esteban / cojear / dos / semana /.

_____

8. mi / padres / tener / un / noticia / imprevisto /.

_____

GRAMMAR I   Comparisons of inequality.

A.   With nouns, adjectives, and adverbs:

más **menos**	noun + adjective adverb	**+ que**	_more_ _less_ _(fewer)_	noun + adjective adverb	_+ than_

Ex.: Ella tiene _más_ libros _que_ yo. (she has _more_ books _than_ I do)
José es _más_ inteligente _que_ yo. (Joe is _more_ intelligent _than_ I am)
Tú escribes _más_ aprisa _que_ él. (you write fast_er_ _than_ he does)
Yo tengo _menos_ pesos _que_ tú. (I have _fewer_ pesos _than_ you do)

Notice that in English short adjectives and adverbs take the comparative ending *-er* rather than the adverb *more: happier, faster, funnier.*

B. With numbers and amounts:

más **menos**	+ **de** + number (amount)	*more* *less*	+ *than* + number (amount)

Ex.: Compré *más de* cinco libros. (I bought more than five books)
Compré *más de* lo que quería. (I bought more than I wanted to)

C. Emphatic way to indicate an exact amount:

no + (verb) + **más que** + (amount) → *only* + (verb) + (amount)

Ex.: *No* tengo *más que* 5 pesos. (I only have 5 pesos)
Tengo *exactamente* 5 pesos. (I have *exactly* 5 pesos)

The first example is more emphatic and more idiomatic than the second one.

D. With verbs:
The expressions *más que* and *menos que* are used after the verb.
Ex.: Ella trabaja *más que* yo. (she works *more than* I do)
Ella pagó *menos que* yo. (she paid *less than* I did)

PRACTICE THE COMPARATIVES   *(Answers, p. 311)*

1. The expressions *más que* and *menos que* are used to compare nouns, verbs, adjectives, or_____. Ex.: *Ellos corrieron más_____ yo.* (than)

2. To compare numbers, the expression_____is used instead of *más que* and_____is used instead of *menos que.* Ex.: *Usted bebió_____cuatro vasos de cerveza.* (more than)

3. How do you complete the sentence *En mi familia tenemos más_____ un carro*? (than)

4. Notice that sometimes it's necessary to compare a general amount rather than an exact number. For example, the idea of *more than you think* is translated into Spanish as _____ *lo que usted piensa.*

5. The English ending *-er* added to an adjective or adverb is translated into Spanish by the full word _____. For example, *she is taller than I am* in Spanish becomes *ella es* _____ *yo.*

6. In Spanish *un, una* are indefinite articles as well as numbers. Therefore, it's incorrect to say *Tienes más que un carro.* The correct way is *Tienes_____ _____ un carro.*

7. If I say *No tengo más que dos pesos,* how many pesos exactly do I have?

   _____

8. If I say *No tengo más de dos pesos,* I probably have fewer than_____ pesos.

9. *Compraron exactamente tres libras* is less emphatic and less idomatic than *No compraron* _____ *tres libras.*

EXERCISES

(Answers, p. 311)

A.   Complete the sentences with the correct comparative form.

1. Paco se fue a casa _____ temprano _____ yo. (earlier than)

2. ¿Tiene usted_____ veinte dólares? (more than)

3. No puedo comprarlo porque tengo_____ un dólar. (less than)

4. Usted estudia_____ su hermano. (more than)

5. Yo tenía $8,00 y pagué $5,00 por la comida. Ahora no tengo_____ _____ $3,00. (only)

6. Mi esposa es_____ alta _____ yo. (taller than)

7. Ellos estudian_____ lo que usted se imagina. (more than)

8. Ustedes compraron_____ libros_____ Graciela. (fewer . . . than)

9. En realidad yo siempre como _____ lo que necesito. (more than)

10. Si usted tiene *exactamente un* televisor, usted *no* tiene _____ un televisor. (only)

B. Combine the sentences according to the example.

Example: Ana compró tres libros. Yo compré dos libros. Ana compró *más libros que* yo.

1. Pablo se rompió dos huesos en el accidente. María se rompió un hueso.

   _____

2. Esteban tuvo un accidente. Graciela no tuvo ningún accidente.

   _____

3. Marcos tiene seis pies de alto. Lola sólo tiene cinco pies y medio. (use *taller*)

   _____

4. José estudia dos horas por la noche. Yo estudio cuatro horas.

   _____

5. Yo estudio cuatro horas todos los días. Ud. piensa que yo estudio sólo dos horas.

   _____

6. Miriam tiene exactamente dos hermanos. No tiene ni más ni menos. (only)

   _____

7. Anita tiene siete dólares en papel. También tiene algunas monedas.

   _____

GRAMMAR II   Comparisons of equality. Superlatives.

A. With adjectives and adverbs:

> **tan** + adjective / adverb + **como** → *as* + adjective / adverb + *as*

> Ex.: María es *tan* alta *como* yo. (Mary is *as* tall *as* I am)
> Ella corre *tan* rápidamente *como* yo. (she runs *as* fast *as* I do)

B.   With verbs:

> (verb) + **tanto** + **como** → (verb) + *as much as*

Ex.: Esteban no fuma *tanto como* tú. (Steve doesn't smoke *as much as* you do)

C.   With nouns:

> **tanto, tanta,**   + (noun) + **como**   *as much*   + (noun) + *as*
> **tantos, tantas**   *as many*

Ex.: No tengo *tanto* dinero *como* tú. (I don't have *as much* money *as* you do)
No trabajo *tantas* horas *como* tú. (I don't work *as many* hours *as* you do)
Compré *tantos* libros *como* tú. (I bought *as many* books *as* you did)

Notice that *tanto/tanta* agree in gender and number with the following noun. Notice also that the distinction between *much* and *many* is not made in Spanish.

D.   Superlatives:
Study the following examples carefully:
a. José es *el más* alto *de* la clase. (Joe is *the* tall*est in* the class)
b. Ella es *la más* alta *de* la clase. (she is *the* tall*est in* the class)
In Spanish it is necessary to change the article *el/la, los/las* according to the gender and number of the noun. Notice that here *in* is translated by *de* rather than *en*.
c. José corre *lo más* rápido posible. (Joe runs *as* fast *as* possible)
In this case the second *as* is not translated in Spanish, and the neuter article *lo* has no translation in English.
d. José está gord*ísimo*./ José está *muy* gordo. (Joe es *very* fat)
The ending *-ísimo/-ísima* is equivalent to the adverb *muy* in Spanish and *very* in English. It is more colloquial to use *muy*.

E.   Irregular comparatives and superlatives: A few adjectives in Spanish have the ending *-or* for the comparative (similar to English *-er*). These adjectives also have special forms for the superlative:

ADJECTIVE	COMPARATIVE	SUPERLATIVE	ENGLISH
bueno	**mejor**	**óptimo**	(better/best)
malo	**peor**	**pésimo**	(worse/worst)
grande	**mayor**	**máximo**	(bigger/biggest)
pequeño	**menor**	**mínimo**	(smaller/smallest)

NOTES:

1. *Mejor* can be used instead of *más bueno,* and *peor* instead of *más malo.*
   Ex.: Tu pluma es *mejor que* la mía.
         Tu pluma es *más mala que* la mía.

2. *Mayor* translates *older* and *oldest* when talking about people, and *menor* translates *younger* and *youngest.*
   Ex.: Mi hermana es *menor que* yo. (my sister is *younger than* I am)

PRACTICE YOUR GRAMMAR   *(Answers, p. 311)*

1. The comparatives *tan/tanto/tanta,* etc., are completed with the word
   _____ which is translated as *as* in English.

   Ex.: *Trabajo tanto_____tú.*

2. *Tanto/tanta* show the same gender and_____as the noun.

   For example, *Tengo_____dedos como tú.* (I have as many fingers as you do)

3. *Tan* is the short form of *tanto. Tan* is used only in front of adjectives
   and_____. For example, *Tu pelo es_____rubio como el mío.*

4. What English word is *not* translated in the expression *as much as?*_____ _____ .

5. How do you translate *older* if we are talking about people?_____.
   The same word translates *oldest* with the article *el/la.*

   Ex.: *Mi hermana es_____de la familia.* (the oldest)

6. How do you say *younger* in Spanish?_____. This word
   changes to the plural *menores.* Ex.: *Tengo dos hermanas_____ _____que yo.*

7. We can use the word _____ instead of *más bueno,* and the
   word _____ instead of *más malo.* Ex.: *Tu casa es* _____
   que la mía. (better)

8. Another way to say *muy lindo* in just one word is _____.
   This is another way to express the *superlative.* Ex.: *Esa chica es muy linda;*

   es _____.

9. How do you complete the sentence *Anita es la más rubia* _____
   la clase? This means that the English preposition *in* is translated by

   _____.

10. How do you translate *lo más pronto posible?* _____

    _____. This means that the Spanish article *lo* is not translated, and the

    English word _____ has no equivalent in Spanish.

11. If you are *optimista* you look for the *best;* in Spanish *Usted busca lo* ___

    _____ *en la vida.* But if you are *pesimista,* you look only at

    lo _____.

12. Since 1972 the maximum speed on United States roads and highways is 55
    mph. You would tell a Spanish tourist that *La velocidad* _____
    es 55 millas por hora.

EXERCISES   *(Answers, p. 311)*

A.   Complete the following sentences.

1. Mi hermano es _____ yo, pero él es _____
   alto _____ yo. (younger)/(as . . . as)

2. Tus patillas no son _____ largas _____ las mías. (as
   . . . as)

3. Elena no trabaja _____ horas _____
   usted. (as many . . . as)

4. Después de clase tengo que irme _____.
   (as soon as possible)

5. José está demasiado gordo; él está _____.
   (very fat)

6. ¿Quién es _____, tu padre o tu madre? (older)

7. Tú no corres_____los atletas. (as much as)

8. Los dedos del pie no son_____grandes_____ los de la mano. (as . . . as)

9. Carlitos no tiene_____hambre_____ yo. (as . . . as)

10. Yo hablo el inglés_____el español. (worse than)

11. Colorado es el estado_____montañoso_____Estados Unidos. (the most . . . in)

12. Otra palabra para decir *muy grande* es_____.

13. Marta y Sofía son_____Elena. (older than)

14. Otra palabra para decir *más malo* es_____.

15. Un_____siempre busca *lo mejor* de las cosas.

16. Un_____siempre ve lo negativo, *lo peor* de las cosas.

B.   Change the comparisons from *tan . . . como* to *más . . . que.*

1. Lola tiene el pelo tan rubio como su hermana.

   _____.

2. Ustedes tienen tantos libros como el profesor.

   _____.

3. Guillermo tiene tanta suerte como su amiga.

   _____.

4. En Alaska hace tanto frío como en Siberia.

   _____.

5. Esta comida es tan ligera como la otra.

   _____.

C.   Translate into Spanish.

1. Meat is as expensive as fish.

   _____.

2. You are younger than I (am).

   _____.

3. My car is as old as yours (is).

_____.

4. Steve is very lame.

_____.

5. I did it as soon as possible.

_____.

6. She works as much as you (do).

_____.

7. They are worse than he (is).

_____.

8. She is the best of them all.

_____.

9. My son is very tall.

_____.

GRAMMAR III   Future Indicative of regular verbs.

A.   Verb forms in the Future tense:

SUBJECT	hablar	comer	vivir	ser	estar
yo	hablar é	comer é	vivir é	ser é	estar é
nosotros -as	hablar emos	comer emos	vivir emos	ser emos	estar emos
tú	hablar ás	comer ás	vivir ás	ser ás	estar ás
él/ella/Ud.	hablar á	comer á	vivir á	ser á	estar á
ellos/ellas	hablar án	comer án	vivir án	ser án	estar án

1. The *stem* of the Future is the whole infinitive: *hablar, comer, ser,* etc.
2. The *endings* are the same for all the verbs: *-é, -emos, -ás, -á, -án.*
3. Notice that all the endings have *acentos* except *-emos*.

B.   Use of the Future forms:
1. We use the Future tense to indicate an action which is supposed to occur some time after the present moment.

   Ex.:   La carta *llegará* mañana. (the letter *will arrive* tomorrow)

2. The forms of the Present Indicative are used very frequently to indicate a future action.

> Ex.: La carta llega mañana. (the letter will arrive tomorrow)

3. The Present Indicative of *ir* followed by *a* and the infinitive of the main verb is used to indicate a future action.

> Ex.: La carta va a llegar mañana. (the letter will arrive tomorrow)

4. Frequency in use of the Future, the Present, and the auxiliary *ir a* differs from country to country; for example, in Spain the Future is used much more frequently than in Latin America.

5. The Future tense is also used to indicate an action that is *probable* at the present moment. There is no direct translation in English.

> Ex.: José estará en su casa ahora. (Joe is probably at home now) Serán las tres de la tarde ahora. (it's probably three o'clock now)

PRACTICE THE FUTURE TENSE

(*Answers, p. 312*)

1. The stem of the Future tense is the whole＿＿＿＿＿＿＿＿＿＿.
   For example, the stem of *comerás* is＿＿＿＿＿＿＿; the stem of *seremos* is＿＿＿＿＿＿＿.

2. The endings are the same for all verbs, but each person has a different ending; for example, *-é* means＿＿＿＿; *-ás* means＿＿＿＿.

3. All the endings have *acento* except the ending＿＿＿＿＿.

4. English needs the auxiliary *will* or the contracted *'ll* to form the Future tense. How do you say *we'll buy?*＿＿＿＿＿＿.

5. The future form *seran* is incorrect; it should be spelled＿＿＿＿.

6. The word *future* describes an action that will take place after the＿＿＿ ＿＿＿＿＿＿＿moment.

7. The Future tense is not the only way to express a future action. In Spanish we can use the＿＿＿＿＿tense forms as well as the Future tense forms. For example, *María llegará mañana* is the same as *María＿＿＿ ＿＿＿mañana.*

8. Another way to indicate a future action is using the Present Indicative of_____followed by *a* and by the infinitive of the main verb. For example, *María va a llegar mañana* is the same as *María*_____ _____*mañana.*

9. The forms of the Future tense are sometimes used to indicate an action that is probable at the moment of speaking. For example, if you are not sure what time it is now, you can guess by saying_____ *las tres.*

10. An idiomatic way of saying *Probablemente José está en casa ahora* is *José*_____*en casa ahora.*

EXERCISES   *(Answers, p. 312)*

A.   Complete the sentences with the correct Future tense form.

1. El verano próximo nosotros_____en Miami. (vivir)

2. Si no llueve mañana, yo_____a la playa. (ir)

3. Después de la clase Esteban_____con su amiga. (encontrarse)

4. Esteban_____con muletas por dos semanas. (caminar)

5. Los médicos te_____el tobillo. (enyesar)

6. Si no hay más problemas, no te_____nada. (pasar)

7. Este codo te_____mañana más que hoy. (doler)

8. El presidente_____en Denver el domingo pró-ximo. (estar)

9. Tú y yo_____felices por muchos años. (ser)

10. Estas rosas_____muy bien cuando se abran. (oler)

11. Nadie sabe exactamente lo que_____mañana. (ocurrir)

12. Si no tienes más cuidado,_____el tobillo otra vez. (torcerse)

B. Change these verb forms from Present to Future. Remember
    that a verb that is irregular in the Present is not necessarily
    irregular in the Future. Look for the infinitive; then add the
    appropriate endings. (Don't forget the *acentos*.) Examples:
    vamos/iremos   soy/seré

1. hablas_____   11. vivimos_____

2. vuelvo_____   12. das_____

3. piensan_____   13. vemos_____

4. estamos_____   14. vas_____

5. somos_____   15. es_____

6. pide_____   16. conozco_____

7. sigo_____   17. empieza_____

8. duele_____   18. divierte_____

9. hueles_____   19. entramos_____

10. eres_____   20. conduzco_____

C. Change the verbs from Preterite to Future. Remember that a
    verb that is irregular in the Preterite is not necessarily irregu-
    lar in the Future. Look for the infinitive and add the proper
    endings. Examples: murió / morirá   piensó / pensaré

1. volvió_____   11. lavaste_____

2. fueron (went)_____   12. diste (dar)_____

3. fueron (were)_____   13. regresé_____

4. hablaron_____   14. murió_____

5. torcí_____   15. durmieron_____

6. cojeé_____   16. siguió_____

7. oyó_____   17. estuvo_____

8. cayeron_____   18. enyesó_____

9. pidió_____   19. me caí_____

10. sirvieron_____   20. creyó_____

Lesson 12

La salud
(Health)

alergia	allergy	**indigestión**	indigestion	**remedio**	remedy
antibiótico	antibiotic	**inyección**	shot	**resfrío**[5]	cold (noun)
camisa	shirt	**mareo**[3]	dizziness	**salud**	health
camiseta	undershirt	**medicina**	medicine	**seguro**	insurance
cura[1]	cure	**músculo**	muscle	**síntoma (el)**	symptom
domicilio	address, home	**náuseas**	nausea	**tarjeta**	card
enfermedad	sickness	**pastilla**	tablet	**temperatura**	temperature
enfermero -a	nurse	**peligro**	danger	**tensión**	pressure
estómago	stomach	**píldora**	pill	**tos (la)**	cough
farmacia	pharmacy	**póliza**	policy	**úlcera**	ulcer
fatiga	fatigue	**pulmón**	lung	**vacuna**	vaccine
fiebre (la)	fever	**radiografía**	X-ray	**vitamina**	vitamin
gripe (la)[2]	flu	**receta**[4]	prescription		

agradecer (c)	to thank	**descansar**	to rest
aliviar	to relieve	**enfermarse**	to get sick
arreglar	to arrange, fix	**molestar**[7]	to bother, annoy
auscultar	to listen with a stethoscope	**quitarse**[8]	to go away, disappear
calmar (se)[6]	to calm, to be quiet	**recetar**	to prescribe
curar	to cure, to heal	**toser**	to cough

alegre	happy, cheerful	**pálido**	pale
enfermo	sick	**preferible**	preferable
médico	medical	**saludable**	healthy

¡Cómo no!	Of course.	**perder el tiempo**	to waste time
a lo mejor	perhaps	**guardar cama**	to stay in bed
tener mareos	to be dizzy	**tomar asiento**	to take a seat

tener tos	to have a cough	**llenar una receta**	to fill a prescription
no tener remedio	to have no solution	**¡Sólo me falta eso!**	That's all I need!

NOTES:

1. *Cura* means *cure* when it's *la cura,* but *el cura* means *the priest* as the person who "cures" or "takes care of" the soul. *Una curita* is a *bandaid.*

2. *Gripe* is feminine: *la gripe;* but some dialects use *la gripa.* The word *influenza* is not Spanish but Italian.

3. *Mareo* is *dizziness.* It comes from *mar* (sea), but it applies to any kind of dizziness. The plural form *mareos* is used more frequently than the singular. We use the expression *tener mareos* and *dar mareos* with the meaning of *to be dizzy.*

4. *Receta* is not only *prescription;* it's also a *cooking recipe.*

5. *Resfrío* is one of the many words for a *cold.* Different dialects use the words *resfriado, catarro, constipado.*

6. *Calmar* means *to calm down,* and the reflexive *calmarse* is *to be quiet.* We also use the expression *tener calma* with the meaning of *to be slow.*

7. *Molestar* is not *to molest* as the spelling suggests, but *to bother, annoy.*

8. *Quitar* is not *to quit* as the spelling suggests, but *to take away, steal.* The reflexive means *to go away, take away,* or *disappear.* Note that *molestar, quitarse, calmarse, aliviarse* are often used in the same form as *gustar*—that is, in the third person.
   Ex.:   A José *le* molesta la tos.   A mí *se me* quita la tos.

EXERCISES   *(Answers, p. 312)*

A.   Write *el/la, los/las* in front of the nouns.

1.____tensión	5.____fiebre	9.____seguros	13.____pulmón
2.____síntoma	6.____camisas	10.____inyección	14.____enfermedad
3.____salud	7.____gripe	11.____cura (cure)	15.____radiografía
4.____mareos	8.____tos	12.____cura (priest)	16.____náuseas

B.   Complete the sentences with the appropriate form of one of the idioms below.

¡Cómo no!	tener tos	tomar asiento
a lo mejor	guardar cama	no tener remedio
tener mareos	¡sólo me falta eso!	perder el tiempo

1. No debes fumar tanto porque_____mucha_____.

2. Estás muy enfermo, por eso debes_____
   por unos días.

3. Tienes que esperar un poco; favor de _____
   por unos minutos.

4. Ya sólo faltan 10 minutos; no podemos _____.

5. No debes salir sola, Carmen, si _____.

6. ¡Siempre tengo mala pata! ¡ahora _____!

7. Ese problema no se puede resolver; _____.

8. Si tengo bastante dinero, _____ voy a Las Vegas.

9. _____; yo puedo ir contigo a la fiesta.

C. Complete the sentences with a word from the list below.

vitamina	radiografía	receta	vacuna	domicilio	fatiga (mareos)
úlcera	salud	tensión	farmacia	pulmones	póliza

1. Es necesario hacer una _____ para saber si el
   hueso está *roto* (broken).

2. La _____ contra la polio salva muchas vidas.

3. Las naranjas y limones tienen mucha _____C.

4. Siempre decimos que la _____ es más importante que el
   dinero.

5. Vamos a la _____ a comprar las medicinas.

6. ¿Cuál es el número de tu _____ de seguro?

7. Mi _____ está en la calle Maldonado.

8. Si sientes _____ debes descansar.

9. Creo que su _____ arterial está alta.

10. El médico escribió una _____ para el paciente.

11. Respiramos el aire por medio de los dos _____.

12. Si tienes una _____ en el estómago no puedes
    comer muchas cosas.

D. Complete the sentences with the correct forms of the Future tense.

1. Si me ayudas, te lo _____ siempre. (agradecer)

2. Si fumas tanto, te _____ de cáncer. (enfermar)

3. Ella_____las maletas más tarde. (arreglar)

4. Estoy seguro que este dolor no te_____más. (molestar)

5. Esta gripe se_____muy pronto. (curar)

6. El doctor te_____unas pastillas. (recetar)

7. José y yo_____el verano próximo. (descansar)

8. Ese dolor se te_____con las píldoras. (quitar)

9. Los niños se_____antes de dormir. (calmar)

E. Write a synonym for each of the following words.

1. resfriado_____ 5. gripe_____

2. dirección_____ 6. contento_____

3. pastilla_____ 7. posiblemente_____

4. por supuesto_____ 8. dar gracias_____

F. Write a related word from the vocabulary.

1. alérgico_____ 13. remediar_____

2. fatigoso_____ 14. receta_____

3. estomacal_____ 15. muslo_____

4. farmacéutico_____ 16. inyectar_____

5. digerir_____ 17. escuchar_____

6. curativo_____ 18. alivio_____

7. pulmonar_____ 19. preferir_____

8. vaca_____ 20. palidecer_____

9. toser_____ 21. alegrarse_____

10. saludable_____ 22. calmante_____

11. peligroso_____ 23. mar_____

12. sintomático_____ 24. asegurar_____

DIÁLOGO *En la consulta del médico*

ENFERMERA: ¿Me da usted su nombre, por favor?
GUILLERMO: ¡Cómo no! Guillermo Cabrera Infante.
ENFERMERA: ¿Domicilio y número de teléfono?
GUILLERMO: Avenida de los Mártires, 28. Mi teléfono es 630-4846.
ENFERMERA: ¿Tiene usted seguro médico?
GUILLERMO: Sí; aquí tiene mi tarjeta con la póliza.

• • •

DOCTOR: ¿Qué le trae por aquí, Señor Cabrera?
GUILLERMO: Un dolor de estómago terrible. No quería molestarlo, pero ya llevo dos días con náuseas, mareos, y este dolor que no se me quita.
DOCTOR: Veo que tiene un poco de fiebre y la tensión arterial alta.
GUILLERMO: ¿Cree Ud. que será una úlcera?
DOCTOR: A lo mejor es el resultado de una indigestión. Quítese la camisa y la camiseta para auscultarlo.
GUILLERMO: ¡Sólo falta que tenga complicaciones en los pulmones!
DOCTOR: No, veo que los pulmones y el corazón están bien. Le voy a poner una inyección para calmar el dolor.
GUILLERMO: ¿Debo guardar cama?
DOCTOR: Sí, por varios días. Puede ser un simple caso de gripe. Le daré una receta y ya verá que con estas píldoras todo se curará.
GUILLERMO: Se lo agradezco mucho, doctor.
DOCTOR: Bueno, a la cama y a descansar. Adiós.

DIALOG *At the Doctor's Office*

NURSE: Your name, please?
WILLIAM: Of course. Guillermo Cabrera Infante.
NURSE: Your address and telephone?
WILLIAM: 28 Avenida de los Mártires. My phone is 630-4846.
NURSE: Do you have medical insurance?
WILLIAM: Yes; here's the card with the policy number.

• • •

DOCTOR: What brings you here, Mr. Cabrera?
WILLIAM: A terrible stomachache. I didn't want to bother you, but I've been nauseated and dizzy for two days, and this pain (that) doesn't go away.
DOCTOR: I see you have a slight fever and high blood pressure.
WILLIAM: Do you think it could be an ulcer?
DOCTOR: Perhaps it's the result of indigestion. Take off your shirt and undershirt so I can listen with the stethoscope.

WILLIAM: All I need is complications in the lungs!

DOCTOR: No, I see your lungs and heart are okay. I'm going to give you a shot to stop the pain.

WILLIAM: Should I stay in bed?

DOCTOR: Yes, for a few days. It might be a simple case of flu. I'll give you a prescription and you'll see that everything will be cured with these pills.

WILLIAM: (I) thank you very much, doctor.

DOCTOR: Well, (go) to bed and rest. Goodbye.

EXERCISES

(Answers, p. 313)

A.   Complete the sentences to form a narrative summary of the dialog.

Guillermo está en la (1)_____del médico. La enfermera le pregunta el nombre, (2) el_____y el teléfono. También le pregunta si tiene (3)_____médico, y Guillermo le da la tarjeta con el número de la (4)_____. Él tiene un dolor terrible de (5)_____pero no quería (6)_____ al doctor. Hace dos días que tiene náuseas y (7)_____. También tiene fiebre y la tensión arterial está (8)_____. El doctor le manda quitarse la camiseta para (9)_____. Los pulmones y el (10)_____están bien, y le pone una inyección para (11)_____el dolor. Guillermo debe guardar (12)_____por varios días. El doctor piensa que puede ser un simple caso de (13)_____, y le da una receta para unas (14) _____que le curarán todo. Guillermo le agradece todo y se va a su casa a guardar cama y a (15)_____, pero antes pasará por la farmacia.

B.   Answer True (T) or False (F).

1.____   La enfermera necesita saber el nombre, el domicilio y el teléfono de Guillermo.

2.____   Guillermo le da el nombre y el domicilio pero no el teléfono por que no lo tiene.

3.＿＿ El domicilio de Guillermo está en la Avenida del Cinco de Mayo.

4.＿＿ Guillermo le da la tarjeta del seguro médico a la enfermera.

5.＿＿ El doctor se llama Cabrera Infante.

6.＿＿ Guillermo tiene mucho dolor de estómago, y siente náuseas y mareos.

7.＿＿ Pero él no tiene fiebre ni tensión alta.

8.＿＿ El doctor no piensa que es una úlcera sino una indigestión o un simple caso de gripe.

9.＿＿ El doctor lo ausculta para ver si hay complicaciones en los pulmones y el corazón.

10.＿＿ Guillermo no quiere inyecciones contra el dolor.

11.＿＿ El doctor le receta unas píldoras y le manda guardar cama por unos días.

12.＿＿ Guillermo está muy agradecido y se va a su casa a descansar.

13.＿＿ En conclusión, Guillermo tiene una úlcera y complicaciones en los pulmones.

C. Complete the sentences with the appropriate word.

1. Lo contrario de *salud* es＿＿＿＿＿＿＿＿＿＿＿＿.

2. Lo contrario de *curarse* es＿＿＿＿＿＿＿＿＿＿＿.

3. Lo contrario de *saludable* es＿＿＿＿＿＿＿＿＿＿.

4. Lo contrario de *baja tensión* es＿＿＿＿＿＿＿＿＿.

5. Lo contrario de *descanso* es＿＿＿＿＿＿＿＿＿＿.

6. Lo contrario de *paciente* es＿＿＿＿＿＿＿＿＿＿.

7. Debajo de la *camisa* nos ponemos la＿＿＿＿＿＿＿＿.

8. En una＿＿＿＿＿＿＿＿＿＿＿podemos ver los huesos de una persona.

9. El doctor siempre quiere saber los＿＿＿＿＿＿＿＿＿ de una enfermedad.

10. Fumar es un＿＿＿＿＿＿＿＿＿＿porque puede causar cáncer.

11. La enfermera toma la＿＿＿＿＿＿＿＿＿＿para ver si uno tiene fiebre.

12. Una enfermedad *incurable* es una enfermedad que no tiene＿＿＿＿＿.

D. Write full sentences using the following words. The words are given in the correct order. Change the infinitives to the Present Indicative, and add articles, prepositions, etc., as needed.

1. Guillermo / tener / mareos / porque / su / presión / estar / alta /.

   _____

2. Lola / estar / pálido / porque / tener / fiebre /.

   _____

3. mí / molestar / dolor / estómago /.

   _____

4. ¿ti / quitarse / dolor / cabeza / con aspirina?

   _____

5. A José / no / aliviarse / tos / con / pastillas /.

   _____

6. A Ud. / doler / músculos / porque / tener / gripe /.

   _____

7. doctor / escribir / receta / paciente /.

   _____

GRAMMAR I   Conditional tense of regular verbs.

A. The forms of the Conditional:

SUBJECT	hablar	comer	vivir	ir	ser
yo	hablar ía	comer ía	vivir ía	ir ía	ser ía
nosotros -as	hablar íamos	comer íamos	vivir íamos	ir íamos	ser íamos
tú	hablar ías	comer ías	vivir ías	ir ías	ser ías
él/ella/Ud.	hablar ía	comer ía	vivir ía	ir ía	ser ía
ellos/ellas	hablar ían	comer ían	vivir ían	ir ían	ser ían

1. The stem of the Conditional is the full infinitive, just as in the Future tense.
   Ex.:   estar/estaría; *ir*/iría; escribir/escribiría

2. The endings are the same for all the verbs: *-ía, -íamos, -ías, -ían*. Remember that these same endings are used in the Imperfect tense of the verbs ending in *-ER* or *-IR*, but the stem of the Imperfect is shorter: *comer/comía/comería; escribir/escribía/escribiría*.

3. Notice that all the forms have *acento* on *ía*.

B. Uses of the Conditional tense: (*would* + verb)

1. The Conditional is used to indicate an action that is supposed to occur some time after a moment in the past, just as the Future refers to an action that occurs after the time of speaking. Notice the parallel between the two tenses.
   Future: Te prometo que *volveré*. (I promise you *I'll be back*)
   Conditional: Te prometí que *volvería*. (I promised you *I would be back*)

2. We also use the Imperfect form of *ir a* followed by the infinitive to indicate the same idea as the Conditional.
   Ex.:   Te prometí que *iba a volver*.
          (I promised you *I was coming back*)

3. We frequently use the Conditional in English to show a *habit* in the past. This conditional must be translated in Spanish by the *Imperfect* because the Spanish Conditional is never used to show a habit.
   Ex.:   When I was in Mexico, I *would speak* Spanish all the time. (*Cuando estaba en México, yo siempre* hablaba *español*.)

C. Conditional of probability:
The Conditional is also used to indicate an action that was *probable* at a past moment, just as the Future refers to probability at the present time.
   Ex.:   José no vino ayer a clase. Iría a la playa.
          (Joe did not come to class yesterday. He probably went to the beach)

PRACTICE THE CONDITIONAL   *(Answers, p. 313)*

1. The stem used in the Conditional tense is the full_____;

   for example, the Conditional of *estar* is_____.

2. The_____of the Conditional tense are the same for all verbs: *ía, íamos, ías, ían*.

3. The Conditional has the same endings as the _____
   tense of the verbs ending in *-ER* or *-IR*. For example, *comía/* _____
   _____.

4. The difference between the Imperfect and the Conditional forms of *vivir*
   is one syllable; the Conditional is always longer: *vivía/* _____.

5. We use the Conditional to show that an action is supposed to happen *after* a
   moment in the _____, just as the Future indicates an
   action that takes place after the moment of speaking.

6. The Conditional tense can be replaced by the _____
   of *ir a* followed by the infinitive. For example, *Me dijo que llegaría tarde* is
   the same as *Me dijo que* _____ *tarde.*

7. The Conditional is used in English to show a habit in the past, just like *used
   to*. In Spanish this conditional use must be translated by the _____
   _____ tense.

8. To indicate probability at the actual moment of speaking, we use the
   _____, whereas to show probability in the past, we use the
   _____.

9. A more idiomatic way of saying *Ella estuvo probablemente en casa* is *Ella*
   _____ *en casa.*

EXERCISES   *(Answers, p. 314)*

A. **Complete the sentences with the correct forms of the Con-
    ditional. Suppose you are a patient and the doctor tells you
    what to do and what not to do.**

El doctor *me dijo ayer* que . . .

1. me _____ pronto de la tos. (curar)

2. me _____ del dolor de garganta. (aliviar)

3. _____ guardar cama por una semana. (deber)

4. él no _____ el tiempo con aspirinas. (perder)

5. él no_____por una semana. (fumar)

6. me_____con una inyección. (calmar)

7. no_____comer carne ni pollo. (deber)

8. no me_____otra vez. (enfermar)

9. _____mejor con un calmante. (descansar)

10. la tos no me_____más. (molestar)

11. el dolor de estómago se me_____. (quitar)

12. él me_____unos antibióticos. (recetar)

13. las cosas se_____pronto. (arreglar)

14. él me_____los pulmones. (auscultar)

15. él me_____a examinar después de una semana. (volver)

B. Change the verbs from Present to Conditional. Remember that a verb that is irregular in the Present is not necessarily irregular in the Conditional. Use the full infinitive as the stem of the Conditional.

1. soy_____   8. vamos_____

2. pido_____   9. pago_____

3. estás_____   10. duerme_____

4. vuelven_____   11. escribo_____

5. pienso_____   12. mueren_____

6. eres_____   13. sigue_____

7. conozco_____   14. oyes_____

C. Now change the verbs from Preterite to Conditional.

1. entré_____   7. cayó_____

2. oyó_____   8. creyeron_____

3. fue (went)_____   9. seguiste_____

4. fue (was)_____   10. compraron_____

5. pidieron_____   11. estuve_____

6. murió_____   12. anduvo_____

GRAMMAR II   Future and Conditional of irregular verbs.

A.   Memorize the following verbs:

	saber		venir	
SUBJECT	Future	Conditional	Future	Conditional
yo	sabr é	sabr ía	vendr é	vendr ía
nosotros -as	sabr emos	sabr íamos	vendr emos	vendr íamos
tú	sabr ás	sabr ías	vendr ás	vendr ías
él/ella/usted	sabr á	sabr ía	vendr á	vendr ía
ellos/ellas	sabr án	sabr ían	vendr án	vendr ían

1.   All the verbs that are irregular in the Future are also irregular in the Conditional, and they show the same kind of change. For example, *sabré* and *sabría* are irregular because they drop the *e* for *saberé* → *sabré* and *sabería* → *sabría*.
2.   Notice that *vendré* and *vendría* are the irregular forms of *venir* rather than *veniré/veniría*. In this case the *i* is replaced by a *d*.

B.   Memorize the Future and Conditional forms of the irregular verbs:

saber	sabré	sabría	querer	querré	querría
poder	podré	podría	venir	vendré	vendría
poner	pondré	pondría	salir	saldré	saldría
caber	cabré	cabría	valer	valdré	valdría
decir	diré	diría	tener	tendré	tendría
hacer	haré	haría	haber	habré	habría

C.   Compound verbs:
There are only twelve simple verbs in the previous list (B), but most of them have compound forms that show the same kind of change. Here is a partial list that you should memorize:

obtener	(to obtain)	suponer	(to suppose)	satisfacer	(to satisfy)
contener	(to contain)	componer	(to compose, fix)	deshacer	(to undo, melt)
detener	(to detain, stop)	proponer	(to proose)	rehacer	(to redo, do it again)
mantener	(to maintain)	imponer	(to impose)	prevenir	(to prevent)
sostener	(to sustain)	oponer	(to oppose)	convenir	(to be convenient)
abstener	(to abstain)	exponer	(to expose)	provenir	(to originate in)

1. The compounds of *decir* are regular in the future and conditional.
   Ex.: *bendecir* (to bless)/*bendeciré; maldecir* (to curse)/
   maldeciré.

2. *Caber* means *to fit, to be room for.*
   Ex.: En mi carro sólo caben cuatro personas.
   (only four persons fit in my car)

PRACTICE THE IRREGULAR FUTURE
AND CONDITIONAL   *(Answers, p. 314)*

1. The Future form of *saber* is not *saberé* but_____. This
   means that the vowel_____has been dropped.

2. The Conditional of *venir* is not *veniría* but_____. This
   means that the letter *i* has been replaced by the letter_____.

3. Every verb that is irregular in the Future tense is also irregular in the
   _____. For example, from *hacer* we have *haré* and

   _____.

4. From the verb *querer,* we have *quería* in the Imperfect. In this case the
   Conditional is not a syllable longer, but one letter longer:_____.

5. *Caber* means *to fit.* How do you say *We won't fit in your VW? No*_____

   _____*en tu VW.*

6. *Satisfacer* is a compound of *hacer* (old Spanish *facer*). If the Future of *hacer*
   is *haré,* the Future of *satisfacer* is_____.

7. If the Future of *tener* is *tendré,* the Future of *contener* is_____

   _____.

8. If the Future of *poner* is *pondré,* the Future of *suponer* is_____

   _____.

9. If the Conditional of *hacer* is *haría,* the Conditional of *rehacer* is_____

   _____.

10. If the Conditional of *poner* is *pondría,* the Conditional of *oponer* is_____

    _____.

EXERCISES

(Answers, p. 314)

A. Complete the sentences with the correct Future form of the verb in parentheses.

1. Anita y yo_____para México el lunes. (salir)

2. Pasado mañana_____una fiesta en mi casa. (haber)

3. El calor del sol_____la nieve. (deshacer)

4. El presidente_____una reglas nuevas. (proponer)

5. Algunos senadores se_____de votar. (abstener)

6. Esa composición tiene muchos errores; usted la_____. (rehacer)

7. ¿Cuánto_____un Cadillac en 1999? (valer)

8. Puedes invitar a Carlos, pero estoy seguro que no_____venir. (querer)

9. Los californianos se_____a otra Proposición 13. (oponer)

10. Estamos seguros que tú_____toda la verdad. (decir)

B. Complete the sentences with the Conditional form of the verb in parentheses.

El doctor *me dijo* que . . .

1. _____que guardar cama por una semana. (tener)

2. él_____escribir una receta. (poder)

3. él me_____un gran favor. (hacer)

4. _____bien de la operación. (salir)

5. él_____los síntomas claramente. (exponer)

6. _____mejores resultados sin fumar. (obtener)

7. él_____lo que me convendría más. (saber)

8. _____saludable si no bebo alcohol. (ser)

9. él me_____la verdad sobre mi enfermedad. (decir)

10. él_____verme otra vez pronto. (querer)

11. él se_____en contacto conmingo. (mantener)

12. _____la pena guardar cama. (valer)

13. él_____una operación pronto. (proponer)

14. la aspirina_____el dolor de cabeza. (prevenir)

15. los antibióticos_____la infección. (detener)

16. la vacuna_____buen resultado. (tener)

C. **You have covered the five different tenses of the Indicative in this order: Present, Preterite, Imperfect, Future, and Conditional. In this exercise, you are given the forms of the Present and the Imperfect. Write the forms of the Preterite, the Future, and the Conditional. Answer in the same person in which you find the Present and the Imperfect.**

PRESENT	IMPER-FECT	PRETERITE	FUTURE	CONDITIONAL
1. vamos	íbamos	_____	_____	_____
2. somos	éramos	_____	_____	_____
3. estoy	estaba	_____	_____	_____
4. dan	daban	_____	_____	_____
5. pido	pedía	_____	_____	_____
6. veo	veía	_____	_____	_____
7. hace	hacía	_____	_____	_____
8. digo	decía	_____	_____	_____
9. oigo	oía	_____	_____	_____
10. cree	creía	_____	_____	_____
11. salgo	salía	_____	_____	_____
12. tiene	tenía	_____	_____	_____
13. vuelve	volvía	_____	_____	_____
14. sé	sabía	_____	_____	_____
15. pongo	ponía	_____	_____	_____
16. oyen	oían	_____	_____	_____
17. es	era	_____	_____	_____
18. huye	huía	_____	_____	_____
19. puedo	podía	_____	_____	_____

PRESENT	IMPER-FECT	PRETERITE	FUTURE	CONDITIONAL
20. quiere	quería	_____	_____	_____
21. hay	había	_____	_____	_____
22. anda	andaba	_____	_____	_____
23. muere	moría	_____	_____	_____
24. sigue	seguía	_____	_____	_____
25. empiezo	empezaba	_____	_____	_____
26. ofrezco	ofrecía	_____	_____	_____
27. pago	pagaba	_____	_____	_____

GRAMMAR III   Familiar commands (tú).

A. Regular commands:
The command forms, or imperatives, are used to give an order or a request. The forms for *affirmative* commands are different from those for *negative* commands.
1. *Affirmative commands.* The form is identical to the third person singular of the Present Indicative hablar/habla; comer/come; escribir/escribe.
Ex.: *Trae* el libro de ejercicios. (*bring* the exercise book)

2. *Negative commands.* Verbs ending in *-AR* take the ending *-es,* and verbs ending in *-ER, -IR* take the ending *-as.* A negative word is needed in front of the verb.
Ex.: *No hables* tanto. (*don't talk* so much)
No comas esa ensalada. (*don't eat* that salad)

B. Irregular commands:
1. All stem-changing verbs contain the same change in the command forms as in the Present Indicative.
Ex.: volver/vuelve/no vuelvas;
pedir/pide/no pidas;
pensar/piensa/no pienses;
dormir/duerme/no duermas

2. Most verbs that are irregular in the first person of the Present Indicative show the same irregularity in the *negative* command forms:

salir/salgo/no salgas	**tener/tengo/no tengas**
conocer/conozco/no conozcas	**oír/oigo/no oigas**
decir/digo/no digas	**huir/huyo/no huyas**

3. Here are eight verbs that are irregular because they either drop the ending completely in the affirmative commands, or they take strange forms (see *saber*):

venir/ven/no vengas	**poner/pon/no pongas**
tener/ten/no tengas	**salir/sal/no salgas**
hacer/haz/no hagas	**ser/sé/no seas**
decir/di/no digas	**saber/sabe/no sepas**

C. Unstressed pronouns with command forms:
   The unstressed pronouns *me, lo, la, te,* etc., follow the affirmative commands and precede the negative commands.

   Ex.: Llámame. (call me)/No me llames. (don't call me)
   Dímelo. (tell it to me)/No me lo digas. (don't tell it to me)

PRACTICE THE FAMILIAR COMMAND FORMS

(Answers, p. 315)

1. We use the command forms (sometimes called *imperative*) to give a direct order. There are two kinds of commands: the formal command, addressed to *usted,* and the familiar command, addressed to _____. We will cover the formal command forms in the next lesson.

2. The affirmative command forms are the same as the third-person forms of the Present_____. For example, *hablar/*_____; *comer/*_____.

3. The verbs ending in -*AR* need the ending_____for a negative command, and all the other verbs need the ending_____. For example, *hablar/no*_____; *escribir/no*_____. Remember that a negative word is needed before the verb.

4. Stem-changing verbs show the same changes in the command forms as in the Present_____. For example, *dormir/duerme/no* _____.

5. Most verbs that are irregular in the first person of the Present Indicative show the same irregularity in the_____ command form. For example, *salir/salgo/no*_____; *traer/traigo/no*_____.

6. A few verbs are irregular in the affirmative command forms because they show no ending. For example, *venir*/_____; *tener*/_____; *salir*/_____.

7. The word *di* is two different things in Spanish: (1) the Preterite of the verb *dar*, when it means_____, and (2) the familiar affirmative command form of *decir*, when it means_____. *Di* never has a written accent.

8. *Sé* is also two different things: (1) the present indicative of *saber*, when it means_____, and (2) the familiar affirmative command form of *ser*, when it means_____. In both cases *sé* needs a written accent.

9. The unstressed pronouns, such as *me, te, le, nos,* follow the _____ _____commands, but precede the_____ _____commands. For example, to translate *Call me* we say_____ _____, and *Don't call me* we say *No*_____.

10. Compound verbs follow the same changes as simple verbs. If the command form of *poner* is *pon,* the command form of *exponer* is_____ (it needs an accent!).

11. If the command form of *tener* is *ten,* the command form of *mantener* is _____ (it needs an accent!).

EXERCISES   *(Answers, p. 315)*

A. Change the following statements to familiar affirmative commands.

Example: Carlos me llama esta noche.
         Carlos, llámame esta noche.

1. Ana viene conmigo a la fiesta._____.

2. Lola me habla en español._____.

3. Luis me escribe a menudo._____.

4. José me dice la verdad._____.

5. Marcos me hace un favor._____.

6. Esteban me oye bien. _____ .

7. Luisa sale temprano hoy. _____ .

8. Felipe se lava las manos. _____ .

9. Carlitos se duerme pronto. _____ .

B. Now change these statements to familiar negative commands.

1. Luisa no llega tarde. _____ .

2. Guillermo no dice nada. _____ .

3. José no me llama hoy. _____ .

4. Lolita no se lava las manos. _____ .

5. Jorge se sienta aquí. _____ .

6. Julia no hace eso. _____ .

7. María no me hace un favor. _____ .

8. Carlos no deshace la maleta. _____ .

9. Anita no me lo compra. _____ .

10. Lucía no lo propone. _____ .

11. Mario no se duerme. _____ .

12. Marcos no se despierta. _____ .

C. Answer the questions, first affirmatively and then negatively, substitute object pronouns wherever possible.

Example: ¿Preparo *la comida?*
Sí, prepára*la*. No, no *la* prepares.

1. ¿Contesto el teléfono?

   Sí, _____ . No, _____ .

2. ¿Lleno esta receta?

   Sí, _____ . No, _____ .

3. ¿Traigo a mi amiga Luisa?

   Sí, _____ . No, _____ .

4. ¿Me lavo las manos?

   Sí,_____. No,_____.

5. ¿Le pido el carro a papá?

   Sí,_____. No,_____.

6. ¿Le digo la verdad a tu amiga?

   Sí,_____. No,_____.

7. ¿Tomo las pastillas ahora?

   Sí,_____. No,_____.

D. Change these familiar commands from affirmative to negative, and vice versa.

Examples: Llámame.   No lo comas.
           No me llames.   Cómelo.

1. Siéntate aquí._____.

2. Dame la cuenta ahora._____.

3. Háblame siempre en español._____.

4. Dímelo todo._____.

5. Arréglate el pelo._____.

6. Bébete el café._____.

7. No te lo tomes todo._____.

8. No la llames temprano._____.

9. No te vistas ahora._____.

10. No lo toques, por favor._____.

11. No lo empieces mañana._____.

12. No te lleves el carro._____.

Lesson 13

En la droguería[1] (At the Drugstore)

acero	steel	**florería**	flower shop	**pescadería**	fish store
alimento	food	**frutería**	fruit store	**sangre (la)**	blood
balanza	scale	**gota**	drop (noun)	**sastre**	tailor
barbería[2]	barbershop	**irritación**	irritation	**sastrería**	tailor shop
calmante	sedative	**jabón**	soap	**talco**	powder
caloría	calorie	**jarabe**	syrup	**tubo**	tube, pipe
carnicería	butcher shop	**líquido**	liquid	**variedad**	variety
dieta	diet	**marca**	trademark, brand	**verdulería**	greengrocer's
diestista	dietitian	**narcótico**	narcotic	**verdura**[3]	vegetable
droga	drug	**panadería**	bakery	**vuelta**[4]	change
droguería	drugstore	**pastelería**	pastry shop	**yogur**	yogurt
ejercicio	exercise	**peluquería**	haridresser's	**zapatería**	shoe store

abusar	to abuse	**convertir (ie, i)**	to convert
acostumbrarse	to get used to	**cortar el pelo**	to cut the hair
adelgazar	to lose weight	**durar**	to last
alimentar	to feed	**gotear**	to drip
balancear	to balance	**padecer (c)**	to suffer
conseguir (i)	to obtain	**preocuparse**	to worry
contener	to contain	**tardar**	to be long
contestar	to answer	**tragar**	to swallow

complicado	complicated	**flaco**	thin, skinny
balanceado	balanced	**gordo**	fat
delgado	thin	**grueso**	fat
drogadicto	drug addict	**inoxidable**	rustproof, stainless
estricto	strict, severe	**reciente**	recent

bajar de peso	to lose weight	hoja de afeitar	razor blade
crema dental	toothpaste	perder peso	to lose weight
estar a dieta	to be on a diet	seguir una dieta	to be on a diet
farmacia de guardia	pharmacy open 24 hours		

NOTES:

1. *Droguería* is also called *farmacia.* In Hispanic countries the *farmacia* is not as large as the drugstore in the United States. It has medicines, perfumes, and other items such as toothpaste, razor blades, and cosmetics.

2. *Barbería* is barbershop, but in some countries the word *peluquería* is used with this meaning (for men only). Here we use *peluquería* or *salón de belleza* for a women's shop. Remember that the *i* in parentheses following *conseguir* means that this verb is irregular with the change of *e* to *i: consigo, consigues, consigue.*

3. *Verdura* is more frequent in the plural form *verduras*, meaning *vegetables.* Some dialects use the word *vegetales, viandas.*

4. *Vuelta* also means *ride, return (regreso), bend.* Here it is the *change* in a money operation. Some dialects use *vuelto* for this meaning.

5. *Contener* is a compound of *tener,* with the same changes: *contengo, contuve, contendré.*

6. *Convertir* changes *e* to *ie,* such as *convierto, conviertes,* and like *sentir,* also changes *e* to *i* in the Preterite: *convirtió, convirtieron.*

7. *Delgado* means *thin; flaco* is used to indicate *very thin, skinny.*

EXERCISES

(Answers, p. 315)

A. **Write the articles *el, la, los, las* in front of the nouns. Remember that nouns ending in *L-O-N-E-R-S* are masculine, and nouns ending in D-IÓN-Z-A are feminine.**

1. ___ sastre
2. ___ vuelta
3. ___ líquido
4. ___ yogur

5. ___ jarabe
6. ___ sangre
7. ___ jabón
8. ___ variedad

9. ___ dietista
10. ___ narcóticos
11. ___ irritación
12. ___ calmante

B. **The Spanish suffix (ending) *ería* is used frequently to indicate the place where a thing is made, or a thing can be bought. For example, café/cafetería; chocolate/chocolatería (a shop where chocolate is made or served).**

¿Dónde compra o dónde consigue usted . . .

1. pescado? _____

2. verduras? _____

3. zapatos?_____

4. cortarse el pelo? (hombres)_____

5. arreglarse el pelo? (mujeres)_____

6. pasteles?_____

7. pan?_____

8. frutas?_____

9. carne?_____

10. flores?_____

11. medicinas?_____

12. hacerse un traje o un vestido?_____

13. tacos?_____

14. libros?_____

15. relojes?_____

C. Complete the sentences with one of the idioms below.

perder peso	hoja de afeitar
seguir una dieta	crema dental
farmacia de guardia	

1. Estas_____son de acero inoxidable.

2. Aunque (although) ya es la una de la mañana, puedes comprar medicinas en

   la_____.

3. ¿Cómo te vas a lavar los dientes sin_____.

4. Para_____rápidamente debes_____

   _____estricta y hacer ejercicio.

D. Review the Future by completing these sentences with the correct Future forms.

1. El viaje de Nueva York a Madrid_____unas seis
   horas. (durar)

2. Tú_____si no dejas de fumar. (padecer)

3. ¿Cuánto tiempo_____en llegar la secretaria? (tardar)

4. Aquí en el banco (ellos) te_____los dólares en pesos. (convertir)

5. Yo_____los boletos si me das el dinero. (conseguir)

6. Nosotros_____si seguimos una buena dieta. (adelgazar)

7. Si llegamos tarde, mamá_____por nosotros. (preocuparse)

8. José, ya te_____al frío en Alaska. (acostumbrar)

9. Usted_____estas píldoras sin *masticar*las (chew). (tragar)

10. Los padres_____a su familia con su trabajo. (mantener)

11. Si llamas tarde, nadie_____el teléfono. (contestar)

E.   Word Families: Write a related word for each of the following.

1. uso_____   7. tarde_____

2. pelo_____   8. diente_____

3. delgado_____   9. volver_____

4. dieta_____   10. verde_____

5. sangría_____   11. óxido_____

6. gota_____   12. alimento_____

F.   Complete the sentences with a word from the list below.

marca	talco	balanza	jabón	jarabe
sangre	tubo	droga	verdura	florería
yogur	caloría	acero	gota	

1. En esta dieta sólo podemos comer 600_____por día.

2. La cocaína es una_____peligrosa.

3. Voy a pasar por la_____para comprar unas rosas para mi mujer.

4. Tú dices que sólo pesas 150 libras, pero aquí está la_____que dice 155.

5. Ford, Toyota, Fiat son _____ de automóviles.

6. Estas hojas de afeitar son de _____ inoxidable.

7. Creo que tu tensión de _____ está un poco alta.

8. Para bañarte necesitas _____ y una toalla.

9. Algunos dietistas dicen que las _____ son mejores que las carnes.

10. Si te molestan los pies, debes ponerte un poco de _____ .

11. El _____ no tiene muchas calorías.

12. Voy a comprar un _____ de crema dental.

13. Los niños prefieren el _____ a las pastillas porque es dulce.

14. Es necesario poner tres _____ de este líquido en los ojos porque los tienes irritados.

DIÁLOGO *En la farmacia*

(Guillermo y Don Tomás son amigos. Guillermo es el mismo paciente de la lección anterior. Don Tomás es el farmacéutico.)

DON TOMÁS: ¡Hola, Guillermo! ¡Hacía mucho tiempo que no te veía! ¿Cómo estás?

GUILLERMO: No muy bien. Tengo un dolor terrible de estómago, con mareos, náuseas, . . .

DON TOMÁS: ¿Ya viste al doctor?

GUILLERMO: Sí, de allá vengo.

DON TOMÁS: ¿Y qué te dijo?

GUILLERMO: Que no parece nada serio, pero que debo guardar cama por varios días.

DON TOMÁS: ¿Y no te recetó nada para el dolor?

GUILLERMO: Sí; aquí está la receta. Llénamela lo más pronto posible.

DON TOMÁS: A ver. No es complicada. Es un calmante. Te la puedo preparar en pastillas o en jarabe.

GUILLERMO: Prepárala en jarabe. Siempre me molesta tragar pastillas. Ese calmante, ¿contiene algún narcótico?

DON TOMÁS: No te preocupes. Este jarabe no te convertirá en drogadicto.

GUILLERMO: Mientras preparas la receta voy a buscar unas cosas que necesito. Un tubo de crema dental, talco para los pies y unas hojas de afeitar.

DON TOMÁS:	Esas hojas son de acero inoxidable. Te deben durar mucho tiempo.
GUILLERMO:	Recientemente me molestan bastante los ojos. ¿Tienes algo para eso?
DON TOMÁS:	¡Cómo no! Te recomiendo estas gotas; deben aliviarte la irritación. Ponte dos gotas antes de acostarte.
GUILLERMO:	Gracias, Tomás. ¿Cuánto te debo?
DON TOMÁS:	Son 122 pesos en total. Gracias, y alíviate pronto.

DIALOG   *At the Pharmacy*

(William and Thomas are friends. Bill is the same patient we had in the previous lesson. Tom is the pharmacist.)

TOM:	Hi, Bill! I haven't seen you in a long time! How are you?
BILL:	Not so well. I have a terrible stomachache, with dizziness, nausea, ...
TOM:	Have you seen the doctor?
BILL:	Yes, that's where I'm coming from.
TOM:	What did he say?
BILL:	That it doesn't seem serious, but that I should stay in bed for a few days.
TOM:	And didn't he prescribe anything for the pain?
BILL:	Yes, here is the prescription. Fill it for me as soon as possible.
TOM:	Let me see. It's not complicated; it's a sedative. I can make it for you in pills or in syrup.
BILL:	Prepare it in syrup. It always bothers me to swallow pills. Does the sedative contain narcotics?
TOM:	Don't worry. This syrup won't turn you into a drug addict.
BILL:	While you fill the prescription, I'm going to pick up a few things that I need. Toothpaste, foot powder, and some razor blades.
TOM:	Those blades are made of stainless steel. They should last you a long time.
BILL:	My eyes have been bothering me a lot recently. Do you have anything for that?
TOM:	Of course! I recommend these drops. They should relieve the irritation. Put in two drops before you go to bed.
BILL:	Thanks, Tom. How much do I owe you?
TOM:	It's 122 pesos all together. Thanks, and I hope you'll feel better soon!

EXERCISES

(Answers, p. 316)

A. Complete the sentences to make a narrative summary of the dialog.

Guillermo habla con su (1)_____Don Tomás que es farmacéutico. Hace mucho tiempo que los dos amigos no se (2)_____ _____. Guillermo tiene un dolor terrible de (3)_____, con náuseas y (4)_____. Él viene de ver al (5)_____. El médico no cree que su enfermedad es cosa (6)_____, pero le recomienda guardar (7)_____por varios días. Guillermo le da la receta a Don Tomás para llenarla lo (8)_____ _____posible. El farmacéutico puede prepararla en pastillas o en (9)_____. Guillermo prefiere el jarabe porque le molesta (10)_____pastillas. El calmante siempre tiene alguna droga, pero esto no convertirá a Guillermo en (11)_____ _____. Mientras Don Tomás prepara la (12)_____ _____, él va a buscar algunas cosas que necesita: un tubo de crema (13)_____, talco para los (14)_____, y unas hojas de (15)_____. Las hojas son de acero (16)_____, y deben durar mucho (17)_____ _____. A Guillermo le molestan los (18)_____ recientemente, y el farmacéutico le recomienda unas (19)_____ que debe ponérselas antes de (20)_____. Guillermo paga 122 (21)_____en total y se va para su casa.

B. Circle the best answer.

1. Si Ud. desea cortarse el pelo va a (la droguería, la farmacia, la barbería, la florería).

2. Si Ud. quiere perder peso debe (seguir una dieta, ver al farmacéutico, tomar narcóticos).

3. Si Ud. quiere lavarse los dientes necesita (jabón, jarabe, crema dental, una marca buena).

4. Si Ud. quiere comer dulces va a (la frutería, la pastelería, la panadería, la verdulería).

5. Si Ud. quiere hacerse un traje va a la (sastrería, pescadería, zapatería, florería).

6. Si Ud. quiere saber su peso necesita una (marca, droga, gota, balanza).

7. Si Ud. necesita bañarse debe tener (yogur, jabón, acero, alimento).

8. Si Ud. tiene la tensión de sangre alta debe (comer más carne, tragar píldoras, tomar alcohol, comer sin sal).

9. Si Ud. tiene los ojos irritados es bueno (comer más calorías, ponerse gotas, leer más).

C. Match the two columns.

1.____ Una cosa que no es *sencilla* es. . . .   A. inoxidable

2.____ Una cosa . . . acaba de ocurrir o pasar.   B. drogadicto -a

3.____ Si usted paga *por todo,* Ud. paga. . . .   C. sastre

4.____ Una persona que está *delgada* no   D. abusar
         está. . . .

5.____ Una persona que está *muy delgada*   E. complicado -a
         está. . . .

6.____ Un metal que no se puede oxidar es. . . .   F. líquido

7.____ Una persona que está *gorda* es lo mismo G. en total
         que. . . .

8.____ Una comida que tiene toda clase de   H. reciente
         alimentos está. . . .

9.____ Una persona que siempre toma cocaína   I. grueso -a
         es un. . . .

10.____ El jarabe no es sólido sino. . . .   J. flaco -a

11.____ *Usar* demasiado de una cosa es. . . .   K. gordo -a

12.____ La persona que sabe hacer trajes es. . . .   L. balanceado- -a

D.   Write full sentences with the words given. Keep the words in the order given. Use the verbs in the familiar command forms. You may need to add words such as articles, prepositions, and object pronouns.

1. Preparar / este / receta / a mí /.

_____

2. No preocuparse / de / ese / problemas /.

_____

3. Ponerse / dos / gota / antes de / acostarse /.

_____

4. Acostumbrarse / a / este / píldoras /.

_____

5. Conseguir / un / balanza / para / pesarse /.

_____

GRAMMAR I   Conjunctions y, e, o, u, pero, sino. Adverbs ending in -mente.

A.   There are two words in Spanish for the word *and: y* and *e*. We use *e* when the following word begins with the sound [i] which corresponds to the letters *i, hi* (remember that the *h* is silent).
　　　Ex.: padre *e* hijo, Daniel *e* Isabel

There are a few words that begin with *hie;* in this case the *hi* sounds like [y] instead of [i] and the conjunction *y* is used.
　　　Ex.: agua *y* hielo (water and ice)

B.   There are two words in Spanish for the word *or: o* and *u*. We use *u* when the following word begins with the sound [o] which corresponds to the spelling *o, ho*.
　　　Ex.: siete *u* ocho, minutos *u* horas, but músculos *o* huesos (muscles or bones)

C.   There are three ways to translate the word *but: sino, pero, sino que*. In order to use *sino*, two conditions are required:
　　1. The first part of the sentence must be *negative.*
　　　　Ex.: No es Pedro *sino* José.
　　2. The two parts of the sentence must be parallel—that is, the contrast must be between two nouns, two adjectives, etc. At the same time the two parts must be on the same level of meaning; otherwise *pero* must be used.

> Ex.: No es gordo *sino* delgado. (fatness and thinness are on the same level)
> No es gordo *pero* es alto. (fatness and height are on different levels)

Sino que is used when the two parts of the sentence contain subject and verb.

> Ex.: No fuma *sino que* (él) bebe, but: No quiere fumar *sino* beber. Remember that subject pronouns are almost always omitted in Spanish.

D. Formation and uses of adverbs ending in *-mente:*
1. Every descriptive adjective becomes an adverb with the ending *-mente* added to the feminine form of the adjective.
> Ex.: inmediato/inmediatamente

2. If the adjective has a written accent, this accent is preserved in the adverb.
> Ex.: fácil/fácilmente; cómico/cómicamente

Actually these adverbs are the only Spanish words with two stresses: one on the adjectival part and the other on the first *e* of *-mente*.

3. If there are two or more adverbs in a sequence, only the last adverb takes the ending *-mente*, but all of them must be feminine.
> Ex.: José habló *clara, concisa* y *amablemente.*

PRACTICE YOUR GRAMMAR

(Answers, p. 316)

1. The usual translation of *and* is *y*, but if the following word begins with the sound [i] we don't use *y* but_____. There are two possible spellings for the sound [i]: _____ and _____ . Ex.: padre e hijo

2. *Hielo* (ice) begins with the sound [y] rather than [i]. Therefore we say *agua* _____ *hielo*. The same rule applies to *oro* _____ *hierro* (gold and iron).

3. We usually translate *or* by *o*, but if the following word begins with the sound [o], we use _____ rather than *o*. The two spellings for the sound [o] are *o* and _____ ; for example, *setenta* _____ *ochenta*.

4. *Pero* and *sino* mean the same thing: *but*. Most of the time we use *pero*. In order to use *sino*, the first sentence must be _____ .
If the sentence is affirmative, *pero* must be used.

5. Another condition for using *sino* is that the two parts of the sentence must be parallel, such as two colors, two nationalities, etc. Ex.: *Ella no es mexicana_____chilena.*

6. *Sino que* is used when both parts of the sentence contain_____ and_____; for example, *Ella no es mexicana_____* _____*es de Chile* (notice that *mexicana* and *de Chile* have the same function: as adjectives describing *ella*).

7. Complete the sentence: *María no desea bailar_____* *sentarse.* The reason for your choice of conjunction is that *bailar* and *sentarse* are not full sentences but infinitives.

8. To form an adverb from an adjective, we add *-mente* to the adjective. If this adjective has masculine and feminine forms, which one do you use as a base?_____.

9. If the adjective has a written accent, is it preserved or dropped?_____ _____.

10. From the adjectives *malo* and *fácil,* we have the adverbs_____ _____and_____.

11. If we have two or more adverbs in a sequence, which one takes the ending *-mente?*_____. Ex.: *Habla_____* _____*y*_____. (clearly and easily)

EXERCISES
(Answers, p. 317)

A.   Translate the words in parentheses.

1. Marta____Isabel son bonitas_____inteligentes. (and)

2. El agua tiene dos elementos: oxígeno____hidrógeno. (and)

3. ¿Cuántos años tiene tu abuela, setenta____ochenta? (or)

4. Dos metales importantes son oro____hierro. (and)

5. Andrés Segovia no toca el violín_____la guitarra. (but)

6. No me importa si son minutos____horas. (or)

7. Aquí no está la entrada del aeropuerto_____la salida. (but)

8. No tomamos la Calle Doce_____fuimos por la Avenida Martí. (but)

9. Esta calle no es para carros_____para *peatones* (pedestrians). (but)

10. María Elena es gordita_____bonita. (but)

11. Carlos vio el STOP_____no se paró. (but)

12. Irma____Nancy son buenas amigas. (and)

B. Form adverbs from the following adjectives.

1. tonto_____.   7. fácil_____

2. reciente_____.   8. difícil_____

3. claro_____.   9. triste_____

4. feliz_____.   10. alegre_____

5. amable_____.   11. bueno_____

6. suave_____.   12. total_____

C. Answer the questions using the cues given. Change the adjectives to adverbs.

Example: ¿A qué hora sale el tren? - (tres P.M./puntual)
Sale a las tres de la tarde puntualmente.

1. ¿Qué hace Ud. cuando su mamá tiene sed? - (llevar/refresco/rápido)

_____

2. ¿Qué hace Ud. cuando está muy cansada? - (sentarse/cómodo/o/acostarse/cama)

_____

3. ¿Cómo podemos llevar estos libros? - (poder/llevar/fácil/en/carro)

_____

4. ¿Qué hace Ud. cuando es el cumpleaños de su amigo? - (gustar/dar/regalo)

_____

5. ¿Qué hace Ud. cuando sus amigos la visitan? - (gustar/servir/bebida/y posible/comida)

_____

GRAMMAR II   Formal commands (usted/ustedes).

A.   Regular verbs:
Verbs ending in *-AR* take the ending *-e* for *usted* and *-en* for *ustedes*.

Verbs ending in *-ER* and *-IR* take the ending *-a* for *usted* and *-an* for *ustedes*. Memorize the chart:

habl ar	com er	escrib ir
habl e Ud.	com a Ud.	escrib a Ud.
habl en Uds.	com an Uds.	escrib an Uds.

The pronouns *usted* and *ustedes* are not required with the command forms, but it is considered more polite to use them.
    Ex.: *Hable usted* en español.

Formal negative and affirmative commands have the same forms.
    Ex.: hablar/hable Ud./no hable Ud.

B. Irregular verbs:
    1. Stem-changing verbs show the same changes in the command forms as in the Present Indicative.
        Ex.: volver/vuelva Ud.;   pedir/pidan Uds.;
           pensar/piense Ud.

    2. Verbs with irregularities in the first person singular of the Present Indicative show the same changs in the formal commands. Study the following chart:

decir	salir	oír	conducir	huir
digo	salgo	oigo	conduzco	huyo
diga Ud.	salga Ud.	oiga Ud.	conduzca Ud.	huya Ud.
digan Uds.	salgan Uds.	oigan Uds.	conduzcan Uds.	huyan Uds.

C. Spelling changes:
    1. Verbs with *z* in the stem change the *z* to *c* before *e*, just as *feliz* changes to *felices*.
        Ex.: empezar/empiece Ud.

    2. Verbs with *g* at the end of the stem add *u* before *e*.
        Ex.: pagar/pague Ud./paguen Uds.;   llegar/llegue Ud./lleguen Uds.

    3. Verbs with *gu* at the end of the stem before *ir* drop the *u* before *a*.
        Ex.: seguir/siga Ud./sigan Uds.

D. Unstressed object pronouns:
Unstressed object pronouns, such as *me, te, lo,* follow the affirmative commands but precede the negative commands.
    Ex.: pensar/piénselo Ud./no lo piense Ud.;
        lavarse/lávese Ud./no se lave usted.

PRACTICE THE FORMAL COMMANDS   *(Answers, p. 317)*

1. Verbs ending in -*AR* change the *a* to _____ for the command with *usted*. The ending for the plural command *ustedes* is _____. Ex.: *hablar/* _____ *Ud.*

2. Verbs ending in -*ER* and -*IR* take the ending ____ for *usted*, and _____ ____ for *ustedes*. Ex.: *comer/* _____ *Ud./* _____ *Uds.*

3. The expression *mande usted* is used in Mexico to ask the speaker for repetition of what he/she said. Actually *mande usted* is the command form of the verb _____ .

4. The stem-changing verbs have the same changes in the formal command forms as in the Present _____. Ex.: *pensar/* _____ *usted.*

5. *Dormir* changes the *o* to *ue* in *duermo, duermes,* etc. The command form for *usted* shows the same change: _____; in the plural, _____ *ustedes.*

6. The Present Indicative of *decir* is *digo.* This same stem appears in the command form: _____ *usted* and _____ *ustedes.*

7. The formal command form of *empezar* is not *empieze Ud.,* but_____ _____ *usted.* The reason is that a Spanish spelling rule never allows *z* in front of_____ .

8. The formal command form of *pagar* is not *page usted,* but_____ *usted.* In order to preserve the hard sound of the *g* in front of *e,* we have to add _____ .

9. The formal command form of *seguir* is not *sigua usted,* but_____ *usted.* The *u* of *seguir* is silent and is not needed infront of *o (sigo)* or _____ .

10. The unstressed object pronouns (*me, te, se, lo,* etc.) follow the_____ _____ command forms, but they precede the _____ _____ command forms.

11. If you want your friend to *call you*, you don't say *Me llame usted,* but

_____ *usted.* If you want to say *Don't call me,* you

would say *No*_____ *Ud.*

12. *Lavarse* is a reflexive verb and it requires the reflexive pronoun. The formal

affirmative command is_____ *usted.* The plural

form is_____ *Uds.*

13. It is interesting to note that parents who usually use the familiar command
forms *(tú)* when addressing their child, switch to a *formal* command when
they are angry at their child in order to keep a certain distance between
them and the child. Therefore instead of telling her child *Lávate las manos,*

an angry mother would say_____ *usted las manos.*

EXERCISES

(Answers, p. 317)

A.   Write the affirmative form of the formal *(usted/ustedes)* commands of the following new verbs.

1. abusar_____
2. alimentar_____
3. balancear_____
4. conseguir_____
5. contestar_____
6. convertir_____

7. cortar_____
8. durar_____
9. padecer_____
10. tragar_____
11. preocupar*se*_____
12. acostumbrar*se*_____

B.   Answer the questions, first affirmatively and then negatively. Substitute object pronouns wherever possible.

Example: ¿Compro esta camisa?

Sí, *cómprela* Ud._____ . No, *no la compre Ud.*_____ .

1. ¿Escribo la carta?

Sí,_____ . No,_____ .

2. ¿Pido más café?

Sí,_____ . No,_____ .

3. ¿Lleno esta receta?

   Sí,_____. No,_____.

4. ¿Me siento en esta silla?

   Sí,_____. No,_____.

5. ¿Pago la cuenta de la comida?

   Sí,_____. No,_____.

6. ¿Trago las píldoras?

   Sí,_____. No,_____.

7. ¿Empiezo la composición?

   Sí,_____. No,_____.

8. ¿Consigo los boletos?

   Sí,_____. No,_____.

9. ¿Me lavo las manos?

   Sí,_____. No,_____.

10. ¿Le compro la soda al niño?

   Sí,_____. No,_____.

C. Suppose that you are a doctor or pharmacist. Use the formal plural command forms (ustedes) to give advice to your patients.

1. No abusar de las aspirinas._____.

2. Tragarse las pastillas._____.

3. Empezar la dieta mañana._____.

4. Guardar cama unos días._____.

5. No tomar café ni soda._____.

6. No fumar nada._____.

7. Lavarse bien los dientes._____.

8. No preocuparse demasiado._____.

9. Acostumbrarse a comer poco._____.

10. Acostarse temprano._____.

11. Dormir 8 horas por lo menos._____.

12. Balancear bien la comida._____.

GRAMMAR III   Present Subjunctive of regular and stem-
changing verbs.

A.   Memorize the following chart:

SUBJECT	habl ar	com er	volv er	pens ar	ped ir
yo	habl e	com a	vuelv a	piens e	pid a
nosotros -as	habl emos	com amos	volv amos	pens emos	pid amos
tú	habl es	com as	vuelv as	piens es	pid as
él/ella/Ud.	habl e	com a	vuelv a	piens e	pid a
ellos/ellas	habl en	com an	vuelv an	piens en	pid an

1.   Verbs ending in -AR take the endings -e, -emos, -es, -en in the
Present Subjunctive, whereas verbs ending in -ER and -IR take
the endings -a, -amos, -as, an. Remember that the formal commands show the same vowel switch: a to e and e to a.
2.   The stem-changing verbs show the same changes in the Present
Subjunctive as in the Present Indicative: o to ue (volver) and e to ie
(pensar).
3.   Notice that pedir changes e to i in all the persons. Morir and
dormir have two kinds of change: o to ue in duerma, duermas,
duerman and o to u in the first person plural: durmamos. Sentir,
divertir, sugerir, and other verbs show two different changes: e to
ie in sienta, sientas, sientan and e to i in verbs like pedir in the first
person plural: sintamos, divirtamos, etc.

B.   In order to correctly form the Present Subjunctive, remember these
spelling changes:

1.   z to c in front of e: comenzar/comience.
c to z in front of a: convencer/convenza.
2.   g to gu in front of e: llegar/llegue.
gu to g in front of a: conseguir/consiga.
3.   c to qu in front of e: practicar/practique.
4.   g to j in front of a: recoger/recoja (to pick up).

NOTE:

The Present Subjunctive is used much more frequently in Spanish than in English.
In the charts above, we saw how the Subjunctive of regular and stem-changing
verbs is formed. In the next lesson, we will cover some of the most common uses of
the Subjunctive.

PRACTICE THE PRESENT
SUBJUNCTIVE
(Answers, p. 317)

1. Verbs ending in *-AR* change the vowel *a* to _____ in the Present Subjunctive, and verbs ending in *-ER* or *-IR* change *e* or *i* to _____.

2. You have probably noticed that the command forms for *usted* and *ustedes* are the same as the forms of the Present_____ in all the verbs.

3. The negative commands for *tú (hablar/no hables tú)* are also the same forms as the Present_____.

   Ex.: *comer/no*_____.

4. *Volver* changes the stem from *volv-* to_____in the Present Indicative as well as in the command forms and the Present _____, except in the first person plural:

   *volvemos/*_____.

5. *Sentarse* changes *e* to *ie* in all the persons of the Present Indicative and Subjunctive, except the first person plural: *me siento/me*_____ (Subjunctive), but *nos sentamos/nos*_____ (Subjunctive).

6. *Pedir* changes the vowel *e* in the stem to_____in all the persons in the Present Subjunctive: *tú*_____*/nosotros*_____

   _____.

7. *Dormir* and *morir* show a double change in the Present Subjunctive: *o* to *ue* in all the persons except in the first person _____: *yo duerma/*

   *nosotros*_____.

8. *Sentir* and similar verbs show a double change in the Present Subjunctive: *e* to *ie* in all the persons except the_____person plural: *yo sienta/*

   *nosotros*_____.

9. Many verbs have spelling changes because they follow general rules of Spanish spelling. These same rules apply to the Preterite. For example, *comenzar* changes *z* to_____in front of *e: comenzar/tú*_____

   _____(Subjunctive.)

10. *Tragar* (to swallow) has a *g* at the end of the stem. It is necessary to add the vowel_____in front of *e* to preserve the hard sound of the *g*: *tragar/yo* _____. (Subjunctive)

11. *Seguir* has a silent *u* at the end of the stem. This *u* disappears in front of *o (sigo)* and in front of_____: *seguir/yo* _____ (Subjunctive).

12. The last *c* of *practicar* and other verbs ending in *-car* change *c* to *qu* in front of the vowel_____. The Present Subjunctive of *practicar* is *yo*_____ _____.

13. Notice that the only difference between the first person of the Preterite and the Present Subjunctive of the *-AR* verbs is the accent: *hablé / hable; llegué/*_____.

EXERCISES

(Answers, p. 318)

A. Write the first person singular of the Present Subjunctive.

1. abusar_____

2. adelgazar_____

3. balancear_____

4. convertir_____

5. alimentar_____

6. divertir_____

7. sentar*se*_____

8. sentir*se*_____

9. torcer (ue)_____

10. servir (i)_____

11. conseguir_____

12. recoger_____

B. Some of the most common uses of the Present Subjunctive will be explained in the next lesson. In this exercise, you will practice one of these uses: the Subjunctive following verbs of *command* or *wish.* In this context, the verb in the Subjunctive is an indirect command. Suppose that the doctor is telling (ordering) patients what and what not to do.

El doctor *quiere que* . . .

1. yo no_____una dieta muy estricta. (seguir)

2. usted_____estas píldoras. (tomar)

3. ella_____temprano. (acostar*se*)

4. nosotros_____mejor. (sentir*se*)

5. ustedes_____a verlo la semana próxima. (volver)

6. tú_____bastante peso. (perder)

7. mi padre_____a trabajar menos horas. (empezar)

8. Marta_____más verduras. (comer)

9. nosotros_____otra receta nueva. (pedir)

10. ustedes_____su cuenta. (pagar)

11. yo_____de este dolor de estómago. (aliviar*se*)

12. tú no_____tanto de tu trabajo. (preocupar*se*)

13. usted_____de que está bien. (convencer*se*)

14. ellos_____más los deportes. (practicar)

15. el niñito_____más horas. (dormir)

16. usted no_____tanto en su enfermedad. (pensar)

17. tú_____cada día mejor. (sentir*se*)

18. los pacientes_____contentos. (estar: ¡necesita acento!)

19. ella no_____otro resfriado. (coger)

20. su hija_____estudiar sin problemas. (poder)

Lesson 14

El autómovil[1]
(The Car)

aceite	oil	**cinturón**	belt	**milla (1.6 km.)**	mile
acelerador	accelerator	**desastre**	disaster	**motor**	engine
acumulador	battery	**embrague**	clutch	**neumático**	tire
alquiler	rent, lease	**faro**	headlight	**parabrisas**	windshield
arranque	starter	**freno**	brake	**parachoques**	bumper
batería	battery	**galón**	gallon	**pedal**	pedal
baúl[2]	trunk	**ganga**	bargain	**placa**	license plate
bocina	horn	**kilómetro**[3]	kilometer	**rueda**	wheel
cacharro	jalopy	**licencia**	license	**seguridad**	safety
calefacción	heating	**llanta**	tire	**tablero**	dashboard
cajuela (Mex.)	trunk	**maletero**[2]	trunk	**tarifa**	fees
capó	hood	**mapa (el)**	map	**velocidad**	speed
carnet	license	**matrícula**	license plate	**volante, timón**	steering wheel

alquilar	to rent, lease	**funcionar**	to work (a machine)
apagar	to turn off	**guiar**	to drive, guide
aparcar	to park	**inflar**	to inflate
arrancar[4]	to start, root	**llenar**	to fill
cobrar	to charge	**manejar**	to drive
conducir[5]	to drive, conduct	**parquear**	to park
desinflar	to deflate	**pinchar**	to get a flat tire
estacionar	to park	**pitar**	to blow the horn
frenar	to brake	**tocar**	to touch, blow the horn

asegurado	insured	**gastado**	worn out
automático	automatic	**lujoso**	luxurious

cómodo	comfortable	**manual**[6]	standard (shift)
destruido	destroyed, in rags	**mecánico**[7]	standard (shift) mechanic
diario	daily	**roto**	broken
disponible	available	**torcido**	twisted, bent

a todo riesgo	at all risk	**olerle mal a uno**	to seem suspicious, to smell fishy
de segunda mano	second-hand	**por ser usted**	just for you
en fin, por fin	in short	**tocar la bocina**	to blow the horn
el limpiaparabrisas	windshield wiper		
a millas por hora	miles per hour	**transmisión** { manual, mecánica, de cambios }	standard transmission
a Kms. por hora	kms. per hour		

NOTES:

1. *Automóvil* is used for *car* in the whole Spanish world, but different words are preferred by different countries: *carro* (Latin America), *coche* (Spain), etc. Although the vocabulary differs from region to region, we usually understand what other Spanish speakers are talking about when they mention the different parts of the car.

2. *Baúl* is the *trunk* of a car and also a large suitcase. In Mexico they use *cajuela,* in Spain *maletero,* which happens also to be the *suitcase carrier,* or *porter.*

3. *Kilómetro* is used in all of Latin America and Spain. It's .62 mile: in other words, one mile is 1.6 kilometers.

4. *Arrancar* is *to start an engine,* but it's also *to root* plants or things.

5. *Conducir* is *to drive* in Spain. Latin America uses *manejar. Conducir* also means to conduct.

6. *Manual* as a noun is a *booklet, notebook.* As an adjective it means by hand; it's used for the "standard" shift, as are *mecánico* and *de cambios.*

7. *Mecánico* is a *mechanic,* a person who knows about engines. As an adjective it means *mechanical* and also *standard* (shift).

EXERCISES   *(Answers, p. 318)*

A.   Write *el, la* in front of these nouns.

1.___ motor	7.___ baúl	13.___ arranque	19.___ parabrisas
2.___ velocidad	8.___ capó	14.___ embrague	20.___ cinturón
3.___ galón	9.___ carnet	15.___ milla	21.___ pedal
4.___ aceite	10.___ placa	16.___ acelerador	
5.___ batería	11.___ mapa	17.___ acumulador	
6.___ alquiler	12.___ volante	18.___ parachoques	

B.   Complete the following sentences with one of the expressions given below.

a todo riesgo	millas por hora	transmisión manual
por fin	olerle mal a uno	el limpiaparabrisas
de segunda mano	tocar la bocina	por ser usted

1. No, este coche no es completamente nuevo; es_____
    _____.

2. El parabrisas está muy sucio; ponga usted_____
    _____.

3. La velocidad máxima en este calle es 35_____
    _____.

4. Después de manejar un día completo,_____
    llegamos a Chicago.

5. ¡Por supuesto! Este carro está asegurado_____.

6. Por favor, no_____ usted_____
    en esta zona de hospital.

7. La tarifa normal es $10,00 diarios, pero_____
    se la bajo a $8.

8. ¡Otra ganga! No lo creo. ¡Esto me empieza a_____
    a mí!

9. No, este coche no es automático; es de_____
    _____.

C.   Write a synonym for each of these words.

1. batería_____   6. conducir_____

2. coche_____   7. matrícula_____

3. aparcar_____   8. neumático_____

4. carnet_____   9. manual_____

5. baúl_____   10. en fin_____

D.   Write a word related to each of the following.

1. alquiler_____   3. arranque_____

2. frenos_____   4. estación_____

5. mano_____   8. función_____

6. pito (whistle)_____   9. intocable_____

7. parque_____   10. conductor_____

E. Complete the sentences with a word from the list below.

llanta	cacharro	pedal	maletero	mapa		gastado	lujoso
carnet	tablero	volante	ganga		cinturón	torcido	diario

1. Ponemos el equipaje en el_____del carro.

2. Usted necesita llantas nuevas porque las que tiene ya están muy_____

   _____.

3. Para manejar ponemos las manos en el_____.

4. Tenemos precios baratos; es una verdadera_____.

5. Para acelerar ponemos el pie en el_____del
   acelerador.

6. Este carro es nuevo, moderno y_____; tiene toda
   clase de comodidades.

7. Nuestras tarifas de alquiler son bajas: 8 dólares_____.

8. Por favor, abróchense los_____de seguridad.

9. Este coche es viejísimo, y está todo roto; es un_____.

10. Si usted no tiene_____de conducir, no podemos
    alquilarle el carro.

11. Usted necesita un_____para manejar por todo el
    país.

12. Mi carro no tiene reloj en el_____, pero tiene
    radio.

13. Después del accidente, todo el parachoques quedó_____

    _____.

14. Es necesario tener las_____bien infladas para
    ahorrar gasolina.

DIÁLOGO   *¡Qué desastre!*

(Un turista de Estados Unidos está en México, y va a una agencia de carros de alquiler para alquilar un coche. Habla con el agente.)

AGENTE: ¿En qué puedo servirle, señor?
TURISTA: Querría alquilar un carro pequeño pero cómodo.
AGENTE: ¿Por cuánto tiempo lo desea, señor?
TURISTA: Por tres semanas.
AGENTE: Sólo tengo uno disponible. Es de segunda mano, pero está en perfectas condiciones.
TURISTA: ¿Automático o de cambios?
AGENTE: De cambios. Así ahorra gasolina.
TURISTA: Mmmm . . . ¡de segunda mano! ¿Cómo están los frenos?
AGENTE: Acabo de ponerlos nuevos, y también la batería, el arranque y el embrague . . . En fin, está como nuevo.
TURISTA: ¿Está asegurado contra todo riesgo?
AGENTE: No, señor. Usted lo alquila y maneja a su propio riesgo.
TURISTA: ¿Cuál es la tarifa diaria?
AGENTE: Normalmente cobro 10 dólares diarios, pero por ser usted se lo dejo en 8. Una ganga, ¿no?
TURISTA: Esta clase de ganga me huele mal. ¿Podría ver el carro antes de alquilarlo?
AGENTE: Por supuesto. Venga Ud. conmigo. Está aquí nomás.

• • •

TURISTA: ¿De segunda mano? Yo diría de "última mano". Las llantas están gastadísimas, los faros rotos, el parachoques todo torcido, los asientos destruidos, el tablero . . .
AGENTE: Pero el motor todavía funciona, señor.
TURISTA: ¡No me diga más! ¡Este cacharro es un verdadero desastre!

DIALOG   *What a Disaster!*

(An American tourist is in Mexico, and goes to a car rental agency to rent a car. He is speaking to the agent.)

AGENT: May I help you, sir?
TOURIST: I would like to rent a small but comfortable car.
AGENT: How long do you want it for sir?
TOURIST: Three weeks.
AGENT: I have just one available. It's a second-hand car, but it's in perfect condition.
TOURIST: Is it automatic or standard shift?
AGENT: Standard. That way you save gas.

TOURIST: Mmmm . . . Second hand! How are the brakes?

AGENT: I just put in new ones, as well as the battery, the starter, and the clutch . . . In short, it's like new!

TOURIST: Is it insured against all kinds of risk?

AGENT: No, sir. You rent it and drive at your own risk.

TOURIST: How much is it per day?

AGENT: Normally I charge $10.00 a day, but I'll give you a special price: $8.00. It's a bargain, isn't it?

TOURIST: This kind of bargain smells fishy to me. Could I see the car before I rent it?

AGENT: Of course. Come with me, sir. It's right here.

TOURIST: Second-hand? I'd say "last hand"! The tires are all worn out, the headlights are broken, the bumper is all bent, the seats are in rags, the dashboard . . .

AGENT: But, sir, the engine still works.

TOURIST: Don't say another word! This jalopy is a total disaster!

CULTURAL NOTE:

This dialog exaggerates a tendency that exists in Hispanic countries. We try to keep cars as long as we can because of the high price of new cars and because the mechanical work involved for repairs is not as expensive as in the United States.

EXERCISES

(Answers, p. 318)

A. Complete the sentences with words from the dialog to make a narrative summary in the past.

Un turista americano fue a una agencia de carros de (1)_____

____para alquilar un carro pequeño pero (2)_____. Él quería

alquilarlo por tres (3)_____. El agente sólo tenía un

carro (4)_____y era de segunda (5)_____,

pero estaba en perfectas (6)_____. El turista le

preguntó si el carro era automático o (7)_____. Como

el carro era de trasmisión manual él podría (8)_____gasolina. El

agente acababa de poner frenos (9)_____, y también batería y

otras cosas, pero el carro no estaba (10)_____. El

turista tenía que alquilarlo y manejarlo a su propio (11)_____. La

agencia cobraba normalmente $10.00 (12)_____, pero

el agente se lo dejó en 8, una verdadera ganga. Al turista no le gustó esta clase de

gangas, y por eso quiso (13)_____el carro antes de alquilarlo. El
agente lo llevó a verlo, y el turista se *asustó* (got scared) de las condiciones del

carro: las llantas estaban (14)_____, los faros estaban

(15)_____, el parachoques estaba (16)_____, los asien-

tos estaban (17)_____. En fin, ¡el cacharro era un

verdadero (18)_____!

B. Answer True (T) or False (F).

1.____ El turista desea alquilar un carro lujoso y grande.

2.____ El turista desea alquilar el carro por tres días para ir a Acapulco.

3.____ El agente dice que sólo tiene un carro disponsible pero que está en
buenas condiciones.

4.____ El agente cree que un carro de cambios ahorra gasolina.

5.____ La tarifa normal de alquiler del carros es 8 dólares diarios.

6.____ Todos los coches de la agencia están asegurados contra todo riesgo.

7.____ El carro tiene los frenos nuevos, pero la batería ya es muy vieja.

8.____ El turista piensa que el carro no es de segunda mano sino de "última
mano."

9.____ Las llantas están muy gastadas, pero los faros están bien.

10.____ El parachoques está torcido y los asientos muy destruidos.

11.____ El agente asegura que el motor todavía funciona bien.

12.____ El turista americano considera que el carro es un desastre.

13.____ En Estados Unidos se usan los carros más viejos que en Latinoamérica.

14.____ Problemente el turista americano alquiló el cacharro.

C. Review the Subjunctive. All the verbs in the vocabulary of
this lesson are regular, except *conducir: yo conduzco/conduz-
ca* (subjunctive). Suppose a friend wants to borrow your car.
You are a good mechanic and you give some advice to your
friend who doesn't seem to know much about cars. Complete

the sentences with the correct form of the Present Subjunctive.

"Oye, Carlos, te doy mi carro; pero quiero que . . ."

1. tú _____ bien antes de llegar a un STOP. (frenar)

2. tú _____ siempre con mucho cuidado. (manejar)

3. tú no te _____ en la *carretera* (road). (pinchar)

4. tú _____ siempre entre las líneas blancas. (aparcar)

5. el motor te _____ sin problemas. (funcionar)

6. tú _____ el depósito de gasolina. (llenar)

7. tú _____ los faros durante el día. (apagar)

8. tú _____ la bocina sólo cuando es necesario. (tocar)

9. tú nunca _____ frente a un hospital. (pitar)

10. tú nunca _____ por el lado izquierdo. (conducir)

11. la batería te _____ sin dificultad. (arrancar)

12. tú nunca _____ demasiado las llantas. (inflar)

13. tú nunca _____ en la zona roja. (estacionarse)

14. tú nunca _____ a más de 55 millas por hora. (correr)

15. tú siempre _____ tu licencia de conducir. (llevar)

D. Word Families: Write a verb or noun related to each of the following adjectives.

1. asegurado_____

2. lujoso_____

3. manual_____

4. disponible_____

5. torcido_____

6. cómodo_____

7. diario_____

8. roto_____

9. gastado_____

10. lleno_____

11. desinflado_____

12. destruido_____

13. pinchado_____

14. aceitoso_____

GRAMMAR I   Irregular verbs in the Present Subjunctive.

A.   Memorize the verbs in the chart:

SUBJECT	sent ir	sal ir	conoc er	ten er	hu ir
yo	sient a	salg a	conozc a	teng a	huy a
nosotros	sint amos	salg amos	conozc amos	teng amos	huy amos
tú	sient as	salg as	conozc as	teng as	huy as
él/ella/Ud.	sient a	salg a	conozc a	teng a	huy a
ellos/ellas	sient an	salg an	conozc an	teng an	huy an

1. *Sentir* is a stem-changing verb with two changes: *e* to *ie* in all the persons except the first person plural *sintamos* which is irregular because it changes *e* to *i* in the stem. Other verbs like *sentir* are *divertir, preferir, sugerir, convertir, mentir* (to lie).
2. *Salir* is irregular because it adds *g* to the stem, as does *tener/ tenga*. Notice that this change also occurs in the Present Indicative: *salgo/tengo*.
3. *Conocer* is irregular because it adds *c* to the stem. Verbs ending in *-cer* and *-cir* have the same change; for example, *conducir, ofrecer* (to offer), *seducir* (to seduce).
4. *Huir* is irregular because it adds *y* to the stem. Other verbs ending in *-uir* have this same change: *excluir, concluir, incluir.*

B.   Memorize this list of irregular verbs:

decir	diga	salir	salga	venir	venga
hacer	haga	valer	valga	haber	haya
traer	traiga	huir	huya	ver	vea
caer	caiga	oír	oiga	ser	sea
poner	ponga	saber	sepa	dar	dé
tener	tenga	estar	esté	ir	vaya

1. Notice that *esté* and *dé* (from *dar*) have an accent.
2. The same irregular forms are used in the formal commands and in the Present Subjunctive.
       Ex.:   traer/traiga usted (command)/yo traiga (subjunctive)
3. Compound verbs have the same irregularities as the simple verbs from which they are derived.
       Ex.:   mantener/mantenga; contraer/contraiga; componer/componga; deshacer/deshaga; contradecir/contradiga; etc.

PRACTICE THE SUBJUNCTIVE   *(Answers, p. 319)*

1. *Sientan* (from *sentir*) is irregular because changes *e* to ____ in the stem, whereas *sintamos* is irregular because the same *e* changes to ____ .

2. *Preferir* is a stem-changing verb like *sentir*. The Present Subjunctive of *preferir* is yo _____ and *nosotros* _____ _____ .

3. *Conocer* and other verbs ending in *-cer, -cir* are irregular in the Present Subjunctive because they add the letter _____ which has the [**k**] sound, whereas the *c* from the infinitive has the [**s**] sound and changes to *z* in front of the *c*.

4. *Producir* is irregular like *conocer*. The Subjunctive is *yo* _____ _____ .

5. *Huir, concluir, incluir* have the same irregularity; they add ____ to the stem. The Subjunctive of *concluir* (to conclude) es *nosotros* _____ _____ .

6. You have heard the expression (and song) *Vaya con Dios*. Actually this is the command form (expressing a wish in this case) of the verb ____ .

7. Only two verbs have written accents in the Present Subjunctive: _____ from *estar*, and ____ from *dar*. However, *tú des, ellos den, nosotros demos* have no accent. *Estés* and *estén* have an accent; *estemos* does not.

8. *Saber* is very irregular because it has *yo sé* in the Present Indicative, *yo supe* in the Preterite, *yo sabré* in the Future, and yo _____ in the Subjunctive.

9. From *hacer* we have *haga* in the Present Subjunctive. *Satisfacer* is a compound of *hacer* (the old *facer*); the Present Subjunctive of *satisfacer* is

_____ .

10. From *venir* we say *venga;* from *prevenir* we say _____ .

11. From *poner* we say *ponga;* from *suponer* (to suppose) we say _____ _____ .

12. From *tener* we say *tenga;* from *mantener* we say _____ .

EXERCISES

(Answers, p. 319)

A. Suppose you are a mechanic, and you have just fixed your friend Luisa's car. You don't want the car to break down again, and you have some advice for Luisa. Complete the sentences with the Present Subjunctive.

"Oye, Luisa, tu carro está en buenas condiciones; pero *espero que* (I hope that). . ."

1. tú no_____con poco aceite en el motor. (manejar)

2. tú_____gasolina a tiempo en el depósito. (poner)

3. tus amigos_____usar bien tu carro. (saber)

4. tus padres no_____que pagar tu cuenta de gasolina. (tener)

5. tú no_____cosas estúpidas con tu carro. (hacer)

6. tú_____oír bien el radio ahora. (poder)

7. tú_____siempre tranquila cuando manejas. (estar)

8. este carro te_____casi como nuevo. (valer)

9. tú nunca_____de un accidente si te ocurre. (huir)

10. tú siempre_____una llanta de *repuesto* (spare). (traer)

11. tú nunca_____a una velocidad excesiva. (ir)

12. tú nunca_____de viaje sin bastante gasolina. (salir)

13. tú siempre_____la velocidad marcada. (mantener)

14. tus amigos_____tan prudentes como tú. (ser)

15. tú nunca te_____mientras manejas. (dormir)

16. nadie_____a causa de un accidente contigo. (morir)

17. tú siempre_____los peligros. (prevenir)

18. tú siempre_____el cinturón de seguridad. (ponerse)

19. nunca más me_____de problemas de tu carro. (decir)

B. The stem-changing verbs show similar changes in different tenses. For example, *pedir* changes to *yo pido* in the Present Indicative, to *él pidió* in the Preterite, and to *yo pida* in the

Present Subjunctive. *Dormir* changes to *yo duermo,* to *él dur- mió* (Preterite) and to *tú duermas* and *nosotros durmamos* in the Subjunctive. Follow the examples and fill in the rest of the chart.

INFINITIVE	PRESENT INDICATIVE	PRETERITE	PRESENT SUBJUNCTIVE
Examples:			
vestirse	me visto	se vistió	nos vistamos
pedir	pido	pidió	pidamos
1. morir	_____	_____	_____
2. dormir	_____	_____	_____
3. divertir	_____	_____	_____
4. preferir	_____	_____	_____
5. sentir	_____	_____	_____
6. convertir	_____	_____	_____
7. servir	_____	_____	_____
8. seguir	_____	_____	_____
9. conseguir	_____	_____	_____
10. mentir	_____	_____	_____

GRAMMAR II   Indicative and Subjunctive in contrast: Information vs. influence.

A. A sentence is often composed of two clauses joined by the conjunction *que* (that). In this case, the *subordinate clause* is dependent upon the *main clause.*

> Ex.: Nosotros sabemos que Roberto es mexicano. (we know [that] Robert is Mexican)
> (main clause)   (subordinate clause)

B. Indicative after verbs of *information:*
1. If the main clause contains a verb of *information,* such as *decir, leer, saber,* the verb in the subordinate clause must be in the *Indicative.* Note *habla* and *necesito* in the following examples:

> Ex.: Ella sabe que Ud. habla español. (she knows [that] you speak Spanish)
> Usted dice que yo necesito una dieta. (you say [that] I need a diet)

2. Here is a partial list of verbs and expressions of *information:*

saber	(to know)	**decir**	(to say)	**reconocer**	(to recognize)
conocer	(to know)	**contar**	(to tell)	**es verdad que**	(it's true that)
informar	(to inform)	**escribir**	(to write)	**es cierto que**	(it's true that)
declarar	(to declare)	**leer**	(to read)	**es claro que**	(it's clear that)

C. Subjunctive after verbs of *influence:*
1. If the main clause contains a verb of *influence*—in other words, a verb that indicates something that is *not a fact,* the verb in the subordinate clause must be in the *Subjunctive* in Spanish. Under the blanket word *influence,* we include verbs that denote *commanding, wishing, forbidding, permission, advice, requesting, suggestion, opposition,* etc.

    Ex.: Ella quiere que yo hable español.

It's important to note that here the subject of the main clause tries to impose his/her will on the subject of the subordinate clause. Therefore, they must be different persons.

If the subject is the same in both clauses, we use the infinitive.

    Ex.:   Ella quiere volver. vs. Ella quiere que tú vuelvas.

2. Here is a partial list of verbs of *influence:*

ordenar	(to order)	**decir**	(to order)	**permitir**	(to permit)	**pedir**	(to ask for)
suplicar	(to beg)	**mandar**	(to command)	**impedir**	(to prevent)	**querer**	(to want)
oponerse	(to oppose)	**esperar**	(to hope)	**sugerir**	(to suggest)	**desear**	(to wish)
escribir	(to write)	**prohibir**	(to forbid)	**dejar**	(to allow)	**gritar**	(to shout)
aconsejar	(to advise)	**insistir**	(to insist)	**preferir**	(to prefer)	**recomendar**	(to advise)

D. Subjunctive with expressions of *influence:*
1. When we say to a person "It's necessary that you do it," we are trying to *influence* that person; in other words, instead of saying "I want you to do it," we are using the impersonal expression *it's necessary.* In Spanish the verb of the subordinate clause must be in the Subjunctive:

    Ex.:   Es importante que lo hagas. (it's important that you do it)

2. Here is a partial list of impersonal expressions of *influence:*

es necesario	(it's necessary)	**es útil**	(it's useful)
es importante	(it's important)	**es inútil**	(it's useless)
es preciso	(it's necessary)	**es conveniente**	(it's convenient)
es bueno	(it's good)	**es aconsejable**	(it's advisable)
es mejor	(it's better)	**es deseable**	(it's desirable)
es malo	(it's bad)	**es imperativo**	(it's imperative)
es peor	(it's worse)	**está prohibido**	(it's forbidden)

E. Verbs of both *information* and *influence:*
You may have noticed that a few verbs were listed previously in *(B)* and *(C)* as verbs of *information* and also as verbs of *influence.* These verbs are *decir, escribir, insistir,* and *gritar.* Actually all of these verbs have a double meaning; for example, *decir* means *to simply state with words* (information) or *to order something* (influence). The difference is illustrated by the use of either the Indicative or the Subjunctive:

(a) Ella dice que tú eres bueno. (Indicative) (she says that you are good)
(b) Ella dice que tú seas bueno. (Subjunctive) (she tells you to be good)

PRACTICE THE SUBJUNCTIVE (Answers, p. 319)

1. A clause that depends on another clause is called a _____

   _____ clause. The independent clause is called the _____ clause.

2. In English the conjunction that joins the main and subordinate clauses is

   that, which can be omitted. In Spanish this conjunction is _____ and it's never omitted.

3. If the main clause contains a verb of *information,* the verb in the subordin-

   ate clause must be in the _____. For example,

   Usted sabe que yo _____ español. (hablar)

4. If the main clause contains a verb of *influence,* the subordinate clause must

   have its verb in the _____. For example, *Usted*

   quiere que yo _____ español. (hablar)

5. By *influence* we mean verbs that denote imposition of will, from a strong *command* to a soft *suggestion.* Note that if the subject is the same in both the main clause and the subordinate clause, neither Indicative nor Subjunctive is needed: the infinitive is the solution. Ex.: Ella quiere comer.

   Compare this with *Ella quiere que tú* _____. (comer)

6. Verbs like *saber, declarar, informar, leer* denote *information.* Therefore the

   verb in the subordinate clause must be in the _____.

7. If you read a notice at work that says *It is important that all of you . . .,* you will probably interpret it as an *order.* How would you complete the sentence

   Es necesario que ustedes _____ *a tiempo?* (llegar)

8. Notice that impersonal expressions like *Es bueno que, Es mejor que,* etc., contain an adjective: *bueno, mejor.* If the adjective in the main clause contains a message of *information* like *cierto, verdad, claro,* the subordinate clause must be completed in the _____. Ex.: *Es cierto que José*_____*español.* (hablar)

9. How do you translate *El director dice que Ud. trabaja mucho*? (*trabaja* is Indicative!)_____.

10. How do you translate *El director dice que Ud. trabaje mucho*? (*trabaje* is Subjunctive!)_____.

EXERCISES   *(Answers, p. 319)*

A.   Complete the sentences with the Indicative or Subjunctive forms.

1. La abuela quiere que el niño_____ temprano. (dormirse)

2. No es necesario que el carro_____nuevo. (ser)

3. Es verdad que ustedes_____bien su carro. (manejar)

4. Espero que todos ustedes_____a tiempo. (llegar)

5. Es cierto que el agente sólo_____un carro disponible. (tener)

6. El turista desea que usted le_____un carro pequeño. (alquilar)

7. Todos reconocemos que Juan_____bueno e inocente. (ser)

8. Mi amiga me escribe que su mamá_____enferma. (estar)

9. Tus padres no permiten que tú_____tarde a casa. (volver)

10. El médico insiste en que el paciente_____las pastillas. (tomar)

11. Es mucho mejor que yo_____con mi amiga. (ir)

12. Es muy importante que tú_____en las vacaciones. (divertirse)

13. Acabo de leer aquí que_____una *huelga* (strike). (haber)

14. El presidente declara que la huelga_____ilegal. (ser)

15. Yo prefiero que usted me_____antes de las 11:00. (llamar)

16. Es verdad que Cecilia _____ en un banco grande. (trabajar)

17. No es bueno que ellos _____ sin usted. (salir)

18. El mecánico dice que Ud. no _____ el aceite a tiempo. (cambiar)

19. El policía no permite que nosotros _____ aquí. (aparcar)

20. Mi esposa prefiere que yo _____ en casa. (comer)

21. Los senadores se oponen a que _____ una *huelga* (strike). (haber)

22. Todos conocemos que tú _____ demasiado. (trabajar)

23. Mi hijo siempre me pide que yo le _____ pasteles. (llevar)

24. ¿Me sugieren ustedes que _____ en tren o en autobús? (venir)

25. Es mejor que tú y yo _____ a vivir juntos. (acostumbrarse)

B. What do teachers expect of the students? And what do students expect of their teachers? Complete these sentences with the correct form of the Subjunctive.

El maestro dice: "*Quiero* que mis estudiantes . . ."

1. _____ (decir la verdad).

2. _____ (llegar a tiempo).

3. _____ (hablar español en clase).

4. _____ (hacer sus *tareas* [homework]).

5. _____ (escribir los ejercicios).

6. _____ (no fumar en clase).

7. _____ (venir preparados).

8. _____ (saber respetarme).

Los estudiantes *esperan* que su maestro . . .

9. _____ (hablar siempre español).

10. _____ (preparar bien las clases).

11. _____ (ser muy alegre)

12. _____ (tener paciencia).

13. _____(terminar a tiempo).

14. _____(empezar a tiempo).

15. _____(mantener disciplina).

16. _____(dar buenas *notas* [grades]).

C. **Complete the sentences with one of the ideas given below. You may need to make a few changes. Decide which is more appropriate: the Indicative or the Subjunctive.**

acostarse tarde	llegar más temprano	visitarme en agosto
tomar una cerveza	volver a la consulta	cambiar el día del examen

1. José vio al médico hace una semana porque tenía mucho dolor en el pecho.

    Todavía no se le quita ese dolor. Es necesario que él_____

    _____ .

2. Mis padres trabajan todos los meses del año excepto agosto. Ayer recibí su

    carta y me dicen que_____ .

3. Carmencita, ya sabes que tienes que empezar a trabajar a las siete y media

    de la mañana. Mira, ya son las 11:30. Es mejor que no_____

    _____ .

4. Ya sabemos el indicativo, el imperativo y parte del subjuntivo; pero necesi-
    tamos más tiempo para aprender tantas palabras nuevas. Por eso hoy le

    vamos a pedir a la maestra que _____ .

5. Hace un calor terrible; te sugiero que nosotros_____

    _____ .

6. Todas la mañanas hay mucho tráfico en la sección donde yo vivo. Siempre
    quiero salir de casa con bastante tiempo, pero necesito tiempo para desayu-
    nar. Pero yo nunca llego tarde. Esta mañana me dice el director que yo

    _____que los otros empleados.

GRAMMAR III   A review of the written accent.

(The accent is first discussed on p. 63)

A. The written accent (ʹ) is used in Spanish to facilitate reading. It is written on the *stressed* vowel of a word according to certain spelling rules. You should be able to hear the *stress* in order to apply most of the rules. For example, if you hear (and say) the stress on *lá* of *lápiz,* you should be able to apply rule *(2)* below and write the accent. By the same token, if you hear the stress on *iz* of *feliz,* you know not to write the accent because of rule *(1).*

B. Three important rules for the written accent:

1. Words with the stress on the *last syllable* need a written accent if the last letter is a vowel or the consonants *n, s.* If the word has only *one* syllable, the rule does not apply.
    Ex.:   comió, menú, estás, estén, café, dieciséis, veintidós, mantén (command form of *mantener*); *but* dio, di, fui, fue, vas, dos, seis, ten.

2. Words with the stress on the *next-to-the-last syllable* need written accent if the last letter is any consonant besides *n* or *s.*
    Ex.:   árbol, fácil, huésped (guest), lápiz, Martínez, álbum, sángüich, estándar; *but* silla, dentistas, libro, once.

3. Words with the stress *two syllables before the last* always need an accent, and the last letter need not be considered.
    Ex.:   águila, número, números, dígame, área.

C. Special cases for the written accent:

1. Whenever the weak vowels *i, u* precede or follow any of the other vowels, *a, e, o* (called strong vowels), the two vowels form *one* syllable, with the stress on the strong vowels. This combination is called a diphthong. For example, *oigo* has two syllables: *oi-go,* with the stress on the first *o.* But sometimes the stress is on the *weak* vowel, *i* or *u;* in this case, the diphthong is broken, and the accent is written.
    Ex.:   oír, día, mío, comían, baúl, Raúl, reúno, dúo. Notice *país* but *paisano; reunir* but *reúnes; maíz* but *maizal* (cornfield); *prohibir* but *prohíbe.*

2. When a word has two or more meanings, one is marked with the accent. This is perhaps the most arbitrary rule. Memorize the spelling along with the meaning:

él (he)	**el** (the)	**más** (more)	**mas** (but)	**sé** (know, be)	**se** (him-herself)
tú (your)	**tu** (your)	**dé** (give)	**de** (of)	**sí** (yes, oneself)	**si** (if)
té (tea)	**te** (you)	**mí** (me)	**mi** (my, mine)	**sólo** (only)	**solo** (alone)

3. Question words need the accent in questions and exclamatory expressions, such as ¡*Qué desastre!* The question words are *cuándo, cómo, dónde, adónde* (also spelled *a dónde*), *cuánto, qué, por qué, para qué, cuál, cuáles, quién, quiénes.* Even when the question is indirect, the accent is needed.

  Ex.:   Quiero saber *cómo* te llamas.

4. The demonstrative words *este, ese, estos,* etc., need an accent when they are used without a noun—that is, when they are used as pronouns.

  Ex.:   Prefiero este libro a aquél.

Neuter *esto, eso, aquello* never take an accent.

PRACTICE THE WRITTEN ACCENT   *(Answers, p. 320)*

1. The accent is written over the _____ vowel of a word. There are a few words without *stress* in Spanish: articles, prepositions, unstressed pronouns, and short forms of the possessives: *mi, tu, su.*

2. If a word ends in a vowel, we write the accent if the stress is on the ____ syllable, but the word must have _____ or more syllables. Ex.: menú, comerá.

3. If a word ends in *n* or *s*, we write the accent if the _____ is on the last syllable. Again, we need two or more syllables. Ex.: *leccion/*

  _____ .

4. *Fue* has only one syllable because the vowel group *ue* is pronounced together in one syllable. Does *fue* need an accent? _____ . Which is correct, *dió* or *dio*? _____ .

5. *Lápiz* needs an accent because the _____ is on the next-to-the-last syllable, and the last letter is a consonant other than *n* or *s*. The plural form *lápices* needs the accent according to a different rule: the stress is _____ syllables before the last.

6. Foreign words follow the same rules for the accent. For example, *sángüich* needs the accent because the stress is on the next-to-the-last syllable, and the last letter is a _____ that is neither *n* nor *s*.

7. Some Spanish dialects say *sángüiche,* and this word needs the accent because the _____ is two syllables before the last, just like *gramática* or *pirámide.*

8. *Diga* doesn't need the accent, but *dígame* needs it because the stress is on *di* which is _____ syllables before the last. In a few cases, there are three syllables before the last, for example, *dígamelo* (tell it to me).

9. *Sí* needs an accent when it means two things: (a)_____, (b)_____ _____. But *si* means____.

10. *Tú* means_____, and *tu* means_____. *Mi* means_____, and *mí* means_____. There is only one *ti*, and it doesn't need an accent.

11. *Yo sé donde vive usted* is not correct; *dónde* needs the accent because it is an indirect_____. Where do you write the accent in ¡*que interesante!*?_____.

12. *Día* and *María* need the accent because the stress is on the vowel_____ and the diphthong is broken. Do you write the accent in *oir*?_____. How about *oiga*?_____.

EXERCISES

(Answers, p. 320)

Write the accent where it is needed.

1. El baul de mi automovil es bastante grande y ayer lo llene de libros.

2. El doctor me receto unas pildoras y me puso una inyeccion de antibioticos.

3. Solamente quiero saber cuando te vas y a donde llevaras a tu familia.

4. Yo compraria ese hotel, pero tu no quieres ayudarme con tu dinero.

5. En este album de fotografias esta toda mi familia con mis papas.

6. Jose prefirio comprar este coche en lugar de aquel.

7. Digame por que no vino a tiempo el dia veintitres de abril.

8. Cristobal Colon descubrio America el doce de octubre de 1492.

9. Todos los indios de America comian maiz y hacian pan con el.

10. Tu carro es automatico, pero esta en pesimas condiciones.

11. No entiendo eso del acento en la ultima silaba; ¿puede explicarmelo?

12. ¡Como no! Para mi, eso esta mas claro que el agua del rio.

13. Te dire que si, porque asi me volveras a invitar a tu cumpleaños.

14. Este te esta mas caliente que ese cafe, pero a mi no me gusta el te.

Lesson 15

En la carretera (On the Road)

autobús[1]	bus	**cumplido**	compliment	**pirámide (la)**	pyramid
autopista	highway	**choque**	crash	**pozo**	well
autoservicicio	self-service	**emergencia**	emergency	**puente**	bridge
avería	breakdown	**engrase**	lubrication	**radiador**	radiator
bienvenida	welcome (noun)	**esquina**	corner	**ranchero**	rancher
bomba	pump, bomb	**estación**	station	**rancho**	ranch
camino	road, way	**intersección**	intersection	**ruina**	ruin
camión[1]	truck, bus	**lana**[2]	wool, money	**stop**[4]	stop
campo	field	**loma**	hill	**surtidor**	pump
carretera	road	**manguera**	hose	**tanque**	tank
cerro	hill	**onda**[3]	wave	**templo**	temple
cruce	intersection	**paisaje**	landscape	**terreno**	terrain
cuadra	block	**parada**	stop	**turismo**	tourism
curva	curve	**petróleo**	oil	**velocímetro**	speedometer

acompañar	to accompany	**doblar**	to turn, bend
asustar (se)	to scare, get scared	**engrasar**	to grease, lubricate
cargar	to load, charge	**limpiar**	to clean
consultar	to consult	**ocupar (se)**[5]	to occupy, take care of
convencer	to convince	**pararse**[6]	to stop, to stand up
cruzar	to cross	**prohibir**	to forbid
cultivar	to cultivate	**resbalar**	to skid, to slip
chocar	to crash	**revisar**	to check, revise
dañar	to damage	**subir**	to go up, climb

atento	polite	**estrecho**	narrow	**prudente**	prudent
breve	short, brief	**fascinante**	fascinating	**quebrado**	abrupt

chistoso	funny	**gentil**	elegant	**ondulado**	wavy, hilly
derecho	right, straight	**güero**	blonde	**recto**	straight
despierto	awake, alert	**listo**	ready, smart	**resbaladizo**	slippery
espontáneo	spontaneous	**petrolero**	oil-producing	**romántico**	romantic

con anticipación	ahead of time	**llanta de repuesto**	spare tire
dar la bienvenida	to welcome	**prestar atención**	to pay attention
estar en onda	to be up to date	**¡Qué casualidad!**	What a coincidence!
freno de emergencia	emergency brake	**traérselas**[7]	to get worse and worse

NOTES:

1. *Autobús* means *bus* in the whole Hispanic world, but different countries use other words: *camión* in Mexico, *guagua* in the Caribbean, *autocar* in Spain, etc.

2. *Lana* means *wool*, but in Mexico it is frequently used in colloquial speech as *money*, similar to American "dough".

3. *Onda* means *wave* (sea, sound). In colloquial Spanish *estar en onda* is *to be up to date*.

4. *Stop* is the international road sign for *stop*. But some countries, (e.g. Mexico) still use the old sign ALTO.

5. *Ocupar* is *to occupy*. *Estar ocupado* means *to be busy*. Th reflexive form *ocuparse de* means *to take care of*.

6. *Parar* and *pararse* mean the same: *to stop*. But in Latin America *pararse* is also *to stand up*. We decide the meaning from the context.

7. *Traérselas* is a colloquial expression, with the reflexive *se* and the pronoun *las,* which doesn't replace anything (just like *le* in *ándale, órale*).
   Ex.: *Este chico se las trae.* (this boy is getting worse and worse)

EXERCISES

(Answers, p. 320)

A. Write *el, la* in front of the nouns.

1. ____ autobús
2. ____ camión
3. ____ cruce
4. ____ avería
5. ____ choque
6. ____ engrase
7. ____ estación
8. ____ paisaje
9. ____ pirámide
10. ____ puente
11. ____ radiador
12. ____ surtidor
13. ____ stop
14. ____ tanque
15. ____ intersección
16. ____ autopista

B. Complete the sentences with one of the expressions from the list below.

con anticipación	freno de emergencia	¡Qué casualidad!
dar la bienvenida	llanta de repuesto	traérselas
estar en onda	prestar atención	

1. ¿Su apellido es Rosicler? pues el mío también: ¡ _____ !

2. Amalia, llevas un vestido y unos zapatos de última moda. Se ve que te gusta _____ .

3. La _____ está en el maletero del carro.

4. No creas que este trabajo es fácil; _____ .

5. Mañana vienen a verme unos amigos de Canadá. Voy a dar una fiesta para _____ .

6. Ese dolor de pecho puede ser serio; creo que debes _____ _____ .

7. Si el freno de pedal no funciona, usamos el _____ _____ .

8. Si vas a hacer un viaje largo, es mejor que lo prepares _____ _____ .

C.   Write a verb related to each of the following nouns.

1. compañero _____   7. choque _____

2. daño _____   8. parada _____

3. cruce _____   9. doble _____

4. ocupación _____   10. engrase _____

5. prohibición _____   11. resbaladizo _____

6. susto _____   12. consultorio _____

D.   Write an adjective related to each of the following verbs.

1. atender _____   5. fascinar _____

2. abreviar _____   6. resbalar _____

3. despertar _____   7. estrechar _____

4. quebrar _____   8. ondular _____

E.   Write a synonym for each of the following.

1. autobús _____   3. cerro _____

2. cruce _____   4. depósito _____

5. accidente _____   8. campo _____

6. bomba _____   9. autopista _____

7. stop _____   10. cuidar _____

F. Complete the sentences with a word from the vocabulary.

1. Para poner gasolina en el tanque usamos la_____
   de autoservicio.

2. En Texas y en Oklahoma hay muchos_____
   de petróleo.

3. Los mexicanos llaman_____a las chicas "rubias."

4. El viento hace muchas_____con las aguas del mar.

5. San Francisco tiene un_____famoso sobre la *bahía* (bay) que
   se llama *Golden Gate.*

6. Ayer se me paró el carro en la autopista; tuve una_____
   en el motor.

7. Es necesario reducir la velocidad en las_____
   peligrosas.

8. Colorado tiene montañas y_____muy
   lindos.

9. Carolina tuvo un accidente terrible;_____ contra un camión.

10. Ponemos agua en el_____del coche para
    enfriar el motor.

11. Los faraones de Egipto y los indios de México construyeron_____
    _____ muy altas.

12. Leemos la velocidad del coche en el_____
    que está en el tablero.

**G. Complete the sentences with the Present Subjunctive of the
     verbs in parentheses.**

   "Antes de empezar el viaje, *es importante que* . . ."

1. un mecánico me_____.
   (*engrasar* el motor)

2. yo_____.
   (*limpiar* bien las ventanillas)

3. un mecánico me _____.
   (*revisar* el aceite)

4. mis padres _____.
   (*ocuparse* de mi perro)

5. yo _____.
   (*consultar* los mapas)

6. tú me _____.
   (*acompañar* a comprar cosas)

7. tú _____.
   (*llenar* el tanque)

8. en una estación de servicio me _____.
   (*inflar* las llantas)

H.   Complete the sentences with a word from the list below.

surtidor	esquina	quebrado	ruina
cerro	petrolero	chistoso	lana
cuadra	estrecho	atento	cumplido
listo			

1. Anita no vive lejos de aquí; hay solamente tres _____.

2. Venezuela y México son dos países muy _____.

3. Carlos es un caballero muy _____ con las damas; siempre
   les dice muchos _____.

4. En España hay muchas _____ romanas de templos,
   puentes, acueductos, etc.

5. Vamos a pasar por un terreno muy _____, con muchos
   cerros y montañas.

6. ¡Cuidado! que la carretera se hace más pequeña porque llegamos a un
   puente muy _____.

7. Don Paco es millonario; él tiene toda la _____ que quiere.

8. La consulta del médico está en la _____ de la calle Martí y
   Miramar.

9. Marta siempre está _____ para cualquier emergencia.

10. Señor, si quiere gasolina tiene que manejar más cerca del_____

    _____ .

11. Johnny Carson y Bob Hope son_____en sus programas
    de televisión.

12. Una montaña chiquita es una loma o _____ .

DIÁLOGO *¡Qué casualidad!*

(Una turista americana decide viajar en autobús desde México hasta
Acapulco. En el autobús se sienta al lado de un joven mexicano.)

AMERICANA: Buenos días, ¿puedo pasar hacia la ventanilla?
MEXICANO: Claro. ¿Hasta dónde va usted, señorita?
AMERICANA: Hasta Acapulco. Es un viaje largo, ¿no?
MEXICANO: Sí, bastante. Pero, ¿qué hace una güera como usted via-
jando en este camión? ¿Dónde está su Cadillac?
AMERICANA: No se crea Ud. que todos los americanos tengamos un
Cadillac. La verdad que me gusta viajar con la gente del
pueblo para conocerla mejor.
MEXICANO: Ándale, pues. Ya verá que este "viajecito" se las trae.
AMERICANA: Eso no me asusta. Estoy lista para cualquier emergencia.

• • •

AMERICANA: ¡Qué lindos campos de maíz!
MEXICANO: Sí, gracias a eso seguiremos comiendo enchiladas, tacos,
tortillas, . . .
AMERICANA: ¡Qué poco romántico es usted! Es mejor que admire la
naturaleza. ¡Mire allá lejos las ruinas de un templo y una
pirámide altísima!
MEXICANO: Sí, sí, muy lindo; pero hablando de otras cosas, ¿de qué
parte de Estados Unidos viene usted?
AMERICANA: De una ciudad pequeña de California. Se llama Calabasas.
MEXICANO: ¡Qué casualidad! Yo tengo un primo allí que trabaja de
camarero en un restaurante.
AMERICANA: ¿No me diga usted que ese restaurante es "El Torito"?
MEXICANO: Efectivamente. Hace ya más de un año que trabaja allí y
está bien cargado de lana. Se llama Carlos.
AMERICANA: ¡Otra casualidad! Yo lo conozco muy bien. ¡Es un chico
bien simpático!

DIALOG   *What a Coincidence!*

(An American tourist is visiting Mexico and decides to travel by bus from Mexico City to Acapulco. She is going to sit down next to a young Mexican man.)

AMERICAN: Good morning. May I sit next to the window?

MEXICAN: Of course. How far are you going, miss?

AMERICAN: To Acapulco. It's a long trip, isn't it?

MEXICAN: Yes, pretty long. But, what's a blonde like you doing traveling in this bus? Where's your Cadillac?

AMERICAN: Don't think all Americans own a Cadillac. The truth is I like to travel with people to know them better.

MEXICAN: Well, then. You'll see that this "little trip" gets worse and worse.

AMERICAN: That doesn't scare me. I'm ready for any emergency.

• • •

AMERICAN: What pretty corn fields!

MEXICAN: Sure; thanks to that we'll keep on eating enchiladas, tacos, tortillas, . . .

AMERICAN: You're not very romantic! It's better to admire nature. Look over there, the ruins of a temple and a very tall pyramid!

MEXICAN: Yes, yes, very pretty. But let's talk about something else. What part of the U.S. do you come from?

AMERICAN: From a small city in California. It's called Calabasas.

MEXICAN: What a coincidence! I have a cousin there who works as a waiter in a restaurant.

AMERICAN: Don't tell me the restaurant is "El Torito"?

MEXICAN: Yes, it is. He's been working there over a year and he is loaded with dough. His name is Carlos.

AMERICAN: Another coincidence! I know him, really well. He's a very nice guy!

EXERCISES

(Answers, p. 321)

A.   Complete the sentences in the past to make a narrative summary of the dialog.

La turista americana decidió (1)_____ en autobús desde

México (2)_____ Acapulco. En el autobús se encontró con un

joven mexicano. La americana quería (3)_____ junto a la

ventanilla, y pidió permiso para pasar. El mexicano se sorprendió de ver una

(4) _____ como ella viajando en autobús. Él pensaba que todos

los americanos (5) _____ un Cadillac. A la americana le gusta-

ba (6) _____ así para conocer mejor a la gente. El mexicano le

dijo que el viaje era bastante largo, que se (7) _____ , pero la

americana le aseguró que ella estaba (8) _____ para cualquier

emergencia. Después de viajar un tiempo por la carretera, la chica observó los

lindos campos de (9) _____ , las ruinas de un templo, y una

(10) _____ muy alta. El mexicano le preguntó de dónde

(11) _____ y ella le contestó que de una pequeña (12) _____

_____ de California, Calabasas. El joven se sorprendió mucho porque él tenía

allí un (13) _____ que trabajaba de (14) _____

y además tenía mucho dinero. La americana conocía muy bien el (15) _____

_____ donde trabajaba su primo Carlos, y también conocía

personalmente a este chico muy (16) _____ .

B. Answer True (T) or False (F).

1. ____ La chica americana no es rubia sino morena.

2. ____ La turista va a viajar desde Mexico hasta Mazlatán.

3. ____ La americana quiere sentarse junto a la ventanilla.

4. ____ El mexicano se sorprende de ver a una joven americana viajando en autobús.

5. ____ Los mexicanos en general piensan que los americanos tienen carros grandes.

6. ____ La chica dice que le gusta el autobús porque puede ver los campos y paisajes.

7. ____ Al mexicano le interesa más el maíz desde un punto de vista práctico: la comida.

8. ____ A la americana le parece romántico el campo, las ruinas, las pirá-mides.

9. ____ La chica dice que vive en una ciudad pequeña de Arizona, Calabasas.

10. ___ El mexicano tiene un hermano que trabaja de camarero en esa ciudad.

11. ___ El nombre del restaurante donde trabaja el muchacho se llama "El Torito."

12. ___ El muchacho trabaja de camarero y gana muy poco dinero.

13. ___ La americana conoce al muchacho que trabaja de camarero, pero no el restaurante.

14. ___ Esta historia sugiere que pocos turistas americanos viajan en autobús.

C. You are driving with a friend. Complete these suggestions with the correct form of the Present Subjunctive.

1. Mira, José, es mejor que nosotros _____ el aceite. (revisar)

2. Te sugiero (I suggest) que te _____ en aquella estación. (parar)

3. Es necesario que tú _____ las vías del ferrocarril. (cruzar)

4. Es muy importante que nosotros _____ a la derecha. (doblar)

5. Será mejor que el carro no _____ con esta agua. (resbalar)

6. Te pido que no _____ esta loma tan rápidamente. (subir)

7. Espero que nosotros no _____ con nada. (chocar)

8. Estamos perdidos. Es bueno que tú _____ con el mapa. (consultar)

9. Espero que nosotros no _____ ninguna avería. (tener)

10. Vamos a parar aquí. Es mejor que tú me _____. (acompañar)

11. Espero que el motor no se _____ con tanto calor. (dañar)

12. Será mejor que nosotros _____ bastante comida aquí. (cargar)

D. Review the formal command forms. Suppose that you are a travel agent. You are making suggestions to a man who is planning a trip to Venezuela.

1. _____ los boletos con tiempo. (comprar)

2. No_____ las cosas para el último momento. (dejar)

3. _____ algunos libros sobre el país que va a visitar. (leer)

4. _____ los mapas del país o la región. (consultar)

5. No_____ demasiado equipaje. Las maletas molestan mucho. (llevar)

6. _____ las maletas con anticipación. (hacer)

7. No_____ su pasaporte ni su dinero en casa. (olvidar)

8. _____ temprano al aeropuerto. (llegar)

9. No_____ un asiento en la sección de fumar. (pedir)

10. No_____ los cheques de viajeros ni las tarjetas de crédito. (perder)

E. Now review the familiar command forms. Use the sentences from the previous exercise, and write only the verb forms.

1._____   6._____

2._____   7._____

3._____   8._____

4._____   9._____

5._____   10._____

GRAMMAR I Indicative and Subjunctive in contrast: perception vs. emotion.

A. If the main clause contains a verb of *perception*, such as *ver*, *oír*, *observar*, the verb in the subordinate clause must be in the *Indicative*. Here are a few verbs and expressions of *perception*:

ver	(to see)	**observar**	(to observe)	**es evidente**	(it's evident)
oír	(to hear)	**notar**	(to notice)	**es claro**	(it's clear)
sentir	(to feel)	**es obvio**	(it's obvious)	**está claro**	(it's clear)

Ex.: Usted ve que ella es rubia. (you can see that she is blonde)
Es evidente que tú estudias. (it's evident that you're studying)

B.   If the main clause contains a verb of *emotion,* the verb in the sub-
     ordinate clause must be in the *Subjunctive.* Verbs of emotion are
     those that denote sadness, happiness, like, dislike, hate, love, anger,
     gratitude, surprise, pity, fear, etc.
          Ex.: Me gusta que usted vaya conmigo. (I like the fact that
                you're going with me)
                Es triste que él esté enfermo. (it's sad that he is sick)

     There must be a change in subject between the two clauses to war-
     rant the Subjunctive. If the two clauses have the same subject, the
     infinitive is used in the second clause. Compare *Siento mucho no ir*
     (I'm very sorry I can't go) with *Siento mucho que tú no vayas* (I'm very
     sorry you can't go).

     Here is a partial list of verbs and expressions of *emotion:*

temer	(to be afraid)	**molestar**	(to bother)	**es triste**	(it's sad)
gustar	(to like)	**asustar**	(to scare)	**es una pena**	(it's a pity)
disgustar	(to dislike)	**agradecer**	(to thank)	**es (una) lástima**	(it's a pity)
agradar	(to please)	**enojarse**	(to get angry)	**es extraño**	(it's strange)
alegrarse de	(to be glad)	**sorprender**	(to surprise)	**es sorprendente**	(it's surprising)
sentir	(to be sorry)	**tener miedo**	(to fear)	**es maravilloso**	(it's marvelous)

C.   Notice the following facts:
     1. *Sentir* has two meanings: (1) *to be sorry,* an emotion, and as such
         requires the Subjunctive; (2) *to feel, to sense,* a perception, and as
         such requires the Indicative.
              Ex.: Siento mucho que estés enfermo. (I'm very sorry that you
                    are sick)
                    Siento por el pulso que estás enfermo. (I feel by your pulse
                    that you're sick)

     2. *Ojalá* means *I hope that,* implying an emotion or a wish. It always
         requires the Subjunctive, and the linking conjunction *que* may be
         omitted.
              Ex.: Ojalá (que) llegues a tiempo. (I hope that you will arrive on
                    time)

PRACTICE THE SUBJUNCTIVE　　　　　　　　*(Answers, p. 321)*

1. If the main clause contains a verb of perception, the subordinate clause must be in the _____. Ex.: *Es evidente que ella* _____ *español.* (hablar)

2. If the main clause contains a verb of emotion, the subordinate clause must be in the _____. Ex.: *Me alegra que tú* _____ *a la fiesta.* (ir)

3. You may remember from the previous lesson that a verb of *information* requires the Indicative. *Perception* is information received through our senses. Also remember that a verb of *influence* requires the _____. Somehow an *emotion* is an influence on somebody, and as such, requires the verb in the _____.

4. Gratitude is a type of emotion. Complete the sentence *José te agradece que* _____ *a verlo.* (venir) (Joe thanks you for coming to see him).

5. *Molestar* is not *to molest* as the spelling suggests, but *to bother,* an emotion of dislike. Complete the sentence *Me molesta que usted* _____. (fumar) (it bothers me that you smoke)

6. *Asustar* (to scare, to be afraid) is an emotion of surprise and fear. Complete the question *¿Te asusta que yo* _____ *a 80 millas por hora?* (manejar) (are you scared that I drive 80 miles an hour?)

7. *Evidente* is related to *ver;* it refers to something everybody can see and understand. Complete the sentence *Es evidente que él* _____ *dinero.* (tener)

8. *Ojalá* is one of the many words that Spanish got from the Arabic language. Originally it meant *may Allah grant that;* but nowadays it means simply *I hope that.* Complete the sentence *Ojalá que no* _____ *mañana.* (llover)

9. In the expression *es una lástima que* (it's a pity that) *una* may be omitted. This certainly denotes a type of emotion and as such requires the subordinate verb in the _____.

10. *Sentir* means *to be sorry,* an emotion, and the subordinate verb must be in the _____. But sometimes *sentir* means *to feel, to sense, to hear,* and as such requires the subordinate verb in the _____.

EXERCISES

A. Complete the sentences with the Present Indicative or Subjunctive as required.

1. Me sorprende que tu amigo no_____cerveza. (beber)

2. Es una lástima que ustedes_____tan tarde. (llegar)

3. Es obvio que ustedes no_____español perfecto. (hablar)

4. El director me asegura que ese alumno_____mucho. (estudiar)

5. Me pone furioso que los estudiantes no_____la lección. (saber)

6. ¿Te gusta que yo_____en tu libro? (escribir)

7. Ya todos vemos que Cristina_____lista para eso. (estar)

8. Es evidente que Ud. no_____ni_____. (fumar, beber)

9. Es muy extraño que tu amiga no te_____por teléfono. (llamar)

10. Ojalá que el coche no_____ninguna avería. (tener)

11. Es claro que esta americana_____viajar con la gente. (querer)

12. Sentimos mucho que Ud. no_____venir mañana. (poder)

13. Me sorprende bastante que tú no_____más vino. (pedir)

14. Ella tiene miedo que el carro se_____en la autopista. (parar)

15. Es maravilloso que Ud._____tan rápidamente. (vestirse)

B. Combine the two sentences using the conjunction *que*. Make all necessary changes and select Indicative or Subjunctive according to the verb in the main clause.

Example: Te gusta mucho. Yo salgo contigo.
Te gusta mucho que yo salga contigo.

1. Me alegro mucho. Mi carro gasta poca gasolina.

_____.

2. Rosaura tiene miedo. Su carro no arranca bien.

    _____.

3. Es muy obvio. Yo no puedo comprar cuatro llantas ahora.

    _____.

4. Ella se pone furiosa. Usted maneja muy rápidamente.

    _____.

C. **Combine the sentences, making all necessary change in the second (subordinate) clause. Select Indicative or Subjunctive according to the verb in the main clause. Remember that when the two clauses have the same subject, the infinitive is used.**

    Examples: Siento mucho. yo / no poder / acompañarlos.
    Siento mucho no poder acompañarlos.
    Siento mucho. Ud. / no poder / acompañarnos.
    Siento mucho que Ud. no pueda acompañarnos.

1. Me sorprende. ella / no ir / de vacaciones / este año.

    _____.

2. Nos alegramos mucho. nosotros / tener / buen trabajo.

    _____.

3. Ustedes esperan. el / carro / no tener / llantas / desinflado.

    _____.

4. Es una lástima. nosotros / volver / a enfermarse.

    _____.

5. Nos molesta mucho. nosotros / oír / ese / música / moderno.

    _____.

6. Agradecemos mucho. tú / cambiar / el aceite / a / el carro.

    _____.

GRAMMAR II   Indicative and Subjunctive in contrast: certainty vs. doubt.

A.   Indicative with verbs of *certainty:*
   1. If the main clause contains a verb of *certainty, belief, sureness,* the verb in the subordinate clause is in the Indicative.
      Ex.: Usted cree que su amiga está enferma. (you believe your friend is sick)
      Yo supongo que ella está enferma. (I suppose that she is sick)

   2. Here is a list of verbs and expressions that are followed by the Indicative:

creer	(to believe)	**imaginarse**	(to imagine)	**no hay duda**	(there is no doubt)
pensar	(to think)	**es cierto**	(it's certain)	**estar convencido**	(to be convinced)
suponer	(to suppose)	**es verdad**	(it's true)	**tener por seguro**	(to be sure)
parecer	(it seems)	**es seguro**	(it's sure)	**tener por cierto**	(to be certain)
es que	(the fact is)	**no dudar**	(not to doubt)	**es claro**	(it's clear)

B.   Subjunctive with verbs of *doubt, disbelief:*
1.   If the main clause contains a verb denoting the idea of *doubt, disbelief,* the verb in the subordinate clause is in the Subjunctive.
      Ex. Usted no cree que ella esté enferma. (you don't believe that she is sick)
      Es posible que llueva mañana. (it's possible that it will rain tomorrow)

   2. Here is a list of verbs and expressions that are followed by the Subjunctive:

dudar	(to doubt)	**es dudoso**	(it's doubtful)
no creer	(not to believe)	**es probable**	(it's probable)
no pensar	(not to think)	**es posible**	(it's possible)
no parecer	(not to seem)	**es imposible**	(it's impossible)
no es que	(it isn't that)	**no es seguro**	(it's not sure)
no suponer	(not to suppose)	**no es claro**	(it's not clear)
no imaginarse	(not to imagine)	**no estar convencido**	(not to be convinced)
hay duda de que	(there is doubt)	**no es verdad**	(it's not true)

   3. There is no clear line between *doubt* and *certainty* in many of the verbs and expressions listed above. Therefore these rules will not apply in every situation.

C.   Indicative and Subjunctive with adverbs of doubt:
      The adverbs of doubt are *quizá (quizás), tal vez, acaso, puede ser,* and they all mean *perhaps, maybe.* They are used with the Indicative or

Subjunctive, according to the degree of doubt or certainty felt by the speaker.

Ex.: Quizás llueve mañana. (perhaps it will rain tomorrow)
(the speaker is almost sure)
Quizás llueva mañana. (perhaps it will rain tomorrow)
(the speaker has his doubts)

PRACTICE THE SUBJUNCTIVE   *(Answers, p. 322)*

1. Verbs and expressions of *doubt* require the verb in the subordinate clause to be in the _____. For example, *Es posible que mi tío* _____ *a visitarme.* (venir) (it's possible that my uncle will come to visit me)

2. Verbs of sureness and belief in the main clause require the subordinate verb to be in the _____. Ex.: *Carlos piensa que yo* _____ *un buen trabajo.* (tener) (Charles thinks that I have a good job)

3. *Suponer* indicates more certainty than doubt. For this reason *suponer* requires the subordinate verb to be in the Indicative. Ex.: *Usted supone que él* _____ *en su casa.* (estar)

4. There is no definite line between doubt and sureness, belief and disbelief. You may have noticed in the lists given in *(A)* and *(B)* on page (292) that many verbs take the Indicative with the affirmative form, and the Subjunctive with the _____ form.

5. One way to emphasize a statement is to add *The fact is that* in front of it. To translate this idea, Spanish uses *Es que* followed by the Indicative. Ex.: *Es que José sabe muy bien el español.* To deny the fact requires the Subjunctive: *No es que José* _____ *bien el español, sino que lo está aprendiendo.* (saber)

6. Adverbs of doubt, such as *quizás, tal vez,* show the Indicative-Subjunctive contrast we are studying in this lesson. When the speaker is almost sure, he/she would use the _____, and if the speaker has doubts he/she would use the _____.

7. Certain expressions like *es claro, es verdad* can be used to give information that is obvious and certain. In this case the dependent, subordinate verb must be in the _____.

8. If you are almost sure that John is Italian, you say *Me parece que Juan* _____ *italiano.* But if you have doubts, you say *No me parece que Juan* _____ *italiano.*

EXERCISES

(Answers, p. 322)

A. Complete the sentences with the Indicative or the Subjunctive as required.

1. Yo pienso que mis padres_____en casa ahora. (estar)

2. Te apuesto que Josefina no_____con Roberto. (casarse)

3. Marta no está convencida de que tú la_____. (querer)

4. Dudamos mucho que Anita nos_____hoy.
   (acompañar)

5. No es que yo_____infalible; pero es que tú siempre_____
   _____tener razón. (ser, querer).

6. Suponemos que este carro_____en buenas condiciones.
   (estar)

7. Estoy seguro que este carro_____poca gasolina. (gastar)

8. ¿Por qué dudas que yo no te_____el dinero que te debo?
   (dar)

9. No hay duda de que ellos_____aprender español.
   (desear)

10. Me parece muy bien que ustedes_____una dieta. (seguir)

11. El doctor piensa que mi enfermedad no_____seria. (ser)

12. Es muy probable que el jueves_____otra vez. (llover)

B. Add the expressions in parentheses to form sentences with two clauses. Follow the example.

Example: Le cuesta mucho dinero arreglar el motor. (dudo)
         Dudo que le cueste mucho dinero arreglar el motor.

1. El muchacho cruza la calle sin problema. (suponemos)

   _____

2. Roberto se ocupa de comprar los boletos. (me parece)

   _____

3. El autobús se para antes del cruce de ferrocarril. (te imaginas)

   _____

4. El mecánico engrasa bien el motor. (no estoy seguro)

_____

5. Tú doblas en la esquina siguiente. (no hay duda)

_____

6. Ella se asusta mucho por la noche. (es posible)

_____

7. El carro resbala mucho cuando llueve. (es que)

_____

8. Nosotros seguimos derecho hasta la catedral. (ella duda)

_____

9. El paisaje de las pirámides es fascinante. (creemos)

_____

10. Estás bien despierto mientras manejas. (quizás)

   (speaker doubts)_____

   (speaker is hopeful)_____

GRAMMAR III   Indicative and Subjunctive in Contrast:
   Adjective and Adverbial clauses.
   Review of the Present Subjunctive.

A.   Indicative-Subjunctive contrast in adjective clauses (Known vs. unknown nouns).
   1. Compare this pair of sentences:
      (a) Tengo una casa que es cómoda. (I have a house that is comfortable)
      (b) Busco una casa que sea cómoda. (I'm looking for a house that is comfortable)
      In (a) we have a *house* that is *known,* and the verb *es* is Indicative; in (b) the *house* is *unknown,* and the verb *sea* is Subjunctive. In both cases the subordinate clauses beginning with *que* describe *una casa* (noun) and are therefore called *adjective* clauses.
   2. Now compare this pair of sentences:
      (a) Aquí hay una chica que habla chino. (there is a girl here who speaks Chinese)

(b) Aquí no hay ninguna chica que hable chino. (there is no girl here who speaks Chinese)

In (a) the speaker states the existence of *una chica* who is known, and therefore *habla* is Indicative. In (b) the speaker denies the existence of *una chica,* in which case the noun mentioned is nonexistent, and therefore *hable* is Subjunctive.

More examples:

Quiero una secretaria que sepa español. (*subjunctive:* the secretary is unknown)

Conozco una secretaria que sabe español. (*indicative:* the secretary is known)

¿Hay una secretaria que sepa español? (*subjunctive:* the secretary is unknown)

B. Indicative-Subjunctive contrast in adverbial clauses:

1. *Indicative to show reality.* An adverbial subordinate clause explains some circumstance of the main clause: time, location, etc. If the main clause shows an action that has already occurred, the verb in the subordinate clause is in the Indicative because it's a real fact or a definite situation.

   Ex.: Te vi cuando saliste de clase. (I saw you when you left the room)

   Me siento mejor después que como. (I feel better after I eat)

   Notice that any action in a *past* tense is already a fact as shown in the first example. The Present Indicative also denotes a real fact when it shows a *habit* as in the second example.

2. *Subjunctive to show unreality.* A future action is one that is only a possibility; it's not *real* yet and is considered hypothetical. When the main clause is in the Future tense, the verb in the subordinate clause must be Subjunctive. Remember that the present tense is often used to show a future action as you can see in the second example that follows.

   Ex.: Te veré cuando llegues. (I'll see you when you arrive)

   Te pago cuando me paguen. (I'll pay you when they pay me)

3. List of adverbial conjunctions that take Indicative or Subjunctive:

cuando	(when)	**mientras**	(while)	**después que**	(after)
donde	(where)	**luego que**	(after)	**siempre que**	(whenever)
como	(as)	**hasta que**	(until)	**en seguida que**	(as soon as)
aunque	(although)	**en cuanto**	(as soon as)	**tan pronto como**	(as soon as)

NOTES:

1. *Mientras* can be used with or without *que.* The tendency today is to omit *que.*
   Ex.: Mamá cocina mientras nosotros vemos televisión.

2. *Antes que* always requires the subjunctive, even to show *reality* in the past.
   Ex.: Te veré antes que salgas. (I'll see you before you leave)

3. We use *después que* and *después de que,* as well as *antes que* and *antes de que.* The tendency today is to omit the preposition *de.*

C. Review of the Present Indicative-Subjunctive Contrast:

INDICATIVE	SUBJUNCTIVE
Information: Ya sé que estás bien.	Influence: Quiero que estés bien.
Perception: Ya veo que estás bien.	Emotion: Me alegra que estés bien.
Certainty: Creo que estás bien.	Doubt: No creo que estés bien.
Known noun: Tengo una casa que es grande.	Unknown noun: Busco una casa que sea grande.
Real fact: Te veo siempre que llegas.	Future fact: Te veré cuando llegues.

PRACTICE THE SUBJUNCTIVE   *(Answers, p. 322)*

1. An adjective is a word that describes a noun. A Subordinate clause that begins with *que* and describes the noun in the main clause is called an

   _____ clause.

2. The adjective clause may describe a *known* noun; in this case the verb is in

   the_____. If the noun described by the clause is

   unknown, the verb must be in the_____.

3. We know that a verb denotes *influence, emotion, doubt,* by the meaning in the dictionary. The use of the Subjunctive in an adjective clause has nothing to do with the meaning of the verb. It has to do with the speaker's knowledge of the noun being described. Complete this sentence: *Carlos necesita un*

   carro que_____poca gasolina. (usar)

4. To state the existence of a noun presupposes some knowledge of that noun.

   Complete this sentence: *Aquí hay una iglesia que_____*
   200 años. (tener)

5. A speaker can mention a noun that is hypothetical or nonexistent. Complete this sentence: *No hay nadie que_____500 años.* (vivir)

6. You ask for information about a noun when you don't know about that noun. Complete the question: *¿Hay alguna persona aquí que_____*
   _____matemáticas? (estudiar)

7. You know about the things you have: your house, your car, etc. Complete this sentence: *Tenemos un perro que_____mucho?* (comer)

8. An adverb gives information about an action, such as when *(mañana)*, where *(aquí)*, etc. If we use a clause rather than an adverb to describe the verb in the main clause, this new clause is called an_____
   _____.

9. If the main clause shows an action that has already occurred, this action is a *reality*. The verb in the adverbial clause must be in the_____
   _____. For example, *Comimos después que mi padre*
   _____. (llegar)

10. A habit is something we repeat many times, and is therefore already a reality. Therefore the subordinate clause must be_____.
    For example, *Usted siempre fuma un cigarrillo después que_____*.
    (comer)

11. A future action is only a possibility; it's not a reality yet. When the main clause is in the Future tense, the verb in the subordinate clause is_____
    _____. For example, *Comeremos después que mi*
    padre_____. (llegar)

12. Complete this sentence: *Vamos a viajar cuando mi padre_____*
    dinero. (tener)

13. *Después de que* is the same as_____.
    Mientras que is the same as_____.

14. *Antes que* always requires the_____, even when we talk about an action in the past. This conjunction is an exception to the rule of reality vs. unreality.

15. Verbs of *influence* require the_____, whereas verbs of *information* require the_____.

16. Verbs of *certainty* are to the *Indicative* as verbs of *doubt* are to the _____

_____ .

17. Verbs of *emotion* are to the *Subjunctive* as verbs of *perception* are to the

_____ .

EXERCISES

(Answers, p. 323)

A. **Complete these sentences with the Present Indicative or Subjunctive as required.**

1. Conozco un parque que_____ muchos árboles. (tener)

2. Compré una casa que me_____ mucho. (gustar)

3. Necesitamos un *equipo* (team) que_____ ganar o perder. (saber)

4. María tiene un amigo que_____ en Nueva York. (vivir)

5. No hay muchos españoles que_____ chino o japonés. (hablar)

6. En Estados Unidos hay 20 millones de personas que_____

_____ español. (hablar)

7. Me molesta mucho que la gente_____ en lugares públicos. (fumar)

8. Teresa tiene un gato que_____ muy lindo. (ser)

9. Quiero comprar una casa que_____ barata. (ser)

10. ¿Hay aquí algún estudiante que_____ francés? (escribir)

11. Tengo miedo que ellos_____ demasiado dinero. (gastar)

12. Es muy cierto que yo no_____ más que inglés y español. (saber)

B. **Replace the verb in the main clause with the verb or expression given in parentheses. Change the sentence to Subjunctive as required.**

Example: Tienen una raqueta buena. (buscar)
          Buscan una raqueta que *sea* buena.

1. Tenemos un profesor que nunca llega tarde. (querer)

_____

_____

2. Hay alguien aquí que estudia italiano. (no hay nadie aquí)

_____

3. Conocemos a una chica que escribe bien a máquina. (necesitamos)

_____

_____

4. Hay muchos turistas que quieren viajar en camión. (no hay ningún)

_____

_____

5. Hay una farmacia que está abierta hasta las 10:00. (no hay ninguna)

_____

_____

6. Tienen una secretaria que es _bilingüe_ (bilingual). (buscar)

_____

C. Translate the sentences into Spanish.

1. We don't know anyone who is going.

_____

2. She needs an apartment that has two bedrooms.

_____

_____

3. There is no one here who plays the guitar.

_____

4. Is there anyone here who has a watch?

_____

5. I am looking for a secretary who wants to work.

_____

_____

D. Use the adverbial conjunctions in parentheses to combine the two sentences. Make all the necessary changes.

Example: Teresa se enfermará. Ella comerá enchiladas. (después que)

Teresa se enfermará después que coma enchiladas.

1. No te olvides de llamarme. Llegarás a la oficina. (antes que)

_____

_____

2. Paco siempre llama al doctor. Tiene mareos. (cuando)

_____

_____

3. Mi mamá me dará algo. Vendrá a verme el domingo. (cuando)

_____

_____

4. Los turistas volverán al hotel. Visitarán las ruinas. (después que)

_____

_____

5. Yo busco la llanta de repuesto. Ud. revisa la batería. (mientras)

_____

_____

6. No podemos comprar un carro nuevo. Recibiremos el préstamo del banco. (hasta que)

_____

_____

7. Me ocuparé de todo. Los niños se dormirán. (tan pronto como)

_____

_____

8. El camarero sirve camarones a José. José termina el aperitivo. (antes de que)

_____

_____

E. Complete the following sentences with the required tense, Indicative or Subjunctive.

1. Yo espero que usted _____ algo en El Rastro. (comprar)

2. No entiendo por qué el _____ a Chicago mañana. (irse)

3. Puedo ver a tu amiga después que yo _____ de clase. (salir)

4. Ya te diré muchas cosas cuando (nosotros) _____ a casa. (llegar)

5. Me sorprende mucho que Mirta no _____ nada. (decir)

6. El mecánico trabaja hasta que se _____ . (cansarse: *to be tired*)

7. Teresa me sugiere que (nosotros) _____ en esta esquina. (cruzar)

8. Todos los días me fumo un *puro* (cigar) después que nosotros _____ _____ . (cenar)

9. Anita me informa que usted _____ a España el verano próximo. (ir)

10. Conozco a una muchacha en la oficina que _____ de Venezuela. (ser)

11. ¿Hay alguien aquí que _____ acompañarme? (poder)

12. No hay nadie aquí que no _____ español. (hablar)

REVIEW EXAM FOR LESSONS 11–15

Part I VOCABULARY

A. Match the two columns. Cross out the article where it is not needed.

1. ___ las pestañas

2. ___ el tobillo

3. ___ el codo

4. ___ las muletas

5. ___ la rodilla

6. ___ la garganta

7. ___ el muslo

8. ___ la tos

9. ___ los mareos

10. ___ la fiebre

11. ___ la pastilla

12. ___ los pulmones

13. ___ las gotas

14. ___ el sastre

15. ___ la sangre

16. ___ el acero

17. ___ la marca

18. ___ la balanza

A. Cuando me duele el estómago me dan muchos . . . .

B. El doctor me recetó . . . para el dolor de estómago.

C. Creo que tiene la tensión de . . . un poco alta.

D. Voy a ir a . . . porque necesito un vestido nuevo.

E. Con tanto fumar debes tener . . . negros del humo.

F. Algunas señoras se pintan . . . .

G. Me duelen los ojos. Voy a ponerme unas . . . .

H. Cuando se tuerce . . . da mucho dolor, y no se puede caminar.

I. Doblamos la pierna en la parte que se llama . . . .

J. Necesitas una . . . si quieres saber tu peso.

K. Tienes dificultad para hablar por la infección de . . . .

L. Doblamos los brazos en la articulación del . . . .

M. El hueso más grande del hombre está en . . . .

N. Si te enyesan la pierna tienes que caminar con . . . .

O. No me gustan las hojas de aluminio; prefiero las de . . . .

P. Para saber si tienes . . . debes ponerte el termómetro.

Q. Con tanta . . . no deberías fumar.

R. No me gusta esa . . . de cerveza; pide otra.

B. Circle the choice that best completes each of the following.

19. Debemos comprar llantas nuevas porque éstas están (desinfladas, torcidas, gastadas, disponibles).

20. Mi carro tiene el acumulador viejo; por eso no (funciona, arranca, toca, pincha) bien.

21. Si no tiene buenos (frenos, cinturones, neumáticos, faros) no puedes ver bien de noche.

22. Vamos a la droguería para (llenar una receta, bajar de peso, ponernos una inyección, estar en onda).

23. Para poder mandarle la cuenta necesito (una radiografía, el domicilio, su cacharro, su matrícula).

24. Si tiene un hueso roto probablemente lo tendremos que (cortar, oler, enyesar, tragar).

25. Debemos estar listos para una emergencia (increíble, gruesa, imprevista, resbaladiza).

26. No puedo llenar el tanque porque la manguera está (doblada, dañada, cargada, ondulada).

27. En un cruce peligroso es mejor (bajar le velocidad, engrasar el motor, subir la loma, aparcar el carro).

28. Cuando se pincha un neumático es bueno tener (un choque con anticipación, una llanta de repuesto, buena la bocina, un puente estrecho)

29. Para que el médico pueda auscultarnos es conveniente (tragarse las pastillas, quitarse la camiseta, guardar cama, seguir una dieta).

30. Vamos a la florería cuando queremos (comprar unas rosas, cortarnos el cabello, conseguir un jarabe, contener la fiebre).

C. Write a synonym for each of the following words.

31. autobús_____, manejar_____

32. farmacia_____, baúl (del carro)_____

33. carnet_____, matrícula_____

34. aparcar_____, manual_____

35. choque_____, detenerse_____

36. autopista_____, cerro_____

37. píldora_____, cruce_____

38. paciente_____, resfriado_____

39. delgado_____, grueso_____

D. One of the four answers is the best; circle the letter.

40. El lunes pasado tuve una avería imprevista en la carretera.
   A. Sí, claro; por eso echas de menos a tus amigos.
   B. Sí, claro; eso te pasa por comprar carros de segunda mano.
   C. Sí, claro; tú siempre tienes buena pata en todo.
   D. Sí, claro; ya veo que tienes un pie enyesado y muletas.

41. Esta mañana me corté terriblemente en la mejilla cuando me afeitaba.
   A. Bueno, me imagino que eso te hizo ver las estrellas.
   B. Eso te pasa por afeitarte con una máquina eléctrica.
   C. Entonces debes ir a llenar una receta en seguida.
   D. Ya veo que tienes todavía un poco de sangre en la mano.

42. Doctor, tengo una tos terrible desde hace una semana y no se me quita.
   A. Lo mejor será que dejes el cigarrillo inmediatamente.
   B. Eso me huele mal. Será mejor que tengas mareos y úlcera.
   C. Eso no tiene remedio. Es preferible que pierdas peso.
   D. Probablemente es una indigestión con complicaciones.

43. Me parece que las tarifas de alquiler son demasiado altas, señor.
   A. Es que aquí solamente alquilamos coches de segunda mano.
   B. Ya veo que usted siempre tiene mala estrella.
   C. Es que todos nuestros carros están asegurados a todo riesgo.
   D. Una razón es que nuestros carros son todos de cambios.

44. Doctor, me dañé bastante la espalda cuando choqué contra el autobús.
   A. Eso te pasa porque probablemente no te pones el cinturón de seguridad.
   B. Sí, ya veo que tienes el tobillo torcido y habrá que enyesarlo.
   C. Eso te pasa porque acabas de poner los frenos nuevos al carro.
   D. Pero ese dolor se te quitará cuando tu seguro pague los daños.

45. ¿Cree usted que todo mi equipaje cabrá en el baúl de su carro?
   A. ¡Cómo no! Usted sabe que mi automóvil es de cambios.
   B. Por supuesto. Yo también llevo tres maletas grandes.
   C. Claro que sí. Mi esposa también lleva dos baúles.
   D. Creo que no. Usted sabe que mi carro es bastante pequeño.

46. Anita, ayer me encontré con un señor muy gentil y me pagó el almuerzo.
   A. Bueno, pues ya sabes que "a mal tiempo, buena cara".
   B. Yo también me encontré con uno muy atento que se las traía.
   C. Me imagino que te casarás con él mañana mismo.
   D. Te felicito. Tú siempre tienes buena estrella.

47. Oiga, señor, aquí se prohíbe estacionar el automóvil.
   A. En ese caso me aparcaré aquí mismo.
   B. Está bien. No me importa pagar la propina.
   C. En ese caso tendré que buscar otro lugar.
   D. No importa. Éste es el carro de mi papá.

48. El turismo representa una buena entrada de dinero en nuestro país, ¿no?
    A. Sí, por eso los turistas americanos viajan en autobús.
    B. Sí, los turistas admiran mucho nuestros paisajes.
    C. Claro, los turistas dejan mucha lana en los hoteles.
    D. ¡Cómo no! los turistas americanos se las traen.

49. ¿Estás prestando atención a la velocidad máxima de 55 millas?
    A. Sí, pero mi póliza de seguro pagará todo.
    B. Sí, pero mis frenos y llantas son nuevos.
    C. Aquí en Texas no hay velocidad máxima.
    D. Sí, pero yo estoy yendo solamente a 50.

50. Doctor, ¿qué me recomienda para este dolor terrible de cabeza?
    A. Que vayas a la pastelería de guardia.
    B. Que te pongas esta inyección de calmante.
    C. Que te pongas unas gotas de jarabe en los ojos.
    D. Que te preocupes más de pagar las cuentas.

PART II GRAMMAR
(Answers, p. 324)

A. Change the verbs in these sentences to the Future. Write only the verb.

1. Ud. tiene que poner gasolina en el tanque. _____

2. ¿Por qué no vuelves mañana a verme? _____

3. Yo no sé qué hacer con este equipaje. _____

4. Ellos no quieren venir en el autobús. _____

5. El padre mantiene a toda su familia. _____

6. Jaimito dice la verdad a sus papás. _____

7. El pueblo no se opone al presidente electo. _____

B. Change the verbs in these sentences to the familiar command form. If the statement is negative, write the negative command. Write only the verb.

8. Teresa viene con nosotros a la fiesta. _____

9. Eduardo no sale con el carro. _____

10. Esteban no va en avión sino en tren. _____

11. Mamá tiene mucha paciencia con nosotros. _____

12. Juanita pone la mesa con cuidado. _____

13. Mario no es cruel con los perros. _____

C. **Change the verbs in these sentences to the formal command form *(usted/ustedes).* Substitute object pronouns (*me, lo,* etc.) wherever possible. Write the entire sentence.**

14. Usted sabe esta lección para mañana. _____

15. Ustedes no vienen tarde a la fiesta. _____

16. Usted me da un regalo para el cumpleaños. _____

17. Ustedes me lo hacen bien. _____

18. Usted no me lo dice. _____

19. Ustedes nos lo traen. _____

20. Usted pide el café con crema. _____

D. **Complete these sentences with the Present Indicative or Subjunctive as required.**

21. Es muy necesario que él_____a tiempo. (llegar)

22. Es muy evidente que tú_____muy atento. (ser)

23. Nadie duda que ustedes_____buena salud. (tener)

24. ¿Te gusta que nosotros te_____*bromas* (tricks)? (hacer)

25. Siento mucho que tu papá no_____vernos. (poder)

26. ¿Es cierto que Teresa_____para Colombia? (irse)

27. Yo no pienso que tú_____tan enfermo. (estar)

28. Es mejor que usted_____en una semana. (volver)

29. Mis padres quieren una casa que_____un jardín grande. (tener)

30. Siempre me siento bien después que_____ocho horas. (dormir)

31. Ellos prefieren que yo_____el carro. (conducir)

32. Mi tía escribe que ella_____a verme pronto. (venir)

33. El doctor te informa que el caso no_____serio. (ser)

34. El director quiere verte antes que_____. (salir)

35. ¿Hay alguien aquí que_____hablar árabe? (saber)

E.   Select the best answer, and circle the letter.

36. En realidad tu amigo no es gordo, . . . es bajito.
    - A. sino
    - B. pero
    - C. excepto
    - D. sino que

37. Aquí hay muchas minas de plata . . . hierro.
    - A. y
    - B. e
    - C. o
    - D. i

38. Prefiero que ustedes . . . en mi viaje de vacaciones.
    - A. me acompañan
    - B. me acompañarán
    - C. me acompañen
    - D. me acompañarían

39. Conozco a una familia que . . . diez niños.
    - A. tenga
    - B. tendría
    - C. tiene
    - D. ten

40. Es una lástima que no . . . más en el sur de California.
    - A. llueve
    - B. llovería
    - C. lloverá
    - D. llueva

41. Yo siempre tenía . . . dinero . . . tú; pero ahora no tengo nada.
    - A. más que
    - B. tanto que
    - C. más como
    - D. tan como

42. Jorge siempre toma una cerveza fría antes que . . .
    - A. coma
    - B. come
    - C. comer
    - D. comería

43. Sentimos mucho que no . . . venir al teatro con nosotros.
    - A. puedes
    - B. podrás
    - C. poderás
    - D. puedas

44. Ella me prometió que . . . aquí a las 8, y ya son las 9.
    - A. estuviera
    - B. estaría
    - C. estará
    - D. esté

45. Tengo dos dólares. Aquí tienes uno; no me queda . . . otro dólar para comer.
    - A. menos de
    - B. pero
    - C. más que
    - D. más de

46. Lolita quiere que . . . la novela este fin de semana.
    A. le lees   C. le leas
    B. la lees   D. la leas

47. Es conveniente que el niño . . . ocho horas diarias.
    A. dormirá   C. duerme
    B. duerma   D. dormiría

48. José me contó que ustedes . . . un verano fantástico en España.
    A. tengan   C. tuvieron
    B. tendrían   D. teniendo

49. A Carolina le agrada que tú . . . en español.
    A. le hablas   C. la hables
    B. la hablas   D. le hables

50. Me parece que la gente de España . . . más baja que la de Estados Unidos.
    A. será   C. sea
    B. sería   D. es

ANSWERS FOR LESSONS 11–15

Lesson 11

Vocabulary

A.
1. el	4. el	7. el	10. los	13. el
2. la	5. las	8. la	11. el	14. las
3. los	6. las	9. el	12. la	15. la

B.
1. echo de menos	3. tengo mala pata	5. ver las estrellas
2. en serio	4. meter la pata	6. tiempo, buana cara

C.
1. dedos	4. escalera	7. nariz	10. cabello	13. codo
2. imprevista	5. párpados	8. espalda	11. hueso	14. frente
3. cojea	6. rodilla	9. ligero	12. muletas	

D.
1. brazo	4. doler (doloroso)	7. patilla	10. cara
2. cuello	5. oler (oloroso)	8. escalera	11. rodilla (rueda)
3. increíble	6. seriedad	9. labio	12. cabello

E.
1. torcí	3. nos encontramos	5. enyesaron	7. ocurrió
2. pasó	4. cojeé	6. dolió	8. olieron

F.
1. párpados	4. rodilla	7. muñeca	10. frente
2. labios	5. hombros	8. hueso	11. mejillas
3. pelo/cabello	6. pecho	9. muslo	

Dialog Exercises

A.
1. encuentran	7. mala pata	13. estrellas
2. enyesado	8. en serio	14. muletas
3. muletas	9. hermana	15. semanas
4. escalera	10. ligero	16. menos
5. torció	11. yeso	17. buena cara
6. deportes	12. huesos	

B.
1. F	3. T	5. F	7. T	9. T	11. T
2. F	4. F	6. T	8. F	10. F	12. T

C.
1. muletas	5. hueso	9. las mejillas
2. la nariz	6. garganta	10. la muñeca
3. (una buena) pareja	7. el codo	
4. deportes	8. imprevisto	

D.   1. Esteban se cayó por la escalera de su casa.

2. Él se torció el tobillo derecho en el accidente.

3. Graciela no creyó a Esteban (a lo) primero. (le creyó)

4. Esteba sintió bastante dolor en la operación.

5. El doctor (le) puso los huesos en su lugar

6. El doctor (le) hizo ver las estrellas a Esteban del dolor.

7. Esteban cojeó por dos semanas.

8. Mis padres tuvieron una noticia imprevista.

Grammar I

Practice   1. adverbs/que   4. más de   7. two

2. más de/menos de/   5. más/más alta que   8. two

     más de   6. más de   9. más que

3. de

1. más . . . que	5. más que (sino)	9. más de
2. más de	6. más . . . que	10. más que (sino)
3. menos de	7. más de	
4. más que	8. menos . . . que	

1. Pablo se rompió más huesos que María.

2. Esteban tuvo más accidentes que Graciela.

3. Marcos es más alto que Lola.

4. José estudia menos (horas) que yo.

5. Yo estudio más de lo que Ud. piensa.

6. Miriam no tiene más que (sino) dos hermanos.

7. Anita tiene más de siete dólares.

Grammar II

Practice   1. como/como   5. mayor/la mayor   9. de/de

2. number/tantos   6. menor/menores   10. as soon as possible/as

3. adverbs/tan   7. mejor/peor/mejor   11. mejor/peor

4. much   8. lindísimo/lindísima   12. máxima

A.   1. menor que/tan . . . como   7. tanto como   13. mayores que

2. tan . . . como   8. tan . . . como   14. peor

3. tantas . . . como   9. tanta . . . como   15. optimista

4. lo más pronto posible   10. peor que   16. pesimista

5. muy gordo (gordísimo)   11. más/de

6. mayor   12. grandísimo

B.   1. Lola tiene el pelo más rubio que su hermana.

2. Ustedes tiene más libros que el profesor.

3. Guillermo tiene más suerte que su amiga.

4. En Alaska hace más frío que en Siberia.

5. Esta comida es más ligera que la otra.

C. 1. La carne es tan cara como el pescado.

2. Tú eres (Ud. es) menor que yo.

3. Mi carro es tan viejo como el tuyo (suyo) (de usted).

4. Esteban está muy cojo (cojísimo).

5. Lo hice lo más pronto posible.

6. Ella trabaja tanto como tú (Ud.).

7. Ellos (as) son peores que él.

8. Ella es la mejor de todos -as.

9. Mi hijo es muy alto (altísimo).

Grammar III

Practice   1. infinitive/comer/ser   5. serán   9. probable/Serán

              2. I (yo)/you (tú)   6. present   10. estará

              3. -emos (first person plural)   7. present/llega

              4. compraremos   8. ir/llegará (llega)

A. 1. viviremos   4. caminará   7. dolerá   10. olerán

   2. iré   5. enyesarán   8. estará   11. ocurrirá

   3. se encontrará 6. pasará   9. seremos   12. te torcerás

B. 1. hablarás   5. seremos   9. olerás   13. veremos   17. empezará

   2. volveré   6. pedirá   10. serás   14. irás   18. divertirá

   3. pensarán 7. seguiré   11. viviremos 15. será   19. entraremos

   4. estaremos 8. dolerá   12. darás   16. concoceré 20. conduciré

C. 1. volverá   5. torceré   9. pedirá   13. regresaré 17. estará

   2. irán   6. cojearé 10. servirán 14. morirá   18. enyesará

   3. serán   7. oirá   11. lavarás 15. dormirán 19. me caeré

   4. hablarán 8. caerán   12. darás   16. seguirá   20. creerá

Lesson 12

Vocabulary

A. 1. la   5. la   9. los   13. el

   2. el   6. las   10. la   14. la

   3. la   7. la   11. la   15. la

   4. los   8. la   12. el   16. las

B. 1. tienes . . . tos   4. perder el tiempo   7. no tiene remedio

   2. guardar cama   5. tienes mareos   8. a lo mejor

   3. tomar asiento   6. sólo me falta eso   9. ¡Cómo no!

C. 1. radiografía   4. salud   7. domicilio   10. receta
    2. vacuna   5. farmacia   8. fatiga   11. pulmones
    3. vitamina   6. póliza   9. tensión   12. úlcera

D. 1. agradeceré   4. molestará   7. descansaremos
    2. enfermarás   5. curará   8. quitará
    3. arreglará   6. recetará   9. calmarán

E. 1. resfrío/catarro/constipado   3. píldora   5. gripa   7. a lo mejor
    2. domicilio   4. ¡cómo no! 6. alegre 8. agradecer

F. 1. alergia   7. pulmón   13. remedio   19. preferible
    2. fatiga   8. vacuna   14. recetar   20. pálido
    3. estómago   9. tos   15. músculo   21. alegre
    4. farmacia   10. salud   16. inyección 22. calmar
    5. digestión (indigestión) 11. peligro   17. auscultar 23. mareo
    6. cura/curar   12. síntoma 18. aliviar   24. seguro (seguridad)

Dialog Exercises

A. 1. consulta 4. póliza   7. mareos   10. corazón 13. gripe
    2. domicilio 5. estómago 8. alta   11. calmar 14. píldoras
    3. seguro   6. molestar 9. auscultarlo 12. cama   15. descansar

B. 1. T   3. F   5. F   7. F   9. T   11. T   13. F
    2. F   4. T   6. T   8. T   10. F   12. T

C. 1. enfermedad 4. alta tensión   7. camiseta   10. peligro
    2. enfermarse   5. fatiga (cansancio) 8. radiografía 11. temperatura
    3. enfermo   6. doctor (enfermera) 9. síntomas   12. cura

D. 1. Guillermo tiene mareos porque su presión está alta.
    2. Lola está pálida porque tiene fiebre.
    3. A mí me molesta el dolor de estómago.
    4. ¿A ti se te quita el dolor de cabeza con aspirina?
    5. A José no se le alivia la tos con pastillas.
    6. A Ud. le duelen los músculos porque tiene gripe.
    7. El doctor escribe una (la) receta al paciente. (le escribe).

Grammar I

Practice 1. infinitive/estaría 4. viviría   7. Imperfect
              2. endings   5. past   8. Future/Conditional
              3. Imperfect/comería 6. Imperfect/iba a llegar 9. estaría

A.   1. curaría   5. fumaría   9. descansaría   13. arreglarían
      2. aliviaría   6. calmaría   10. molestaría   14. auscultaría
      3. debería   7. debería   11. quitaría   15. volvería
      4. perdería   8. enfermaría   12. recetaría

B.   1. sería   5. pensaría   9. pagaría   13. seguiría
      2. pediría   6. serías   10. dormiría   14. oirías
      3. estarías   7. conocerías   11. escribiría
      4. volverían   8. iríamos   12. morirían

C.   1. entraría   4. sería   7. caería   10. comprarían
      2. oiría   5. pedirían   8. creerían   11. estaría
      3. iría   6. moriría   9. seguirías   12. andaría

Grammar II

Practice   1. sabré/e   5. cabremos   9. reharía
             2. vendría/d   6. satisfaré   10. opondría
             3. conditional/haría   7. contendré
             4. querría   8. supondré

A.   1. saldremos   3. deshará   5. abstendrán   7. valdrá   9. opondrán
      2. habrá   4. propondrá   6. rehará   8. querrá   10. dirás

B.   1. tendría   5. expondría   9. diría   13. propondría
      2. podría   6. obtendría   10. querría   14. prevendría
      3. haría   7. sabría   11. mantendría   15. detendrían
      4. saldría   8. sería   12. valdría   16. tendría

C.   1. fuimos/iremos/iríamos   15. puse/pondré/pondría
      2. fuimos/seremos/seríamos   16. oyeron/oirán/oirían
      3. estuve/estaré/estaría   17. fue/será/sería
      4. dieron/darán/darían   18. huyó/huirá/huiría
      5. pedí/pediré/pediría   19. pude/podré/podría
      6. vi/veré/vería   20. quiso/querrá/querría
      7. hizo/hará/haría   21. hubo/habrá/habría
      8. dije/diré/diría   22. anduvo/andará/andaría
      9. oí/oiré/oiría   23. murió/morirá/moriría
      10. creyó/creerá/creería   24. siguió/seguirá/seguiría
      11. salí/saldré/saldría   25. empecé/empezaré/empezaría
      12. tuvo/tendrá/tendría   26. ofrecí/ofreceré/ofrecería
      13. volvió/volverá/volvería   27. pagué/pagaré/pagaría
      14. supe/sabré/sabría

Grammar III

Practice   1. tú
2. Indicative/habla/come
3. es/as/hables/escribas
4. Indicative/duermas
5. negative (familiar)/salgas/traigas
6. ven/ten/sal
7. I gave/say (tell)
8. I know/be
9. affirmative/negative/Llámame/me llames
10. expón
11. mantén

A.
1. Ana, ven	4. José, dime	7. Luisa, sal
2. Lola, háblame	5. Marcos, hazme	8. Felipe, lávate
3. Luis, escríbeme	6. Esteban, óyeme	9. Carlitos, duérmete

B.
1. Luisa, no llegues	5. Jorge, no te sientes	9. Anita, no me lo compres
2. Guillermo, no digas	6. Julia, no hagas	10. Lucía, no lo propongas
3. José, no me llames	7. María, no me hagas	11. Mario, no te duermas
4. Lolita, no te laves	8. Carlos, no deshagas	12. Marcos, no te despiertes

C.
1. Sí, contéstalo. No, no lo contestes.	5. Sí, pídeselo. No, no se lo pidas.
2. Sí, llénala. No, no la llenes.	6. Sí, dísela. No, no se la digas.
3. Sí, tráela. No, no la traigas.	7. Sí, tómalas. No, no las tomes.
4. Sí, lávatelas. No, no te las laves.	

D.
1. No te sientes aquí.	7. Tómatelo todo.
2. No me des la cuenta.	8. Llámala temprano.
3. No me hables siempre en español.	9. Vístete ahora.
4. No me lo digas todo.	10. Tócalo, por favor.
5. No te arregles el pelo.	11. Empiézalo mañana.
6. No te bebas el café.	12. Llévate el carro.

Lesson 13

Vocabulary

A.
1. el	4. el	7. el	10. los
2. la	5. el	8. la	11. la
3. el	6. la	9. el (la)	12. el

B.   1. pescadería   6. pastelería   11. droguería (farmacia)
      2. verdulería   7. panadería   12. sastrería
      3. zapatería.   8. frutería   13. taquería
      4. barbería   9. carnicería   14. librería
      5. peluquería   10. florería   15. relojería

C.   1. hojas de afeitar   3. crema dental
      2. farmacia de guardia   4. perder peso/seguir una dieta

D.   1. durará   4. convertirán   7. se preocupará   10. mantendrán
      2. padecerás   5. conseguiré   8. acostumbrarás   11. contestará
      3. tardará   6. adelgazaremos   9. tragará

E.   1. abusar   4. dietista   7. tardar   10. verdura (verdulería)
      2. peluquería 5. sangre   8. dental (dentista)   11. inoxidable
      3. adelgazar   6. gotear   9. vuelta.   12. alimentar

F.   1. calorías   5. marcas   9. verduras   13. jarabe
      2. droga   6. acero   10. talco   14. gotas
      3. florería   7. sangre   11. yogur
      4. balanza   8. jabón   12. tubo

Dialog Exercises

A.   1. amigo   5. doctor (médico)   9. jarabe   13. dental   17. tiempo   21. pesos
      2. ven   6. seria   10. tragar   14. pies   18. ojos
      3. estómago   7. cama   11. drogadicto   15. afeitar   19. gotas
      4. mareos   8. más pronto   12. receta   16. inoxidable   20. acostarse

B.   1. barbería   4. pastelería   7. jabón
      2. seguir una dieta   5. sastrería   8. comer sin sal
      3. crema dental   6. balanza   9. ponerse gotas

C.   1. E   4. K/I   7. I   10. F
      2. H   5. J   8. L   11. D
      3. G   6. A   9. B   12. C

D.   1. Prepárame esta receta a mí.   4. Acostúmbrate a estas píldoras.
      2. No te preocupes de esos problemas.   5. Consigue una balanza para pesarte.
      3. Ponte dos gotas antes de acostarte.

Grammar I

Practice   1. e/i/hi   5. sino   9. preserved
             2. y/y   6. subject/verb/sino que 10. malamente/fácilmente
             3. u/ho/u   7. sino   11. the last one/clara/fácilmente
             4. negative   8. feminine

A. 1. e   4. y   7. sino   10. pero
    2. e   5. sino   8. sino que   11. pero
    3. u   6. u   9. sino   12. y

B. 1. tontamente   4. felizmente   7. fácilmente   10. algremente
    2. recientemente   5. amablemente   8. difícilmente   11. buenamente
    3. claramente   6. suavemente   9. tristemente   12. totalmente

C. 1. Le llevo un refresco rápidamente.
    2. Me siento cómodamente o me acuesto en la cama.
    3. Pueden llevarlos fácilmente en el carro. (Los pueden . . .)
    4. Me gusta darle algún regalo (un regalo).
    5. Me gusta servirles bebida y posiblemente comida.

Grammar II

Practice   1. e/en/hable   6. diga/digan   11. Llámeme/me llame
    2. a/an/coma/coman   7. empiece/e   12. lávese/lávense
    3. mandar   8. pague/u   13. Lávese
    4. Indicative/piense   9. siga/a
    5. duerma/duerman   10. affirmative/negative

A. 1. abuse   4. consiga   7. corte   10. trague
    2. alimente   5. conteste   8. dure   11. preocúpese
    3. balancee   6. convierta   9. padezca   12. acostúmbrese

B. 1. escríbala/no la escriba   6. tráguelas/no las trague
    2. pídalo/no lo pida   7. empiécela/no la empiece
    3. llénela/no la llene   8. consígalos/no los consiga
    4. siéntese/no se siente   9. láveselas/no se las lave
    5. páguela/no la pague   10. cómpresela/no se la compre

C. 1. No abusen   4. Guarden cama   7. Lávense   10. Acuéstense
    2. Tráguense   5. No tomen   8. No se preocupen   11. Duerman
    3. Empiecen   6. No fumen   9. Acostúmbrense   12. Balanceen

Grammar III

Practice   1. e/a   6. i/pidas/pidamos   11. a/siga
    2. Subjunctive   7. plural/durmamos   12. e/practique
    3. Subjunctive/no comas.   8. first/sintamos   13. llegue
    4. vuelv-/Subjunctive/volvamos   9. c/comiences
    5. siente/sentemos   10. u/trague

A.   1. abuse   4. convierta   7. se siente   10. sirva
          2. adelgace   5. alimente   8. se sienta   11. consiga
          3. balancee   6. divierta   9. tuerza   12. recoja

B.   1. siga   5. vuelvan   9. pidamos   13. se convenza 17. te sientas
          2. tome   6. pierdas   10. paguen   14. practiquen   18. estén
          3. se acueste   7. empiece   11. me alivie   15. duerma   19. coja
          4. nos sintamos   8. coma   12. te preocupes 16. piense   20. pueda

Lesson 14

Vocabulary

A.   1. el   5. la   9. el   13. el   17. el   21. el
      2. la   6. el   10. la   14. el   18. el (los)
      3. el   7. el   11. el   15. la   19. el (los)
      4. el   8. el   12. el   16. el   20. el

B.   1. de segunda mano   4. por fin   7. por ser usted
      2. el limpiaparabrisas   5. a todo riesgo   8. oler mal
      3. millas por hora   6. toque . . . la bocina 9. transmisión manual

C.   1. acumulador   5. maletero (cajuela)   9. de cambios (mecánico)
      2. carro (automóvil)   6. manejar (guiar)   10. por fin
      3. estacionar (parquear) 7. placa
      4. licencia   8. llanta (goma)

D.   1. alquilar   5. manual   9. tocar
      2. frenar   6. pitar   10. conducir
      3. arrancar   7. parquear (aparcar)
      4. estacionar   8. funcionar

E.   1. maletero   4. ganga   7. diarios   10. carnet   13. torcido
      2. gastadas   5. pedal   8. cinturones 11. mapa   14. llantas
      3. volante   6. lujoso   9. cacharro   12. tablero

Dialog Exercises

A.   1. alquiler   7. de cambios   13. ver
      2. cómodo   8. ahorrar   14. gastadísimas
      3. semanas   9. nuevos   15. rotos
      4. disponible   10. asegurado   16. torcido
      5. mano   11. riesgo   17. destruidos
      6. condiciones   12. diarios (por día)   18. desastre

B. 1. F   4. T   7. F   10. T   13. F
    2. F   5. F   8. T   11. T   14. F
    3. T   6. F   9. F   12. T

C. 1. frenes   4. aparques   7. apagues   10. conduzcas   13. te estaciones
    2. manejes   5. funcione   8. toques   11. arranque   14. corras
    3. pinches   6. llenes   9. pites   12. infles   15. lleves

D. 1. asegurar (seguro)   5. torcer   9. gastar   13. pinchar
    2. lujo   6. comodidad 10. llenar   14. aceite
    3. mano   7. día   11. desinflar (inflar)
    4. disponer   8. romper   12. destruir

Grammar I

Practice   1. ie/i   5. y/concluyamos   9. satisfaga
             2. prefiera/prefiramos   6. ir   10. prevenga
             3. c   7. esté/dé   11. suponga
             4. produzca   8. sepa   12. mantenga

A. 1. manejes   5. hagas   9. huyas   13. mantengas   17. prevengas
    2. pongas   6. puedas   10. traigas   14. sean   18. te pongas
    3. sepan   7. estés   11. vayas   15. duermas   19. digas
    4. tengan   8. valga   12. salgas   16. muera

B. 1. muero/murió/muramos   6. convierto/convirtió/convirtamos
    2. duermo/durmió/durmamos   7. sirvo/sirvió/sirvamos
    3. divierto/divirtió/divirtamos   8. sigo/siguió/sigamos
    4. prefiero/prefirió/prefiramos   9. consigo/consiguió/consigamos
    5. siento/sintió/sintamos   10. miento/mintió/mintamos

Grammar II

Practice   1. subordinate/main   6. Indicative
             2. que   7. lleguen
             3. Indicative/hablo   8. Indicative/habla
             4. Subjunctive/hable. 9. The principal says that you are working a lot.
             5. comas   10. The principal tells you to work a lot.

A. 1. se duerma   8. está   15. llame   22. trabajas
    2. sea   9. vuelvas   16. trabaja   23. lleve
    3. manejan   10. toma (tome)   17. salgan   24. venga
    4. lleguen   11. vaya   18. cambia   25. nos acostumbremos
    5. tiene   12. te diviertas 19. aparquemos
    6. alquile   13. hay   20. coma
    7. es   14. es   21. haya

B. 1. digan   5. escriban   9. hable   13. termine
    2. lleguen   6. no fumen   10. prepare   14. empiece
    3. hablen   7. vengan   11. sea   15. mantenga
    4. hagan   8. sepan   12. tenga   16. dé

C. 1. vuelva a la consulta   4. cambie el día del examen
    2. me visitan (visitarán) en agosto   5. tomemos una cerveza
    3. te acuestes tarde   6. llego más temprano

Grammar III

Practice   1. stressed   4. No/dio   7. stress   10. you/your/my/me
           2. last/two   5. stress/two   8. two   11. question/qué
           3. stress/lección 6. consonant (ch) 9. yes/oneself/if 12. i/Yes/No

Exercise   1. baúl/automóvil/llené
           2. recetó/píldoras/inyección/antibióticos
           3. cuándo/dónde/llevarás
           4. compraría/tú
           5. álbum/fotografiías/está/papás
           6. José/prefirió/aquél
           7. dígame/por qué/día/veintitrés
           8. Cristóbal Colón/descubrió América
           9. América/comían/maíz/hacían/él
           10. automático/está/pésimas
           11. última/sílaba/explicármelo
           12. Cómo no/mí/está/más/río
           13. diré/sí/así/volverás
           14. té/está/más/café/mí/té

Lesson 15

Vocabulary

A. 1. el   5. el   9. la   13. el
    2. el   6. el   10. el   14. el
    3. el   7. la   11. el   15. la
    4. la   8. el   12. el   16. la

B. 1. Qué casualidad   4. se las trae   7. freno de emergencia
    2. estar en onda   5. darles la bienvenida 8. con anticipación
    3. llanta de repuesto   6. prestarle atención

C. 1. acompañar   4. ocupar   7. chocar   10. engrasar
    2. dañar   5. prohibir   8. parar   11. resbalar
    3. cruzar   6. asustar   9. doblar   12. consultar

D. 1. atento   3. despierto   5. fascinante   7. estrecho
    2. breve   4. quebrado   6. resbaladizo   8. ondulado

E. 1. camión (autocar) (guagua)   5. choque   9. carretera (autovía)
    2. intersección   6. surtidor   10. ocuparse de
    3. loma (colina)   7. parada (alto)
    4. tanque   8. terreno

F. 1. manguera   4. ondas (olas)   7. curvas (lomas)   10. radiador
    2. pozos   5. puente   8. paisajes   11. pirámides
    3. güeras   6. avería   9. chocó   12. velocímetro

G. 1. engrase   3. revise   5. consulte   7. llenes
    2. limpie   4. se ocupen   6. acompañes   8. infle

H. 1. cuadras   4. ruinas   7. lana   10. surtidor
    2. petroleros   5. quebrado   8. esquina   11. chistosos
    3. atento/cumplidos 6. estrecho 9. lista   12. cerro

Dialog Exercises

A. 1. viajar   7. las traía   13. primo
    2. hasta   8. lista   14. camarero
    3. sentarse   9. maíz   15. restaurante
    4. güera (americana)   10. pirámide   16. simpático
    5. tenían (eran dueños de)   11. venía
    6. viajar   12. ciudad

B. 1. F   4. T   7. T   10. F   13. F
    2. F   5. T   8. T   11. T   14. T
    3. T   6. F   9. F   12. F

C. 1. revisemos   4. doblemos   7. choquemos   10. acompañes
    2. pares   5. resbale   8. consultes   11. dañe
    3. cruces   6. subas   9. tengamos   12. carguemos

D. 1. compre   3. lea   5. lleve   7. olvide   9. pida
    2. deje   4. consulte   6. haga   8. llegue   10. pierda

E. 1. compra   3. lee   5. lleves   7. olvides   9. pidas
    2. dejes   4. consulta   6. haz   8. llega   10. pierdas

Grammar I

Practice   1. Indicative/habla   6. maneje
             2. Subjunctive/vayas   7. tiene
             3. Subjunctive/Subjunctive   8. llueva
             4. vengas   9. Subjunctive
             5. fume   10. Subjunctive/Indicative

A. 1. beba   5. sepan   9. llame   13. pidas
    2. lleguen   6. escriba   10. tenga   14. pare
    3. hablan   7. está   11. quiere   15. se vista
    4. estudia   8. fuma/bebe   12. pueda

B. 1. Me alegro mucho que mi carro gaste poca gasolina.
    2. Rosaura tiene miedo que su carro no arranque bien.
    3. Es muy obvio que yo no puedo comprar . . .
    4. Ella se pone furiosa de que usted maneje muy rápidamente.

C. 1. Me sorprende que ella no vaya de vacaciones este año.
    2. Nos alegramos mucho de tener un buen trabajo.
    3. Ustedes esperan que el carro no tenga las llantas desinfladas.
    4. Es una lástima que nosotros volvamos a enfermarnos.
    5. Nos molesta mucho oír esa música moderna.
    6. Agradecemos mucho que (tú) cambies el aceite al carro.

Grammar II

Practice   1. Subjunctive/venga   5. sepa
             2. Indicative/tengo   6. Indicative/Subjunctive
             3. está   7. Indicative
             4. negative   8. es/sea

A. 1. están (estarán)   4. acompañe   7. gasta   10. siguen (sigan *as an influence*)
    2. se casa   5. sea/quieres 8. dé   11. es
    3. quieras   6. está   9. desean 12. llueva

B. 1. Suponemos que el muchacho cruza . . .
    2. Me parece que Roberto se ocupa de . . .
    3. Te imaginas que el autobús se para . . .
    4. No estoy seguro que el mecánico engrase . . .
    5. No hay duda que tú doblas . . .
    6. Es posible que ella se asuste . . .
    7. Es que el carro resbala . . .
    8. Ella duda que nosotros sigamos . . .
    9. Creemos que el paisaje de las pirámides es . . .
   10. Quizás estés despierto . . ./quizás estás despierto . . .

Grammar III

Practice   1. adjective   5. viva
           2. Indicative/Subjunctive   6. estudie
           3. use   7. come
           4. tiene   8. adverbial clause

9. Indicative/llegó   13. después que/mientras

10. Indicative/come   14. Subjunctive

11. Subjunctive/llegue   15. Subjunctive/Indicative

12. tenga   16. Subjunctive

17. Indicative

A.
1. tiene	4. vive	7. fume	10. escriba
2. gusta	5. hablen	8. es	11. gasten
3. sepa	6. hablan	9. sea	12. sé

B.
1. Queremos un profesor que nunca llegue tarde.
2. No hay nadie aquí que estudie italiano.
3. Necesitamos una chica que escriba bien a máquina.
4. No hay ningún turista que quiera viajar en camión.
5. No hay ninguna farmacia que esté abierta hasta las 10:00.
6. Buscan una secretaria que sea bilingüe.

C.
1. No conocemos a nadie que vaya.
2. Ella necesita un apartamento que tenga dos dormitorios.
3. No hay nadie aquí que toque la guitarra.
4. ¿Hay alguien aquí que tenga reloj?
5. Yo estoy buscando una secretaria que quiera trabajar. (Busco)

D.
1. No te olvides de llamarme antes que llegues a la oficina.
2. Paco siempre llama al doctor cuando tiene mareos.
3. Mi mamá me dará algo cuando venga a verme el domingo.
4. Los turistas volverán al hotel después que visiten las ruinas.
5. Yo busco la llanta de repuesto mientras Ud. revisa la batería.
6. No podemos comprar un carro nuevo hasta que recibamos el préstamo del banco.
7. Me ocuparé de todo tan pronto como se duerman los niños.
8. El camarero sirve camarones a José antes de que (José) termine el aperitivo.

E.
1. compre	5. diga	9. va (irá)
2. se va	6. canse	10. es
3. salga	7. crucemos	11. pueda
4. lleguemos	8. cenamos	12. hable

REVIEW EXAM

Vocabulary

A. 1. F   5. I   9. A   13. G   17. R
    2. H   6. K.   10. P   14. D   18. J
    3. L   7. M   11. B   15. C
    4. N   8. Q   12. E   16. O

B. 19. gastadas   25. imprevista.
    20. arranca   26. dañada
    21. faros   27. bajar la velocidad
    22. llenar una receta   28. una llanta de repuesto
    23. el domicilio   29. quitarse la camiseta
    24. enyesar   30. comprar unas rosas

C. 31. autocar (camión/guagua)/conducir (guiar)
    32. droguería/maletero (cajuela)
    33. licencia/placa
    34. estacionar (parquear)/mecánico (de cambios)
    35. accidente/pararse
    36. carretera (autovía)/loma (colina)
    37. pastilla/intersección
    38. enfermo/resfrío (catarro) (gripe -a)
    39. flaco/gordo

D. 40. B   43. C   46. D   49. D
    41. A   44. A   47. C   50. B
    42. A   45. D   48. C

Grammar

A. 1. tendrá   3. sabré   5. mantendrá   7. opondrá
    2. volverás   4. querrán   6. dirá

B. 8. ven   10. no vayas   12. pon
    9. no salgas 11. ten   13. no seas

C. 14. sepa   16. déme   18. no me lo diga   20. pídalo
    15. no vengan   17. háganmelo   19. tráigannoslo

D. 21. llegue   25. pueda   29. tenga   33. es
    22. eres   26. se va   30. duermo   34. salgas
    23. tienen   27. estés   31. conduzca   35. sepa
    24. hagamos   28. vuelva   32. viene (vendrá)

E. 36. D   40. D   44. B   48. C
    37. A   41. A   45. C   49. D
    38. C   42. A   46. C   50. D
    39. C   43. D   47. B

Appendix I

Regular Verbs

Infinitive

habl ar, to speak   *com er,* to eat   *viv ir,* to live

Present Participle

habl ando, speaking   *com iendo,* eating   *viv iendo,* living

Past Participle

habl ado, spoken   *com ido,* eaten   *viv ido,* lived

Indicative—Simple Tenses

Present

I speak/do speak/ am speaking/will speak	I eat/do eat/ am eating/will eat	I live/do live/ am living/will live
habl o	com o	viv o
habl amos	com emos	viv imos
habl as	com es	viv es
habl a	com e	viv e
habl an	com en	viv en

Imperfect

I was speaking/spoke	I was eating/ate	I was living/lived
habl aba	com ía	viv ía
habl ábamos	com íamos	viv íamos
habl abas	com ías	viv ías
habl aba	com ía	viv ía
habl aban	com ían	viv ían

Preterite

I spoke/did speak	I ate/did eat	I lived/did live
habl é	com í	viv í
habl amos	com imos	viv imos
habl aste	com iste	viv iste
habl ó	com ió	viv ió
habl aron	com ieron	viv ieron

Future

I will speak	I will eat	I will live
hablar é	comer é	vivir é
hablar emos	comer emos	vivir emos
hablar ás	comer ás	vivir ás
hablar á	comer á	vivir á
hablar án	comer án	vivir án

Conditional

I would speak	I would eat	I would live
hablar ía	comer ía	vivir ía
hablar íamos	comer íamos	vivir íamos
hablar ías	comer ías	vivir ías
hablar ía	comer ía	vivir ía
hablar ían	comer ían	vivir ían

Subjunctive—Simple Tenses

Present

I speak/do speak, etc.	I eat/do eat, etc.	I live/do live, etc.
habl e	com a	viv a
habl emos	com amos	viv amos
habl es	com as	viv as
habl e	com a	viv a
habl en	com an	viv an

Imperfect

I was speaking/spoke		I was eating/ate		I was living/lived	
habl ara	habl ase	com iera	com iese	viv iera	viv iese
habl áramos	habl ásemos	com iéramos	com iésemos	viv iéramos	viv iésemos
habl aras	habl ases	com ieras	com ieses	viv ieras	viv ieses
habl ara	habl ase	com iera	com iese	viv iera	viv iese
habl aran	habl asen	com ieran	com iesen	viv ieran	viv iesen

Commands

speak	eat	live
habl a (tú)	com e (tú)	viv e (tú)
habl e (Ud.)	com a (Ud.)	viv a (Ud.)
habl en (Uds.)	com an (Uds.)	viv an (Uds.)

Indicative—Compound Tenses

Present Perfect

I have spoken		I have eaten		I have lived	
h e		h e		h e	
h emos		h emos		h emos	
h as	hablado	h as	comido	h as	vivido
h a		h a		h a	
h an		h an		h an	

Past Perfect

I had spoken		I had eaten		I had lived	
hab ía		hab ía		hab ía	
hab íamos		hab íamos		hab íamos	
hab ías	hablado	hab ías	comido	hab ías	vivido
hab ía		hab ía		hab ía	
hab ían		hab ían		hab ían	

Future Perfect

I will have spoken		I will have eaten		I will have lived	
habr é		habr é		habr é	
habr emos		habr emos		habr emos	
habr ás	hablado	habr ás	comido	habr ás	vivido
habr á		habr á		habr á	
habr án		habr án		habr án	

Conditional Perfect

I would have spoken		I would have eaten		I would have lived	
habr ía		habr ía		habr ía	
habr íamos		habr íamos		habr íamos	
habr ías	hablado	habr ías	comido	habr ías	vivido
habr ía		habr ía		habr ía	
habr ían		habr ían		habr ían	

Subjunctive—Compound Tenses

Present Perfect

I have spoken		I have eaten		I have lived	
hay a		hay a		hay a	
hay amos		hay amos		hay amos	
hay as	hablado	hay as	comido	hay as	vivido
hay a		hay a		hay a	
hay an		hay an		hay an	

Past Perfect

I had spoken		I had eaten		I had lived	
hub iera		hub iera		hub iera	
hub iéramos		hub iéramos		hub iéramos	
hub ieras	hablado	hub ieras	comido	hub ieras	vivido
hub iera		hub iera		hub iera	
hub ieran		hub ieran		hub ieran	
hub iese		hub iese		hub iese	
hub iésemos		hub iésemos		hub iésemos	
hub ieses	hablado	hub ieses	comido	hub ieses	vivido
hub iese		hub iese		hub iese	
hub iesen		hub iesen		hub iesen	

Appendix II

Irregular Verbs

(Only the tenses in which the verbs are irregular are included here)

Andar, To Walk, Go

Preterite: anduve, anduvimos, anduviste, anduvo, anduvieron.
Imperfect Subjunctive: anduviera (anduviese), anduviéramos, anduvieras,
    anduviera, anduvieran.

Caber, To Fit

Present Indicative: quepo, cabemos, cabes, cabe, caben.
Preterite: cupe, cupimos, cupiste, cupo, cupieron.
Present Subjunctive: quepa, quepamos, quepas, quepa, quepan.
Imperfect Subjunctive: cupiera (cupiese), cupiéramos, cupieras, cupiera,
    cupieran.

Caer, To Fall

Present Indicative: caigo, caemos, caes, cae, caen.
Present Subjunctive: caiga, caigamos, caigas, caiga, caigan.

Conducir, To Drive, Conduct

Present Indicative: conduzco, conducimos, conduces, conduce, conducen.
Preterite: conduje, condujimos, condujiste, condujo, condujeron.
Present Subjunctive: conduzca, conduzcamos, conduzcas, conduzca, conduzcan.
Imperfect Subjunctive: condujera (condujese), condujéramos, condujeras, condu-
    jera, condujeran.

Conocer, To Be Acquainted, Know

Present Indicative: conozco, conocemos, conoces, conoce, conocen.
Present Subjunctive: conozca, conozcamos, conozcas, conozca, conozcan.

Construir, To Build

Present Indicative: construyo, contruimos, construyes, contruye, construyen.
Present Subjunctive: construya, construyamos, construyas, construya, construyan.

Dar, To Give

Present Indicative: doy, damos, das, da, dan.
Preterite: di, dimos, diste, dio, dieron.
Imperfect Subjunctive: diera (diese), diéramos, dieras, diera, dieran.

Decir, To Say, Tell

Present Indicative: digo, decimos, dices, dice, dicen.
Preterite: dije, dijimos, dijiste, dijo, dijeron.
Future: diré, diremos, dirás, dirá, dirán.
Conditional: diría, diríamos, dirías, diría, dirían.
Present Subjunctive: diga, digamos, digas, diga, digan.
Imperfect Subjunctive: dijera (dijese), dijéramos, dijeras, dijera, dijeran.
Command: di (tú), diga (Ud.), digan (Uds.)
Present participle: diciendo
Past participle: dicho

Estar, To Be

Present Indicative: estoy, estamos, estás, está, están.
Preterite: estuve, estuvimos, estuviste, estuvo, estuvieron.
Present Subjunctive: esté, estemos, estés, esté, estén.
Imperfect Subjunctive: estuviera (estuviese), estuviéramos, estuvieras, estuviera, estuvieran.

Haber, To Have (Auxiliary)

Present Indicative: he, hemos, has, ha, han.
Preterite: hube, hubimos, hubiste, hubo, hubieron.
Present Subjunctive: haya, hayamos, hayas, haya, hayan.
Imperfect Subjunctive: hubiera (hubiese), hubiéramos, hubieras, hubiera, hubieran.
Future: habré, habremos, habrás, habrá, habrán.
Conditional: habría, habríamos, habrías, habría, habrían.

Hacer, To Do, Make

Present Indicative: hago, hacemos, haces, hace, hacen.
Preterite: hice, hicimos, hiciste, hizo, hicieron.
Present Subjunctive: haga, hagamos, hagas, haga, hagan.

Imperfect Subjunctive: hiciera (hiciese), hiciéramos, hicieras, hiciera, hicieran.
Future: haré, haremos, harás, hará, harán.,
Conditional: haría, haríamos, harías, haría, harían.
Command: haz (tú), haga (Ud.), hagan (Uds.)
Past participle: hecho

Ir, To Go

Present Indicative: voy, vamos, vas, va, van.
Imperfect Indicative: iba, íbamos, ibas, iba, iban.
Preterite: fui, fuimos, fuiste, fue, fueron.
Present Subjunctive: vaya, vayamos, vayas, vaya, vayan.
Imperfect Subjunctive: fuera (fuese), fuéramos, fueras, fuera, fueran.
Command: ve (tú), vaya (Ud.), vayan (Uds.)
Present participle: yendo

Oír, To Hear, Listen

Present Indicative: oigo, oímos, oyes, oye, oyen.
Present Subjunctive: oiga, oigamos, oigas, oiga, oigan.

Poder, To Be Able, Can

Present Indicative: puedo, podemos, puedes, puede, pueden.
Preterite: pude, pudimos, pudiste, pudo, pudieron.
Present Subjunctive: pueda, podamos, puedas, pueda, puedan.
Imperfect Subjunctive: pudiera (pudiese), pudiéramos, pudieras, pudiera,
    pudieran.
Future: podré, podremos, podrás, podrá, podrán.
Conditional: podría, podríamos, podrías, podría, podrían.
Command: puede (tú), pueda (Ud.), puedan (Uds.)
Present participle: pudiendo

Poner, To Put, Place, Set

Present Indicative: pongo, ponemos, pones, pone, ponen.
Preterite: puse, pusimos, pusiste, puso, pusieron.
Present Subjunctive: ponga, pongamos, pongas, ponga, pongan.
Imperfect Subjunctive: pusiera (pusiese), pusiéramos, pusiera, pusieran.
Future: pondré, pondremos, pondrás, pondrá, pondrán.
Conditional: pondría, pondríamos, pondrías, pondría, pondrían.
Command: pon (tú), ponga (Ud.), pongan (Uds.)
Past participle: puesto

Querer, To Wish, Want, Love

Present Indicative: quiero, queremos, quieres, quiere, quieren.
Preterite: quise, quisimos, quisiste, quiso, quisieron.

Present Subjunctive: quiera, queramos, quiereas, quiera, quieran.
Imperfect Subjunctive: quisiera (quisiese), quisiéramos, quisieras, quisiera, quisieran.
Future: querré, querremos, querrás, querrá, querrán.
Conditional: querría, querríamos, querrías, querría, querrían.

Saber, To Know

Present Indicative: sé, sabemos, sabes, sabe, saben.
Preterite: supe, supimos, supiste, supo, supieron.
Present Subjunctive: sepa, sepamos, sepas, sepa, sepan.
Imperfect Subjunctive: supiera (supiese), supiéramos, supieras, supiera, supieran.
Future: sabré, sabremos, sabrás, sabrá, sabrán.
Conditional: sabría, sabríamos, sabrías, sabría, sabrían.

Salir, To Go Out, Leave

Present Indicative: salgo, salimos, sales, sale, salen.
Present Subjunctive: salga, salgamos, salgas, salga, salgan.
Future: saldré, saldremos, saldrás, saldrá, saldrán.
Conditional: saldría, saldríamos, saldrías, saldría, saldrían.
Command: sal (tú), salga (Ud.), salgan (Uds.)

Ser, To Be

Present Indicative: soy, somos, eres, es, son.
Imperfect Indicative: era, éramos, eras, era, eran.
Preterite: fui, fuimos, fuiste, fue, fueron.
Present Subjunctive: sea, seamos, seas, sea, sean.
Imperfect Subjunctive: fuera (fuese), fuéramos, fueras, fuera, fueran.
Command: sé (tú), sea (Ud.), sean (Uds.)

Tener, To Have

Present Indicative: tengo, tenemos, tienes, tiene, tienen.
Preterite: tuve, tuvimos, tuviste, tuvo, tuvieron.
Present Subjunctive: tenga, tengamos, tengas, tenga, tengan.
Imperfect Subjunctive: tuviera (tuviese), tuviéramos, tuvieras, tuviera, tuvieran.
Future: tendré, tendremos, tendrás, tendrá, tendrán.
Conditional: tendría, tendríamos, tendrías, tendría, tendrían.
Command: ten (tú), tenga (Ud.), tengan (Uds.)

Traer, To Bring

Present Indicative: traigo, traemos, traes, trae, traen.
Preterite: traje, trajimos, trajiste, trajo, trajeron.
Present Subjunctive: traiga, traigamos, traigas, traiga, traigan.
Imperfect Subjunctive: trajera (trajese), trajéramos, trajeras, trajera, trajeran.

Valer, To Be Worth

Present Indicative: valgo, valemos, vales, vale, valen.
Present Subjunctive: valga, valgamos, valgas, valga, valgan.
Future: valdré, valdremos, valdrás, valdrá, valdrán.
Conditional: valdría, valdríamos, valdrías, valdría, valdrían.

Venir, To Come

Present Indicative: vengo, venimos, vienes, viene, vienen.
Preterite: vine, vinimos, viniste, vino, vinieron.
Present Subjunctive: venga, vengamos, vengas, venga, vengan.
Imperfect Subjunctive: viniera (viniese), viniéramos, vinieras, viniera, vinieran.
Future: vendré, vendramos, vendrás, vendrá, vendrán.
Conditional: vendría, vendríamos, vendrías, vendría, vendrían.
Command: ven (tú), venga (Ud.), vengan (Uds.).
Present participle: viniendo

Ver, To See, Watch

Present Indicative: veo, vemos, ves, ve, ven.
Imperfect Indicative: veía, veíamos, veías, veía, veían.
Present Subjunctive: vea, veamos, veas, vea, vean.
Past participle: visto

Appendix III

Stem-changing Verbs

1. *e* to *ie* and *o* to *ue:*

Pensar, To Think, Plan

Present Indic.: pienso, pensamos, piensas, piensa, piensan.
Present Subj.: piense, pensemos, pienses, piense, piensen.

Volver, To Return

Present Indic.: vuelvo, volvemos, vuelves, vuelve, vuelven.
Present Subj.: vuelva, volvamos, vuelvas, vuelva, vuelvan.

Some common verbs of this type are:

querer (ie), to wish, love	*volar* (ue), to fly
sentar (ie), to sit down	*mostrar* (ue), to show
tener (ie), to have	*llover* (ue), to rain
empezar (ie), to start, begin	*jugar* (ue), to play
entender (ie), to understand	*encontrar* (ue), to find
cerrar (ie), to close	*doler* (ue), to hurt
nevar (ie), to snow	*contar* (ue), to count, tell
negar (ie), to deny	*costar* (ue), to cost
perder (ie), to lose	*acostarse* (ue), to go to bed
despertarse (ie), to wake up	*acordarse* (ue), to remember
comenzar (ie), to start, begin	*recordar* (ue), to remember

2. Double change: *e* to *ie* or to *i,* and *o* to *ue* or to *u.*

Preferir, To Prefer

Present Indic.: prefiero, preferimos, prefieres, prefiere, prefieren.
Present Subj.: prefiera, prefiramos, prefieras, prefiera, prefieran
Preterite: preferí, preferimos, preferiste, prefirió, prefirieron.
Imperfect Subj.: prefiriera (prefiriese), prefiriéramos, prefirieras, prefiriera, prefirieran.
Present participle: prefiriendo

Dormir, To Sleep

Present Indic.: duermo, dormimos, duermes, duerme, duermen.
Present Subj.: duerma, durmamos, duermas, duerma, duerman.
Preterite: dormí, dormimos, dormiste, durmió, durmieron.
Imperfect Subj.: durmiera (durmiese), durmiéramos, durmieras, durmiera,
      durmieran.
Present participle: durmiendo

   Other verbs with similar changes in the stem are:
divertirse (ie, i), to enjoy oneself
sentir (ie, i), to feel, be sorry
morir (ue, u), to die
mentir (ie, i), to lie

3. *e* to *i:*

Pedir (i), To Ask For

Present Indic.: pido, pedimos, pides, pide, piden.
Present Subj.: pida, pidamos, pidas, pida, pidan.
Preterite: pedí, pedimos, pediste, pidió, pidieron.
Imperfect Subj.: pidiera (pidiese), pidiéramos, pidieras, pidiera, pidieran.
Present participle: pidiendo

   Other *-ir* verbs of this type are:
servir (i), to serve
seguir (i), to follow
repetir (i), to repeat
vestirse (i), to dress oneself
conseguir (i), to obtain, get
corregir (i), to correct

4. Verbs with spelling changes

1. Verbs in *-zar* change *z* to *c* before *e*.

Empezar, To Begin

Preterite: empecé, empezamos, empezaste, empezó, empezaron.
Present Subj.: empiece, empecemos, empieces, empiece, empiecen.
Command: empieza (tú), empiece (Ud.), empiecen (Uds.)
Like *empezar: comenzar* (to begin), *especializar* (to specialize), *organizar,* (to
      organize), *cazar,* (to hunt).

2. Verbs in *-cer* change *c* to *z* before *o* and *a.*

Vencer, To Defeat

Present Indic.: venzo, vencemos, vences, vence, vence.
Present Subj.: venza, venzamos, venzas, venza, venzan.
Like *vencer: convencer* (to convince).

3. Verbs in *-car* change *c* to *qu* before *e*.

Buscar, To Look For

Preterite: busqué, buscamos, buscaste, buscó, buscaron.
Present Subj.: busque, busquemos, busques, busque, busquen.
Like *buscar: explicar* (to explain), *sacar* (to take out), *tocar* (to touch, play
    music), *practicar* (to practice).

4. Verbs in *-gar* change *g* to *gu* before *e*.

Llegar, To Arrive

Preterite: llegué, llegamos, llegaste, llegó, llegaron.
Present Subj.: llegue, lleguemos, llegues, llegue, lleguen.

5. Verbs in *-guir* change *gu* to *g* before *o* and *a*.

Seguir, To Follow

Present Indic.: sigo, seguimos, sigues, sigue, siguen.
Preterite: siga, sigamos, sigas, siga, sigan.
Like *seguir: conseguir* (to get), *distinguir* (to distinguish).

6. Verbs in *-ger, -gir* change *g* to *j* before *o* and *a*.

Coger, To Take, Seize

Present Indic.: cojo, cogemos, coges, coge, cogen.
Present Subj.: coja, cojamos, cojas, coja, cojan.
Like *coger: escoger* (to choose), *recoger* (to pick up), *dirigir* (to direct, go to),
    corregir (to correct), *elegir* (to elect).

7. Verbs in -aer, eer, -uir change *i* to *y* when *i* is unstressed between two vowels.

Leer, To Read

Preterite: leí, leímos, leíste, leyó, leyeron.
Imperfect Subj.: leyera (leyese), leyéramos, leyeras, leyera, leyeran.
Present participle: leyendo
Like *leer:* caer (to fall), *creer* (to believe), *traer* (to bring), *huir* (to flee), *incluir* (to
    include), *excluir* (to exclude).

Vocabulary

SPANISH-ENGLISH

Nouns ending in the letters L-O-N-E-R-S are masculine, and nouns ending in D-IÓN-Z-A are feminine. The exceptions to this rule are marked (m) or (f). Some cognates are not included in this list.

A

abrazar, embrace
abrir, to open
abrocharse, to fasten
abuela, grandmother
abuelo, grandfather
aburrido, bored, boring
abusar, to abuse
acabar, to finish
    ____ *de*, to have just + participle
acaso, perhaps
acción, action
aceite (m), oil
acelerador, accelerator
acero, steel
acompañar, to accompany
acostumbrarse, to get used to
actual, present/now
actualmente, nowadays
acuerdo, agreement
    de ____, agreed
acumulador, battery
adelgazar, to lose weight
además, besides
aduana, customs
aerolínea, airline
aeropuerto, airport
afeitar, to shave
    hoja de ____, razor blade
agradar, to please
agradecer, to thank
agradecido, thankful
agua, water
    hacer la boca ____, to make one's
    mouth water
aguacate, avocado
águila, eagle
ahora, now
ahorrar, to save
ahorro, saving
    cuenta de ahorros, savings account
ajo, garlic

alegrarse de, to be happy
alegre, happy
alergia, allergy
algo, something
alimentar, to feed
alimento, food
aliviar, to relieve
allí, there, over there
almorzar (ue), to eat lunch
almuerzo, lunch
¡*aló!*, hello!
alquilar, to rent lease
alquiler (m), rent lease
alto, high
    ¡*alto!*, stop!
amable, kind, nice
amarillo, yellow
ancho, wide
andar, to walk
andén (m), platform
antes de, before
antibiótico, antibiotic
anticipación, (*con* ____), ahead of time
antiguo, ancient old
antigüedad, old times, ancient times
antipático, unpleasant, mean
año, year
apagar, to turn off
aparcar, to park
aparecer, to appear
apartamento, apartment
aperitivo, aperitif
aprender, to learn
apretado, tight
apretar (ie), to tighten, to be tight
aquí, here
árbol, tree
arraigar, to take root, to settle
arrancar, to start the engine, to root up
arranque, starter
arreglar, to arrange, fix
asado, broiled, roasted

337

asar, to broil, to roast
ascensor, elevator
asegurado, insured
asegurar, to insure, to affirm
así que, so that
asiento, seat
asustar, to scare, frighten
atender (ie), to take care of, to assist
atento, polite
atrasado, late
atún (m), tuna
aumentar, to increase
aunque, although
auscultar, to listen with a stethoscope
autobús, bus
automático, automatic
autopista, highway, toll road
autoservicio, self-service
avería, breakdown
avión (m), airplane
avisar, to warn, to remind
ayer, yesterday
ayudar, to help
azafata, stewardness
azúcar (m/f), sugar

B

bailar, to dance
baile, dance
bajar, to go down
    ____*de peso*, to lose weight
bajo, low, short
balanceado, balanced
balanza, scale
banana, banana (Latin America)
banco, bank
baño, bathroom, bath
bar, bar
barato, cheap, inexpensive
barbilla, chin
barbería, barbershop
bastante, enough
batería, battery (Latin America)
baúl, trunk
beber, to drink
bebida, drink
bienvenida, welcome
    *dar la*____, to welcome
billete, ticket, bill
blanco, white
blusa, blouse

boca, mouth
bocadillo, sandwich
bocina, horn
    *tocar la*____, to blow the horn
boleto, ticket (Latin America)
bomba, pump, bomb
bonito, pretty
botella, bottle
botana, tid-bit, snack (Mexico)
botón, button
botones, bellboy
brazo, arm
breve, short
buscar, to look for

C

caballero, gentleman
    *ropa de*____, men's wear
cabello, hair
cabeza, head
cacharro, jalopy
cada, each
caer, to fall
caja, box, cash register
cajero, teller
cajuela, trunk of the car (Mexico)
calefacción, heating
caliente, hot
calmante, sedative
calor, heat
caloría, calorie
callarse, to be silent
calle (f), street
cama, bed
    *guardar*____, to stay in bed
camarera, waitress
camarero, waiter
camarón, shrimp (Latin America)
cambiar, to change
camino, road
camión, truck, bus (Mexico)
camisa, shirt
camiseta, undershirt
campo, field
capó, hood
cara, face
cargar, to load
carne (f), meat
carnet (m), license
carnicería, meat shop
caro, expensive

carretera, road
carro, car (Latin America)
casa, house
casado, married
casarse, to marry
casi, almost
casualidad, coincidence
   por____, by coincidence
cebolla, onion
ceja, eyebrow
celebrar, to celebrate
celoso, jealous
cena, supper
cenar, to eat supper
centavo, cent (Latin America)
céntimo, cent (Spain)
cerca, near
cerdo, pig
cerrar (ie), to close
cerro, hill
cerveza, beer
champán, champagne
chequera, check book
chimenea, fireplace
chiste, joke
chistoso, funny, comical
chocar, to crash
choque, crash, accident
chuleta, chop, steak
ciento, one hundred
   por____, percent
cigarrillo, cigarette
cintura, waist
cinturón, belt
claro, clear
cliente, customer
cobrar, to charge, to get paid
coche, car (Spain)
cochecama, sleeping car
cochecomedor, dining car
cocina, kitchen
codo, elbow
cojear, to limp
cojo, lame, crippled
comedor, dining room
comenzar (ie), to begin, start
comer, to eat
cómico, funny, humorous
comida, food, meal
¿cómo?, how?
   ¡*____no!*, of course

cómodo, comfortable
compañero, friend, schoolmate
competencia, competition
competir (i), to compete
complicado, complicated
compra, buy
   ir de____, to go shopping
comprar, to buy
comprender, to understand
con, with
concluir, to conclude
condimentar, to season
conducir, to drive (Spain), to
   conduct
confirmar, to confirm
conmigo, with me
conocer, to be acquainted with,
   to know
conseguir (i), to get, to obtain
construir, to build
contar (ue), to count, to tell
   pagar al contado, to pay cash
contener, to contain
contestar, to answer
convencer, to convince
convenir, to be convenient
convertir, (ie, i), to convert, change
cordero, lamb
correr, to run, jog
cortar, to cut
corto, short
crema, cream
   ____dental, toothpaste
cruce, intersection
cruel, cruel, mean
cruzar, to cross
cuadra, (city) block
cuadro, picture
cuarto, room, fourth
cuello, neck, collar
cuenta, bill, account
   ____corriente, checking account
   ____de ahorros, savings account
culpar, to blame
cultivar, to cultivate, grow
cumpleaños, birthday
cumplido, compliment
cumplir, to fulfill
cura (f), cure
cura (m), priest
curva, curve

D

dañar, to damage
dar, to give
 ——*a*, to face
débil, weak
decir, to say
 ——*que sí*, to say yes
dedo, finger, toe
dejar, to leave, to permit
dejar de, to stop
delgado, thin
delicioso, delicious
demorar, to delay
deporte, sport
derecho, right, straight
desastre, disaster
desayunar, to eat breakfast
desayuno, breakfast
descansar, to rest
descontento, unhappy
descubrir, to discover
descuento, discount
descuidar, to neglect
desde, from
 —— ... *hasta*, from ... to
desear, to wish, desire
deshacer, to undo, to melt
 ——*la maleta*, to unpack the suitcase
desinflar, to deflate
desocupado, free, vacant
despierto, awake
después, after
destruido, destroyed, in rags
destruir, to destroy
detener, to detain, stop
devolver (ue), to return, give back
diario, daily (adj.)
diente, tooth
dieta, diet
dietista, dietitian
difícil, difficult
dinero, money
dirigirse a, to go (straight) to
discutir, discuss
disfrutar, to enjoy
disponible, available
distinguido, distinguished
divertido, enjoyable
divertirse (ie, i), to have a good time
divisa, foreign money

doblar, to turn, to bend
doble, double
doler (ue), to hurt, to ache
domicilio, address, home
domingo, Sunday
dormir (ue, u), to sleep
dormitorio, dormitory, bedroom
droga, drug
drogadicto, drug addict
droguería, drugstore
ducha, shower
durar, to last
duro, hard

E

echar, to throw
 ——*de menos*, to miss
ejercicio, exercise
electricidad, electricity
electrotrén, electric train
eliminar, to eliminate
embrague, clutch
emergencia, emergency
empleado, employee
encantar, to like, to charm
encargar, to take charge of
encender (ie), to light
encontrar (ue), to find
enfermarse, to get sick
enfermedad, sickness
enfermero, nurse
enfermo, sick
engrasar, to lubricate
engrase, lubrication
ensalada, salad
enseguida (en seguida), right away
entender (ie), to understand
enterarse, to find out
entero, entire
entonces, then
entrada, entry way, ticket
entrar a/en, to enter
entregar, to deliver
entremés, appetizer
entrenar, to train
envolver (ue), to wrap
enyesar, to put on a cast
época, season, epoch
equipaje, luggage
equivocarse, to be mistaken
escalera, staircase

escaso, scarce
escribir, to write
escritorio, desk
ese/esa, that
eso, that
espalda, back
espejo, mirror
esperar, to wait, hope, expect
espeso, thick
esposa/esposo, spouse
esquí, ski
esquiar, to ski
esquina, corner
estación, station
estacionamiento, parking
estacionar, to park
estar, to be
este/esta, this
esto, this
estrecho, narrow
estrella, star
   tener mala____, to be very unlucky
   ver las estrellas, to feel a terrible
   pain
estudiar, to study
estupendo, fantastic
estúpido, stupid
éxito, success
exportar, to export

F

fácil, easy
   ____de, easy to
factura, bill
falta, mistake, need
   sin____, without fail
faltar, to miss, to fail
farmacia, pharmacy
faro, headlight
fascinante, fascinating
fatiga, fatigue
fecha, date
felicidad, happiness
felicidades, congratulations
feliz, happy
feo, ugly
ferrocarril, railroad
fiebre (f), fever
fiesta, party, holiday
filete, steak
fin, end

a fines de, by the end of
   por (en)____, finally
firmar, to sign
flaco, thin
flan, custard
flor, flower
florería, flower shop
frenar, to brake
freno, brake
frente (f), forehead
frente (m), front
fresco, fresh, cool
frijol, bean
frío, cold
fruta, fruit
fuerte, strong
funcionar, to work
fumar, to smoke
fútbol, soccer

G

galón, gallon
gana/ganas, desire
   tener____, to feel like
   dar la____, to feel like
ganancia, earnings
ganar, to win, to earn
ganga, sale, bargain
garaje, garage
garganta, throat
gastado, worn out
gastar, to spend, to wear out
gasto, expense
gato, cat
giro postal, money order
gordo, fat
gota, drop
gotear, to drip
gracioso, funny
grande, large, big
grasa, grease, fat
gratis, free ($)
gratuito, free ($)
gripe (f), flu
grueso, thick
guante, glove
guapo, handsome
guardar, to keep, to hold
guardia, guard, policeman
   farmacia de____, all-night pharmacy
güero, blonde (Mexico)

guiar, to guide
guisante, pea
gustar, to like

H
haber, to have (auxiliary)
habitación, room
hablar, to speak
hacer, to do/make
——*caso*, to pay attention
——*la maleta*, to pack the suitcase
hambre (f), hunger
hasta, until
helado, ice cream
hermana, sister
hermano, brother
hielo, ice
hierro, iron (metal)
hija, daughter
hijo, son
hindú, Hindu
hipoteca, mortgage
hombre, man
hombro, shoulder
hora, hour
horario, schedule
hoy, today
hueso, bone
huir, to flee

I
ida, departure, going
——*y vuelta*, round trip
billete de——, one-way ticket
iglesia, church
importar, to matter, to import
imprevisto, unexpected
impuesto, tax
incluir, to include
incluso, even
increíble, incredible
indigestión, indigestion
inesperado, unexpected
inflar, to inflate
ingenioso, witty
inicial, initial
inoxidable, rustproof
inspeccionar, to inspect
intercambiar, interchange
interesar, to interest, to matter
invitación, invitation

invitado, guest
invitar, to invite
inyección, shot, injection
ir, to go
——*a pie*, to go on foot

J
jabón, soap
jamón, ham
jarabe, syrup
jardín, garden
jarra/jarro, pitcher
joven, young
jueves, Thursday
jugar, to play (a sport)
jugo, juice
junto a, next to

K
kilogramo/kilo, kilo (two pounds)
kilómetro, kilometer

L
labio, lip
lámpara, lamp
lana, wool, money (Mexico)
langosta, lobster
lápiz (m), pencil
largo, long
lata, can
lavaplatos (m), dishwasher
lavar, to wash
lección, lesson
leche (f), milk
lechuga, lettuce
leer, to read
lejos, far
lento, slow
letrero, sign
libre, free
al aire——, in the open air
libro, book
licencia, license
ligero, light
limpiaparabrisas, windshield wiper
limpiar, to clean
limpio, clean
lindo, pretty
listo, ready, smart
litera, berth
loco, mad, fool

*volverse*_____, to get mad
locomotora, train engine
loma, hill
lujo, luxury
    *de*_____, luxurious
lujoso, luxurious
luna, moon
    _____*de miel*, honeymoon
lunes, Monday
luz, light

LL
llanta, tire
llave (f), key
llegada, arrival
llegar, to arrive
llenar, to fill
lleno, full
llevar, to take
llevarse bien, to get along
llover (ue), to rain
lluvia, rain

M
madre, mother
maíz (m), corn
maleta, suitcase
    *hacer la*_____, to pack
    *deshacer la*_____, to unpack
maletero, trunk (of the car)
maletero, porter
maletín, briefcase
malo, bad
mamá, mom
mandar, to send, to command
manejar, to drive (Latin America)
manguera, hose
mano (f), hand
mantequilla, butter
manual, standard shift
manzana, apple
mañana, tomorrow, morning
mapa (m), map
mar, sea
marca, trademark
marearse, to get dizzy
mareo, dizziness
marisco, seafood
martes, Tuesday
matar, to kill
matrícula, license plate, registration

matrimonio, marriage
mecánico, mechanic
mediano, average (adj.)
medianoche, midnight
medicina, medicine
médico, doctor, medical
medio, half
mediodía, noon
mejilla, cheek
mejor, better
(a) menudo, often
mercado, market
merecer, to deserve
merienda, afternoon snack
merendar (ie), to eat a snack
mes, month
mesa, table
meter, to put into
miércoles, Wednesday
milagro, miracle
milla, mile (1.6 kilometers)
mirar, to look at
misterio, mystery
molestar, to bother
moneda, coin, currency
morir (ue, u), to die
mostrar (ue), to show
motor, engine
mover (ue), to move
mozo, bellboy, waiter
mucho, much, a lot
mudarse, to move
mueble, furniture
muerte, death
mujer, woman, wife
muleta, crutch
mundo, world
muñeca, wrist, doll
música, music
músculo, muscle
muslo, thigh

N
nacer, to be born
nadar, to swim
naranja, orange
nariz, nose
náusea, nausea
necesario, necessary
necesidad, need
necesitar, to need

negro, black
nervioso, nervous
neumático, tire
nevar (ie), to snow
nieta, granddaughter
nieto, grandson
nieve (f), snow
niña, girl
noche, night
   *por la*____, at night
nombre, name
novia, fiancée, bride
novio, fiancé, bridegroom
nube (f), cloud
nublado, cloudy
nuevo, new
   *de*____, again

O

o, or
o . . . o, either . . . or
ocupado, busy
ocuparse, to take care of
ocurrir, to occur, happen
odiar, to hate
ofrecer, to offer
oír, to hear, to listen
ojo, eye
oler (ue), to smell
   ____ *mal a uno*, to look suspicious
olvidar, to forget
onda, wave
   *estar en*____, to be up to date
ondulado, wavy, hilly
ordenar, to order
oreja, (outer) ear
oro, gold
oscuro, obscure, dark

P

padecer, to suffer
padre, father
padres, parents
paella, paella (seafood dish with rice)
pagar, to pay
   ____ *al contado*, to pay cash
   ____ *a plazos*, to pay in installments
país, country
paisaje, landscape
palabra, word
pálido, pale

pan, bread
panadería, bakery
pañuelo, handkerchief
papa, potato (Latin America)
   ____*frita*, french fries
papá, dad
papel, paper
paquete, package
par, pair, couple
para, for
parabrisas, windshield
parachoques, bumper
parada, stop
paraguas, umbrella
parar, to stop
parecer, to seem
pared, wall
pareja, couple (of people)
pariente, relative
párpado, eyelid
parquear, to park
participar, to share
partida, departure
pasaje, ticket
pasajero, passenger
pasar, to pass, to happen
pastel, cake, pastry
pastelería, pastry shop
pastilla, pill
pata, leg (of an animal)
   *meter la*____, to make a mistake
   *tener mala*____, to be unlucky
patilla, sideburn
pavo, turkey
pecho, breast
pedal, pedal
pedir (i), to ask for
pelo, hair
   *tomar el*____, to pull one's leg
peligro, danger
peluquería, hairdresser's
pensar (ie), to think, to plan
pensión, boarding house
pepino, cucumber
pequeño, small
pera, pear
perder (ie), to lose
   ____*el tiempo*, to waste time
perdonar, to pardon
permitir, to allow, to permit
pero, but

pertenecer, to belong
pescadería, fish store
pescado, fish
peseta, peseta (Spain's currency)
peso, peso, weight
pestaña, eyelash
petróleo, oil
petrolero, oil-producing
piano, piano
picante, hot, spicy
pie, foot
piel, skin, leather
pierna, leg
píldora, pill
pinchar, to get a flat tire
piscina, swimming pool
piso, floor, story
pista, road, way
pitar, to blow the horn
placa, license plate
plancha, iron, grill
    a la ____, on the grill
plata, silver, money
plátano, banana (Spain)
plato, dish
playa, beach
plaza, square
plazo, period of time
    pagar a plazos, to pay in install-
    ments
pluma, pen, feather
pobre, poor
poco, little
poder (ue), to be able, can
póliza, policy
pollo, chicken
poner, to put, set
    ponerse a, to start to
    ponerse ropa, to put on clothes
por, for, through, by, along
    ____ *día*, per day
    ____ *eso*, because of that
porcentaje, percentage
porque, because
postre, desert
pozo, well
precio, price
precioso, precious, pretty
preferir (ie, i), to prefer
préstamo, loan
prestar, to loan

presupuesto, budget
primo/prima, cousin
prisa, hurry
probar (ue), to try, to taste, to try on
producir, to produce
prometer, to promise
propina, tip
    dar dinero de—, to tip
propósito, purpose
    a ____, on purpose, by the way
proteger, to protect
próximo, next
puente, bridge
puerco, pig
puerta, door, gate
pulmón, lung
punto, point, dot
    a ____, on the dot
    en ____, sharp (with time)

Q

que, that, which, who
¿qué?, what?
    ¿ ____ *hay?*, what's new?
quejarse de, to complain about
querer (ie), to want, love
queso, cheese
quien, who
    ¿de quién?, whose?
quitar, to take away
quitarse, to take off

R

ración, serving, order
radiografía, X-ray
ranchero, rancher
rapidez, fastness
rápido, fast
raro, rare, strange
rato, a while
razón, reason
    tener ____, to be right
razonable, reasonable
recado, message
receta, prescription, recipe
recetar, to prescribe
reciente, recent
reconocer, recognize
recordar (ue), to remember
refresco, refreshment
refrigerador, refrigerator

regalar, to give a present
registrarse, to register (in a hotel)
reloj, watch, clock
remedio, remedy
    *no hay*____, there is no solution
    (de) repente, suddenly
res (f), beef, livestock
resbaladizo, slippery
resbalar, to slip
resbaloso, slippery
reservar, to make a reservation
resfriado, cold (n)
resfrío, cold (n)
revisar, to check
revista, magazine
rico, rich
riesgo, risk
    *a todo*____, at all risk
ritmo, rythm
robar, to steal
rodilla, knee
rojo, red
romper, to break
ropa, clothes
    ____*interior*, underwear
rosado, pink
roto, broken
rueda, wheel
rumbo, direction
    ____*a*, toward

S

sábado, Saturday
sabor, taste, flavor
saber, to know
sabroso, tasty
sacar, to draw, to take out
salida, exit, departure
salir, to leave
salsa, sauce
salud, health
saludable, healthy
sangre (f), blood
sangría, wine cooler
sángüich, sandwich
sastre, tailor
sastrería, tailor shop
satisfacer, to satisfy
seco, dry
sed, thirst
seguir (i), to follow

seguridad, safety
seguro, insurance
seguro, (adj.), sure, safe
semana, week
semejante, similar
sencillo, simple, single
sentarse (ie), to sit down
sentir (ie, i), to feel, to be sorry
señalar, to point out
ser, to be
serio, serious
    en ____, seriously
servir (i), to serve
silbar, to whistle
silla, chair
síntoma, symptom
simpático, nice, cute
sobrar, to be left
sobre, on top of, about
sobrina, niece
sobrino, nephew
sol, sun
solamente, only
solo, alone
sólo, only
solomillo, sirloin
soltero, single
sombrero, hat
sonar (ue), to sound, to ring
soñar (ue), to dream
sopa, soup
sospechar, to suspect
sospechoso, suspicious
subir, to climb, to get on
sucio, dirty
suegra, mother-in-law
suegro, father-in-law
sueldo, salary
sueño, sleep, dream
suerte, luck
sugerir (ie, i), to suggest
superar, to overcome
supermercado, supermarket
(por) supuesto, of course
sur, south
surtidor, pump

T

tablero, dashboard
talco, powder
también, also

tanto, so, so much
taquilla, ticket window
taquillero, ticket agent
tardar, to last
tarde, afternoon, late
tarifa, fee
tarjeta, card
    ____ *de crédito*, credit card
taxista, cab driver
té, tea
tejado, roof
tema (m), theme, topic
templo, temple
temprano, early
tender (ie), to tend to
tener, to have
    ____ *que*, to have to
tensión, pressure
tercero, third
ternera, calf, veal
terreno, terrain, land
tía, aunt
tiempo, time, weather
    a ____, on time
tienda, store
tierno, tender
tierra, land
timón, steering wheel
tinto, red (wine)
tío, uncle
típico, typical
tirar, to throw, to pull
toalla, towel
tobillo, ankle
tocadiscos, record player
tocar, to touch, to play music
todavía, still, yet
todo, all
    sobre ____, above all
tomar, to take
tomate, tomato
torcer (ue), to twist
torcido, twisted, crooked
torta, cake
tortilla, omelette, tortilla
tos (f), cough
toser, to cough
trabajar, to work
    ____ *de*, to work as
traducir, to translate
traer, to bring

traérselas, to get worse and worse
tragar, to swallow
tranvía, trolley, street car
tratar de, to try to
(a) través, through
tren, train
triste, sad
tubo, pipe

U
úlcera, ulcer
usar, to use
útil, useful

V
va, it goes
    ¡*qué* ____*!* of course not
vaca, cow
vacío, empty
vacuna, vaccine
vagón, car, wagon
valer, to be worth
    ____ *la pena*, to be worthwhile
valioso, expensive, worthy
valor, courage
variedad, variety
varios, several, various
vaso, (drinking) glass
vegetales, vegetables
vela, candle
velocidad, speed
velocímetro, speedometer
vender, to sell
venir, to come
ventana, window
ventanilla, small window, airplane
  window
ver, to see, to watch
verdad, truth
verdadero, true
verde, green, unripe
verdulería, vegetable store
verdura, vegetable
vez, time
    a veces, sometimes
    de vez en cuando, from time to time
vía, way, railroad tracks
viajar, to travel
viaje, travel, trip
viajero, traveler
viejo, old

viernes, Friday
vino, wine
visitar, to visit
vista, view, sight
vivir, to live
volante, steering wheel
volar (ue), to fly
volver (ue), to return, to turn
vuelo, flight
vuelta, turning, ride, change ($)

vuelto, change ($)

Y

ya, already, now
yeso, plaster, cast

Z

zanahoria, carrot
zapatería, shoe store, shoe-repair shop
zapato, shoe

ENGLISH-SPANISH

A

able, capaz
   to be ____, poder
about, sobre, a eso de
above, arriba, sobre
abuse (to), abusar
accept (to), aceptar
accompany (to), acompañar
account, cuenta
   checking ____, cuenta corriente
   savings ____, cuenta de ahorros
action, acción
actually, en realidad
address, dirección, domicilio
after, después de
afternoon, tarde (f)
afterwards, después
agreed, de acuerdo, conforme
ahead, adelante
   ____ of time, con anticipación
airline, aerolínea
airplane, avión (m)
airport, aeropuerto
all, todo
   above ____, sobre todo
allergy, alergia
allow (to), permitir, dejar
almost, casi
already, ya, todavía
also, también
although, aunque
ancient, antiguo
   ____ times, antigüedad
ankle, tobillo
annoy (to), molestar
answer (to), contestar, responder
answer (noun), respuesta
apartment, apartamento, piso
aperitif, aperitivo
appear (to), aparecer
apple, manzana
arm, brazo
armchair, sillón
arrange (to), arreglar
arrival, llegada
arrive (to), llegar
ask (to), preguntar
ask for (to), pedir (i)
at, a/en

   ____ noon, a mediodía
   ____ midnight, a medianoche
attention, atención
   to pay ____, hacer caso, prestar atención
aunt, tía
automatic, automático
available, disponible, vacante, desocupado
average, promedio, medio
avocado, aguacate
awake, despierto
awake (to), despertar
away, lejos

B

back, detrás, espalda
bad, malo
bakery, panadería, pastelería
balance (to), balancear
banana, banana, plátano
bank, banco
barber, barbero
barbershop, barbería, peluquería
bargain, ganga, venta
bath, baño
bathe (to), bañarse, ducharse
bathroom, baño, servicio
battery, batería, acumulador
be (to), ser, estar
beach, playa
bean, frijol
beautiful, lindo, bonito, precioso, hermoso
because, porque
   ____ of that, por eso
bed, cama
   to stay in ____, guardar cama
bedroom, alcoba, dormitorio, recámara
beef, res (f), carne de res, carne de vaca
beer, cerveza
before, antes
beforehand, de antemano
begin (to), empezar (ie), comenzar (ie)
   to ____ to, ponerse a
believe (to), creer
bellboy, botones, mozo
belong (to), pertenecer
belt, cinturón

bend (to), doblar
berth, litera
besides, además
better, mejor
big, grande
bill, billete, cuenta, factura
birthday, cumpleaños
black, negro
blame (to), culpar
block, cuadra
blond, rubio, güero (Mexico)
blood, sangre (f)
blouse, blusa
blow (to) the horn, pitar, tocar la
    bocina
boarding-house, pensión
bone, hueso
book, libro
bored, aburrido
boring, aburrido
born (to be), nacer
bother (to), molestar
bottle, botella
brake (to), frenar
brake, freno
brand, marca
bread, pan
break (to), romper
breakdown, avería
breakfast, desayuno
    to eat___, desayunar
breast, pecho
bridge, puente
briefcase, maletín
bring (to), traer
broken, roto
brother, hermano
budget, presupuesto
build (to), construir
building, edificio, construcción
busy, ocupado
but, pero
butter, matequilla
button, botón
buy (to), comprar
buy, compra
by, por, para

C
cake, tarta, torta, pastel
calorie, caloría

can (verb), poder (ue)
can (noun), lata
candle, vela
car, carro, coche, vagón
    sleeping___, cochecama
    dining___, cochecomedor
card, tarjeta
    credit___, tarjeta de crédito
carrot, zanahoria
cash, dinero
    to pay___, pagar en efectivo, pagar
    al contado
cashier, cajero, cajera
cashier register, caja
cast, yeso
    to put on a___, enyesar
cat, gato
celebrate (to), celebrar
cent, *centavo*/céntimo
    percent, por ciento
chair, silla
champagne, champán
chance, oportunidad, casualidad
change (to), cambiar
change, cambio, vuelta, vuelto
charge (to), cobrar
    to take___, encargarse de
cheap, barato
check (to), revisar, facturar
checkbook, chequera, talonario
cheerful, alegre
cheese, queso
chest, cómoda, pecho
chicken, pollo
chin, barbilla, barba
chop, chuleta
church, iglesia
cigarette, cigarrillo
city, ciudad
clean, limpio
clean (to), limpiar
clear, claro
clerk, empleado, empleada
climb (to), subir
clock, reloj
close to, junto a
close (to), cerrar (ie)
clothes, ropa, vestimenta
cloud, nube
cloudy, nublado
clutch, embrague

coin, moneda
coincidence, coincidencia, casualidad
cold, frío, resfriado, resfrío
come (to), venir, ir
    _____ *back,* volver (ue), regresar
    _____ *in,* entrar
comfortable, cómodo
complain (to), quejarse de
compliment, cumplido
conclude (to), concluir
conduct (to), conducir
congenial, simpático
congratulate (to), felicitar
congratulations, felicidades
contain (to), contener
convert (to), convertir (ie, i)
cook, cocinero, cocinera
cook (to), cocinar
cool, fresco
corn, maíz (m)
corner, esquina
cough, tos (f)
cough (to), toser
country, país
couple, par, pareja
course, curso
    of _____ , por supuesto, ¡cómo no!
cousin, primo, prima
cow, vaca
crash, choque
crash (to), chocar
cream, crema
    ice _____ , helado
crippled, cojo
cross (to), cruzar
crutch, muleta
cucumber, pepino
currency, dinero, moneda
    foreign _____ , divisa
custard, flan
customer, cliente
customs, aduana
cure (to), curar
cute, gracioso/simpático

D
daily, diario
damage (to), dañar, estropear
dance, baile
dance (to), bailar
danger, peligro

dark, oscuro
dashboard, tablero
date, fecha
    to be up to _____ , estar en onda, estar
    al día
daughter, hija
day, día (m)
decide (to), decidir
deflate, pincharse, desinflarse
delay (to), tardar, demorar
delicious, delicioso, sabroso
deliver (to), entregar
departure, salida, partida
deposit, depósito, garantía
deserve (to), merecer
desk, escritorio, pupitre
    front _____ , recepción
dessert, postre
destroy (to), destruir
die (to), morir (ue, u)
diet, dieta
    to be on a _____ , estar a dieta
dietitian, dietista
difficult, difícil
dining room, comedor
dirty, sucio
disappear, desparecer
discontent, descontento
discount, descuento
dish, plato
dishwasher, lavaplatos
disaster, desastre
discover, descubrir
dizziness, mareo
dizzy, mareado
    to get _____ , marearse
do (to), hacer
door, puerta
double, doble
dream, sueño
dream (to), soñar (ue)
dress (to), vestirse (i)
drink, bebida
drink (to), beber
drip (to), gotear
drive (to), manejar, conducir
drop, gota
drug, droga
    _____ *addict,* drogadicto
    _____ *store,* droguería, farmacia
dry, seco

E

each, cada
eagle, águila
ear, oído, oreja
early, temprano
easy, fácil
_____*to do,* fácil de hacer
eat (to), comer
_____*supper (to),* cenar
elbow, codo
electric, eléctrico
_____*train,* electrotrén
electricity, electricidad
elevator, ascensor
eliminate (to), eliminar
embrace (to), abrazar
employee, empleada, empleado
empty, vacío
end, fin
   by the_____of, a fines de
engine, motor, locomotora (del tren)
enjoyable, simpático, agradable, divertido
enough, bastante
entire, entero, todo
entry way, entrada
epoch, época
even, incluso, aún
every, todo, todos
excellent, excelente, sin par
exciting, emocionante
exit, salida
expense, gasto
expensive, caro, costoso
eye, ojo
eyebrow, ceja
eyelash, pestaña
eyelid, párpado

F

face, cara
face (to), dar a (un lugar)
(without) fail, sin falta
fall, otoño
fall (to), caer
family, familia
far, lejos
fascinating, fascinante
fast, rápido
fasten (to), abrocharse, ponerse
fastness, rapidez

fat (noun), grasa
fat (adj.), gordo, grueso
father, padre, papá
father-in-law, suegro
fee, tarifa, impuesto
feed (to), alimentar
feel (to), sentir (ie, i)
_____*like,* tener ganas de
fever, fiebre (f)
fiancé, novio
fiancée, novia
field, campo
fill up (to), llenar
finally, finalmente, por fin
find (to), encontrar (ue), hallar
   to_____out, enterarse, descubrir
finger, dedo
fireplace, chimenea
first, primero
fish, pescado
fish (to), pescar
_____*store,* pescadería
fit (to), caber
fix (to), arreglar
flavor, sabor, gusto
flee (to), huir
flight, vuelo
floor, piso
flower, flor (f)
flower shop, florería
flu, gripe (la), gripa
fly (to), volar (ue)
follow, seguir (i)
food, comida, alimento
foolish, loco, tonto
foot, pie
forbid (to), prohibir
forehead, frente (f)
foreign, extranjero
_____*money,* divisa
forget (to), olvidar
free, gratis ($), gratuito ($)
free, libre, desocupado
frequently, frecuentemente, a menudo
fresh, fresco
Friday, viernes
fried, frito
from, de, desde
_____ *. . . to,* desde . . . hasta
fruit, fruta
fruit store, frutería

fulfill (to), cumplir
funny, chistoso, divertido, gracioso
   to have fun, divertirse, pasarla bien
furniture, mueble, muebles

G

garden, jardín
garlic, ajo
get (to), obtener, conseguir (i)
   to____sick, enfermarse
   to____out, salir
   to____in, entrar
girl, chica, muchacha
give (to), dar
   to____as a present, regalar
glass (drinking), vaso, copa
glove, guante
go (to), ir, irse
   to____down, bajar
   to____up, subir
granddaughter, nieta
grandfather, abuelo
grandmother, abuela
grandson, nieto
grease, grasa
   to____, engrasar
green, verde
green pea, guisante
grill, plancha
   on the____, a la plancha
guitar, guitarra

H

hair, pelo, cabello
   to cut the____, cortar el pelo
hairdresser's, peluquería
half, medio, mitad
ham, jamón
hamburguer, hamburguesa
hand, mano (f)
handsome, hermoso, guapo
hang (to), colgar (ue)
happen (to), pasar, ocurrir
happiness, alegría, felicidad
happy, feliz, alegre, contento
   to be happy, alegrarse de
hard, duro, difícil
hat, sombrero
hate (to), odiar
have (to), tener, haber (auxiliary)
   to____just, acabar de

head, cabeza
headlight, faro
heal (to), curar
health, salud
healthy, saludable
hear (to), oír
heat, calor
heating, calefacción
hello!, ¡aló!, ¡dígame!, ¡hola!
help (to), ayudar
here, aquí
high, alto
highway, carretera
hill, loma, cerro
hilly, ondulado
home, casa, hogar
hood, capó
horn, bocina
   to blow the____, tocar la bocina
hose, maguera
hot, caliente
hot (spicy), picante
hour, hora
house, casa, domicilio
hunger, hambre
   to be hungry, tener hambre
hurt (to), doler (ue)

I

Ice, hielo
   ____cream, helado
in, en, dentro
   ____short, en fin, por fin
include (to), incluir
increase (to), aumentar
incredible, increíble
inflate (to), inflar
inspect (to), inspeccionar
installment, plazo
   in____s, a plazos
insurance, seguro, aseguranza (Mexico)
insure (to), asegurar
interchange, intercambio
interest, interés
   to be interested, interesar
intersection, cruce, intersección
invite (to), invitar

J

jalopy, cacharro
jealous, celoso

juice, jugo
just, justo (adj.)
just, justamente (adv.)
   to have ____, acabar de
   ____ *now*, ahora mismo

K

key, llave (f)
kilometer, kilómetro
kind, amable, simpático
kitchen, cocina
knee, rodilla
know (to), conocer, saber

L

lamb, cordero
lame, cojo
landscape, paisaje
large, grande
late, tarde (adv.)
late, atrasado (adj.)
learn (to), aprender
left (to be), sobrar
leg, pierna
   to pull one's ____, tomar el pelo
lemonade, limonada
leave (to), salir
lettuce, lechuga
license, carnet, licencia
light, luz
light (to), encender (ie)
light (adj.), ligero
like, como
like (to), gustar, agradar, encantar
   to feel ____, tener ganas de
limp (to), cojear
lip, labio
listen (to), oír, escuchar
little, pequeño
   a ____, un poco
live (to), vivir
living room, sala
load (to), cargar
loan, préstamo
loan (to), prestar
lobster, langosta
long, largo
look (to), mirar, ver
   to ____ *for*, buscar
   to ____ *like*, parecer
lose (to), perder (ie)

   to ____ *weight*, adelgazar
lot (a lot), mucho
love (to), querer (ie), amar, gustar
low, bajo
lubricate (to), engrasar, lubricar
luggage, equipaje
lunch, almuerzo
   to eat ____, almorzar (ue)
lung, pulmón
luxurious, lujoso, de lujo

M

mad, loco, furioso, enojado
magazine, revista
make (to), hacer
man, hombre, caballero
market, mercado
marriage, matrimonio, casamiento
marry (to), casarse
   to ____ *to*, casarse con
matter (to), importar, interesar
meal, comida
measurement, medida
medical, médico
medicine, medicina
meet (to), reunirse, encontrarse,
   conocer
meeting, reunión
melt (to), deshacer
message, mensaje
mile, milla (1.6 kilometers)
   ____ *per*, por milla
milk, leche (f)
   ____ *store*, lechería
mirror, espejo
mistaken, equivocado
   to be ____, estar equivocado
Monday, lunes
money, dinero, fondos
month, mes
morning, mañana
   tomorrow ____, mañana por la
   mañana
mortgage, hipoteca
mother, madre, mamá
mother-in-law, suegra
mouth, boca
move (to), mover (ue), mudarse
muscle, músculo
must, deber

N

narrow, estrecho
near, cerca, cerca de
necessary, necesario, preciso
necessity, necesidad
neck, cuello
need, necesidad, falta
need (to), necesitar, faltar
   that's all I ____!, ¡sólo me
   falta eso!
neglect (to), descuidar
nephew, sobrino
nervous, nervioso
new, nuevo, otro
next, siguiente
   ____to, junto a
nice, simpático, amable
niece, sobrina
night, noche (f)
   at____, por la noche
   midnight, medianoche
nose, nariz
now, ahora
   right____, ahora mismo
   up to____, hasta ahora
   from____on, desde ahora, a partir de
   ahora
nurse, enfermero, enfermera

O

obtain (to), obtener, conseguir (i)
occupy (to), ocupar
occur (to), ocurrir, pasar
offer (to), ofrecer
oil, aceite, petróleo
   ____well, pozo de petróleo
old, viejo, antiguo
   to be____, tener años
omelette, tortilla
one, uno, una
one-way-ticket, boleto de ida
onion, cebolla
only, sólo, solamente
open, abierto
open (to), abrir
orange, naranja
order (an), orden, mandato
order (to), mandar, pedir,
   ordenar
over, sobre, otra vez

P

pack (to), hacer (la maleta)
pale, pálido
paper, papel
pardon (to), perdonar, disculpar
   ____me, discúlpeme
parent, padres
park (to), aparcar, estacionar, parquear
parking, estacionamiento, aparca-
   miento
party, fiesta
pass (to), pasar
passenger, pasajero
passport, pasaporte
pastry, pastel, dulce
pay (to), pagar
   to____cash, pagar en efectivo, al contado
peace, paz
pear, pera
pen, pluma, bolígrafo
pencil, lápiz (m)
people, gente, país
percent, por ciento
percentage, porcentaje
perhaps, tal vez, quizás, acaso
pharmacy, farmacia, droguería
pig, puerco, cerdo
pill, píldora, pastilla
pink, rosado
pipe, tubo
pitcher, jarra, jarro
plan (to), planear, pensar
plate, placa, matrícula
platform, andén
play (to), jugar (ue), tocar música
police, policía
policy, póliza
polite, atento, educado
poor, pobre
pork, puerco, cerdo
porter, mozo, maletero
powder, talco
preferable, preferible
prescribe (to), recetar
prescription, receta
present (adj.), actual
pressure, presión, tensión
pretty, lindo, bonito
price, precio
priest, cura (m), sacerdote

protect (to), proteger
prudent, prudente
pull (to), tirar
    to___one's leg, tomar el pelo
pump, bomba, surtidor
put (to), poner
    to___on clothes, ponerse (ropa)

Q

quick, rápido
quickly, rápidamente, de prisa
quiet, tranquilo, calmado
    to be___, calmarse

R

railroad, ferrocarril, vía
rain, lluvia
rain (to), llover (ue)
rare, raro, extraño
razor blade, hoja de afeitar
read (to), leer
ready, listo, preparado
reason, razón
reasonable, razonable
recent, reciente
recognize, reconocer
record, disco
    ___player, tocadiscos
red, rojo
red (wine), tinto
reduce (to), reducir, perder peso
refreshment, refresco
refrigerator, refrigerador, nevera
register (to), matricularse (in school)
register (to), registrarse (in a hotel)
relative, pariente
relieve (to), aliviar
remedy, remedio
remember (to), recordar (ue), acordarse
    (ue)
rent, alquiler, renta
rent (to), alquilar
request (to), pedir (i)
rest (to), descansar
return (to), volver (ue), regresar
rice, arroz (m)
rich, rico
right, derecho, correcto
    to be___, tener razón
    to the___, a la derecha
ring (to), sonar (ue)

risk, peligro, riesgo
    at all___, a todo riesgo
road, camino, carretera
roast (to), asar
roasted, asado
roof, tejado
room, cuarto, recámara, habitación
    bathroom, alcoba, dormitorio, re-
    cámara, habitación
    bedroom, baño, servicio, aseo
    living room, sala, salón
    ___service, servicio a los cuartos
root, raíz
    to take___, arraigar
    to___up, arrancar
rosé, rosado
round-trip, viaje de ida y vuelta
rough, duro, abrupto
ruin, ruina
run (to), correr
rust, óxido
    ___proof, inoxidable
rusty, oxidado

S

sad, triste
safe, seguro
safety, seguridad
salad, ensalada
salary, salario, sueldo
sale, venta, liquidación
    on___, en venta
salesman, vendedor
saleswoman, vendedora
sandwich, sangüich, bocadillo
satisfy (to), satisfacer
Saturday, sábado
sauce, salsa
save (to), ahorrar
saving, ahorro
    savings account, cuenta de ahorros
say (to), decir
    ___yes, decir que sí
scarce, escaso
scare (to), asustar
    to be scared, estar asustado
schedule, horario
school, escuela
schoolmate, compañero de escuela
sea, mar
    to get___sick, marearse

seafood, mariscos
season, estación, temporada
season (to), sazonar, condimentar
seat, asiento
   to take a____, tomar asiento
sedative, calmante
see (to), ver
seem (to), parecer
self, uno mismo
self-service, autoservicio
sell (to), vender
send (to), mandar, enviar
serious, serio
seriously, en serio, seriamente
serve (to), servir (i)
share (to), participar
sharp (adv.), en punto
shirt, camisa
shop, tienda
shop (to), comprar
   to go shopping, ir de compras
short, corto, breve
   in____, en conclusión, en breve, en
   fin
shot, inyección
shoulder, hombro
shower, ducha (bath)
shrimp, camarón, gamba
shut (to), cerrar (ie)
   to____up, callarse
sick, enfermo
   to get____, enfermarse
sickness, enfermedad
sideburn, patilla
sight, vista
sign, letrero, anuncio
sign (to), firmar
silly, tonto, estúpido
silver, plata
similar, semejante
simple, sencillo, simple
single, soltero
sirloin, solomillo, lomo
sister, hermana
sit (to), sentarse (ie)
   to____down, sentarse (ie)
ski (to), esquiar
skid (to), resbalar
skin, piel
skinny, flaco
skirt, falda

sleep (to), dormir (ue)
   to fall asleep, dormirse
slip (to), resbalar
slippery, resbaladizo, resbaloso
small, pequeño
smell (to), oler (ue)
smoke (to), fumar
snack, bocadillo, botana, entremés,
   tapa
snow, nieve
snow (to), nevar (ie)
soap, jabón
soft, suave, tierno
solve (to), resolver (ue)
some, un poco de, algunos
something, algo
son, hijo
sound, sonido
sound (to), sonar (ue)
soup, sopa
south, sur
spare tire, llanta de repuesto
speed, velocidad
speedometer, velocímetro
spend (to), gastar
spicy, picante
spouse, esposo, esposa
sprain (to), torcer (ue)
square, plaza
staircase, escalera
stairs, escalera
stand (to), ponerse de pie, pararse
   can't____it, no poder ver
start (to), arrancar (el motor), empezar
   (ie)
starter, arranque (del motor)
steak, filete, bistec, bisté, chuleta
steel, acero
steering wheel, volante, timón
stewardess, azafata, aeromoza
still, todavía
stomach, estómago
stop, parada, escala, stop
stop (to), parar, detenerse
store, tienda
straight, derecho
strange, extraño, raro
street, calle (f)
strict, estricto
strong, fuerte
study (to), estudiar

suddenly, de repente, de pronto
suffer (to), sufrir
sugar, azúcar (m/f)
suggest (to), sugerir (ie, i)
suit, traje
suit (to), convenir
suitcase, maleta
sun, sol
Sunday, domingo
sunny, soleado
   to be____, hacer sol, haber sol
supermarket, supermercado
supper, cena
   to eat____, cenar
surround (to), rodear
suspect (to), sospechar
suspicious, sospechoso
   to look____, oler mal a uno
swallow (to), tragar
sweet, dulce
swim (to), nadar
symptom, síntoma (m)
syrup, jarabe

T

table, mesa
tablet, píldora
tailor, sastre
   ____shop, sastrería
take (to), tomar, coger
   to____out, llevarse, sacar
   to____to, llevar
   to____care of, cuidar, atender (ie)
talk (to), hablar, charlar
tall, alto
tank, tanque, depósito
taste, sabor, gusto
taste (to), saborear, gustar
   to____like, saber a
tasty, sabroso, delicioso
tax, impuesto
taxi driver, taxista
tea, té
telephone, teléfono
tell (to), decir (i)
tend to (to), tender a (ie)
tender, blando, suave, tierno
terrain, terreno
thank (to), agradecer, dar las gracias
thankful, agradecido
that, que

theme, tema (m)
then, entonces, luego
there, allí, allá, ahí
thigh, muslo
third, tercero
thirst, sed
thirsty, sediento
   to be____, tener sed
throat, garganta
   sore____, dolor de garganta
through, por, a través
   to be____, acabar, terminar
throughout, por todo, a través de
Thursday, jueves
ticket, billete, boleto, entrada
   ____window, taquilla
   ____agent, taquillero
time, tiempo
   on____, a tiempo
tire, llanta, neumático, goma
   spare____, llanta de repuesto
tip, propina
toe, dedo del pie
today, hoy
tonight, esta noche
tooth, diente
tooth paste, crema dental, pasta dental
touch (to), tocar
tourism, turismo
tourist, turista
toward, hacia
towel, toalla
town, ciudad, pueblo
train, tren
translate (to), traducir
travel (to), viajar
travel, viaje
traveler, viajero
tree, árbol
trip, viaje
trolley, tranvía
try (to), probar (ue)
   to____on, probarse (ue)
   to____to, tratar de
truck, camión
true, verdadero, cierto
   to be____, ser verdad, ser cierto
truly, verdaderamente, ciertamente
trunk, baúl, maletero (car), cajuela
  (car)
truth, verdad

tube, tubo
Tuesday, martes
tuna, atún
turkey, pavo, guajolote (Mexico)
turn (to), doblar
   to____off, apagar
   to____on, encender (ie)
   to be one's____, tocarle a uno
twist (to), doblar/torcer (ue)
twisted, torcido, doblado
typical, típico

U

ugly, feo
ulcer, úlcera
umbrella, paraguas, sombrilla
uncle, tío
uncongenial, antipático
undershirt, camiseta
understand (to), entender(ie), comprender
undo (to), deshacer
unexpected, inesperado, imprevisto
unlucky, con mala suerte
   to be____, tener mala pata, tener mala suerte
unpack (to), deshacer (la maleta)
until, hasta
use (to), usar

V

vacant, desocupado, vacante
vacation, vacación, vacaciones
vaccine, vacuna
valuable, valioso
value, valor, costo, coste
varied, vario, diverso
variety, variedad
veal, carne de ternera, ternera
vegetable, vegetal
violent, violento
visit, visita
visit (to), visitar
vitamin, vitamina

W

wagon, coche, vagón
waist, cintura
wait (to), esperar
   to____on, atender (ie)
waiter, camarero, mesero, mozo

waitress, camarera, mesera
walk (to), caminar, andar
want (to), desear, querer (ie)
warn (to), avisar, aconsejar
waste (to), echar a perder
watch, reloj
   wrist____, reloj de pulsera
watch (to), ver, mirar
water, agua
wave, onda, ola
wavy, ondulado
way, camino, vía
   this____, por aquí
   by the____, a propósito
weak, débil
wear (to), llevar, ponerse
   to____out, gastar
weather, tiempo
Wednesday, miércoles
week, semana
welcome, bienvenida, acogida
welcome (to), dar la bienvenida
well, bien
what, lo que
what?, ¿qué?
wheel, rueda
   steering____, volante, timón
where, donde
whistle, pito
whistle (to), pitar
white, blanco
whole, todo, entero
wide, ancho
wind, viento
   to be windy, hacer viento, haber viento
windshield, parabrisas
window, ventana, ventanilla
wine, vino
   ____cooler, sangría
wiper, limpiaparabrisas
with, con
witty, ingenioso
wool, lana
woman, mujer
wonderful, maravilloso
word, palabra
work, trabajo, empleo, puesto
work (to), trabajar
world, mundo
worn out, gastado

worry (to), preocuparse
worse, peor
worth, valor
worthwhile, valioso
　　to be___, valer la pena
wrap (to), envolver (ue)
wrist, muñeca
write (to), escribir

Y

yellow, amarillo
yes, sí
yesterday, ayer
yet, todavía
　　not___, todavía no
yogurt, yogur
you, tú, usted, ustedes
young, joven
your, tuyo, suyo